Events Management

Contemporary events management is a diverse and challenging field. This major new introductory textbook is the first to fully explore the multi-disciplinary nature of events management, and provides students with all the practical skills and professional knowledge needed to succeed in the events industry.

The book covers every type of event studied on an events management course, including areas as diverse as sports, music, the arts, corporate events, tourism, and the public and voluntary sectors. It introduces all the key issues facing the contemporary events industry, from health, safety and risk management to sustainability and developing a market-oriented business, with every topic brought to life through vivid case studies, personal biographies and examples of best practice from the real world of events management.

Written by a team of authors with many years' experience working in the events industry, the book introduces the practical skills required in every core functional area of events management, such as marketing, finance, project management, strategy, operations, event design and human resources. A companion website for the book includes a dazzling array of additional teaching and learning features, including self-test questions, video interviews with key industry figures and PowerPoint slides for each chapter. *Events Management: An introduction* is the essential course text for any events management programme.

Charles Bladen is Programme Leader in Events Management at the University of Greenwich.

James Kennell is Director of the Economic Development Resource Centre at the University of Greenwich, where he is also Senior Lecturer in Tourism and Regeneration.

Emma Abson is Senior Lecturer on the Events Management BA programme at the University of Greenwich.

Nick Wilde is an expert in sports marketing and sporting events management, with research interests in international sports marketing, which he has taught in many overseas institutions.

Events Management

An introduction

Charles Bladen, James Kennell,
Emma Abson and Nick Wilde

Routledge
Taylor & Francis Group

LONDON AND NEW YORK

First published 2012
by Routledge
2 Park Square, Milton Park, Abingdon, Oxon, OX14 4RN

Simultaneously published in the USA and Canada
by Routledge
711 Third Avenue, New York, NY 10017

Routledge is an imprint of the Taylor & Francis Group, an informa business

British Library Cataloguing-in-Publication Data
A catalogue record for this book is available from the British Library

Library of Congress Cataloging in Publication Data
Bladen, Charles.
Events management : an introduction / Charles Bladen...[et.al.]. –1st ed.
p. cm.
1. Special events--Management. I. Title.
GT3405.B63 2012
394.2068–dc23
2011043776

ISBN 978-0-415-57742-7 pbk
ISBN 978-0-415-57741-0 hbk
ISBN 978-0-203-85297-2 ebk

Typeset in Sabon and Frutiger
by Keystroke, Station Road, Codsall, Wolverhampton
Printed and bound by Ashford Colour Press Ltd, Gosport, Hampshire

Contents

Contents

Endorsements

'The *Events Management* book by the tutors at the University of Greenwich is a well structured book suitable for most events management degree courses, especially at levels 4 and 5. This is because it is a practice-based resource that includes all the main types of special events and key issues in the field. From a pedagogic perspective, there are useful case studies, examples of best practice and a supporting website, as well as relevant concepts and theories. As such, the book compares favourably with other titles in the field, and I have no hesitation in recommending this textbook for events management degree courses.'
Liam Higgins, Southampton Solent University, UK

'*Events Management: An introduction* is a comprehensive text that provides in-depth discussion, case studies, international examples and coverage of all of the major elements of the body of knowledge required for both students of event management and those seeking to enter the industry. For current industry practitioners it provides insights into the theoretical underpinnings to their own professional practice. I recommend the text to both my undergraduate and postgraduate students here at Flinders University and recommend it to you as the perfect introduction to the study of events and how they are managed.'
Steve Brown, Flinders University, Australia

'*Events Management: An introduction* is a comprehensive and fully up to date guide to the events industry. Students and teachers will find the book's accessible style, practical examples and guides to further reading given in each chapter very helpful. The authors are to be congratulated on their collegiate and multi-disciplinary approach which has led to a substantial contribution to the field of event management literature.'
Tom Lunt, London Metropolitan University, UK

'The textbook and its authors certainly cover much contemporary ground here and there is a progressive and logical flow to the text which marries theory to practice. The linkages of real world industry voices to rich examples and case studies is very refreshing and keeps all issues raised both relevant and live. It is an enjoyable and engaging read. I recommend that all students studying events management have a copy to hand for continued reference throughout their studies.'
Phil Williamson, Liverpool John Moores University, UK

Images

Figures

Tables

Case studies

List of case studies

Acknowledgements

Charles Bladen: For Kim, Sol, Owen and Freya and Alan and Barbara.

James Kennell: Thanks to Abi, Lyra and Aphra.

Emma Abson: I'd like to thank my family, friends and colleagues for their support during this project.

Nick Wilde: To all of my friends, family and colleagues around the world who have supported me in my career, with a special mention for my brother Phil Holden, as well as Rory Miller, Orlando Salvestrini, Fernando de Tomaso, Omar Larrosa, Alan Dennington and Trevor Williams. Finally to Ellie Ghassemi, the love of my life, you are my inspiration and I love you with all of my heart.

A Visual Tour of *Events Management: An introduction*

Pedagogical features

Events Management: An introduction offers a variety of ways to help lecturers introduce this exciting discipline, and to engage students and help them understand key concepts and issues.

CHAPTER AIMS
Each chapter opens with a series of key learning outcomes that students will be able to attain after reading the chapter. They serve to ensure more focused learning and teaching.

> **1.1 Aims**
>
> By .... chapter, the student will be able:
>
> - To describe .in characteristics of events.
> - To explain t .ition and history of events.
> - To analyse t .ture of the contemporary events industry.
> - To underst .ok relationships between the events industry and the education sector.
> - To navi .ok in order to develop their knowledge of event management.

FIGURES, TABLES AND IMAGES
The text uses a rich mix of figures, tables and images to represent important concepts and issues, creating an inviting visual design.

CASE STUDIES
International case studies are included in each chapter, illustrating the chapter topic area through a focused presentation of events management on the ground. Case studies are supplemented by study activities asking students to engage actively with the material. See *List of case studies* for full details.

> **CASE STUDY 3.2**
>
> ### Notting Hill Carnival
>
> **Location:** Lo .don, UK
> **Event type:** co .munity festival
> **Attendees:** app .imately one million
>
> .horities imposed a 6.30 p.m. curfew on the 2009 Notting Hill .t was an attempt to prevent the kind of street violence that had .vious year's carnival, when around fifty police officers were .gs of rioters and looters. The council also restricted sound system .nival .35 decibels – a move that was welcomed by the 10,000 residents living near the carnival route (140 decibels had been recorded in 2008).
>
> A council report highlighted significant problems in the management of the

STUDY ACTIVITIES

The book fosters an active learning approach through discussion points and activities interspersed throughout each chapter. These can be used as the basis for class discussion, or developed into essay questions or research projects.

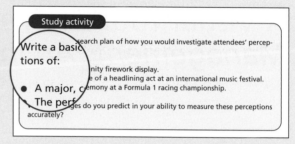

Study activity

Write a basic ...search plan of how you would investigate attendees' perceptions of:

...nity firework display.
...e of a headlining act at an international music festival.
● A major, c...emony at a Formula 1 racing championship.
The perf...

...ges do you predict in your ability to measure these perceptions
accurately?

INDUSTRY VOICES

Each chapter features insight and commentary from a senior figure in the field of events management, providing a definitive 'real life' edge to this introductory textbook. Voices come from a range of companies and organisations, from sponsorship consultants to security advisers, communication executives to mega-event programmers.

Industry voice

Tracie Carlsund, Jet Set Sports

...an incessant buzz in my ear; it won't go away. I suddenly realise
There ...one vibrating under my pillow. A glance at the clock shows
it is my ... earpiece into my ear, I hear loud music, celebratory cheers
2.30 a.m...sed client manager on the phone: 'Hi there, my client wants
...er party tomorrow night, in addition to the planned itinerary
Slidi...ts, sightseeing, lunch and dinner for the rest of the guests. Is
...a high...get some additional staff to assist for the evening?'
At this point I am up, pulling my spreadsheets off the side-table, pen in hand,
and through bleary eyes scanning the next day's staff allocations. I then shoot
off, in rapid fire, a series of questions, all of which I need answers for now, to
ensure we can: a) find staff who are the best fit for the dinner/client; b) find

CHAPTER SUMMARIES

A concise overview of each chapter – perfect to consolidate learning, or as a useful tool for student revision.

7.5 Summary

To gain an und...randing of what event consumers require from an event experience, it is
necessary to inv...ate what role the event plays in their lives, and which emotions are
associated with t...perience. Events are about lifestyle, excitement and escapism from day-
to-day life; they...e memorable and an important ingredient in the lives of attendees. This
...quires a ne...ch to research and marketing planning to ensure that organisers cater
...d key stakeholders who can contribute to the success of the event. Event
...re that research is at the heart of everything they do when planning an
...work hard to develop the event's brand image and must be willing to improve

FURTHER READING

Each chapter concludes with a list of key scholarly books and articles that will provide additional treatment of the theories and concepts covered. Students will find this list particularly helpful for developing and researching papers and other assignments.

Further reading

...T. and Anderson D. E. (2002), Environmental Factors Associated with
Fink, J. S., Tra...ce and Sport Consumption Behaviour: Gender and Team Differences,
Spectator At...uarterly, 11: 8–19. This important article explores sports fans' con-
Sport Marke......rting events and features the previously under-researched area of female
sumption du...Virtually Free Marketing, London: A & C Black. This is an important
attendanc...ers the important issues relating to social media, an increasingly crucial
...management.
O'Neill, M., Getz, D. and Carlsen, J. (1999) Evaluation of Service Quality at Events: The 1998
Coca-Cola Masters Surfing Event at Margaret River, Western Australia, *Managing Service
Quality*, 9 (3): 156–165. This is one of the first articles to consider the importance of service

Companion Website

 http://www.routledge.com/cw/bladen

Events Management: An introduction will also include a comprehensive companion website of online resources for both students and lecturers. These include:

Student Resources

- Annotated further reading for each chapter to provide an accessible gateway to in-depth information on key issues highlighted.
- Various tools used by events management professionals to provide further insight into the realities of the industry.
- Multiple Choice Questions for each chapter for students to test their understanding.
- Further discussion questions for each chapter, which can be set as assessment tasks or used to prompt seminar or in-class discussions.

Lecturer Resources

- PowerPoint presentations for each chapter to provide lecturers with a ready-made foundation for their lecture preparation. The files can be downloaded and annotated.

Chapter 1

Introduction to events management

Contents

1.1 Aims

By the end of the chapter, the student will be able:

- To describe the main characteristics of events.
- To explain the evolution and history of events.
- To analyse the structure of the contemporary events industry.
- To understand the relationships between the events industry and the education sector.
- To navigate this book in order to develop their knowledge of event management.

1.2 Introduction

This chapter, in addition to introducing the rest of the book, is intended to set the scene for the reader in terms of the crucial role of events in human history through to the present day. It emphasises events as artefacts of human culture that have only recently developed into a fast-growing and influential industry. This chapter also intends to provide an analysis of the business environment within which the events industry operates. Some of the contemporary questions that are raised by this fast development of the industry, and the education provisions designed to serve it, will be introduced for development throughout subsequent chapters.

1.3 What is an event?

There are various answers to this question, depending on the viewpoint of the person defining it. There are many definitions of 'events', available from various academic writers such as Getz (2007) and Goldblatt (2008). As such definitions become more detailed, their real-world application becomes more problematic. Thus, this book provides a general definition as follows:

> Events are temporary and purposive gatherings of people.

It follows that 'Events Management', as a field of industrial practice, should be defined as:

> The organisation and coordination of the activities required to achieve the objectives of events.

The aims of this text are to discuss and evaluate the management of these activities in the context of various and common types of events within their wider industrial and societal context. In order to do this, a clearer discussion of the features of events which make them distinct from more general business activities is required.

Events generally possess the following characteristics:

- They are temporary in nature.
- They are gatherings of people.
- They are often displays of ritual.
- They are, in some sense, unique occurrences.

Though these points may seem rather obvious, the more we observe the phenomena of events in our society, and their influence on our business and social lives, the more we could be forgiven for finding inconsistencies between these basic descriptors and that which we witness daily in the media, our neighbourhoods and even our own families.

1.3.1 Events are temporary

Events differ from other, more common, organisational activities because they possess a finite beginning and end. Managers and students probably agree that most events have a start time, a programme and a finishing time. Though this is certainly true of managed events, it is generally not the case with 'spontaneous events', which generally take place without much specific planning.

However, though it is necessary to plan times and programmes for the successful delivery of a planned event, many events are not planned at all. These 'spontaneous' displays of ritual can vary widely in nature and expression. This was seen in 1997 following the death of Diana, Princess of Wales, in a sudden motor vehicle accident. The occurrence, which shocked the British nation, led to two different types of events taking place. The first was the formal, managed funeral ceremony, befitting a member of the royal family. The other was the informal outpouring of grief on the streets of the capital by 'ordinary' people. The formal event possessed all the characteristics familiar to a planned event: there was pomp and ceremony, music and

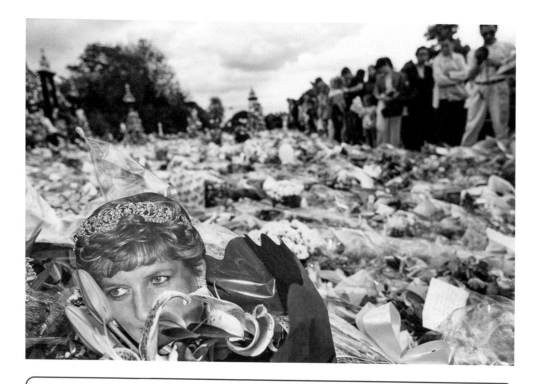

Image 1.1 Pile of flowers and people mourning the death of Princess Diana
Source: Andy Hall/Edit/ Getty Images

speeches, crowds, processions, and the British Union Flag at Buckingham Palace was even lowered to half mast for the first time ever (BBC 2005). However, millions of people also displayed their grief publicly the day after the organised funeral at a variety of more spontaneous gatherings which involved acts such as the building of makeshift shrines, the walking of Princess Diana's favourite park routes, and the placing of flowers at associated venues, such as royal residences and the Harrods retail store, the company with which her deceased partner was associated (Ibrahim 1997).

There are also important differences between events and the attractions in or around which they are held. Getz (2007) focuses on the differences between events and permanent attractions, such as historical venues (although many events take place for a pre-planned period at such venues). For example, permanent art galleries, such as the Prado in Madrid, regularly hold events to display works by grand masters for a limited period only. Such events can last for several weeks, or even as long as a year, but whilst their attraction to tourists is clear, their limited duration still places them in the category of events.

1.3.2 Events are gatherings of people

So far, we have established that events are comprised of people, though numbers of such attendees may vary considerably. As with Diana's funeral, a clear definition of an event attendee is obviously easier to define in certain situations than in others. Somebody attending a sports or music event is unlikely to be allowed to enter without a ticket, whether paid for or not. However, as will be discussed in Chapter 10, mega-events include in their scope entire locations, destinations and even the whole world in the form of international media coverage.

Events can involve single people as the focus, as in the case of concerts by solo music celebrities, or the 'Speaker's Plinth', as discussed in the following case study.

CASE STUDY 1.1

The Speaker's Plinth event

Location: Trafalgar Square, London, UK
Event type: cultural event
Attendees: 2400 participants, approximately 1 million visitors and a worldwide media audience

The Speaker's Plinth was the fourth of its kind and was unveiled in Trafalgar Square on 6 July 2009. Conceived by the artist Antony Gormley, the plinth was designed as a display of the ordinary, living people among emblems celebrating the nation's dead heroes.

Trafalgar Square, known to many as a world-class tourist attraction itself, was selected because of its open space, fame and distinctive statues and other monuments to historical figures, such as Admiral Horatio Nelson, leader of the victorious Royal Navy at the Battle of Trafalgar.

The 100-day event involved 2400 British people who were randomly chosen by lottery from around the country to mount the plinth and do anything they wanted for their allotted time of one hour, as long as it was legal. During that period of time, the individual was observed by onlookers, at least some of whom were baffled by the occurrence.

The result was that each person appearing on the plinth became a constituent of Gormley's 'One-on-One' art exhibit, as well as potentially stimulating individual comment and possible notoriety in their own right. Those chosen for the exhibit varied wildly in appearance and performance. As the *Daily Telegraph* (1 August 2009) remarked:

> Take the girl who dressed up as a mermaid, complete with tail and modesty scallop shells, in an attempt to highlight overfishing; the aquatic scientist Oliver Parsons-Barker whose 'poo costume' was lovingly created to draw attention to the global shortage of clean water; or the woman who beheaded red roses with a curved pruning knife to symbolise female genital mutilation in Africa.

The artist's raison d'être for the event was that it would promote greater levels of social engagement for the British population. The event gained continued television coverage on Sky Arts and could be viewed on webcam throughout. The unintended impacts of the event included complaints that the traditional nature of Trafalgar Square was damaged by some of the displays and that it needlessly promoted anti-social behaviour, already a huge national concern.

Source: Woods 2009

Study activity

1 Which are the main groups of people being gathered by this event? How do you think they differ in terms of their perceptions of what is happening?
2 What do you think are some of the possible event planning aspects that need to be considered for this event?
3 What are your ideas about potential future developments of the plinth event concept?

As can be seen from this example, events can comprise both planned staging elements and unplanned spontaneity. Scale and formality of events can vary considerably, as can the levels of ritual display.

When considering such events as gatherings, we should also consider the impacts of more recent technologies on these otherwise age-old practices. Certainly, web conferencing – the ability through media to share information from widespread geographic locations – has progressed in terms of effectiveness and popularity in recent years. In a sense, the participants gather without travelling.

Applications of web conferencing include meetings, training events, lectures and presentations, and they have the advantage of being real-time and potentially of being recordable, which is a valuable service for many businesses. Among the downsides of web conferencing is technological failure, which can fast make a promising event a complete 'non-event'. This is particularly frustrating for organisers of larger web conferences as the technology is rarely under their direct control. This is also the case for the associated propriety software, which must usually be downloaded beforehand by all parties involved.

Webinars or webcasts have been born of these technologies, making possible one-way mass presentations to international audiences, although webinars tend to be more interactive than webcasts. Workshops can also be held effectively by organisers using online tools.

Despite certain alarmist suggestions that web conferencing may end 'real' conferencing completely, it tends to be used more as a supplement to face-to-face contact, rather than its replacement. The 'Industry Voice' at the end of this chapter – leading industry figure Howard Evans – discusses some of the questions raised by this and other event-based technologies in more detail. One of the main limitations of web conferencing is that it cannot replace the richness of face-to-face interactions.

1.3.3 Events are often displays of ritual

Humans are the most socially evolved species on the planet. As such, we develop social interactions beyond our family structures which can trigger the need for events. According to Maslow (1943), these social needs relate to other human needs, as is shown in Figure 1.1:

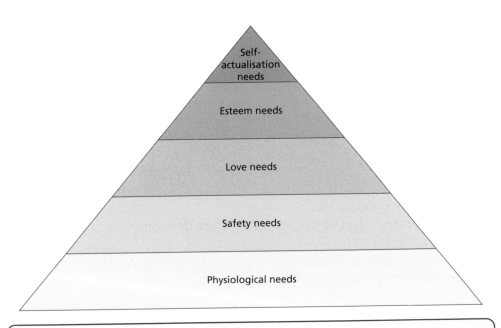

Figure 1.1 Maslow's hierarchy of needs
Source: Adapted from Maslow 1943

As this early model suggests, humans are on a journey to the achievement of self-actualisation, which relates to the ultimate fulfilment of one's potential. Initially, physiological needs, followed by safety needs, should be satisfied before a person can go about satisfying their needs for love and belonging to a social group. Clearly these latter needs are partially fulfilled through family ties and social relationships, but they also could be said to form the main motivating factor behind the age-old practice of holding events.

Events are characterised by rituals, symbols and artefacts which themselves denote meaning. For example, one has only to consider the average wedding event, which will likely be composed of various costumes, food and drink, speeches and behaviours which denote the meanings of the culture in question. More discussion of how these meanings can be designed is provided in Chapter 3.

1.3.4 Events are unique occurrences

Events, because they are not permanent, are held at different times, in different locations and for different reasons. Even the same event held annually can differ considerably in its characteristics. These features make every event, in a sense, unique. As will be discussed in Chapter 14, this makes planning for event legacy particularly challenging, as the enduring things left over after the event are often very difficult to predict.

1.4 The challenge of events management

The previous discussion raises some important challenges for anybody seeking to manage the delivery of an event. Whether the reader is an event professional, a student or somebody reading because of more general interest, they could be forgiven for concluding that a coherent understanding of the events industry and its effective 'management' is almost impossible due to its breadth, complexity and fast-moving nature. Definition and categorisation of different events has been attempted and has resulted in some common labels, including mega-events, cultural events, special events, corporate events and sporting events.

Although such clean categorisation of events should enable their management requirements to be easily communicated, in practice it seems that these labels are often too broad and unclear to be useful. For example, many of the special events upon which Goldblatt (2010) bases his discussions could be categorised in several different ways. Whilst clearly recognising such problems, we decided to use many of these classifications as chapter headings. Industry professionals do still use many classifications, such as 'special events', to define certain event concepts; but terms such as 'corporate events' are widely recognised to encompass a variety of concepts, such as conferences, exhibitions or brand experience events, which are generally more useful in conveying their ideas.

However, this book focuses on the systematic project management of the practices relating to the delivery of a variety of events. As discussed in Chapter 2, the origination, planning and delivery of events, regardless of their classifications, tend to require similar frameworks, based upon existing events management theory.

1.5 The place of events in human history and human cultures

Despite the obvious advantages of clear and definite information, particularly to those embarking on new study of this exciting and fast-evolving field, it is worth remembering that events management is largely the modern-day practice of age-old expressions of human social interactions and activities. Before commencing an understanding of some of the mechanics of modern-day events management, a more historical view of their development through the ages may enable the reader to put contemporary events management into the context of its origins.

Ancient texts, such as the Christian and Jewish Old Testaments, record the early practice of festivals. These were enshrined in law and primarily took the form of the seven feasts of Israel, where the people of the nation gathered seven times throughout the year in religious celebration and remembrance. Various customs and rituals were practised, from the eating of the Passover feast through to the offering of sacrifices. Variations of these different feasts are still practised today. World religions, such as Islam, later developed annual pilgrimages – such as the *hajj* to Mecca (see Chapter 8) – which currently presents a number of significant crowd safety challenges. Religious observance in Greece gave rise to the first, ancient Olympic Games. Modern-day festivals, such as Christmas and Halloween, also have their roots in such observance, whether pagan or otherwise. (Faith events as a whole are discussed further in Chapter 11.)

The development of modern-day events from ancient origins is illustrated in the Case study 1.2.

CASE STUDY 1.2

The Dragonboat (Duanwu) Festival

Location: Beijing, China
Event type: cultural festival
Attendees: 3,110,000

This festival is said to have originated to commemorate the suicide of a popular Chinese poet, Qu Yuan, in 278 BC. Part of its traditional ritual reportedly involved attendees dropping rice into the river where Qu Yuan was supposed to have died to ensure the fish had enough food to eat so that they would not eat the poet's body.

In 2008, following a reported decrease in popularity of a traditional Chinese version of Valentine's Day and the continuing celebration of Christmas, particularly among young people, the Chinese government decided to revive traditional festivals as a way of promoting Chinese culture. It stated: 'At a time of cultural globalization in the world, the revival of traditional festivals will help boost Chinese traditional culture, easy and friendly personal relations and harmonious social environment, and will help build cohesive affinity among the

Image 1.2 Chinese celebrate the Duanwu Festival
Source: China Photos / Getty Images

Chinese nation promoting reunification across the Taiwan Straits' (*China People's Daily* 2008). This statement was accompanied by a call for festivals such as the Dragonboat Festival to be well organised and contemporary in approach, and to involve the younger, business sector of the population.

The modern-day Dragonboat Festival has markedly changed from its roots many centuries ago. It is now characterised by the eating and drinking of traditional foods and wines, as well as racing the boats. There has even been the development of such racing in other countries across the world. The festival has a different delivery, more in line with a faster pace of life, particularly among younger Chinese businesspeople.

Source: Dragonboatnet 2011

Study activity

1 Research the Dragonboat Festival online and compare and contrast some of its ancient and modern-day characteristics. What do you think are the main reasons for any changes or new developments?

2 Choose a similar, more familiar festival to you and establish its:

- *Origins*. How did it come about? What were the original reasons for it being held?
- *Main rituals*. What are the reasons for these?
- *Modern developments*. How has the event changed from its origins to its present expression? What are the reasons for these changes?

1.6 The events industry: what business are we in?

In Case study 1.2, one of the reasons for the modernisation of the event from its traditional origins was the changing culture and other aspects of the way people live as members of a fast-developing, global economy. These changes were highlighted by the Chinese government, which saw festivals as a useful vehicle for revisiting and promoting traditional Chinese culture and values in the face of encroachment by external ones.

Festivals are generally common forms of cultural practice and, although many have long histories, the majority have been founded in the much more recent past (Getz 2005). The International Festivals and Events Association estimates that there are over 4.5 million recurring festivals worldwide per year (IFEA 2009).

Events have a substantial impact on the UK national economy. In 2010, a report entitled 'Britain for Events' was compiled by leading industry figure Tony Rogers on behalf of the Business Visits and Events Partnership. The report revealed that:

- The sector is worth over £36 billion per annum to the national economy. Business visitors spend on average £131 per day – £72 more than the amount spent by leisure visitors – while visitors to UK exhibitions from overseas spend £193 more per day than leisure visitors to Britain.
- Trade transacted at exhibitions and other business events held in the UK is conservatively estimated to be worth over £100 billion.
- There are over 25,000 businesses in the sector, which sustain at least 530,000 full-time equivalent (FTE) jobs.

The economic impact of the various types of events is shown in Figure 1.2.

Total value £36.1bn			
Corporate events	Cultural events and festivals	Sports events	Outdoor events
£30.3bn	£2.3bn	£2.3bn	£1bn

Figure 1.2 The value of Britain's events industry by sector

Source: Adapted from *Britain for Events Report* 2010

1.7 The role of the event manager

The increasing importance of the events sector to the national economy means that there is a greater need than ever for trained specialists to plan, organise and deliver what are sometimes mammoth events. As with most professionalising fields, there has been some discussion of the traits, attributes and skills that the modern-day event manager needs to possess. Their leadership style and qualities are discussed in depth in Chapter 2, and the skills they need to apply are touched upon in many of the subsequent chapters. These newer industry requirements generate questions about how such skills are acquired and the role of events management education in the professionalisation of future event managers.

CASE STUDY 1.3

Is events management a profession?

Presumably, most readers and practitioners in the field would immediately confirm, without reservation, that it is indeed a profession. In fact, many of us speak of the 'events management profession' all the time. Yet, we rarely compare it to other, more traditional professions – such as doctors, accountants and teachers. Part of the problem in referring to the events field as 'a profession', and to its managers as 'professionals', lies in the historical definitions of such terms, which are probably now quite outdated.

In 1859, Sir Lionel Bertram provided one such early English definition, which spoke of 'a calling by which gentlemen, not born to the inheritance of a gentleman's allowance of good things, might ingeniously obtain the same by some exercise of his abilities' (in Trollope 1859: 88). This was a reference to the privileged who lacked personal wealth or means and were therefore required to work to support themselves. This elitist model seems to stem mainly from an outdated system of class-based power which is certainly no longer as strong in most Western economies. Its proponents used their knowledge of their field to exert power over those who needed their services. This, in turn, was used to justify their salaries and to protect their own and their associates' incomes from unqualified entry by newcomers to the field.

Since these early days, this view of professionalism has become outmoded due to cultural, social and technological changes in society. In the 1950s, Greenwood (1957) called for occupations to be seen in a more complex way – as exhibiting specific attributes that could be viewed as the practical manifestations of the concept of professionalism. This view represented a more dynamic process, which writers such as Wilensky (1964: 144) termed 'professionalization':

> Professionalization . . . refers to a process and there is sometimes the explicit argument put forward that this process occurs as a determinate sequence of events; that in the process of professionalization an occupation

passes through predictable stages of organizational change, the end-state of which is professionalization.

This process of professionalisation provided advantages for many occupations that had not previously been acknowledged as true professions, and later in the article Wilensky suggested that there was a gradual professionalisation of everyone as all occupations sought similar status. However, as few were able to agree on what constituted 'a professional', Millerson's (1964a) study established six core traits:

1   Skill based on theoretical knowledge.
2   The provision of training and education.
3   Testing the competence of members.
4   Organisation.
5   Adherence to a professional code of conduct.
6   Altruistic service.

However, such definitions have the danger of the profession defining itself.

Wilensky (1964) categorised the process of the development of a profession into five stages:

1   The emergence of a full-time occupation.
2   The establishment of a training school.
3   The founding of a professional association.
4   Political agitation directed towards the protection of the association by law.
5   The adoption of a formal code.

Later, Hoyle and John (1995) argued that freedom from government control was imperative to any true profession. Such a view suggests the need for a professional association – to regulate the profession under the protection of the law, exert collective responsibility and maintain integrity and thus behave autonomously.

The debates over what constitutes a professional and a profession, and the course by which a bona-fide profession might be established, and the extent to which everyone might be considered 'a professional' continue. However, it seems to be a crucial step in the evolution of the international events industry, the future role of the event manager and the evolving role of events education and certification.

Source: Adapted from an unpublished paper by C. Bladen and A. McKechnie

> ### Study activity
>
> 1 In your opinion, to what extent is events management a profession? Use evidence to support your answer.
> 2 How far does the present approach of defining the attributes of the events management profession resemble the various approaches presented in this case?
> 3 How might professionalism be more effectively achieved in events management?

1.8 The events profession and education

There are thousands of institutions worldwide which offer formal qualifications and training in events management. These have widely varying emphases, levels of required practical work experience to be undertaken by students, delivery styles and types of resulting qualifications. Some of these variations have developed as artefacts of the institutions' individual national education systems. Others are as a result of the particular and practical nature of events education when compared to other disciplines. Certainly, as industry requirements become more clearly articulated and understood, and education providers work more in tandem with them, increased cohesion between the planned educational outcomes of events management study programmes and employers is likely to emerge.

Chapter 5 discusses the establishment of events employee attributes in more detail, and it should be stressed that preparation for a lifelong career in the events industry will likely involve the need for graduates to possess more than just the skills and competences required by employers at the entry level to graduate employment. There has been some effort on the part of academics to build a clear Event Management Body of Knowledge (EMBOK) model (see http://www.embok.org). This model attempts to integrate skills in event domains of practice with the values by which they should be practised and the systems of working at each stage of an event's management. It is further explained and evaluated in relation to event design in Chapter 3, but, because of its rather holistic approach, it has proven challenging to use as a practical basis for events education programme design.

The obvious limitations of EMBOK have led organisations such as the Canadian Tourism Human Resource Council to spearhead the development of an industry-led alternative – EMICS: Event Management International Competency Standards project (CTHRC, 2011).

CASE STUDY 1.4

Developing an international events management competency project

Location: Canada

The CTHRC used existing national standards from participating countries, materials from the Event Management Body of Knowledge (EMBOK) and cutting-edge research to create a comprehensive summary of the knowledge, skills and attitudes needed to manage an event expertly anywhere in the world. Once completed, the standards were subjected to a rigorous, large-scale validation by events practitioners from over twenty countries in 2009.

With the standards complete, the CTHRC and the EMICS stakeholders turned their attention towards developing a professional, internationally recognised certification programme. Launched in Canada in the autumn of 2010, the Emerit Event Management certification programme consists of an exam, a practical evaluation and on-the-job experience.

An international benchmark, the EMICS credential transcends borders and event disciplines, allowing the mutual recognition of transferable qualifications. Employers will appreciate that Emerit-certified events professionals have met standards set by international industry experts and events professionals will have access to opportunities throughout the globe.

As opportunities for worker mobility increase, so will opportunities for learner mobility. Post-secondary institutions are already starting to adopt EMICS as a tool for informing new and existing curricula. 'Our industry has suffered from the lack of a formal career path', says Didier Scaillet, Chief Development Officer at MPI. 'The Standards correct this situation by providing a robust, relevant, and globally consistent framework for the development of competencies through academic and training offerings.'

Several international education institutions have officially adopted the standards into their curriculum. It is hoped that training opportunities such as EMICS benefit developing countries in particular and that such a curriculum will help event professionals create jobs and contribute to their country's economic growth as they draw investors and tourists to their regions with well-executed, professional events.

Following the successful launch of its first international standard and certification, the CTHRC will focus on developing a complementary international Event Management Qualification Framework. This framework will illustrate different career paths available to both students and experienced professionals. Consultations with industry professionals and educational institutions will be ongoing and volunteers are always welcome.

Source: CTHRC 2011

1.9 How this book is structured

The overarching aim of this book is to provide a working knowledge of the field of events management. This chapter has given a general summary of the development of the present-day industry, and has outlined some of the fundamental questions for both students and practitioners in the field. The following section provides an overview of the remainder of the book.

This book has been designed to cover the wide variety of events that make up the subject matter of most events management courses, as well as to provide practical event planning and event management skills and knowledge. There is a brief outline of each chapter below.

To support students in developing their understanding of the topics covered, a number of features have been included in each chapter:

- clearly stated aims at the start of each chapter;
- international case studies;
- student activities; and
- suggestions for further reading.

Many industry-focused features are also available on the book's companion website.

1.9.1 Chapter1: Introduction

This first chapter analyses the role and significance of events from historical times until the present day. It sets out how events have evolved and describes the current state of the events industry. Importantly, it also contains this summary section, setting out the book's structure. When researching any aspect of event management, this chapter will provide a key starting point from which the rest of the text can be navigated.

1.9.2 Chapter 2: Managing event projects

This chapter analyses events as projects, with specific features that need to be planned, managed and evaluated in order for a successful event project to be delivered. As projects, events generally have fixed budgets, precise timelines and limited resources, including employees, suppliers, venues and volunteers. In this chapter, students will be introduced to the principles of project management and shown how these principles can be applied to events. This chapter discusses these techniques outside of the simple application of limited, functional management theories and argues that, when applied correctly, event project management can produce better and faster results to plan and deliver events.

1.9.3 Chapter 3: Event design and production

Event design, as a core process in events management, is rarely covered outside of logistical considerations in the events literature. This chapter evaluates the value of a range of social and psychological approaches to understanding the event experience and explores how these can be applied in the design of events to produce authentic and exciting attendee experiences. Working through this chapter will help event managers design events from the initial concept through to design development and production considerations.

1.9.4 Chapter 4: Event operations

This chapter follows logically from the previous one. Operational planning begins once the event concept has been decided upon, a venue has been chosen and the event has been designed and a project plan put in place. To deliver an event successfully, event managers must consider all its elements and determine the resources, skills and equipment needed to deliver them. This chapter covers all aspects of operational planning and management, including the legal external environment – the consideration of legalities, regulations, licences, permits and contracts involved when managing an event – and the event logistics, including the logistical planning for both customers and on-site at venues.

1.9.5 Chapter 5: Managing the event human resource

This chapter provides an overview and analysis of core human resource management issues in the events industry, including recruiting, motivating and rewarding staff, the role of volunteers in events, and the requirements of key legislation affecting the human resource function of event management. The relationship between event organisations and their staff will be considered from the perspective of the 'pulsating organisation'. Finally, the issues of professionalism in the contemporary events industry will be evaluated.

1.9.6 Chapter 6: Event finance

Financial management is vital to the success of an event and forms a core area of competence for any event manager. This chapter examines the key aspects of event finance, at a variety of scales, helping readers develop their knowledge of important financial terms and methods. Having read it, event managers should be able to write, interpret and present financial documents that will be required by colleagues, internal and external stakeholders and clients.

1.9.7 Chapter 7: Event marketing

As the events industry has grown, so has the wealth of research and practical guidance on how to market events. This chapter sets out the key areas of marketing, such as market analysis, marketing planning, marketing techniques, control methods and evaluation. As well as these established areas of event marketing, the chapter also explores the role of sponsorship within the events industry and the advantages and challenges that this presents to event managers. Connections are made in this chapter between the development of the marketing function for modern events, the scope for communication of sponsorship messages to specific audiences and the significant cost recovery potential to event managers of developing relationships with sponsors.

1.9.8 Chapter 8: Event health, safety and risk management

Historically, issues of health and safety have been perceived as a bureaucratic burden on event managers and organisations. In recent years, however, a number of high-profile accidents and disasters have occurred that have highlighted the importance of developing excellence in the management of health, safety and risk for organisations, their staff and event attendees. As well as this focus from within the industry, governments and other regulatory agencies have promoted and enforced new legislation and standards on the events industry with which organisations must comply or face hefty financial and even criminal penalties. Individual event managers have a significant responsibility to deliver events that reflect this new reality, and this chapter evaluates key areas of risk facing event managers before offering important techniques for managing these.

1.9.9 Chapter 9: Sporting events

In this chapter, the specific characteristics of sporting events are analysed. Such events have been hugely significant in the development of the events industry and continue to feature prominently on the events landscape – from the smallest community competition to mega-events with billions of dollars of turnover. The chapter considers the factors affecting attendance at sports events, the behaviour of spectators, and how the sports events sector has developed to meet the changing profile of audiences – who may attend in person or form part of the huge global sports media audience. Issues of crowd management and venue design – in which sports events are at the cutting edge of development – are explored in detail.

1.9.10 Chapter 10: Mega-events

Mega-events, such as the Olympic Games and World Expositions, have become features of the global economic and cultural landscape. Governments compete to bring them to their cities to catalyse economic, social and cultural change. This chapter analyses the rise of the mega-event as a device for promoting development and regeneration, and examines vital aspects of the management of these global media events, including the bidding process, resourcing, media, security and event tourism.

1.9.11 Chapter 11: Events in the public and third sectors

In this chapter, the differences between the private, public and third sectors of event organisations are explained. The public and third sectors operate in a different context to the profit-seeking private sector, which has been the focus of the majority of events management texts. Building on the material found elsewhere in this book on key aspects of events management that are applicable to events in all sectors of the economy, this chapter attempts to highlight the particular characteristics of third sector and public sector events and the different nature and style of managing their success. We analyse types of events that are unique to these sectors – including consultations, fundraising events, political events and faith events – along with issues such as the political impacts of public sector events and the funding challenges facing third sector event organisations.

1.9.12 Chapter 12: Corporate events

The corporate events sector is extremely broad and diverse. This chapter introduces readers to this complexity, exploring the success factors and challenges for meetings and conferences, incentives, networking events, corporate hospitality, exhibitions and trade shows. As well as analysing the different forms of corporate events, the chapter presents an analysis of the corporate event consumer and looks at influences on the contemporary corporate events industry from the perspectives of both suppliers and consumers.

1.9.13 Chapter 13: Cultural events and festivals

This chapter provides an overview of the cultural events and festival sector of the events industry. Cultural events and festivals can often be understood only with reference to the relationship that they have to the expressions of individual and group identities and cultures, and this chapter provides a categorisation of cultural events from this perspective, as well as an overview of arts and entertainment events. In addition to this categorisation, we discuss management approaches to cultural events that are specific to this sector, including audience development and specialised marketing techniques.

1.9.14 Chapter 14: Event impacts, sustainability and legacy

The impact of events is central to both events management education and the sustainable management of the events industry. This chapter analyses the economic, environmental and social impacts of events and provides techniques for the management and evaluation of these impacts. The concepts of sustainability and sustainable events are introduced in this chapter and put into the context of the global economic crisis. We also propose a new model of sustainable economic development that offers a novel perspective on the future growth of the events industry.

1.9.15 Chapter 15: Events and the media

The relationship between events and the media is critical, both in terms of how events are represented in the media and how event managers make use of the media to communicate with their stakeholders. Media coverage of an event can shape how that event is perceived, with positive and negative implications for how the event is managed. This chapter explores the ways in which event managers can obtain and shape media messages. Understanding how the media operates and how to develop positive relationships with journalists and editors, and how to work with new forms of social media, can be vital in delivering a successful event.

Industry voice

Howard Evans, managing director, the Conference Business

How was it twenty-five years ago?

Anyone getting into the events business more than twenty-five years ago did so through four main channels: associations; magazine or newspaper publishers; hotels and banqueting venues; and the corporate sector. Associations and similar bodies produced the largest numbers of events, to inform and educate their memberships. Technical and trade publishers started organising conferences and exhibitions to make a little more money out of their readers and advertisers. The journalists wrote the selling copy and found the speakers while their advertising departments did the marketing. Hotels and banqueting venues saw that events could fill their banqueting spaces and bedrooms. Banqueting managers were quickly re-badged as 'event managers', usually with no training. Large public companies had always held Annual General Meetings for their shareholders but were finding that staff conferences could incentivise employees and instil company messages at the same time.

I came into the business when working for the Financial Times Group, first as a journalist and later as a publishing manager. FT conferences were short of an overseas conferences manager and as I had travelled a lot in an earlier life in the navy and seemed plausible, I was offered the job. It was much better paid than publishing, so I took it. It was that easy then.

The FT was and still is a major player in high-level business conferences, organising more than fifty a year, about of a third of them overseas. FT conferences were like cruise liners of the time: stately, expensive and exclusive. As only top executives could afford to attend them, they replicated the best business schools with brilliant minds – without audio-visual technology support – talking to other brilliant and important people. Splendid lunches with cocktails and wine bisected the day.

What has happened since?

At one level, surprisingly little has changed in the events business in twenty-five years. The four organiser groupings have changed a bit, with associations now including government agencies and political and pressure groups. Publishing companies have generally spun off their events departments into separate and often larger companies than the original parents. The hotels and venue sector now offers more organising skills and inputs than before. Corporate events have widened their scope to cover shareholder, employee and customer communications. 'Experiential' training courses – learning through doing – are replacing many classroom-based courses as employees are encouraged to find better leadership and team-working qualities through shared experiences.

The big change has been in the way data technology is now used in the events business. Presentations once on 35mm slide carousels have been replaced with a memory stick in a data projector and the outputs of the event are now distributed via websites, DVDs and online rather than in heavy, expensive volumes of conference proceedings. Technology has liberated the events business so that delegates or visitors can select what they want to receive, in which format and when.

Where are we today?

In a quarter of a century the events business in Britain, Europe and the rest of the world has boomed. What was once an exclusive product is now available to virtually everyone in some format. You don't have to be a scientist or in business to go to a conference or exhibition for your area of interest.

The events growth worldwide has been driven by travel becoming so much cheaper. It can be cheaper and more convenient to hold your event overseas than at home. Travelling from London to Italy can be as quick and the same price as a train journey from London to Plymouth.

What does the future hold?

Some pessimists have been predicting the end of the events business as we know it for a long time. We have the technology to replace people meetings with cyber conferences or events.

A few years ago, virtual conferences and exhibitions were promoted as the next big thing in events. IT and marketing wizards created online conferences where you could hear or download the presentations of the event. The virtual exhibition – which had a floor plan and list of exhibitors – followed. The exhibitors' offers were also available onscreen. Virtual conferences failed because they did not connect people with each other or with any shared experience. The excitement of human contact is at the heart of the events business.

The skills and talents needed by the event organiser of the future will continue to be creativity, an understanding of how human contact works, and the skill to harness the latest technology to these ends.

1.10 Summary

This chapter has discussed the evolution of events as part of human culture, from their historical foundations to their present-day status as part of a prominent global industry which is a major revenue earner for entire national economies. This rapid and substantial contemporary development has included the revival of many traditional events in a modern-day context, as well as the introduction of many new events, all of which demand knowledgeable, qualified and professional event managers to deliver them.

All of the chapters in this book present basic definitions and descriptions of the key management practices presently employed in the events industry and then link these to the most important theoretical and management frameworks used to inform their successful practice. As event academics and practitioners, the authors have taken care to reflect present industry thinking and practice, whilst simultaneously attempting to challenge anything that might be considered outdated or inconsistent. In such cases, new or adapted models and theories have been proposed in order to stimulate debate and new practice in this fast-moving, international industry. To supplement this approach, many industry leaders and practitioners have been chosen to share their experiences in the 'Industry Voice' sections.

Further reading

EMBOK (2011) Introduction [online]. Available from: http://www.embok.org. Accessed 29 June 2011. EMBOK is a recognised model of the core competences required by event managers that has been applied in the industry and to the study of the field.

Getz, D. (2008). Event Tourism: Definition, Evolution, and Research. *Tourism Management*, 29 (3): 403–428. This is a very useful article for gaining an overview of the study of events and also includes references to many important sources.

Maslow, A. H. (1943) A Theory of Human Motivation, *Psychological Review*, 50 (4): 370–396. Available from: http://psychclassics.yorku.ca/Maslow/motivation.htm. Accessed 29 June 2011. This article is the source of Maslow's 'Hierarchy of Needs' model, which is a recurring feature of management literature.

Chapter 2

Managing event projects

Contents

2.1 Aims

By the end of this chapter, the student will be able:

- To understand the importance of event project management to the international events industry.
- To explain the organisational issues that must be taken into consideration when managing event projects.
- To relate event project management to conventional event planning theories and practices.
- To explain the processes related to effective event project management throughout the event cycle.

2.2 Introduction

Following the discussion in the previous chapter about the variety of events specialists are responsible for organising, we come to more of the essential considerations when planning, delivering and evaluating such projects. As projects, events generally have fixed budgets, precise timelines, and limited resources, including employees, suppliers, venues and volunteers. Organisers of such events are therefore responsible for the management and delivery of projects. Project management has developed processes and techniques to help plan, organise, lead and control events, and it can be used to make event projects more successful. This chapter discusses these techniques outside of the simple application of limited, functional management theories and argues that, when applied correctly, event project management can produce better and faster results to plan and deliver events.

2.3 Events as projects

Projects are distinct from the day-to-day processes of an organisation. As Pinto (2010: 25) observes: 'Project work is continually evolving, establishes its own work rules, and is the antithesis of repetition in the workplace.' Events are projects because they are of limited duration, require a degree of coordination of tasks towards goals, usually have a fixed budget, and are unique occurrences. Whilst each event requires a combination of the management functions discussed throughout this book, they are different from most business processes in that they do not generally exhibit the ordinary day-to-day processes of most organisations. For example, even fairly small event offices in hotels or conference centres can organise a wide variety of one-off events. Even though several wedding events might, to some extent, have similar features, different influences – such as the bride and groom's specific requirements, attendance size, desired service style, budget and programme – may make each event distinct. Although a single event manager may lead all these separate events, they will be classified as distinct projects.

As can be seen in Figure 2.1, most events exhibit the characteristics of projects. This tendency generally increases with the size and scale of the event. Each of the characteristics of events are expanded in the subsections below.

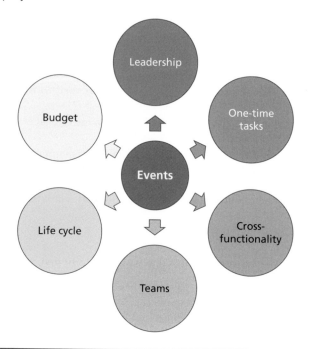

Figure 2.1 The characteristics of events as projects

2.3.1 Leadership

Events are often the ultimate responsibility of one lead event manager who coordinates specialist functions. The centralised and hierarchical nature of the leadership role can depend upon the scale of the event. A mega-event, such as the Olympic Games, has a national planning committee ultimately accountable to its international parent, whilst corporate events are often under the direct leadership of a single event manager. There will be more discussion of this unusual leadership role later in this chapter.

2.3.2 Budget

Events almost always have specific budgets allocated to them. As discussed in Chapter 6, the accurate calculation of such budgets will often include difficult predictions of fixed and projected variable costs in relation to forecasted attendee numbers. Such calculations cannot be considered reliable if made in isolation from other important project factors, such as schedules, timelines and project life-cycle stages. For example, cuts in government funding will inevitably curtail the provision and/or scale of public sector events.

2.3.3 Life cycle

Each event has a defined beginning and end within its life cycle. There are a variety of life cycles proposed in the field of project management to aid managers in distinguishing key phases throughout a project's life. However, the models of business cycles used by such industries as engineering and software development tend to accommodate the tendency in such industries for the phases of each cycle to be definitively completed, leading to the definite beginning of the next phase. Event project managers do not often have this luxury, as they are required to handle multiple tasks, contractors and other (often complex and interrelated) factors simultaneously. This is particularly the case with large exhibitions, which can often take two years to plan and execute for delivery over a single week. In practice, this means that major exhibition organisers are likely to find themselves managing both this year's and next year's events at the same time. An international organisation such as Gartner, which operates across a number of continents at any one time, often has to have team members who are geographically spread working on a variety of different projects at any given time. This demands effective communications, which makes project management software packages, such as Microsoft Project, and international databases imperative, so that team members can alter event details and send immediate project updates to their colleagues through the company's international intranet.

2.3.4 Tasks

Events often require the performance of tasks that will not be repeated, even in recurring annual events. The complexity of certain larger events means that even seemingly simple tasks or functions – such as catering, volunteer recruitment or themeing – must be approached in a distinct manner in order to reinforce the uniqueness of a particular event from year to year. This obviously becomes even more complicated when an event moves location or venue, even if the concept of an annual event remains consistent. Add design and production elements (discussed in Chapter 3), and the tasks become even more complex and variable for different events. Successive Summer and Winter Olympics organising committees have often found it difficult to learn from past events because, although the basic format of such mega-events remains constant, many of the problems and complexities differ due to changes in the city where the event is being held and such factors as culture, government legislation and even the basis on which initial bids by individual cities are made.

2.3.5 Cross-functionality

Event organisations are likely to be required to work cross-functionally, without formal authority. This principle mainly depends on the type of event project being managed and the corresponding organisational structure required for optimal effectiveness and efficiency of execution. In other words, as most industries have clearly needed to adopt project management techniques in order to improve their performances, event managers have always, in a sense, been project managers due to an ongoing need for them to have versatile skills in a number of key business areas in order to be successful. Indeed, as this book suggests throughout, event project managers do not have the luxury of simply being good financial managers, as they must also be effective marketers and human resource managers – and almost anything else that's required!

2.3.6 Teams

Events require working teams to be brought together only for the duration of a particular project. Most event organisations tend to vary their approach towards formality of event leadership and the corresponding organisational structure; it is not uncommon for the make-up of teams employed on particular events to vary according to a variety of factors. Goldblatt (2005) applies Toffler's (1990) discussion of the 'pulsating organisation' to events, particularly in relation to the fluctuating numbers of volunteers required throughout the events cycle. Events such as trade exhibitions have often staggered delegate registration, giving priority to trade deals on the first day, the general public on the second day and students towards the end of the third day. Obviously, this is based on trade considerations, but it can result in some exhibitors leaving early and there being a need for fewer volunteers and other workers. These workers are required in larger numbers for the event set-up and breakdown, but not in the middle of the event. Thus, this organisation 'pulsation' takes place in accordance with the event cycle.

2.3.7 The event project life cycle

Events have a distinct timeline and life cycle. In Figure 2.2, Silvers demonstrates the link between an event's stages – from initiation to closure – and the levels of activity associated with these stages throughout an event's life, from start to finish. This classification has proven generally useful to event project managers in order to understand levels of activity required at the progressive stages of an event's conception, research, planning, delivery and evaluation (see Chapter 1).

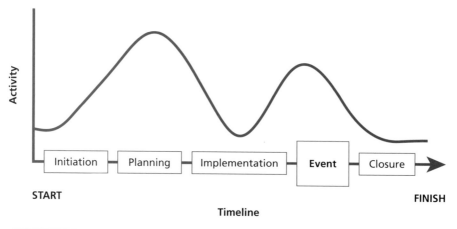

Figure 2.2 The event project life cycle
Source: Silvers 2007: 159

2.4 Project management perspectives

When considering how to apply project management to events, a project leader should consider their overall perspective. As discussed by Kolltveit *et al.* (2007), there are six major perspectives to project management, all of which can be applied directly to the management of the event project.

- The *task perspective* focuses on the delivery of the event as specified, on time and within the set budget. Certainly, it is important to clients that such projects as corporate events and weddings meet the criteria specified beforehand as they represent the most tangible and measureable success factors for the event. Any event project team will need to focus on the scope of the event concept and operations, as well as clear targets, measureable results for evaluation, high levels of ongoing project supervision and tangible event legacy criteria.

This has certainly been the approach thus far with the types of modern mega-events described in Chapter 10. These events, such as the Olympic Games, focus on the tangible measures necessitated by the adoption of the task perspective to events.

- The *leadership perspective* to event projects depends upon theories of leadership styles, communication styles and processes, decision-making, management of team characteristics and organisation, clear allocations of team members' functions and responsibilities, interim milestone delivery dates, reviews and feedback.
- The *stakeholder perspective* to event projects is heavily used in the events industry and focuses on identification of key stakeholder groups and the management of their relations to ensure event success.
- The *transaction-cost perspective* to event projects views the production of an event as a commercial transaction and mainly focuses on governance of the project and its cost structure with particular reliance upon contracts and innovation.
- The *systems perspective* to event projects views the event as an overall holistic system, rather than made up of individual, functional components such as marketing, finance, design and so on.
- The *business-by-project perspective* to event projects views events as individual investments which yield returns or benefits in their own right. This perspective relies upon investment methods and portfolio management, among others. Whilst this approach is probably more common with the development of technological innovations through business start-ups, most large event management companies, to some extent, maintain proprietary interests over a series of different event product concepts at any one time.

Kolltveit *et al.* (2007) found that the writers in the general project management field centre on the leadership and task perspectives. Certainly, the main perspectives adopted by events management writers to date tend to be based mainly on project tasks and stakeholder perspectives. It is argued that more investigation should be made into the relevance of the other perspectives

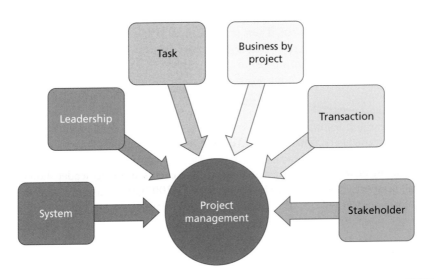

Figure 2.3 Perspectives on project management
Source: Adapted from Kolltveit *et al.* 2007: 4

to the field, in particular those related to event leadership, due to the specific nature of the event planner's role as project manager of complex and highly variable events.

2.4.1 The emerging importance of projects

The origins of project management can be traced back to its use during large-scale government projects in the nineteenth century. This then advanced in the building projects initiated as a result of the Second World War, moving project management towards the form that is used in events management today. The field developed its own project management body of knowledge (PMBOK) and its own professional qualifications, such as the Project Management Professional (PMP) certification.

2.4.2 The core competences of an event project manager

By applying the information provided by the PMP certification (see LaBrosse 2007: 99–100), we can see that an effective event project manager requires a variety of diverse yet interrelated core competences which should be applied throughout the event project stages of initiation, planning, implementation, delivery and closure.

Event managers need to be able to select suitable projects and, in the event of multiple products, they must be able to prioritise between them in relation to the requirements of their organisation. Such prioritisation will likely be related to strategic factors and overall feasibility. Initiation of the project will require the event manager to be able to assemble the initial project team and stakeholders, which may include provisional agreements from key personalities associated with the event, such as top entertainers, leading sponsors, specialised designers and producers, as well as possible donors and benefactors in the case of voluntary and fundraising events. An event manager's ability to initiate an event project also relies upon their skill in developing an effective project contract so that further planning may proceed.

The event project manager will need to be a competent project planner of the event's key delivery milestones, processes and reviews to ensure the project is kept on track through effective ongoing performance measurement. There is also a need to highlight possible areas of conflict between different functions of the event team in these areas. They will be a project leader throughout the event, careful to make sure they capitalise on the skills of others who are involved in the project, and deciding when specific areas should be contracted out to other event specialists.

The event project manager will need to be competent to manage the event's scope, schedule, cost, procurement and resources. The risks to the satisfactory and successful delivery of the event itself (as opposed to 'risk management' of the health, safety and welfare of those associated with it, as covered in Chapter 8) will need to be accurately assessed and managed in the form of insurance and contingencies. As the planning and delivery of the event progresses, required changes will need to be identified and managed, aided by associated performance tracking and reporting. Communication should be facilitated via appropriate media throughout the event. In particular, stakeholders may need to be kept up to date with developments and teams involved in meetings to foster a constructive atmosphere of teamwork, consultation and feedback. Communication skills will also include the ability to negotiate with all parties associated with the event, both inside and outside the project organisation. The event project manager will eventually need to evaluate the overall accomplishment of the event's objectives and legacy, as well as document these findings.

2.5 Event project definition, organisation and framework

Following the foregoing discussion of events as projects and the various approaches an event manager might take towards them, it is now important to consider the most effective type of organisational structure for the event.

2.5.1 Functional and project-led organisations

Event organisations are often temporary and differ slightly, depending on the project concerned. They will have a structure with predefined reporting relationships, functional 'departments' and systems to carry out the project. *Functional organisations* group members of staff who perform similar tasks into departments, as is shown in Figure 2.4.

Project-led organisations group people into temporary teams for the duration of a project. The events industry clearly comprises both types of organisation. Certainly, an international event venue, such as Excel in London, has a functional infrastructure of departments responsible

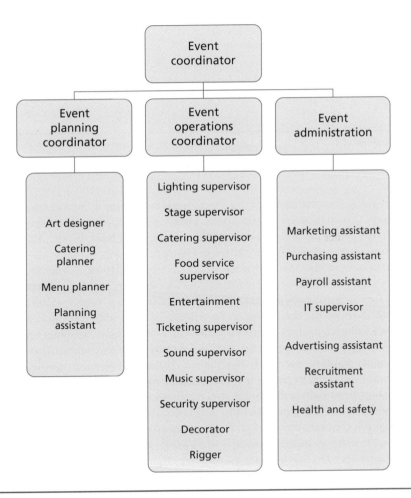

Figure 2.4 Functional event organisation

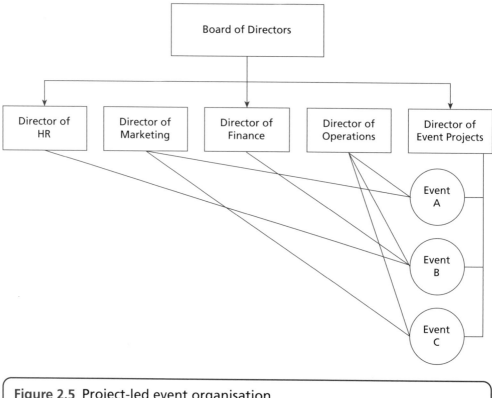

Figure 2.5 Project-led event organisation

for such activities as financial management, operational management, human resource management and so on. No doubt event organisations, such as Gartner – a project-led organisation – will use different people on different events as the concept and brief dictate. An example of a project-led organisational structure is shown in Figure 2.5.

Matrix organisations combine functional and project-led structures in order to perform both focuses at the same time, as illustrated in Figure 2.6. This structure enables both a project-led and a functional approach to events, so it is particularly suitable for this industry. However, it should be noted that in order for the matrix to be project-led, it is important that authority and responsibility for important event project elements – such as budgetary and other resource control – reside with the project manager at the event level rather than the functional manager of the department under which the event is being delivered. Failure to adopt this approach will tend to weaken the matrix and relegate the event project manager to the more minor role of administrator.

It may be tempting to adopt the matrix structure without reservation, considering its appeal in combining the best of both functional and project-led structures. In many cases, this structure does indeed profit the event in question, but there can also be a number of problems with it. In particular, the decision-making processes of an event, particularly during the delivery stage, often have to be very flexible in order to respond immediately to sudden crises or changes in the event's micro or macro environments. The matrix approach often slows down these processes as the project group is required to spend too much time in consultation across areas of responsibility before reaching a consensus. This can lead to serious delays and severe, yet unnecessary, project failures.

Figure 2.6 Matrix event organisation

1 List the strengths and weaknesses of each of the above event organisation structures.
2 Discuss the most suitable organisation type for each of the following:

- A venue specialising in wedding events.
- An event production company involved in creating and delivering one-off corporate events for a variety of leading brand clients.
- The planning committee of the 2018 World Cup.

2.5.2 Project leadership

Whether an event organisation uses a functional, project-led or matrix structure for its events, its choice will, for the most part, dictate the type of leadership which is most practical for that particular structure. The leadership of the organisation, along with its structure, will in turn heavily influence its project culture, which will have its own influences on the delivery of the event itself. According to Pinto (2010: 130), project leadership 'involves inspiring, motivating, influencing, and changing behaviours of others in pursuit of a common goal'. Event project leadership therefore differs from management and administration tasks and responsibilities, which are mostly functional, and focuses on the actions of an individual in their relationship with others who are involved in the event.

Kurt Lewin – one of the pioneers of analysing organisations – carried out research into leadership styles. In their 1939 paper, Lewin *et al.* identified three main, prevailing leadership styles which shaped

- authoritarian;
- democratic; and
- laissez-faire work environments.

Authoritarian work environments are led by an autocratic leader who makes decisions on behalf of the team and divides work tasks and processes accordingly, providing critique of the team's performance whilst often not engaging closely with either the team or its activities. Democratic work environments have leaders who consult team members to arrive at consensus regarding important decisions, offering guidance as required, as well as praise and constructive criticism throughout. Laissez-faire work environments have little tangible leadership input, with the leader allowing all major decisions to be made and executed by the team members themselves. The latter demonstrate 'free rein' and receive little input or feedback from the leader.

Study activity

1 Which of Lewin's work environments above would be best for:

   (a) encouraging motivation and participation by event team members?
   (b) encouraging innovation?

2 What are the advantages and disadvantages of each?
3 Which type of leadership would you prefer to be following? Why?
4 Complete Table 2.1, adding 'High' or 'Low' to each cell.

Table 2.1 Leadership styles

	Leadership style		
	Autocratic	Democratic	Laissez-faire
Time required for decision-making			
Scope for innovation			
Promotion of participation			
Team member motivation			

	Autocratic	Democratic	Laissez-faire
Ability of team members to voice disagreement			
Scope for leader to make mistakes			
Direct/formal communication			
Open team discussion			
Quality of decision-making			
Clarity of mission			

These main traditional leadership styles can certainly be useful in a general sense to inform leaders of event projects, even in reference to the discussions that have hopefully resulted from the completion of the above activity. However, subsequent developments in leadership theory have been more specific to project management itself. Whilst it remains useful for students of events management to consider the administrative and process tools we will review later in this chapter, understanding this rather dated emphasis is not the prime focus of researchers in the project management field.

Turner *et al.* (2009) found that project success was increasingly linked to leadership competences rather than tools and techniques, as had been previously thought. This finding built on the work of Dulewicz and Higgs (2005), which isolated three main project leadership styles: goal-orientated leadership; involving leadership; and engaging leadership. Goal-orientated leadership, which involves the 'management by objectives' approach to events espoused by leading authors in the field (e.g. Bowdin *et al.* 2011; Goldblatt 2005; Shone and Parry 2010), appears more useful in environments that remain mainly stable in nature. However, many event practitioners might suggest that an event project can be quite an unstable context for management, perhaps due to the intangibility of the perceived end product and the fluidity of the context in which it is being delivered. Involving leadership therefore may be more suitable to deal with the transitory features common to event project organisation. Industry managers often find definitions, plans, resources and many other important project variables in a state of flux. Finally, the engaging leadership approach appears impractical for anything other than the smallest or most specialised event teams, due to the transformative nature of the leadership role and the level of corresponding employee commitment that is required. The particular attributes and competences of such leaders are discussed later in this chapter.

2.5.3 Project organisation

Any event project manager must have the ability to form teams, as this is vital to the success of any event's production. (The management of event teams is discussed in depth in Chapter 5.) However, simply selecting team members and placing them in functional groups is often not the most efficient or effective means to staff an event, as this does not suit the common structure of the event organisation. It may also stifle the creativity of design described in Chapter 3. Therefore, team members and their formal and informal interrelationships should ideally reflect accommodation of the cross-functional activities associated with the events industry. For example, the event's security detail will often also be involved in safety and customer service provision, so the team should be constructed to enable these important and interrelated capacities.

Teams and teamwork are usually more effective than individuals in event projects because:

- They allow more to be achieved as they can accomplish a much wider range of tasks and workloads.
- Team members usually have a wider range of skills, specialisations and thought processes which can be drawn upon in the solution of event problems.
- Teams often make better decisions.
- They often provide a better environment for motivation and can support each other better.
- They are more open to risk-taking as risk is spread across more people associated with an event.

According to Maylor (2010: 248–249), effective project teams require:

- clear goals
- a results-driven structure
- competent team members
- unified commitment
- a collaborative climate
- standards of excellence
- external support and recognition
- effective leadership.

For further discussion of important issues related to team management in events, including team culture, roles, motivation and evaluation, see Chapter 5.

2.6 Project parameters

2.6.1 Project scope

Project scope (although this term is rarely used) is probably the largest area in current events management literature. Most process diagrams, including Figure 2.7, tend to relate to 'event planning'. This figure incorporates the main scope aspects, which, according to Pinto (2010: 157), include concept development, statement of scope, work authorisation, scope reporting, control systems and project close-out.

The problem statement commonly clarifies the reason why the event is taking place, including what it intends to achieve. This can vary even when the same event is held in consecutive years at the same venue. It is vital to gather accurate information – on both the internal and the external operating environments – in the event planning stage. These important activities can take months – or even years, in the case of mega-events – and often form the largest part of the overall feasibility study for the event.

2.6.2 Project requirements and constraints

Constraints to the event's staging, financing and other practical issues need to be considered, as do contingencies and alternatives. Alternative designs, themes, venues and entertainment options are often considered at this point in the event concept's development.

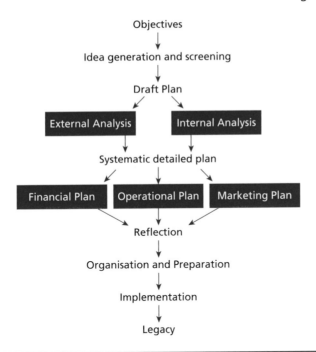

Figure 2.7 Event planning process
Source: Shone and Parry 2010

2.7 Stakeholder requirements and needs

Stakeholder analysis is currently an important topic in events literature, with a much wider definition of the number of parties affected by an event's activities preferred to the narrower, profit-orientated definition used by other business-related fields. In other words, events' often wide-ranging influence and impact on communities and nations make it necessary to consider the needs of all parties affected by them in stakeholder analysis, whether they actively participate or not. This project stage will therefore include the analysis, monitoring and evaluation of the needs and requirements of investors, employees and attendees who seek to benefit from the event's delivery, as well as those of local area residents who may even try to avoid the event and its impacts completely, yet are greatly affected by them. This topic is discussed in depth in Chapter 14.

2.8 The project objective statement

Event objectives form the key direction for the following stages of the project's planning, delivery and evaluation. These objectives provide specifics for concept screening and feasibility analysis and form the overall direction of activities for the project team and associated event contractors to arrive at the accomplishment of the event's outcomes. These must be specific and measurable, where possible, in order to be effective indicators by which the event can be conceived, kept on track, effectively delivered and evaluated. To aid this, Doran's (1981) popular SMART acronym is often used to describe effective event project objectives:

- Specific
- Measureable
- Assignable
- Realistic
- Time-related.

Though not at all scientific, this acronym is a useful guide to the formation of useful objectives. As with any business system, the project objectives will only ever be as effective as the team that sets them, but making them as clear and communicable as possible will help to ensure their effective decoding by important stakeholders, contractors and others associated with the effective outcome of the event.

There is a great deal of discussion about the suitability of the 'management by objectives' approach in events management projects. Certainly, if a project team were to set, achieve and evaluate its own objectives, that may be circular and self-fulfilling. However, the sheer scope of certain events and their potential for instability demand the clear formulation and communication of an effective project objective statement, albeit one that might be modified as the project progresses.

Study activity

Set effective objectives for an event of your choice. Make sure they are specific and measurable. Can their achievement be evaluated effectively by a third party? Check the objectives with someone else. What improvements might be made?

2.9 Project planning

2.9.1 Work breakdown structures

For even the smallest events, most managers will agree that – contrary to the linear nature of several of the popular event planning models that are currently in use – the process of an event project involves a variety of interrelated tasks and functions that need to be broken down into smaller, more clearly distinguishable and easier-to-manage subsections. This work breakdown structure is essentially the basis for the EMBOK model, and it once again attempts to 'departmentalise' event activities into the previously criticised functional structure. On the other hand, it is reasonable to suggest that the successful future of the event management industry depends upon employees who can understand the working dynamics of the smaller elements of event work breakdown.

Work breakdown is important in event projects for several reasons. It enables a clear link to be established between objectives and the tasks required to achieve them; it allows those tasks to be practically divided into functional responsibilities; and it makes progress more tangible for those participating in the event's delivery and for its stakeholders. It also enables more effective evaluation and cost allocation.

2.9.2 Project schedules

Time is a crucial resource in the management and delivery of event projects, not least because event dates often cannot be moved on account of venue availability, other resource availability and the need for up-front procurement payments and deposits. The flexibility of the aforementioned factors also makes delays more likely than in other project-related industries.

2.9.3 Resource breakdown structures

The main event project resources can be broken down into:

- *People* – including the expertise and skills of event specialists, such as designers, specialist entertainers, decorators, those associated with specialist staging activities as well as front-line personnel engaged in customer service delivery and other interactions.
- *Facilities* – including the venue, site and associated amenities, which can also include location and even destination attributes that contribute greatly to the success of any event.
- *Equipment* – including all plant and machinery, from transportation vehicles through to cooking equipment, lighting rigs, sound systems, scaffolds, portable dance floors, toilets and even personnel uniforms.
- *Finance* – as discussed in Chapter 6 and below.
- *Materials* – including anything that can be used to make something else, such as timber, decorations, foodstuffs and paints.

2.10 Project optimisation

2.10.1 Critical path analysis methodology

Critical path analysis requires the analysis of all project tasks. Task dependency – that is, the relationship between the completion of one task before another can be commenced – also needs to be carefully considered. The construction of the critical path analysis of an activity network usually begins with breaking down the activities necessary for the planning of an event and estimating as accurately as possible the earliest and latest start times and duration of each. This can then be represented as shown in Figure 2.8.

By noting each event activity using the above method, the activities can then be represented as an activity network, displaying the relationships and dependencies of tasks to each other. The values in the bottom left of the boxes can be calculated in order to determine how long the project will take. The critical path is the longest path through the dependent activities. (Refer to the companion website for a worked example.)

Critical paths often incorporate elements of contingency planning, also known as capacity constraint buffers (CCB) – a reserve of resources allocated to project tasks that can be drawn upon to facilitate the achievement of particular targets if things do not go according to plan. For example, project managers of specialist corporate events that use an event producer as a central agent for all concept development, design and logistical arrangements will need to protect them as a resource at each stage of the project process. This becomes even more necessary if the producer is working on a number of different projects simultaneously. A CCB must be applied to protect the producer's time as they transition from one part of a single project to another, or one project to the next.

Figure 2.8 Activity notation

2.11 Project evaluation and review techniques

An event project requires ongoing evaluation and review to avoid delays and to manage ongoing changes. Such delays or changes might result in undesirable increases in costs in other types of project, but in event projects they might be lethal to effective delivery.

2.11.1 Evaluation criteria

It is important that the event project team has methods in place to ensure the ongoing evaluation of project scope in terms of its continued adherence to the parameters set by the event objectives. These controls will concern each of the financial, marketing, design and operational areas associated with the event and will need to be supported by relevant documentation of such aspects as expenditure and communication to ensure the initial plan is being adhered to and not changed without authorisation.

Such concerns will also extend to the ongoing monitoring of the event's macro and micro environments. For example, international events rely heavily on attendance by visitors who arrive by air. Any major changes in airline pricing, perhaps as a result of government taxation or direct market factors, may therefore greatly affect potential ticket purchases before the event and may require some corresponding strategic changes to be made.

2.11.2 Review techniques

The event project will require continual evaluation throughout its life cycle. In particular, many event projects are heavily reliant on stakeholder involvement and their promised legacy. They are also commonly subjected to ongoing, critical media scrutiny. These factors, in addition to the usual financial requirements associated with non-event projects, such as return on investment and protection of profits, demand that regular systems are in place to evaluate achievement of the event's key deliverables. The basic process of event project evaluation involves four main reflective stages (see Figure 2.9).

Key event areas which will require evaluation will likely include activity tasks, project milestones and budgetary indicators. Milestones, whilst being clear enough for all team members

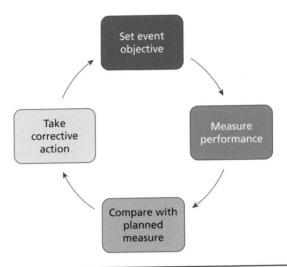

Figure 2.9 The event project evaluation cycle

to understand, present problems if the project suffers serious delays. In such cases, the shortfalls are often revealed too late for them to be remedied effectively. One common way of evaluating and tracking project baselines is with the use of Gantt charts, as shown in Figure 2.10.

The evaluation of any event project depends upon the effective definition and use of critical success factors. Pinto (2010) classifies these factors into:

- project mission
- top management support
- project plans and schedules
- client consultation
- personnel
- technical tasks
- client acceptance
- monitoring and feedback

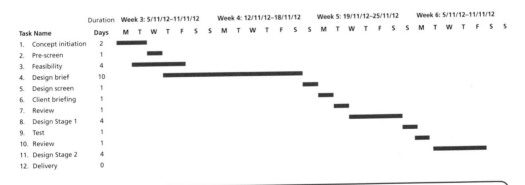

Figure 2.10 Event project tracking Gantt chart

- communication
- troubleshooting.

2.12 Project crashing

Project crashing in events refers to speeding up the delivery process. This becomes necessary when costs can be saved, and when competitor offerings seem likely to steal innovation or successfully imitate other aspects of competitive advantage. Finishing event production early can significantly cut development costs, which may be distinctly advantageous, particularly if this development process has fallen far behind schedule.

The process of project crashing in events might involve increasing the productivity of the existing events team, increasing the resources allocated to the event – which can be in the form of more people, plant and/or equipment – or altering working methods. One way in which crashing can be accomplished is by using more efficient technology for such activities as project meetings, information sharing, ongoing team communication and operational concerns, such as ticketing, sales and reporting. As the project team becomes more liable for financial penalties due to delivery delays, project crashing will likely become more attractive. Crashing can also be achieved by simply contracting out event-related tasks to third-party agencies, thereby freeing up internal resources for reallocation elsewhere. Of course, such outsourcing generates its own set of problems.

> ### Study activity
>
> You have decided to crash an event project in order to save costs. Discuss some of the problems associated with contracting out your event management functions to third parties.

2.13 Project risk management

2.13.1 Definition of project risk management

Pinto (2010: 221) defines risk management as: 'the art and science of identifying, analysing, and responding to risk factors throughout the life of a project and in the best interests of its objectives'. In this section, we shall discuss risk management in terms of the successful completion – or otherwise – of an event project. (Risks associated with the health, safety and welfare of event attendees and employees shall be discussed in depth in Chapter 8. Entrepreneurial risk management, which includes consideration of monetary loss and gain, shall be discussed in Chapter 6.)

Anyone who has worked on even the simplest event project will recognise the complications caused by the unpredicted intervention of problems relating to resources, timings and changes, particularly in the context of the uncontrollable macro environment. The ultimate success of such event projects invariably rests on the project team's ability to solve or lessen the impact of these problems. It cannot be argued that a successful project simply faces fewer problems than an unsuccessful one. It is much more likely that the successful project manager has accurately predicted potential hazards that may come along throughout the project's schedule and has implemented satisfactory contingency measures well in advance. Thus, the art of successful event project risk management lies in the manager's ability to predict the future as accurately as possible.

In order to predict intervening variables before they cause serious problems, event organisers need to ask themselves:

● How might these problems present themselves?
● What will be the symptoms or signs that such problems are occurring?
● What are the likely consequences of doing nothing?
● If something needs to be done, what should it be?

The above questions form part of an internal and external analysis of the event organisation's environment, as discussed in Chapter 1.

2.13.2 Classification of project risk management

Risks need to be assessed in terms of their potential impact on the success of the project and where the source of their control lies. Wysocki (2007) divides risk into the following four categories:

● technical
● project
● organisational
● external.

Projects sometimes fail because suitable technical resources, such as people, expertise or equipment, are unavailable. For example, in production-driven events (as discussed in Chapter 3), there is often inevitable dependence on the creativity of the design team. Staff changes, resignations, disagreements and even illness or death can cause key team members to leave important projects, resulting in significant gaps. In such cases, it is often not a simple case of replacing one person or role with another. For example, two event industry design directors may be considered of equal calibre, but they may have significant creative differences in the way they approach a project.

Charity events often rely on a steady stream of willing volunteers to maintain effective delivery levels, but failure to attract a suitable profile of volunteer can have a serious impact on the success of event projects.

2.13.3 Use of buffers

Though work tends to fill the time available, event project managers can use time and cost buffers in order to offset the impact of several of the aforementioned problems. As their names suggest, cost buffers are extra funds that can be allocated in emergencies, while time buffers are extra hours that can be allocated before the project delivery deadline to offset delays in the schedule. Such buffers are often employed in traditional projects and they frequently help managers overcome problems, but the constraints of event projects can mean that buffers are sometimes ineffective in this sphere. For example, the project managers for the Glastonbury Festival have decided not to hold the world-class, internationally renowned music festival in 2012 due to resource shortages which they say are due to the almost contemporaneous staging

Image 2.1 Portaloos at an event
Source: Jeff Corwin / Getty Images

of the London 2012 Olympic Games. According to one article, the key resources which will be in short supply are police officers and portable toilets (Nicholl 2010).

2.14 Project cost breakdown structures

2.14.1 Total costs

Costing of event projects will likely emphasise price, cost or profit, depending on which is the most relevant to the project in question. It can generally be approached from a top-down or an add-on perspective, depending on whether a fixed budget is provided. Costs will usually be forecasted for events using fixed and variable costs for the resource groups listed earlier in this chapter, which will be subtracted from the forecasted revenues eventually gained from ticket sales made at target prices. Clearly, there are complications to this approach which relate to returns on investment, cash-flow considerations and other event-specific finance issues (covered in more depth in Chapter 6). However, it should be noted that the conventional project management methods regarding cost management tend not to be directly applicable to event projects because the latter rarely present opportunities for guaranteed financial returns. Moreover, cost reductions can rarely be achieved by simple labour reductions (as is possible in other project-based industries), because of the labour-intensive nature of event projects. Also, many events are produced for the not-for-profit and public sectors.

2.14.2 Cost monitoring

For cost monitoring to be successful, the event project manager must allocate costs correctly to each of the project tasks. These should then be reported at regular intervals by the individuals in charge of the relevant tasks' completion. In particular, it is essential with events that contractors are paid correctly, that ongoing expenses are carefully monitored and centrally authorised, and that costs are correctly allocated to the relevant departmental budgets.

2.15 Project implementation

Project implementation concerns the delivery of the event from its live opening to its close. This will involve the practical completion of all the processes related to the tasks with all their associated considerations covered so far in this chapter. The main articulation of this phase of an event will be incorporated into the events programme, which will include a statement beforehand of all the activities that are to be carried out, with the clear assignment of responsibilities for each. Depending on the type of event being staged, the project manager may decide to use a responsibility chart for each of the event programme elements, with an associated time schedule for their completion, as well as other relevant programme details, such as locations and other resource information. Each part of the event's delivery will require ongoing monitoring and reporting systems that should be as simple and user-friendly as possible. These will enable each party to implement their aspects of the work schedule successfully and to take effective remedial action if required. The major evaluative criteria the event manager is most likely to be concerned with include the completion of event delivery tasks, timings and associated cost controls. The more forthcoming and useful this review, the more likely it is that the project manager will be able to remedy shortfalls in these important areas. Remedies may well include the application of predetermined, contingent strategies that will often need to be applied in coordination with the most important event stakeholders. As complicated as these processes may sound, their successful implementation will depend directly on the soundness of the initial event project plan. They might well concern unforeseen circumstances stemming from the event's macro environment, such as adverse weather conditions or terrorist attacks, which may require the overall strategic direction of the event to be significantly altered or even abandoned altogether.

2.16 Project shut-down

Event project shut-down can prove much quicker to implement than its initiation. An events-focused adaptation of Turner's (1999) framework for finishing work can be useful here, and includes the following elements which can be applied to event completion:

- Produce checklists of outstanding work.
- Hold frequent meetings of event teams to ensure that close-down problems are identified and solved.
- Release event personnel from certain teams as they are no longer required, then either reassign them to other parts of the close-down or release them from the project completely.
- Create a specific event close-down 'task-force' to complete outstanding work.
- Close-down contractors and suppliers that are no longer required to avoid unnecessary cost.
- Support the event project manager with a deputy with finishing skills.

Considering the aforementioned importance of stakeholder management, event objectives and planned legacies, it is also important for evaluations of the event to be documented, including its problems, achievements and benefits. Some large event project management organisations, such as Gartner, also elicit attendee feedback through formal research processes, such as interviews and focus groups, at this stage of an event. Overall event evaluation will certainly be required for events that have involved the investment of public funds and those attracting a high degree of media coverage. It is also useful for events that will be repeated. Therefore, the project manager should ensure that the relevant information is planned for well before the event is delivered.

Disbanding event teams can be problematic if not planned well in advance. Many event personnel can experience concerns about future employment, so there can be a tapering of team morale. Some event organisations try to combat this by holding debriefing meetings and end-of-event parties, which may include recognition and rewards for performance achievement.

2.17 The required competences of an event project leader

Following this in-depth analysis of the tasks of an event project leader, it is logical to present a brief consideration of some of the competences needed to lead an event project effectively. Several studies (e.g. Dulewicz and Higgs 2005) suggest that an effective project leader should possess the intellectual, emotional and managerial capacities outlined in Table 2.2.

Table 2.2 Event project leader competences

Intellectual	Emotional	Managerial
Critical analysis and judgment	Self-awareness	Engaging communication
Vision and imagination	Emotional resilience	Managing resources
Strategic perspective	Motivation	Empowering
	Sensitivity	Developing
	Influence	Achieving
	Intuition	
	Conscientiousness	

CASE STUDY 2.1

The big bank project

Location: Various, UK
Event type: corporate event

One of the unique challenges associated with providing professional events management case studies is the competitive nature of this fast-growing industry and the resulting confidentiality that often surrounds examples of outstanding industry practice. However, the following is a real-world, industry case of event project management in action. It is based on the day-to-day activities of a major, international events management company, which cannot be named for proprietary reasons.

Project background

In 2008, a major UK banking-services company commissioned the events management company to stage a series of sixteen events over a five-month period. These were to take place around the country and would consist of welcome drinks, dinners, networking and inspirational after-dinner speakers. Each of these events was differentiated by its design, which was usually related to its speaker or to the venue, so, for instance, there were wine tours, book signings and unique musical entertainment experiences.

The event management company liaised throughout the project with the bank's central marketing team as its key contact, and each event was hosted by a regional director and attended by staff from the local area, which usually consisted of the top sales team. Guests were selected by the bank from their most important local business customers and professional contacts, including solicitors, lawyers and accountants who had the potential to introduce future new business to the company. The overall intentions were to enhance the bank's brand image, to create opportunities to 'upsell' to existing customers and to cultivate new business.

The events were held in a variety of venues around the British Isles, such as the Crypt at the Bleeding Heart in London, the Custard Factory in Birmingham, the National Railway Museum in Leeds, Mercedes-Benz World, a Devon vineyard, and various prestigious, five-star hospitality establishments. Such venues were selected either specifically to reflect regional preferences or to initiate a new local directive, such as the opening of new bank branches.

General project considerations

As liaison took place with one main, central contact in the client's marketing department, every decision was made in conjunction with this contact. This involved regular meetings as well as daily phone calls and emails. The events

Image 2.2 The National Railway Museum in Leeds
Source: Gary Cralle / Getty Images

company also worked with five regional directors, while each of the sixteen areas had one key contact who was responsible for coordinating with them on the delivery of events.

There was an overall budget in excess of £250,000, from which the events company was required to deliver all events and, of course, obtain their fee. The events themselves were free to attend and were considered 'not-for-profit'. Each event had its own allocated budget, but there was fluidity between these as long as the overall figure was not surpassed.

Project management outline

The following outline for the project was agreed:

- Receipt of client brief.
- Management team meetings and feasibility testing (can we deliver – financial considerations, staffing, costs and so on).
- Decision to pitch.
- Pitching project:

    ○ creative ideas and concept development
    ○ proposal document

    ○ pitch content
    ○ pitch processes and practice
    ○ pitch.

- Decision.
- Procurement and feasibility testing (by the client).
- Project management of project:

    ○ planning.

- Client and stakeholder contact.
- Finance.
- Design.
- Marketing.
- Risk and health and safety.
- Venues.
- Suppliers.
- Human resource management – choosing and training staff.
- Critical path development:

    ○ implementation
    ○ evaluation.

Project management approach

The project was approached holistically: the client viewed the events as part of one cohesive 'Inspirational Speakers' series. A project plan for the entire series was formed, which outlined the general processes and the date and specific details of each event. However, as the series was made up of sixteen events, each event had its own project plan. Within each of these mini-plans, individual components of the events also had their own, even smaller project plans that focused on specific aspects, such as the venue, guest list, budget, suppliers and client information.

Series project management

The entire project had a large management plan. The main project management areas for the entire project were:

- Client contact and administration.
- Staff:

    ○ roles and responsibilities of existing staff
    ○ deployment of internal marketing/design staff to support project
    ○ recruitment and training of staff to work at the events.

- Finance:

  - maintenance of overall budget and each individual event budget to ensure no overspend, and to ensure finance exists to pay the event organisation's fees
  - payment term negotiations – from client and for suppliers
  - analysis of resources
  - return on investment.

- Suppliers:

  - supplier selection – audio-visual contracts, speaker contracts and venue negotiations.

- Marketing and design of entire project.
- Evaluation and feedback to client.

As each individual event required its own project plan, it was also managed independently of the series. The process began with the central client contact introducing the event company to the regional director, who in turn introduced the event company to the local contact. The event company and the local contact then worked together to decide on an event date, venue and inspirational speaker. At that stage, the project was broken down into individual components, with plans devised for the venue, other suppliers, client, guests and budget. These plans were issued as Gantt charts to ensure the event company and client knew what had to be done, and by when. The event company also used critical paths to ensure that all elements of each component were delivered effectively and on time. These critical paths enabled the event company to implement all the processes required in the planning of the event.

Client plan

- Communication lines set up – weekly telephone meetings, daily email exchange.
- Liaison on key decisions – venue, speaker, date, other entertainment or unique element.
- Budget discussions.
- Decision to proceed with event.
- Client staff attendance – which staff are attending?
- Guest list generation – which guests do staff wish to invite? Address details collated.
- Client staff briefing and training – how to behave at the events.
- Client staff joining instructions issued.

- Post-event evaluation.
- Post-event feedback and budget collation.

Guest plan

- Data gathered from client.
- Invite designed.
- Invite sent out.
- Invite chased.
- Invite responses collated.
- More invites sent if necessary.
- Final invite responses collated.
- Guest list created.
- Seating plan drawn up.
- Guests joining instructions issued.
- Dietary requirements gathered.
- Venue informed of numbers and details.
- Guests reminded of event.

Venue plan

- Selection – identification, venue visit, negotiation, approval.
- Room layout.
- Catering – menu tasting, menu selection.
- Beverages – priced and selected.
- Budgets and projected costs.
- Staffing.
- Bedroom booking.
- Health, safety and risk assessments.
- Guest numbers confirmed.
- Seating plans supplied.
- Themeing and design elements.

Supplier plans (excluding venue)

- Initial briefs sent to suppliers – audio-visual, speakers, entertainment.
- Quote received.
- Prices negotiated.
- Suppliers secured.
- Briefs issued.
- Approval of any stage sets/lighting/sound/entertainment content and so on.
- Liaison as required.

Budget plan

- Initial budget development.
- Budget control and monitoring.
- Budget evaluation.

Implementation

Once all the planning stages listed above had been completed, the event company was able to implement each event. Again, this required a plan of its own – the company used an event timeline, production schedules and briefing document (including contacts, seating plans and site maps) that enabled all staff (client, event company, venue and other suppliers) to understand the event fully. Timelines started from the evening before the event and listed, by role and time, each action that needed to happen during the set-up, delivery and breakdown of the events. Production schedules provided clear guidance on when every element of the event took place.

Evaluation

Evaluation of each event had two approaches – both the guests and the client were asked to give feedback. This was collated into one large document which included all sixteen events and offered a comprehensive evaluation of each event and of the series as a whole. This document also included profit and loss, and budget evaluation. It included the benefits offered to the client's business, any challenges experienced and critical recommendations for the future. Evaluation of whether the series had met its objectives was also presented.

Industry voice

Laura Shishani, events officer, Royal Parks, London, UK

The event projects I'm responsible for at Royal Parks are often complicated and detailed. As manager and coordinator of all the events that take place in Kensington Gardens and Hyde Park, it's important always to remember the broader purpose of these spaces. These parks are all about providing green, open spaces for use by the public and they are places where people can escape from the hustle and bustle of central London. The parks are non-profit-making organisations and we manage different scales of project – small and large-scale events – all income from which is reinvested into the parks. That way we can maintain the natural beauty and keep it in stunning condition for the members of the public, by making sure the trees and the wildlife are taken care of.

I generally take care of all the small event projects single-handedly. They are held every weekend from February to October and consist of charity sponsored walks and runs which can each have up to a thousand participants. We also hold sporting tournaments which are often low-key, company events as well as large-scale picnics, and bandstands by local schools and other music groups.

Major event projects include input from park management and external agencies, such as the Adidas Women's Challenge and the Race For Life, which can take eight months of planning. Music projects such as the Wireless Festival, including celebrities such as Bruce Springsteen, can attract an audience of up to 60,000. We'll also host the triathlon events for the London 2012 Olympics with external agencies such as the local authority and the Metropolitan Police.

An event project begins when an event organiser calls my office and we attempt to establish project feasibility, and whether or not it fits park guidelines. The next step, a full, formal proposal, includes the event's concept, dates and timings. We need to decide which park is suitable for the event, as each park has its particular character. We also need to understand what the organisers' experience of holding events of this kind is and we ask for references related to two of their previous events. We also want to know what they are setting up in the park and for how long, as they must qualify for a parks licence which is issued by the local council for every event. We will also check their proposed set-up and breakdown, how many vehicles they intend to bring into the park, the expected size of audience, numbers of toilets, marquees, and whether their predicted ratios are correct. We basically want to know whether they know what they're doing. Other important project considerations for our organisation includes whether the tickets are affordable, whether the promotional material is suitable, making sure particular social groups are not being excluded from attending, security and safety proposals, suitability of suppliers, etc. We establish whether park conditions are suitable on the proposed dates. Another key project consideration is the organisers' management arrangements for subcontracting, so that we can establish the overall suitability of their management structure for the project. We start planning for next year's events sometimes twelve months in advance, though even smaller events take at least five months' lead time. We want to make sure that nothing occurs as a result of the event to harm the Royal Parks' brand. We also check with ordinary park users and other important stakeholders, to make sure there will be no damage to the park or its wildlife.

Monthly meetings are held in the run-up to the event with the organisers, park management, local residents, other stakeholders, and we enlist the support of the Licensing Safety Advisory Group (LSAG). This coordination group often consists of around twenty experts from the main agencies associated with the event's planning and delivery, including Westminster Council, Transport for London, the emergency services, and the first-aid organisation Saint John's Ambulance.

Daily disruption fees for the event need to be bonded, a contract signed by all agencies and signed off by the LSAG before the park land is handed over for the period of the licence. We conduct daily site inspections to check all is going to plan, that activities are being carried out safely and that correct safety clothing is being worn. This continues until the night before, when an all-agency, full-site inspection takes place to sign off the event.

The Event Liaison Team (ELT) oversees the entire festival and consists of a representative of each of the key agencies who are situated in a unit next to the stage as the control centre. All decisions during the event are made there and all its members are fully familiar with what is happening at the event and when. For example, if an incident occurs during the event and the first-aiders need to get an ambulance to a particular location, they will radio through to me as the representative for Royal Parks to explain where the incident is and I will advise the most efficient route for the ambulance. It sounds longwinded but in practice it is very slick and works like clockwork, aided by CCTV throughout. It's a crazy little office, but great fun to work in. It's long hours, but working behind the scenes gives me such a different view of the event from the one I had as a festival-goer growing up. In those days, I had no idea of the spectacular arrangements involved.

Safety is always the highest priority during egress of the event. Up to 60,000 festival-goers all leaving at once don't really know where they are, are often drunk and need to be looked after by us, even outside the park. An egress meeting is held with police and organisers, as well as Transport for London. Sometimes we request that Park Lane is closed due to the massive risk posed by so many people. We also check tubes are open, closing times are extended if required, lighting is provided, as is direction from stewards.

Following this, a 'hot debrief' is held into the early hours of the morning, involving all agencies for purposes of evaluation, perhaps requiring changes for the next day.

The breakdown of the event often involves large lorries taking the site down and requires daily checks to make sure organisers stick to the schedule and do no damage to the park, and we finally go round with cameras for a full site inspection. A few months later there is a full debrief and we ask 'Will we hold this event again?' We are always tweaking, changing and improving things before we start planning for next time.

I absolutely love my job. If you are dedicated, have lots of energy, enjoy the buzz of the event in progress, are hardworking and don't mind long, unsociable hours, you can also have time for fun and chill-out time. In addition, there are the bonuses of networking, understanding new job roles, as well as the thought and planning that go into such major event projects.

2.18 Summary

This chapter has attempted to demonstrate that events are projects, yet they are managed quite differently from projects in other industries. The importance of proper application of project management to the international events industry should now be apparent. Proper application depends on an initial understanding of the difference between the organisational structures and processes of event organisation when compared to other types of business. Whilst it is clearly possible to relate project management to many of the conventional event planning theories and practices discussed elsewhere, the particular processes related to effective event project management throughout the event cycle should be noted.

Further reading

Doran, G. T. (1981) There's a S.M.A.R.T. Way to Write Management Goals and Objectives, *Management Review*, November: 35–36. This is the often-quoted, foundational paper for understanding SMART objectives, which is definitely required reading for any student of events management.

Kolltveit, B. J., Karlsen, J. T. and Gronhaug, K. (2007) Perspectives on Project Management, *International Journal of Project Management*, 25: 3–9. This paper provides a fuller discussion of our basic summary of project management perspectives and gives useful models for understanding how to apply project management to events.

Pinto, J. K. (2010) *Project Management*, New Jersey: Pearson. This book is a thorough overview of project management and includes many models and supporting examples from a variety of industries.

Silvers, J. R. (2007) *Risk Management for Meetings and Events*, London: Elsevier. This book is particularly useful for those wanting to understand more about project management and especially the risks associated with projects.

Chapter 3

Event design and production

Contents

3.1 Aims

By the end of this chapter, the student will be able:

- To explain the relationship between the event production steps of concept, design and staging.
- To develop an understanding of events design as the production of experiences rather than the management of staging elements.
- To describe the common elements of the event attendee experience.

3.2 Introduction

Event design and production are among the greatest challenges facing the events specialist. As clients continue to demand ever more memorable and remarkable events for their participants, it is left to the event designer to fulfil the brief and the event producer to deliver desired outcomes. However, event design and production are difficult processes which are also embodied in the wider activities associated with planning events.

Event design and production are distinct sets of activities from each other and are different skills from what are widely regarded as the functions of management. They therefore do not rely on more specific management processes discussed in the previous chapter; instead, they are generally creative and artistic, as well as being strongly grounded in traditional design principles.

'Event design' simply refers to the mental creation of an event before it takes place, first in the mind of the designer and then as it is communicated to those responsible for its production. 'Event production' therefore refers to the subsequent action of manufacturing or engineering an event's delivery, based on its initial design.

However, when approaching this topic with a view to successful industry practice, it is worth noting that the literature about event design and production is sparse, and that there are wide differences among industry practitioners about how to approach both areas. This chapter attempts to unravel some of the controversy and confusion relating to this important topic. Literature about processes and procedures in the industry has led to what many view as a 'managementisation' of what should be the production of authentic event attendee experiences. This emphasis has also led to confusion over event design and production. Practitioners and academics have generally focused on staging and logistics when discussing both of these elements. What is really required from *design* is the clear establishment of an initial event concept, with corresponding design development following. Event *production* then involves putting this design into practice, using practical staging elements.

3.3 Current views of event design

What makes an event such as the Chelsea Flower Show, held in London each year, so striking and memorable? Visitors to this world-class event not only see many interesting flowers, as the name of the event promises; they also smell their fragrances, interact with certain exhibits, and notice particular, highly prized showpieces that they seldom forget afterwards. Car shows have been the motoring industry's traditional way to contact customers and gain media coverage for several decades. However, these have recently been surpassed by newer experiences, such as *Top Gear* events, which combine shows about cars with celebrities, humour and other forms of innovative entertainment. Event designers and producers are invariably behind such memorable events.

However, there is no standard definition of the word 'design', as its sense varies depending upon the application in question. It is commonly thought that design precedes practice and that mental conception is done before something is produced. We can therefore suggest that event design involves the conception of an intended event experience with the intention of delivering it through event production.

Yet, there currently seems to be much misunderstanding among industry managers, academics and students about events as designed experiences. This is based on a traditional view that events are delivered through the staging of catering, entertainment, customer service delivery, lighting and sound, and so on. The assumption is that the collection and correct use of these items guarantees an event's success. Another assumption is that planning is the main function of an event manager. The combination of these two assumptions has resulted in the design component of many events being ignored, leading to an often haphazard collection of staging elements and a 'hope for the best' that they will all work together correctly. However, event design and production are different from the event management functions described in the previous chapter. Certainly, setting clear event objectives and outcomes (e.g. Goldblatt 2005) as part of an overall process of planning (e.g. Shone and Parry 2010; Watt 1998) is important. However, the creative part of delivering memorable attendee experiences has tended to remain practically shrouded in mystery for those aspiring to learn its art, despite the urgent need for its greater consideration (e.g. Getz 2007). As the practical field progresses, and academics begin to understand more about how to instruct students who are new to the field, the present use of traditional management models to inform both areas will give way to the use of clearer event design language and more tailor-made theories to explain it.

Other possible reasons for the absence of sophisticated models of event design include the wide diversity of event types and outcomes, and uncertainty about the importance that customers place on different elements of their experience when judging the success of an event. Certainly, it could be argued that the burgeoning popularity of a variety of worldwide events management study programmes has created a need for seemingly concrete theories and models to be applied and communicated in coherent 'how-to' contexts for acquisition by budding students seeking to enhance their future employability. Perhaps, too, more seasoned professionals hope to add more of a theoretical dimension to their day-to-day work. However, the applied body of research which specifically informs the field of events education, though growing yearly, remains scant.

3.4 Events as designed experiences

3.4.1 Events as part of the growing experience economy

In Chapter 1, the diverse scope of events was discussed, and it was established that it is often difficult to categorise, or even define, what they are. However, one common thread is shared by all events: they are experiences for those who attend them. For instance, masses of attendees flock to the annual Glastonbury music festival, not because they cannot see its extensive, televised coverage, but because attending offers a particular experience that cannot be gained elsewhere. Many music performers have compensated for the earnings they have lost through illegal music downloading by switching their emphasis to performing at live events. This phenomenon has seen previously retired acts reforming to play at large music event venues, such as the O2 in London.

In general, events – whether formally managed or not – can be viewed as forming part of what Pine and Gilmore (1999) call the emerging 'experience economy'. In a social, cultural and technical transition, our society, which used to be concentrated on the consumption of products, now consumes a much higher proportion of services. The third phase of this consumption evolution has resulted in those services being delivered to customers as part of an overall, packaged experience.

Thus, the focus for event companies has changed over time. The modern events industry is changing and moving away from traditional approaches. So, for instance, Top Gear Live is very different from traditional motor shows, which were largely simple presentations of manufacturers' products. Potential customers and enthusiasts could view these cars and obtain information about them as they were consistent, durable products. The products, in turn, were being exhibited by company employees who, as service providers, customised their service offering depending on the requirements and expectations of their customers. However, Top Gear Live turned this product and service relationship into an experience through the designed and produced event. This redefined the car event and produced a prosperous franchise for the organisers, who now hold five such events worldwide.

There has also been recent growth in the popularity of music and cultural festivals, increased media coverage of sporting and mega-events and an increasing reliance on the strategic value of faith, voluntary and corporate events to promote brand relationships. The modern international events industry is a crucial component of this new social architecture. All of this seems to support Jensen's (1999) observations that, as consumers of such experiences, we seem to be living in a developing 'dream society', where our perceptions of value, recognition of rarity and willingness to justify premium expenditure focus on the ability of successful business organisations to produce unique customer experiences. With such profound social and industrial changes, one could argue that the traditional management practices of the twentieth century need reconsideration.

3.4.2 The event production process

Event planning is often presented as a rather simple process that comprises stages that build on each other towards the achievement of specified objectives. Watt (1998), Shone and Parry (2010) and Bowdin *et al.* (2006) all adopt this perspective. However, event design is more of a creative set of activities that can often appear chaotic in its development due to its need to be revised. These activities are embodied in the 'spirit' of the event planning process. However, because *doing* event design and *learning* event design often involve very different outcomes, the specific explanation of what event design involves has proved difficult to explain. Anybody who has worked closely with expert event designers will often be impressed by how different their thinking processes and verbalisation are, compared with those involved in more structured businesses, such as accountancy or law. It often seems that the 'out-of-the-box thinking' that is associated with design is difficult to put into ordinary speech.

Edward De Bono (1976) highlighted that thinking encompasses not only the *logical* and *analytical* types of thinking that we seem to spend so much of our studies and work lives practising and perfecting, but *lateral* thinking, particularly in creative or artistic work. The way these three types of thinking interact is shown in Figure 3.1.

Lateral thinking involves the movement value of ideas. It is often concerned with taking an initial idea as a starting point and moving to the creation of new ideas. De Bono (2006) proposes four types of thinking tools to facilitate this process:

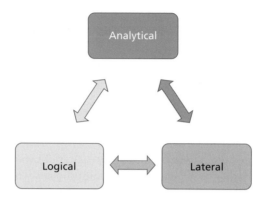

Figure 3.1 Three types of thinking
Source: Adapted from de Bono 1976

- *idea-generating tools* that are designed to break current thinking patterns, routine patterns, the status quo;
- *focus tools* that are designed to broaden where to search for new ideas;
- *harvest tools* that are designed to ensure more value is received from idea-generating output; and
- *treatment tools* that are designed to consider real-world constraints, resources and support.

The realisation that artistic endeavour requires creative thinking processes is not new, particularly to those associated with the arts and the creative industries. However, the nature of the outcomes associated with events often requires much more final measurement of tangible success. Much traditional business school education, particularly in the Western world, is concerned with the development of critical reasoning skills, relating to the evaluation of true statements and the questioning of errors – skills which mainly require analytical and logical thinking processes. Whilst critical reasoning is obviously an important skill for event management specialists to develop and use in their work, it is much less useful for the event designer, whose 'craft' concerns the accomplishment of business outcomes through creative problem-solving.

3.4.3 The need for event designers to develop reflective practice

If the path to effective experience design in events cannot be satisfactorily pursued through the channels of traditional analytical, logical and therefore critical thought processes provided by mainstream business management practice and education, then the methods employed should maybe attempt to incorporate more creative processes, perhaps providing more opportunity to utilise right-brain functions. Certainly, the tasks normally associated with day-to-day event planning often need to be rethought because of the particular requirements of reflective design.

Donald Schön (1987) proposed that a 'reflective practicum' is needed in order to develop 'education for artistry'. This represents a departure from the delivery and use of school knowledge and a move towards the use of reflection in action. For event designers to develop creative design practice which applies the tools of experience design 'outside the box' of conventional management activities, there is a need to articulate the difference between the two spheres of design knowledge, as compared in Table 3.1.

Table 3.1 Comparison of 'school knowledge' and 'reflection in action' in event design

Event design according to 'school knowledge'	Event design according to 'reflection in action'
Designer relies upon critical reasoning – that is, the designer completes a preset schedule of logical steps.	Designer 'knows' in action – that is, various approaches are creatively synthesised using familiar pre-existing models from familiar past representations (e.g. culture) and other design settings in new combinations according to the design concept until an intuitive goal is reached.
The design process can be 'managed' or controlled according to predictability and bureaucracy. This allows the project to be constantly evaluated according to goals, timelines and tangible, measureable standards.	The design process becomes difficult for external parties and stakeholders to evaluate clearly. Measures of 'quality' are mainly perceived and realised from the reflective point of view of the designer.
The designer uses formal, commonly agreed categories of knowledge to inform the design process. This usually relies on a common body of knowledge and clearly 'right answers' which can be clearly articulated.	There is more of a view that design is somewhat about knowing more than we can say. Sensory design, in particular, often cannot be satisfactorily verbalised and also is not simply an intellectual activity.
The designer may view the design environment and its experience as separate from everyday life.	The designer may help the event attendee to coordinate everyday knowledge in action with other forms of privileged or received knowledge.
The designer's theory and experience are considered valuable, with higher levels of theory being brought to design having higher status. Design knowledge is also 'molecular', not interconnected, and there is a view of a more 'set' way and rigid answer to the set design task. Often there are single or set methods towards the required outcome.	The reflective designer uses on-the-spot experimentation, thinking what they are doing as they are doing it. The designer allows himself/herself to be surprised and puzzled, responding to the puzzle as it progresses and unfolds, resetting the problem as appropriate. Separate methods are used, depending on the problem, including the invention of new ways to achieve outcomes in different projects. Overall, the practice is less of a method, more of an art.
'Junk' categories are created for people who do not receive the design and event concept as expected.	The designer attempts to meet the attendee at their level of understanding.

3.4.4 Content-based versus production-driven events

Berridge (2006) distinguished the traditional processes of management from the design 'component' required to ensure the success of production-driven, creative events. This view has recently gained popularity among events academics and practitioners alike.

Building upon the model of creative and reflective practice for event design, it is logical to question the dominance of the linear event planning process models in which design seems to figure only as an implied part. In a more detailed discussion of this topic, Berridge (2006) highlights the fundamental distinction between management and design of event experiences.

Of course, linear models, such as those proposed by Shone and Parry (2010), should not be completely discarded, particularly in favour of a seemingly random replacement. It is simply hoped that there might be a proposition made that may assist the theoretical operationalisation of the design 'function' or component of the overall event planning process. Thus, the creative component of event design is carried out on the basis of a rationale for each event which is based on traditional planning tools. The place of design in events is illustrated in Figure 3.2.

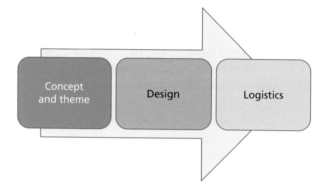

Figure 3.2 The three-stage event design model

CASE STUDY 3.1

Chelsea Flower Show

Location: London, UK
Event type: cultural event
Attendees: 157,000

How do event designers successfully meet the challenge of keeping a century-old flower show relevant to contemporary society, as well as engaging the senses of international flower enthusiasts as diverse as prison inmates and the Queen of England?

The Royal Horticultural Society of Great Britain (RHS) holds an international flower show each year at the Royal Hospital, Chelsea, London. Its 2010 show

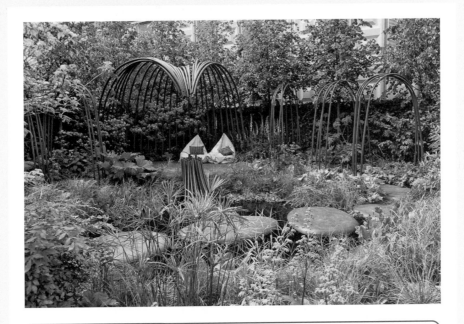

Image 3.1 The British Heart Foundation garden at the 2011 Chelsea Flower Show

Source: Chris Jackson / Getty Images

was sponsored by M&G Investments, and attendees paid ticket prices ranging from fourteen to forty-five pounds. After eighty-eight years at its current venue (and almost 150 in total), the show is still viewed as the most important event in the horticultural calendar, showcasing the finest examples of horticultural excellence and setting the latest trends in gardening, particularly as it is the first event of the London summer social season. With enormous media attention and longer exhibitor waiting lists than ever, there seems to be no sign of public appetite for the event abating: in 2010, tickets sold out in record time.

The previous year's event had been greatly affected by the worldwide economic downturn, with recession-busting measures applied to many of the gardens. In contrast, the 2010 show had a community theme, and the RHS also used the event to mark the International Year of Biodiversity. Potential weather problems were a concern in the run-up to the show, as England had experienced its coldest winter for thirty years. The bad weather, including very late frosts, caused problems for gardeners, and plants were three to four weeks behind schedule, which led organisers to fear that there would be no flowers ready to display. Nevertheless, these problems were overcome, and for five days in May, the grounds of the Royal Hospital were transformed into fifteen spectacular show gardens and twenty-one inspirational small gardens. In total, six hundred exhibitors from the best nurseries and growers around the world were in attendance.

The flower show is essentially a large theatrical production. The designers and the show director work hard to create a theme which garden contributors can respond to in order to create a memorable experience for each visitor. In 2010, the community theme inspired the contributors to create gardens which spoke to the senses. As Tim Richardson reported for the *Daily Telegraph*:

> There is a transcendent feel to Chelsea's show gardens this year, as if the designers were offering us a dose of much-needed escapism in the form of immersive spaces, 'such stuff as dreams are made of', as Shakespeare put it in *The Tempest* . . . In place of 'design solutions' or 'ideas to steal' for our own gardens, there is plenty this year that could be described as expansive, dreamy or evocative of foreign climes.

The show gardens ensured that this theme echoed throughout the event. For instance, one garden was created by the Motor Neurone Disease Association and inspired by the scientist Stephen Hawking. Its designer represented the feelings of people when they are diagnosed with the condition by including a dark swirling water feature, whilst a curved stone folly signified sanctuary. A garden called Ace of Diamonds used twenty million pounds' worth of precious stones (replaced with fakes for the public viewings) and 2010 saw the largest-ever show garden – the Eden Project's Places of Change – which was created by prison inmates and homeless people with no prior gardening experience.

The show boasted a large number of contributors, and many of the show gardens had prestigious designers. Stories of clashes among designers and rows over the use of technology and design elements abound each year, and 2010 was no exception. Height restrictions for trees had been eased a few years earlier, and some designers started to use groves and canopies to enclose and define their spaces. This has apparently led to turf wars between neighbouring designers (Richardson 2010), creating obvious headaches for event organisers, but simultaneously stimulating increased press coverage and a marked improvement in some of the show's garden spaces.

In 2010, in addition to the traditional plant sale, there was a range of shops selling the most innovative gardening products and accessories. There were also displays of floral design from some of the UK's best-known florists and flower arrangers, showcasing the latest trends in floral fashion. Educational displays in the Great Pavilion demonstrated 'The Power of Plants', and RHS experts were on hand to answer any gardening questions and queries.

The main staged elements of the show were complemented by a host of restaurants, bars and cafés which provided places to sit, relax and enjoy refreshment in an extraordinary venue. All of this, from the show gardens and the main exhibition through to the smallest coffee shop, was overseen by the show director and the event designers to ensure there was cohesion and continuity between all aspects of the event and that the staging elements did not interfere with the heavily designed guest experience.

The show director, Stephen Bennett, said:

> We're noticing an increase in demand from both consumers wanting to visit RHS shows and organisations recognising the opportunities to promote through them. RHS Chelsea has a significant financial impact across the gardening industry, with garden centres, growers and design consultancies all achieving growth in business because of the RHS show activity. I hope this is a key indicator that 2010 will be a strong year for horticulture . . . For consumers you're aligning yourself with a good charitable cause and world-class, show-stopping event with immense networking and promotional opportunities.
>
> Sources: BBC website; RHS website; RHS 2009, 2010; Richardson 2010

3.5 Concept and theme

3.5.1 Event concept

The concept of an event and its theme, whilst different steps in the design process, are cohesive aspects, with the theme essentially becoming the main 'vehicle' through which the outcomes of the event are to be achieved. Goldblatt (2005) provided a useful framework, named the '5Ws', which has become the bedrock of most events, whether content-based or production-driven in nature (see Figure 3.3). The 5Ws are explained by Goldblatt as the essential questions which should be asked and answered as the basis for any event before further decisions should be made.

Whilst these questions have their own context in the overall planning of the event and form the basis of widely accepted event planning frameworks, such as the one proposed by Shone and Parry (2010), they pose particular problems for the event designer in terms of the overall event outcomes to be accomplished by its design.

The focus on event attendees' experiences, as opposed to the simple management of an events process, is a major departure from the traditional practice of gathering together various logistical elements, such as catering, entertainment, sound, light and service, in the hope that somehow, with the right timings and programme, an experience will be had by those who attend. Instead, the focus is on the psychology of event attendees and what will be achieved in their own experience. Whilst in the planning context (covered in Chapters 1 and 2) these five questions and their answers lead the quest for the establishment of event feasibility, they present the event designer with more complex, creative problems to solve. In design terms, the reason why the event should be held becomes a question about what is to be achieved in the experience of its attendees. The event stakeholders often become agents in the creative process of design, which, whilst often requiring accommodation by the event designer, can prove troublesome, making the design process more complex due to the need to consider the additional opinions

Figure 3.3 The 5Ws of the event concept
Source: Adapted from Goldblatt 2005: 44

of interested, yet not necessarily expert, parties. The venue, date and time of the event, though often dictated to the designer, become crucial features of design which either complement or hinder the cohesion with the theme and other important aspects of the event's delivery. The event product, or 'take-home', relates to the psychological, physical or even spiritual experience attendees should remember and perhaps reflect on or act upon after the event.

With respect to the event product, the design outcomes can be divided into cognitive, affective, decisional and psychomotor domains. Cognitive outcomes relate to the use of attendees' minds and may involve learning, which could include the delivery and assimilation of new knowledge. For example, an exhibition might seek to inform the public about the life and achievements of a particular historical figure. This would involve the conveyance of various types of information suitable for absorption by attendees, which could be retained in their memories. Affective outcomes relate to appealing to the emotions of attendees and can include their registration of new awareness, surprise, excitement or even fear. Certainly, new awareness and appreciation of social issues, such as environmental sustainability, can be successfully achieved in event attendees by using suitable emotional stimuli, such as personal appeals and visual materials. Decisional outcomes relate to attendees making choices, such as those concerned with new purchases, voting or supporting causes. Psychomotor outcomes relate to physical activities, such as running marathons, playing sports or making political protests.

Once the answers demanded by the 5Ws have been ascertained, the relevant particulars from the outcome domains might then be decided and articulated, and the designer can set specific design objectives. Once these have been decided, this concept can be linked to an appropriate theme.

3.5.2 Theme

Defining this important term from the existing literature has proved problematic. Authors such as Goldblatt (2005) and Monroe (2005) tend to apply the term in relation to a more traditional concept of the 'themed event', perhaps denoting a national flavour to food, entertainment, decor and other staging aspects. Getz (2007: 223) has provided the clearest definition so far, stating: 'A "theme" is a unifying idea or concept which gives meaning to the event, or is the object of celebration or commemoration.' Therefore, the theme, often established with the participation of stakeholders, is assigned with a view to being a dictating influence over all aspects of subsequent event design. This is contrary to the more traditional view presented by Bowdin *et al.* (2006), which places themeing at the centre of logistics, without the key mediation of the distinct role of design in the production of event attendee experiences.

A more helpful analogy might be the use of genre in film and theatre production, which has been used to convey ideas and meanings more efficiently between directors, writers, costumers and all other parties responsible for every aspect of design. Part of the necessity for the use of genre was the difficulty associated with conveying ideas verbally. Words often convey linear thoughts and prove problematic in communicating creative ideas. As a result, directors developed forms of communication based upon visual media, such as storyboards. They also learned to talk to others responsible for important aspects of the creative process by using such genre-based terms and concepts as 'horror', 'romance', 'action' and so on. This filtered into the marketing communication messages of studio advertising in order that potential viewers of movie products might obtain clear ideas about particular offerings. Architectural firms have done something similar for many years when communicating complicated building-design concepts to clients and other stakeholders through such devices as concept boards and scale models.

Similarly, in the case of event design, the parties involved are often unable to convey design ideas and instructions clearly without 'leakage' of meaning, potential loss of detail, and serious risk of potentially expensive design errors and client misunderstandings. Therefore, in addition to the theme being a central idea by which all the other elements of design can be determined, it serves as an effective communication medium.

However, themeing has thus far been approached at a level of complexity little more sophisticated than that offered by the existing tourism and hospitality management literature. For example, Getz (2007) briefly combines the topic with programme design; Malouf (1999) provides themeing advice ranging from table plans to options for napkin folds; Goldblatt (2005) includes a section about themed events which offers suggestions about suitable design elements for events ranging from 'Hooray for Hollywood' through to 'Dickens of a Christmas'; and Monroe (2005) provides a more extensive glossary of event themes including, 'M.A.S.H.', 'Dinosaur Dance' and 'Roman Empire'. Only Berridge (2006) has attempted to incorporate the components of theme into a clearer conceptual framework which appears wholly inseparable from the design process itself and its planned outcomes.

Just as the big Hollywood studio system of the last century was often accused of 'recycling' standardised and mass-produced art forms for general public consumption, the events industry might now be accused of developing its own standardised forms. This has led to some concern about inauthentic, artificially produced events.

As an important part of this ongoing debate, Brown and James (2004) discuss the potential risk of what they term 'ritual sacrifice' in the events industry. They argue that in its haste to become recognised as a mature field and profession, the industry has started to deviate unconsciously from its roots – the age-old foundations of events which were discussed in Chapter 1. These events were 'grassroots' cultural experiences which developed over centuries as authentic expressions of social community gatherings. Brown and James argue that these natural and often spontaneous expressions of social existence have been replaced by inauthentic, artificial, 'packaged' consumer experiences that serve no purpose but to generate profits.

CASE STUDY 3.2

Notting Hill Carnival

Location: London, UK
Event type: community festival
Attendees: approximately one million

When the local authorities imposed a 6.30 p.m. curfew on the 2009 Notting Hill Carnival (NHC), it was an attempt to prevent the kind of street violence that had blighted the previous year's carnival, when around fifty police officers were injured by gangs of rioters and looters. The council also restricted sound system levels to 135 decibels – a move that was welcomed by the 10,000 residents living near the carnival route (140 decibels had been recorded in 2008).

A council report highlighted significant problems in the management of the event. In particular, stewards were recruited fewer than three weeks before the carnival. The consequent danger facing the event, which can attract as many as a million people over the course of three days, could be that it would come under much closer scrutiny in future years from the authorities, leading to further pressure to control it.

Image 3.2 The Notting Hill Carnival
Source: Olly Scarff / Getty Images

The NHC started in 1964 as a hallmark event in which recent immigrants, mainly from Trinidad, could celebrate their cultural heritage and the abolition of slavery in 1833. However, over forty years later, the ethnic composition of London had changed dramatically and the Greater London Authority was under pressure to support a wider range of cultural events on an already stretched budget. For example, an event entitled 'Caribbean in the Park' targeted families who did not want to expose their children to the overcrowding associated with the NHC.

While the NHC still enjoys popular support and is a significant contributor to the local economy, many believe that the original message of the carnival has been diluted and that many attendees are not aware of its origins. Some argue that it is simply yet another free event in the annual calendar, and that this is the key motivation for many attendees. Even members of the carnival's original ethnic communities have started to question what they see as some artificial representations of their cultures, including dress, dance, music and food. What was originally a celebration of freedom and an opportunity for people to participate spontaneously has become more regulated, which in itself poses a threat to the carnival (Burr 2006). Is this iconic event in danger of losing popularity or can the organisers encourage the next generation of the African Caribbean community to continue to support it?

Sources: Burr 2006; GLA 2004

As is discussed in more detail in Chapter 13, some produced events do still provide an escape for attendees from their usual routines; and Chapter 12 highlights the essential part that event production plays in disengaging attendees from their normal thought processes, thereby allowing them to enter into new relationships and experiences that are often related to unfamiliar branding concepts.

Pine and Gilmore (1999: 36) counter Brown and James's criticism by stating: 'There's no such thing as an artificial experience. Every experience created within the individual is real, whether the stimuli be natural or simulated.' Thus, whilst some in the marketing community continue to discuss more effective ways to deliver standardised products in customised service environments, the event industry's focus on the production of attendee experiences requires more consideration of an artificially produced 'experiencescape' in which the attendee is able to engage in his or her personalised experiences at three operational levels of design (see Figure 3.4).

As Figure 3.4 demonstrates, the event attendee is often consuming standardised, tangible products, such as a branded soft drink, which is delivered to them through the medium of customised service provided by event employees, such as waiting or sales counter staff, within a personalised experiencescape which incorporates ambience, fragrances, light, space and other design aspects. It should be remembered that such attendees will always form their own personalised experience, which will often be as a result of stimuli that are artificially produced by the activities of the event organisation. These experiences will be positive or negative with respect to the achievement of the intended event outcomes. It is therefore the responsibility of

Figure 3.4 Three levels of the 'experiencescape'

the event designer to ensure that the experience which is personalised by each attendee mirrors these event objectives as closely as possible.

3.5.3 Inadequacy of the service design research

Since the 1980s, several useful models for the design, delivery, measurement and recovery of customer service have been proposed. Foremost among these has been Zeithaml *et al.*'s (2006) model of service gaps and their associated measurement using the SERVQUAL questionnaire tool. Obviously, the events industry remains, in many respects, a service industry; but whilst the measurement of gaps in customer satisfaction related to service delivery remains relevant, its use as an instrument of customer experience measurement appears limited from an event designer's viewpoint. Such scientific methods are as inadequate in their capacity to evaluate the successful design and delivery of event experiences as they are in their measurement of people's opinions about art exhibits, or their views about theatrical productions. Major event organisations, such as Gartner, have attempted to address these issues through the use of flexible, one-to-one interviews with key event attendees following major productions. Event evaluation will be discussed in greater detail in Chapter 14, but it seems that much more research is required into new ways to research the creative impacts of 'wow' factors on event attendees' perceptions of events and memory formation, in particular.

Study activity

Write a basic research plan of how you would investigate attendees' perceptions of:

- A major, community firework display.
- The performance of a headlining act at an international music festival.
- The awards ceremony at a Formula 1 racing championship.

What challenges do you predict in your ability to measure these perceptions accurately?

3.5.4 Experience blueprinting

It is therefore proposed that designers of the event experience clearly articulate, at least for their own reference, a 'blueprint' of intended attendee experiences throughout the event. This approach is an adaptation of Zeithaml *et al.*'s (2006) initial application of blueprinting to service design, which attempts to articulate service delivery actions, such as employee scripts, interactions and their associated performance standards. It is suggested here that the experience blueprint for an event includes similar details, though it should be supplemented by clear reference to the 'activities' of the various sensory stimuli involved in the design, such as programme, staging and timing elements, as well as their intended outcomes, such as attendees' memory formations, emotional flow, engagement and so on.

Such blueprinting of planned experiences should be carried out for the whole of the event cycle, which cannot be limited simply to the timelines required for operational delivery, but need to be centred on the experiences the attendee has at each stage. Just as marketers often find it essential to view a simple purchase as a multi-staged cognitive and emotional process, so event designers need to predict and design for the multi-phased nature of experience before, during and after events. Clawson's (1963) multi-phased nature of experience model helps to isolate some relevant, key stages of the attendee's experience (see Figure 3.5).

It is also practical to suggest that some of the marketing and sponsorship issues discussed in later chapters should be carefully considered here to ensure cohesion of the event's design in relation to its overall branding and competitive positioning, as well as the service delivery aspects common to ticket sales and pre-event advertising, which form important aspects of Clawson's 'anticipation' stage of attendee experience.

3.5.5 Attendee absorption and immersion

Any proposed blueprint, though subject to change as the event delivery progresses, should clearly provide an understanding of the levels of immersion and/or absorption, as well as the participation requirements and activities of attendees. Once again, such considerations should mirror the requirements of the event concept and will be informed by, and in turn inform, its chosen theme, thereby influencing the design of the event. Pine and Gilmore's (1999) 'experience realm' model helps us to understand these basic combinations of immersion and absorption, with participation levels at various stages of the event experience (see Figure 3.6).

Figure 3.5 Three key stages of the multi-phased nature of experience

Source: Adapted from Clawson 1963

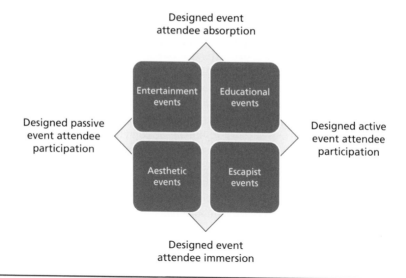

Designed event
attendee absorption

Designed passive
event attendee
participation

Entertainment
events

Educational
events

Aesthetic
events

Escapist
events

Designed active
event attendee
participation

Designed event
attendee immersion

Figure 3.6 The event experience realm
Source: Adapted from Pine and Gilmore 1999: 30

'Participation' can be active or passive, depending on whether event attendees directly influence the experience being produced. Classical music concert events generally involve little audience participation until the final applause, whereas the annual London Marathon depends upon its attendees' (the runners') active participation throughout. 'Absorption' involves 'occupying a person's attention by bringing the experience into the mind', whilst 'immersion' is 'becoming physically (or virtually) a part of the experience itself' (Pine and Gilmore 1999: 31). The combination of these elements produces the four 'experience realms': entertainment, educational, aesthetic and escapist events.

This model is not intended to depict a static rationale for an event, but refers to different levels of participation combined with absorption or immersion at different points of the event, depending on the prescribed outcomes of each stage. The level of participation by attendees at events needs to be carefully designed beforehand to ensure their appropriate level of engagement. Additionally, failure to implement the correct level of immersion can lead to serious shortfalls in attendee engagement, resulting in inadequate satisfaction. It might also be worth noting that attendees sometimes attempt 'unauthorised' immersion of themselves in experiences that are mainly intended for absorption, such as football matches, the outcomes of which have suffered as a result of pitch invasions. In such cases, designers, planners and even contract agents, such as law enforcement officers, need to ensure that steps are taken to minimise such disruptions.

3.6 Understanding event experiences

The previously discussed view of the role of the event designer therefore moves away from the traditional approach of simply planning events using logistics and focuses more on clearly defining the required experiences that attendees are intended to have in relation to the planned outcomes and objectives set for the event, as well as the levels of required participation and immersion or absorption at its different stages.

3.6.1 The role of sensory experience

The basis of event attendee experience formation is sensory stimulation. Authors such as Goldblatt (2005), Monroe (2005) and Getz (2007) acknowledge the necessity of appealing to attendants' senses of sight, hearing, taste, touch, speech and emotions within the experience environment of the event. However, they tend to revert to lists of sensory categories and associated logistical options, without much explanation of their use or how they stimulate attendees to form experiences. The EMBOK model (http://www.embok.org) and the corresponding website of leading events industry authority Julia Silvers (http://www.juliasilvers.com) categorise design in the events industry as follows:

- content design
- theme design
- programme design
- environment design
- production design
- entertainment design
- catering design.

Silvers also attempts to develop each of these categories by adding various logisitical options under the heading of 'Management'. Not referring to EMBOK specifically, but more to the historical tendency of such lists, Berridge (2006: 34) observes:

> Oddly these are not always aligned with detailed examples of their use. Or any further explorations of the types of experiences that might be subsequently created. This is a common characteristic of academic study of events in general, to produce checklists of what could be included without necessarily any accompanying explanation of how they should be used or what they will produce.

3.6.2 Basic event attendee psychology

Bearing in mind that sensory stimulation provokes a psychological formation of experience in event attendees, general reference to some basic theories of psychology is appropriate here. Though it is not within the scope of this text to explain or critique these approaches fully, their importance and application to the design of event attendee experiences is crucial to the understanding of event design by the event designer.

3.6.2.1 Behaviourism

Behaviourism, one of the earliest schools of popular psychology, proposes that individuals learn through conditioning as a result of stimuli in their environment (see Figure 3.7)

This school of learning is based on two main theories: classical conditioning and operant conditioning. Classical conditioning was developed through experimentation on dogs by Ivan Pavlov (1927) and involved associative learning. Pavlov was able to demonstrate that individuals' responses to naturally occurring stimuli – such as smelling food, which leads to the response of increased hunger – could be modified through conditioning to become a conditioned response associated with a modified stimulus. For example, when attendees arrive at a dinner event, they usually expect to eat at some later point. Seeing or smelling attractive food will obviously stimulate hunger and appetite, but the event designer can also use various sensory cues in the environment which are not directly related to food to condition the attendees to

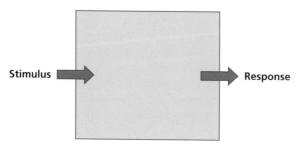

Need to understand stimuli

Stimulus   Response

Figure 3.7 The stimulus–response mechanism

anticipate certain levels of luxury or extravagance in the pleasurable experiences awaiting them. Canapés, fine champagne and the dress, formality and attentiveness of the food service staff can all cause a conditioned response, as can table linens, cutlery and accompanying music.

B. F. Skinner's (1957) theory of operant conditioning – a development of Pavlov's classical theory – demonstrated that individuals can learn as a result of punishment and reward from external stimuli, as is shown in Table 3.2.

This approach focuses on a person's response to stimuli and can be used with the correct corresponding reinforcement to modify behaviour. For example, attendees at an event often need to pass through processes which they do not consider to be satisfying or central to their overall event experience. These processes can include long queuing periods, compliance with security or other necessary crowd management procedures. Correct design can stimulate an appropriate response to verbal, visual or other cues which can instruct attendees in their required behaviours. Formally dressed security personnel can reinforce the need for adequate compliance with bag checks at events where there are valuable artefacts, camera use at art exhibitions or even physical examinations for weapons at football matches. Queuing configuration design can play a large part in the ambience of an event, reinforcing attendees' satisfaction levels and first impressions.

Table 3.2 Basic summary of stimulus–response via operant conditioning

	Outcome of conditioning	
	Increase behaviour	*Decrease behaviour*
Positive stimulus	Positive reinforcement (add stimulus)	Response cost (remove stimulus)
Negative stimulus	Negative reinforcement (remove stimulus)	Punishment (add stimulus)

3.6.2.2 Psychoanalysis

The work of Sigmund Freud, Carl Jung and other popular psychoanalysts can help the event designer to access previous experiences and associations from an event attendee's background and especially their childhood. Many design strategies used to stimulate event attendee immersion encourage the use of basic and familiar instincts, often delivered in unfamiliar contexts. For example, businesses often use paintball competitions for team-building events, which could be little more than the re-enactment of school play. Dressing up in costume is common in events as diverse as carnivals, graduation ceremonies and Halloween. The gamut of childhood emotions, including fear, euphoria and competitiveness, can be variously called upon in event contexts by the appropriate design of sensory stimulation. As human beings, many of these instincts are experienced at an almost primal level, and they can be enhanced by the tastes and textures of foods, food service, familiar music, colours and even smells. These can be used to stimulate attendees' memories, which in turn stimulate the required sensory outcomes. The deeper meanings of cultural symbols, rituals and contexts are discussed later in this chapter.

3.6.2.3 Cognitivism

Cognitive psychologists such as Carl Rogers and Donald Schön extended the humanist agenda which resulted from the practical applications of the theories of the two foregoing psychological schools to propose that humans are sentient beings capable of forming their individual meanings from the world around them. The relevance of reflective processes to the design of event experiences has already been discussed in some detail with respect to the role of designer, but similar application could be made to the process by which event attendees make meaning of their experiences for themselves. Of course, this approach will rely, in part, on those that have been perviously mentioned; but attendees' past experiences will greatly influence how they process a particular event's stimuli.

3.6.3 Sensory perception

An event designer should recognise the application of the above schools in association with the role of perception. Perception refers to the interpretation of the information we receive through our five senses. Attendees at events constantly receive stimulation through visual, auditory, olfactory, tactile and gustatory cues in various amounts and combinations, depending on the particular event in question. It is the perception of our environment that distinguishes us from other mammals. Gestalt psychology, which is concerned with 'the whole', suggests we organise stimuli into groups according to four main types: similarity, proximity, continuity and closure. This means event attendees group items based upon how similar they are, how close they are to each other, according to continuous patterns, and they form their own interpretations of familiar objects to create their own experiences.

Perceptual constancy allows event attendees to maintain their view of an object even though it changes in terms of size, shape and brightness. *Visual perception* allows us to interpret size, texture, overlap, shading, height, clarity and depth. It is therefore an important consideration when designing events. For example, attendees associate groups of dishes on a wedding buffet table in terms of food groups, such as seafood, salad and vegetarian options, or visual indication of likely flavours, such as cultural specialities or desserts. They will expect to see a progression of courses on the table – from hors d'oeuvres, to fish courses, main courses and desserts. Colours will provide indications of variety of ingredients, possible freshness and potentially important differences between flavours of diverse items, such as cheeses. Cleanliness of the surroundings will be visually perceived. Grandeur of the setting can be communicated by the visual perception of the silver plate on the guest cutlery and the texture and brightness of the linen on the table. Though psychologists and philosophers understand more about visual perception than they do about any other type of perception, it is still crucial for the event designer to consider carefully its interaction with the other senses.

Auditory perception is the ability to identify, interpret and attach meaning to sound. Sounds are what we hear (Maclachlan 1989) – internal sensations which we experience directly as a result of public occurrences in the outside world of the event. For example, loud music in a club can generate feelings of euphoria in one attendee and a physical headache in another. The response might be even more extreme: in 2009, a student suffered sudden arrhythmic death syndrome (SADS) at a club event which may well have been caused by the loud, bass-heavy music (http://www.dailymail.co.uk, 8 December 2009). Though a great discussion surrounds the nature of sounds in relation to the objects that produce them and the act of hearing, it is sufficient for our purposes here to state that objects produce distinct sounds and event attendees use the distinction between those sounds to make sense of their environment and the occurrences within them. With this in mind, the effects of music on human experience have been recognised since time immemorial. The effectiveness of themes can be reinforced or compromised by the suitability of the accompanying music and sound system logistics. Obviously, some events revolve around music, which means that organisers have to be very careful about the type of music that they play. For instance, Glastonbury's organisers have recently been heavily criticised for inviting popular music artists to perform. Music was a key design feature of the opening ceremony of the 2004 Olympic Games in Athens, as designers took the unusual step of asking DJ Tiësto to design the accompanying soundtrack in an attempt to give the proceedings a contemporary feel and attract a younger audience.

The other main senses involved in event design, though less well documented, are still crucial to the success of the event. *Olfactory design* involves appealing to the event attendees' sense of smell. This has probably been the fastest-developing area of experience design thanks, in part, to its use by fast-food, retail, hospitality and leisure companies. *Gustatory design* – relating to the sense of taste – has been used by those providing catering at events for millennia, and it continues to be important today. *Tactile design* involves the stimulation of the attendees' sense of touch to achieve outcomes in the psychomotor realm.

3.6.4 Memory

As attendees return home, the main residual effects of an event's concept and outcomes remain in their memories. Sometimes, whole societies can share a powerful collective memory of a particular event. It is therefore crucial that the most important moments in an event are signposted and distinguished from the often huge quantity of other, more peripheral information and stimuli. If this is done well, attendees will form and retain lasting memories of the event. It is vital in this process that various subsections of the experience are carefully designed and programmed. The psychological aspects of such subsections include sense of time, excitement and mood, ambience and emotional flow (these are discussed at length by Berridge (2006)). These are often carefully combined to produce 'wow' factors – sensory crescendos when attendee consciousness reaches its peak. Such wow factors are usually designed moments when the raison d'être of the event is signified to all participants. For example, the captain of the World Cup-winning team raises the trophy in triumph as the high point and culmination of the whole tournament. Similarly, the torch-lighting ceremony of the Olympic Games often attracts the largest international media viewership. Another example is when a film awards ceremony schedules a specific moment to recognise a famous director for their lifetime achievement and contribution to the art form. Sometimes, though, wow factors are unplanned, such as the famous moment during Live Aid when Bono, lead singer of the rock band U2, rescued a spectator from being crushed against security railings to create an iconic, collective, cultural memory of a key event high point.

3.7 Event staging and logistics

Having decided the event concept and the specific design characteristics, it becomes much more straightforward for the event designer to draw together a cohesive system of logistics in order to deliver the experience to event participants. Hopefully, the foregoing discussion has highlighted the importance of adhering to this order of design elements. First, the event's outcomes must be clarified; next, the design elements that will deliver those outcomes on a sensory level can be determined. Finally, the specific staging elements – such as timings, programming, service, audience participants, queuing arrangements, entertainment, sets and decorations, plants and flowers, seating design, table settings, catering and food service, lighting and rigging, colours and themes, sound, and use of technology – can be definitively set, planned and delivered.

Industry voice

David Clement, creative director, live events

As a male, I obviously have a limited ability to multi-task. As a creative director working on the corporate side of live events, I have no choice – I have to be flexible to shifting deadlines, ever-changing client needs, tight budgets requiring flexible solutions and the constant search for 'new', 'fresh' and 'engaging'. Live communication projects have a habit, like buses, of coming along in pairs or not at all, which can sometimes make serving different clients' needs at the same time a real challenge. All clients, regardless of scale of budget or event, like to think of themselves as unique and first in line for service. And if we're doing our job properly, that's an impression we like to maintain; it obviously takes much longer to search out new business than to maintain and grow that from an existing source.

However, if we're honest, not all clients are equal in their ability to plan, brief or communicate. A cynic might even suggest a client gets the job he, she or they deserve. For the ones who say 'We've always done it that way and we'd like another one just the same, please . . . only different' the industry is more than happy to oblige. For the ones in search of something more original and effective in terms of face-to-face communication, live events is one of the most innovative, diverse and dynamic industries, with suppliers (by that I mean crew) who as the unsung heroes – and often in defiance of health and safety regulations – will walk through walls to get the job done. The producer in me knows that the two key elements in any event project which will determine its relative success or failure are the quality of the brief at the start and the quality of the crew on the day to make it happen.

However, with all this talent, energy and new technology to tap into, why aren't more events as ground-breaking or innovative as they could be? Well, in part because every event has or should have its own specific objectives, which in turn may or may not require something radically different. Every year, though, it seems a greater proportion of my time in corporate event design and production is taken up redefining and simplifying the initial client's instructions before we even think about getting on site.

For example, once upon a time, before the age of PowerPoint, agencies produced 35mm slides for speaker support, which meant they had control over design and layout in order to best serve speaker needs. Once presenters began to design their own visual support – and, for fear of missing anything out, began to throw their whole script content in as well – the picture became far more complex and confusing. As a result, audiences are often faced with a tennis match of options, falling between the choice of image on screen or live presenter on stage. My job, and that of my fellow event designers these days, is often not so much a process of building up elements but rather stripping them back or down to the bare essentials, to ensure the take-out message for attendees is as focused and effective as possible.

Extend the thought to staging, lighting, live action and projection, and the same principle applies. The strong, memorable idea with impact trumps the detailed, busy programme every time. It all comes back to the clarity and focus of the client brief at the start, enabling the creative team to become the fountain rather than the filter. As the project gets under way, the concept gathers speed and size as it snowballs downhill – involving and inspiring technicians and suppliers along the way – generating real impact when it finally reaches its target audience. And it's with this kind of potential that the event design process can really begin.

3.8 Summary

This chapter has attempted to provide a clear introductory overview to a topic which is crucial to the success of designed and production-driven events, yet about which there is much misunderstanding and confusion. The relationship between the event production steps of concept, design and staging has been highlighted, with a focus on events as the production of experiences rather than the simplistic, yet common, management of staging elements. This has been discussed from the perspective of the event attendee's experience, with a focus on the psychological outcomes of design and production.

Further reading

Berridge, G. (2006) *Event Design for Experience*, Oxford: Butterworth-Heinemann. This well-written book provides a thorough, literature-based review of several of the concepts discussed in this chapter.

Brown, S. and James, J. (2004) Event Design and Management: A Ritual Sacrifice?, in Ian Yeoman *et al.* (eds) *Festival and Events Management*, Oxford: Butterworth-Heinemann. This seminal chapter provides an interesting and critical discussion of cultural authenticity and the wider implications of escapist events.

Jensen, R. (1999) *The Dream Society: How the Coming Shift from Information to Imagination Will Transform Your Business*, New York: McGraw-Hill. Though not directly related to the events industry, Jensen's thoughtful and well-written book discusses the movement away from tangible products and services to the demand by consumers for the designed experience, and the importance of storytelling and other methods used by the modern-day marketers of such offerings.

Pine, B. J. and Gilmore, J. H. (1999) *The Experience Economy*, Cambridge, MA: Harvard Business Review. A foundational text for anybody interested in models of experience design, which also provides many examples from a variety of consumer industries.

Chapter 4

Event operations

Contents

4.1 Aims

By the end of this chapter, students will be able:

- To explain the key elements of event operations.
- To evaluate the need for event operations within the wider framework of event planning.
- To discuss the external legal framework and frameworks that events operate within.
- To recognise the importance of contracts and to understand the basic contractual require-
ments for events.
- To analyse individual event requirements from a logistical perspective.

4.2 Introduction

Operational planning takes place after the strategic plans have been put in place – the event manager has developed a concept, tested it for feasibility (using situational analysis and market segmentation), chosen a venue, considered the event design and drawn up a strategic project plan. The next stage is to develop and implement the operational plan.

Operational planning consists of a set of plans for each key aspect of managing an event. It is the detailing of the skills and resources needed to deliver an event (Bowdin *et al.* 2010) and must therefore consider all areas central to event delivery. The event manager must consider all elements of the event and decide what resources, skills and equipment will be needed to deliver them – this, in a nutshell, is event operations. As every event is different and individually

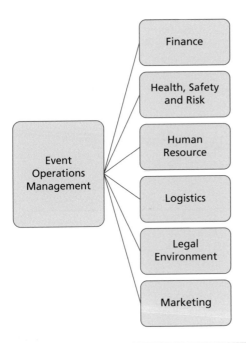

Figure 4.1 The key areas of managing event operations

complex, there is no set formula for which operations will need to be planned. However, we can generalise, to some extent. Typical areas for planning include decisions around a staffing strategy; plans that cover the organisational approach to marketing and sponsorship; operational planning to evaluate health, safety and risk factors; and financial control systems. All of these issues are key event operations requirements and are therefore explored in detail in the chapters that follow this one. Figure 4.1 shows the key areas of operational management.

In addition to these key operational areas, the planning process of an event must consider a wider range of operations. This chapter will focus on the legal external environment – the consideration of legalities, regulations, licences, permits and contracts involved when managing an event – and event logistics – including the logistical planning for both customers and on-site at venues/event sites.

Study activity

Draw a model that demonstrates the event planning process as described in the book so far. It should include the order of the processes and indicate how one element feeds into another. Include the following areas:

- The planning process:

  ○ event concept development including 5Ws and SMART event objective setting
  ○ event design
  ○ event feasibility testing including SWOT/PEST analysis
  ○ event project planning.

- The operations process:

  ○ financial planning
  ○ health, safety and risk
  ○ human resource management
  ○ logistical operations
  ○ the legal environment
  ○ marketing.

4.3 The legal environment

The consideration of and adherence to legalities is seen as the key to secure operations (Shone and Parry 2010). It is therefore essential that event managers keep abreast of the legal framework and relevant events legislation. Goldblatt (2008: 379) suggests four primary reasons for complying with laws and regulations: 'to protect your legal interests, to abide by ethical practices, to ensure the safety and security of your event stakeholders, and to protect your financial investment'. It is also important to comply in order to avoid adverse legal consequences, such as being sued for negligence or losing permits and licences that allow you to operate in the industry.

Legislation changes continually and there are many issues that cannot be fully explored here, so it is essential that event managers keep up to date with the ever-changing legal landscapes. Laws also vary from country to country. However, there are some common legal themes that event managers need to consider. (More information on legal requirements for events can be found in Chapter 8; particular attention should be paid to the various Health and Safety at Work Acts, which underpin much events legislation.)

4.3.1 Event ownership and duty of care

'Who owns the event?' is one of the key questions in the legal external environment. As Bowdin *et al.* (2010) point out, establishing who owns the event is a crucial point – whoever owns the event has legal responsibility and is therefore liable; and liability opens up the event owner to potential claims of negligence and costly litigations. The legal owner of the event could be the event manager, the organising body, the event organisation, the event committee or even the client. The question of ownership is vital to establishing outcomes in legal situations, as potentially negligent activities can lead to expensive and drawn-out litigation processes, and can ultimately have disastrous impacts on the event owner. It is therefore important that the answer is established from the outset – ownership of the event should be implicit throughout all pitching, proposals and contractual negotiations. Issues surrounding intellectual property (who owns the idea or concept) should also be established at the start of any event.

Once the ownership of the event is established – and the responsibility (liability) in the eyes of the law is therefore apparent – the event owner is endowed with a duty of care. Duty of care is a fundamental legal principle that, when applied to events, means 'taking all reasonable care to avoid acts or omissions that could injure employees, contractors, users, participants and visitors' (Bowdin *et al.* 2010: 339).

Study activity

In fifty words or less, explain why the principles of duty of care and event ownership are integral to the events industry.

4.3.2 Equality Acts

Event managers need to ensure that their event is accessible to all members of society. In the UK, legislation exists in order to ensure that events are accessible. This is known as the Equality Act of 2010, and it legislates against discrimination across a number of protected characteristics. Of the eight protected characteristics (age, race, religion, sex, disability, pregnancy, sexual orientation and marriage/civil partnerships), disability is one of the key concerns for event managers. It is unlawful for a service provider to discriminate against a disabled person by refusing to supply any service that it provides for other members of the public (Bowdin *et al.* 2010). In real terms, this means that event managers must consider issues relating to access to venues, ensuring that disabled guests have access to all services offered and fair treatment of disabled employees. Other countries have similar laws and legislations, and it is advisable that event managers keep abreast of these and seek advice on how to adhere to them. In the USA, laws such as the Civil Rights Act of 1964, the Equal Pay Act of 1963 and Title 1 of the Americans with Disabilities Act of 1990 need to be considered. Websites such as www.equality. gov.uk (UK), www.eeoc.gov (US Equal Employment Opportunity Commission), www.hreoc. gov.ac (Australian Human Rights Commission) and www.india.gov.in (Indian Fundamental Rights) are invaluable tools for the event manager seeking further information.

4.3.3 Sustainable events

The BS8901 standard was developed in the UK in November 2007 specifically for the events industry, in order for all aspects of events to be measured in terms of their sustainability. The standard sets out a system that helps organisations to consider the economic, environmental and social impacts of organising their events and ensures that every choice made, from the transportation of goods through to the contents of the delegate pack, are designed to be as ecologically and socially responsible as possible.

However, BS8901 is a standard, not a legal requirement, which is an important distinction. A standard sets out a framework of good practice; if an event organisation is granted the standard, it will be certified as meeting the BSI standard. But the law does not insist that it must comply with the standard.

On an international level, the International Standards Organisation is to create a new standard in 2012. This standard, ISO 21121, seeks to ensure that the international events industry will address social, economic and environmental impacts. It already has a project committee (ISO/PC 250) in place, and thirty countries are involved as participants or observers (Quainton 2010). The aim is to have one internationally recognised framework for the implementation of sustainability in events. (Sustainability is covered in detail in Chapter 14.)

4.4 Insurance

Events are susceptible to any number of issues that are often outside the event organisation's control. Disasters, such as an outbreak of a contagious disease (for example, bird and swine flu in Asia and South America, respectively, and foot and mouth in the UK) or extreme weather conditions (such as flooding or blizzards), can have severe effects on an event's performance. The industry has witnessed a shift towards a larger number of claims made from attendees who have injured themselves at an event or who make claims when they perceive the event to be unsatisfactory – perhaps due to the cancellation of the main act or a change of venue. Event insurance is therefore now seen as essential, and it has become one of the key issues for the industry.

Event insurance will typically cover such items as cancellation of the event, venue bankruptcy, non-appearance of celebrities, failure to vacate the venue, damage to property or premises, legal liabilities, damage to equipment, and public liabilities (Shone and Parry 2010).

The importance of event insurance was illustrated when Unique Events was forced to cancel the New Year's Eve 2006 celebrations in Edinburgh, Scotland, due to severe weather. Fortunately, the company had sufficient cancellation insurance to cover ticket refunds and any financial loss (Francisco 2008); the picture would have been very different if the organisers had not taken out this policy. Cancellation is usually the very last option for event organisers, though – often, they will approach their insurance company to fund preventative action. Insurance companies will often cover smaller amounts that enable the show to go on: for instance, they might make funds available for extra transport to ensure that guests can beat transport strikes, or to a change of venue at the last minute. Both organisers and insurers will obviously explore such options in preference to cancellation of the whole event.

Insurance that covers theft, fire, weather and workers' compensation is also important, as is public liability (sometimes known as personal accident) insurance and property damage insurance. Any special insurance for particular elements of the event should also be acquired (for example, marquees often require special insurance and events that take place outside can sometimes ask for weather insurance) and consideration should be given to event equipment and property cover to ensure that any hired equipment is covered. Many insurance policies exclude terrorist attacks and 'acts of God' (typically defined as acts that are outside of human control, such as natural disasters).

Event managers should also always check that suppliers – such as the artists, venue, audio-visual suppliers, entertainment agencies, staffing agencies and so on – have their own insurance and liability cover and are in compliance with industry and legal regulations.

Insurance policies and the clauses within them are often very specific and should be read carefully. It is also important to give the insurers the right information. Equipment used on site will need to be detailed carefully: for example, expensive musical instruments are often not

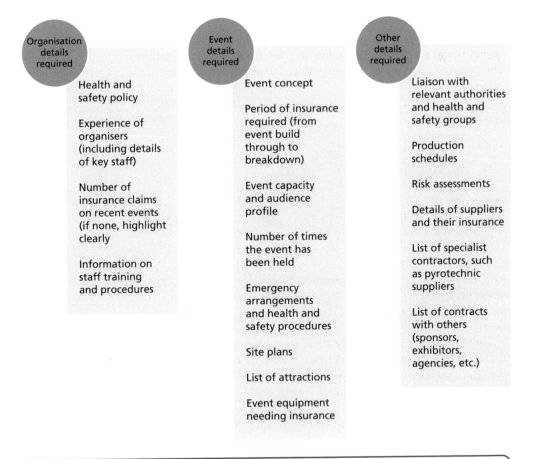

Figure 4.2 Details insurance companies require
Source: Adapted from EventScotland 2006

covered by standard insurance policies. Figure 4.2 provides a sample checklist of information that the insurance company or brokers will require.

Event insurance should therefore be in place for the entire planning process and, in order to gain the correct cover, insurance requirements should be investigated in good time, preferably with an insurance broker or with specialist event insurance companies (Shone and Parry 2010). It is advisable to aim to confirm event insurance two to three months before and certainly no less than one month before the event date (EventScotland 2006).

4.5 Regulations, licences and permits

No matter which country an event is organised in, there are myriad regulations with which the event manager must comply. These regulations change from country to country, and indeed from region to region (regulations are often governed by local authorities or regional councils). Generally, the larger the event, the more regulations, licences and permits that will be required. It is important to note that the event organiser is legally required to obtain the right permits and licences, and failure to do so may well result in fines and penalties. It should also be noted that authorities have the right to cancel events if the right permits are not obtained.

An example of this can be seen with the Lapland West Midlands event (nicknamed 'Blunderland' by the industry press in the UK), which was cancelled just a few days before it was due to open in 2008. In part, this was due to the organisers' failure to apply for an entertainment licence from South Staffordshire District Council (Francisco and Quainton 2008).

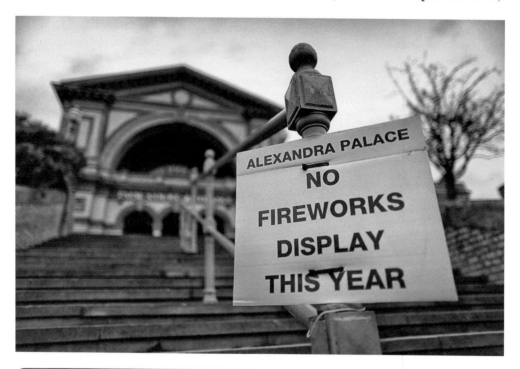

Image 4.1 Councils across Britain cancel firework displays due to government spending cuts
Source: Peter Macdiarmid / Getty Images

Just days before the event was cancelled, another event by the same organisation (LaplandUK) – Lapland New Forest – was cancelled amid claims from visitors that it did not live up to promises made on the website. In 2010, LaplandUK was placed into administration, with its founders blaming bad weather for the company's problems – ironic for an attraction that relied on snow.

It is perhaps easier for event managers to consider the event components that need licences and permits, rather than to try to keep abreast of the ever-changing regulations. Therefore, below, we suggest some of the event elements that may need permits or licences. As each event varies significantly, the list is dictated by the event design and the event product. However, once established, this list can act as a standard plan that merely needs revising and evaluating every time the event is repeated. Again, it should be stressed that many of these licences are legal requirements, so event managers should check carefully.

Event managers should consider the following issues and the regulations, permits and licences that might apply to each one:

- alcohol consumption
- food handling
- staffing
- noise
- building regulations/standards
- fire precautions
- health and safety at work
- first-aid regulations
- lifting equipment and manual handling operations
- occupancy levels
- music and performance rights and licences
- intellectual property
- electricity at work
- environmental protection
- signs and signal regulations
- waste disposal
- street trader or temporary market trader licences
- street closures
- public entertainment licences
- Criminal Record Bureau checks (required for events involving minors; similar police checks are required internationally).

As Bowdin *et al.* (2010) suggest, the principal rule is that the event manager should carry out careful research in order to ensure they understand and comply with all regulations that relate to their event. It should also be noted that the amount of time taken to identify and comply with regulations can vary enormously – the process should be started at the earliest point in order to deal with such issues as delays in the granting of licences.

A list of resources that will help to identify relevant health and safety legislation is given in Chapter 8.

Study activity

You are organising a live music gig for 150 attendees in your town or city. The venue has a dedicated music event space which holds a maximum of 175 people. Write a list of the key event components that might have regulatory considerations and those which might require a permit or licence. Then, using the internet as your primary resource, research the regulations and obtain information about which permits or licences will be needed.

4.6 Events contracts

'The contract is the documentation of the relationship between the event and the various stakeholders' (Bowdin *et al.* 2010: 330); it is an agreement that sets out the responsibilities between two or more parties and it is legally binding. Typically, contracts are written; oral contracts are becoming less common in the industry, as all stakeholders understand the need to have formal contractual obligations in order to guard against future problems.

4.6.1 Contract law

Contract preparation and execution are vital parts of the events management role, so it is important that event managers understand the key terms used within them. Goldblatt (2008: 311–314) defines the key terms of an events contract as:

- *Parties* – names of parties must be clearly defined.
- *Offer* – 'the offer is the service or product tendered by one party to another', including consulting services, products, entertainment, sponsorship deals and so on.
- *Consideration* – the consideration clause defines what one party will provide the other upon acceptance of an offer. This is usually money or rights.
- *Acceptance* – 'when both parties accept an offer, they execute (sign) the agreement confirming that they understand and agree to comply with the terms and conditions of the agreement'.

Matthews (2008) offers a comprehensive breakdown of the requirements of contract provision. He suggests that a contract is made up of two main parts: terms and conditions, and the clauses. *Terms and conditions* are considered essential to the contract and include contact information (including legal names, full addresses and so on); event details (including venue, specifics of product/services, additional requirements, details of general liability and additional insurance, and compliance with regulations and standards); financial information (including details of cancellation and compensation, plus taxes and deposits); rider information.

Clauses comprise the fixed part of the contract. They define and expand upon the terms and conditions, and might include:

- *Cancellation* – usually this is expressed as a percentage of the total value of the contract, which is payable upon cancellation by either party. Cancellation policies usually operate on a sliding scale, with 100 per cent of the contract value within fourteen days of the event date.

- *Force Majeure* (act of God) – this clause removes liability from the contracted party should they be prevented from delivering their obligations due to an act of God. Acts of God are defined as unavoidable circumstances that are outside of the party's control – in event contracts, they tend to relate to the weather, natural disasters, transportation issues and terrorism.
- *Billing* – including payment terms and schedules.
- *Insurance* – including details of insurance held by the contracted parties.
- *Indemnification* – protection of the contract signatory against losses incurred by an event. Liability clauses are also included and are important for events, as many suppliers will not expose themselves to liability and will attempt to remove this clause. Event managers are advised to seek legal advice on this clause, as it relates closely to insurance and can invalidate policies and contracts.

(List adapted from Goldblatt 2008)

Figure 4.3 Event contracts may be required for a number of suppliers and providers

Venue

Sponsorship/exhibition

Audio-visual (including lighting and sound)

Entertainment/artist

Catering (including food and beverage suppliers)

Event structures (marquees/staging, set building, fencing, etc.

Security and staffing

Event production

Decor, design and theming (including florists, furniture suppliers, etc.

Hospitality provision

Technology providers

Marketing/PR agencies

Whilst these lists and generalisations are useful as a background to event contracts, some contracts are vital to the successful delivery of an event and require special consideration. These are listed in Figure 4.3 and explored in more detail in the following sections.

4.6.2 Venue contracts

The venue contract is one of the most complex contracts. It contains many specific clauses and, when dealing with these agreements, a number of issues must be taken into consideration. Again, these are usually legally binding. They can be summarised as:

1 Cancellation clauses, including details of refunds available and costs payable in the event of a cancellation by either party.
2 Payment terms, including deposit details and payment schedules.
3 Full details of costs and estimated event spend at the venue (including projected food and beverage costs, room hire charges, furniture and linen hire, tips and service charges, taxes, set-up charges and so on).
4 Attrition clause, which sets out the food and beverage minimum spend. If your customers do not attend, the event organiser will be required to pay this fixed fee. If the venue is a hotel, and the contract includes room bookings, there will be an attrition clause regarding the minimum number of rooms that must be paid for, even if they are not occupied.
5 Provision of personnel and security, including overtime rates and numbers of staff required.
6 Access times and overrunning clauses, including date of event, start and end times, service times for food and beverages.
7 Venue damage, including indemnification, insurance, liability issues, licences and permits.

The venue contract should be viewed as an opportunity for the event organiser to negotiate rates and charges. Particular attention should be paid to the payment terms. Getting this right will ease cash flow and ensure financial stability throughout the event process. The venue is often the largest expense on an events budget, so ensuring that the payment schedule allows the event manager to generate some revenue before meeting the majority of the costs will help prevent cash-flow issues.

Similarly, cancellation terms and penalties need close attention and are often open to negotiation. Contracts with venues also usually set out the minimum numbers required for the event – this figure represents the least number of guests the event organiser must pay for, no matter how many guests actually attend. It should *always* be negotiated, as it is usually possible to cut it by 10–20 per cent. Event managers should also look closely at food and beverage prices, which are often highly negotiable and may contain hidden costs, such as the supply of linen, chairs and tables, which can be easily removed.

Figure 4.4 shows a sample venue contract.

4.6.3 Entertainment contracts

Entertainment contracts are agreements drawn up between the event organiser and those people supplying the entertainment. Typical entertainment options include after-dinner speakers, celebrities, bands, DJs, singers, cabaret acts, masters of ceremonies, comedians, magicians and musicians. Special considerations for this type of contract will include non-attendance, exclusivity (the prevention of headline acts performing at similar events around the same time), cancellation terms for either party and insurance clauses.

Booking Contract   **Ref: 203**

Cancellation Terms

Unless otherwise agreed in writing by the University, these conditions apply and are additional to any specific agreement concluded for the hiring of University Premises and/or Facilities.

1. Definitions

"Hirer" means the company, entity, institution or person hiring the Premises and/or Facilities from the University. "Premises" means all premises which are being hired by the Hirer (including car parks and grounds).
"University" means University of Greenwich.
"Facilities" means all services, equipment and apparatus belonging to or provided by or on behalf of the University to the Hirer.

2. Booking, Deposit and Confirmation

2.1 The submission of a Hiring Agreement does not constitute a hiring. The University reserves the right to decline an application at its sole discretion.

2.2 This Agreement shall not be effective until the potential hirer has submitted a signed Hiring Agreement and paid a non-refundable deposit for the Hire of Premises and/or Facilities to the University and the University has accepted such Hiring Agreement.

2.3 The Hiring Agreement sets out the amount of non-refundable deposit(s) and the date(s) by which such deposit(s) shall be paid by the Hirer. The Hirer acknowledges that if the University does not receive the non-refundable deposit (s) by or before the relevant date(s), the Premises may be hired to a third party or become non-available. The non-refundable deposit(s) will be based on minimum number of guests or attendees.

The Hirer agrees that the initial pre-paid deposit(s) are non-refundable and non-transferable in the event of the booking being cancelled for whatever reason.

2.4 All catering will be undertaken by the University unless agreed prior in writing by the parties. Final confirmation of the number of guests or attendees for catering purposes must be received by the University one week before the start of the period of hire.

3. Charges, Deposits and Payment

3.1 The charges for the Facilities and the Premises will be communicated to the Hirer prior to or at the time of booking and will be set out in the University Hiring Agreement.

3.2 The Hirer agrees that these charges may be increased by the University between the time of booking and the period of hire in the event of any increase in the costs to the University of providing the Facilities and/or Premises for reasons beyond the University's control.

3.3 The University shall issue (after the period of hire) a final invoice for the charges for the hire of the Premises and/or Facilities plus any applicable VAT, less any deposit(s) already pre-paid by the Hirer. The Hirer shall pay the outstanding amount within 30 days from the date of the invoice.

4. Cancellation and Charges

4.1 All cancellations must be submitted in writing to the University. Failure to confirm cancellation in writing may result in the Hirer being liable to pay the full amount of the estimated charges for the hire.

4.2 Unless minimum numbers are guaranteed by the hirer and stated on the hiring agreement the following shall apply; if the hire is cancelled or the number of guests or attendees is reduced:

a) 365 days or more before the date of hire, there is no charge other than the initial non-refundable deposit (if applicable)
b) between 364 and 180 days before the date of hire, there will be a 20% charge of the estimated total amount.
c) between 179 and 90 days before the date of hire, there will be a 40% charge on the estimated total amount.
d) between 89 and 15 days before the date of hire, there will be a 60% charge on the estimated total amount.
e) 14 days or less before the date of hire, there will be a 100% charge on the estimated total amount.

Notwithstanding the above, the University may, at its sole discretion and in any case after the period of hire, refund part of the initial pre-paid deposit(s) if the same Premises are hired to a third party.

4.3 In addition to the amounts set out in clause 4.2 above, the Hirer shall reimburse the University in full for any expenses already incurred or committed by the University (with the Hirers consent) for or on behalf of the Hirer including but not limited to musicians, florists, equipment hire, catering and accommodation.

4.4 Neither the University nor any body responsible for the management of the University shall be held liable or required to pay compensation to the Hirer or any third party for any loss or damage sustained as a result of or in any way arising out of the cancellation of the hiring.

4.5 The hire charges relate to the times of the booking. The Hirer will be responsible for ensuring that the Premises are vacated by the finishing time agreed at the time of the hiring. In addition to the rights and remedies that the University may have against the Hirer, if an event continues beyond these times the Hirer will incur additional hire charges.

4.6 In any case, the University reserves the right to enter the Premises and terminate any event which extends beyond the contracted times of hire without any liability to the Hirer.

5. Liability

5.1 Where the Hirer is an unincorporated association, the person or any member, servant or agent thereof signing the Hiring Agreement or such other document requesting the use of the Premises and/or Facilities undertakes personal liability for all charges in respect of the hiring and for the compliance with the terms of the Agreement. The liability of the unincorporated association and such person or any member, servant or agent thereof shall be joint and several.

5.2 The Hirer shall indemnify and keep indemnified the University against all actions, claims, demands, costs and expenses of any nature which may be brought against or suffered by the University as a result of or in connection with the use of the University Premises and/or Facilities by the Hirer, its guests or any other attendees. For the avoidance of doubt, the Hirer shall be responsible for any damage, other than fair wear and tear, to University property (or that belonging to any individual or organisation).

Figure 4.4 A sample venue contract

Note: This is an example of part of the terms and conditions section of a booking contract.

Booking Contract   Ref: 203

5.3 The University accepts no liability for any interruption or curtailment of the hiring as a result of the actions of any third party (including any guests or attendees of the event organised by the Hirer), howsoever caused.

5.4 In no circumstances will the University be liable or accept any responsibility for loss of or damage to any personal property, car or other vehicle (or the contents thereof) which may be brought or left within the premises.
All persons using the University's Premises or Facilities must take their own precautions to protect their property.

5.5 The University reserves the right to let other parts of its Premises and/or Facilities to other persons or organisations simultaneously with the hiring and accepts no liability for the actions, omissions or conduct of such other persons or organisations.

5.6 The University's maximum aggregate liability in contract, tort or otherwise (including any liability for any neglect, act or omission) howsoever arising out of or in connection with this Agreement in respect of any one or more incidents or occurrences shall be limited to a sum equal to the charges paid by the Hirer to the University under this Agreement.

5.7 The University shall not be liable for any indirect, special, incidental, or consequential loss or damage nor for any loss of business or profit.

5.8 The limitations set out in clause 5 shall apply to the extent permitted by law. Nothing in this Agreement shall exclude or restrict either party's liability for death or personal injury resulting from the negligence of that party or to any extent not permitted by law.

5.9 The University will require the Hirer to take out such insurance policies as the University may reasonably deem appropriate in respect of the hire.

6. Health and Safety and Conduct

6.1 The Hirer shall comply and must ensure that all guests and attendees and any person entering the Premises comply with any applicable health and safety laws and regulations (including the Health & Safety at Work Act 1974) and any of the University's health and safety guidance, policies, procedures or rules.

6.2 The University reserves the right to cancel the hire, upon notice to the Hirer (and without any liability thereof), if the University reasonably believes that any condition contained in this Agreement is or may be breached or that the safety of persons or property is or may be endangered as a direct or indirect result of the hiring.

6.3 The Hirer shall be solely responsible for keeping and maintaining proper order, for observing fire, safety and security regulations at all times and for providing efficient supervision on the occasion of the hire (including controlling and regulating the ingress and egress of all persons attending the event).

6.4 The Hirer must ensure that any University Premises are maintained in a clean and tidy state at all times during the hire. If any parts of the Premises are in disorder at commencement of the hire, this should be reported to a member of University staff immediately.

6.5 In the event of any damage, the University may make good the damage and the Hirer, by acceptance of the hiring, will thereby be deemed to have undertaken to pay the cost of such reparation.

6.6 The Hirer shall not install and use on the University's premises any electrical appliance, amplification equipment or lighting fittings without the prior written permission of the University. The Hirer is wholly responsible for the safety of such installation at all times whilst it remains on the University's Premises and for any injury caused to any person or property arising in connection with such installation and usage. Consent by the University to such installation and usage does not imply the safety or suitability for use of the said installation or acceptance by the University of liability for damage or injury arising in connection with the said appliance.

6.7 The Hirer must ensure that no child under the age of 14 years is admitted on the University's premises unless during the whole time such child is accompanied by an adult person, (minimum requirement of one adult per 10 children).

6.8 All persons under the age of 18 years (and over 14 years) must be under the control of at least one adult who should be clearly identifiable as such and who will be held responsible for any actions or liabilities incurred by such persons, (minimum requirement of one adult per 15 children).

6.9 University property shall not be moved except with prior written permission of an authorised officer of the University.

6.10 Smoking is not permitted in any part of the University except areas which are clearly designated.

6.11 No pets or other animals, except guide dogs, are permitted on University premises without prior written permission of the University.

6.12 The authorised representatives of the University shall have free access to the Premises at all times.

6.13 No part of the Premises may be sublet, or reassigned by the Hirer to any third party.

7. Overnight Accommodation

Where the hire includes use of the University premises as overnight accommodation the Hirer shall:

(a) provide the University with a full list of persons who will be resident on the hired premised overnight not less than 7 days before the commencement of hire;

(b) ensure the hired overnight accommodation is used only by persons specified on said nominal list unless agreed prior in writing by the University;

(c) receive keys on the day of arrival no earlier than 16.00 and

(d) vacate the room and return the key(s) by 09.00 on the day of departure.

8. Licensing Considerations

8.1 The Hirer must ensure that the maximum number of persons permitted to be present in any indoor facility under the licensing arrangements shall not be exceeded at any time.

8.2 No alcoholic liquor, food or other refreshments, other than those supplied by the University, shall be sold or consumed by the Hirer (or any of the guests or attendees) on the University premises without the prior written consent of the University. Alcoholic liquor shall only be consumed on the premises upon prior written approval of the University and subject to the obtaining of any specific licence that may be necessary.

Figure 4.4 A sample venue contract (contd.)

Particular attention should be paid to the non-attendance – or 'no-show' – clause in the contract, as artists pulling out of an event at the last minute – or simply not showing up – can be a major problem for event organisers. Having a clause that clearly states the implications of a last-minute cancellation will go some way to protecting the event organiser and will at least result in financial remuneration, if not artist replacement.

Another key element of the entertainment contract is the rider. This is usually attached to the contract (hence the name: it 'rides' the contract) and specifies particular demands that the event organiser needs to meet. These can include audio-visual and technological requirements and hospitality demands (specific food, drink, room layouts and so on). Silvers (2004) suggests that riders can run to a hundred pages or more and often contain sensitive material, such as how an entertainer achieves a specific effect. Rider requests should be carefully examined as they are often used by entertainment suppliers to increase their fees, making them extremely costly for event organisers. Event organisers should therefore enlist the help of talent buyers or agents – and should acquire legal advice from solicitors – before negotiating entertainment contracts.

4.6.4 Sponsor and exhibitor contracts

Contracts with sponsors and exhibitors are unique as they refer to a one-off relationship and the obligations that stem from that relationship. Sponsors and exhibitors are usually brought on board by a specialist sales representative and they will often draw up contracts directly. However, it is essential that the event manager directly responsible for event delivery reads these contracts carefully prior to signing to ensure that all the specifics are deliverable. Special considerations for sponsor and exhibitor contract agreements include:

- exclusivity (no other sponsors/exhibitors from the same sector can be involved)
- hospitality rights, including complimentary tickets
- branding on marketing collateral and on-site brand presence
- cancellation terms, including if the event is cancelled and if the sponsor/exhibitor wishes to terminate the relationship
- payment terms – payment is preferable upon signage of the contract
- length of contract – contracts can often cover a relationship lasting for a number of years (sponsorship of a repeat event over a three-year period, for example). These contracts need to be carefully considered in order to ensure that the event will be able to deliver all obligations each year.

4.6.5 Other supplier contracts

Events involve dealing with a large number of suppliers, and each of these relationships should be legally supported through the provision of a contract. Suppliers include audio-visual, security, catering, staging, florists, marquee and furniture, staffing agencies, technology providers and marketing and PR agencies.

These contracts need to be carefully worded to ensure that there is protection for either party if the event is cancelled, and also to ensure there is provision and protection in the case of non-supply by a supplier.

4.6.6 Supplier selection

Suppliers for events are often selected via a tendering process which involves a request for proposals (RFP) to a number of competing organisations. This typically includes a description of the event concept, details of the event plan as they currently stand and an outline of any particular business problems. It will also include a full outline of the requirements of the supplier. These RFPs are sent to a variety of organisations offering the services required, with a deadline for submissions. The potential suppliers will review the request and decide if they wish to bid for the contract. If they decide to go ahead, they submit a proposal, which will include specific suggestions on how to meet the needs and wants of the event organiser and, depending on the type of work, may also include creative solutions to business problems outlined in the proposal. A small selection of these organisations will then be invited to pitch their proposal at a meeting, and from this the event manager will pick their preferred supplier.

Once the preferred supplier has been identified, it is often necessary to go through procurement. This is the process of making a buying decision (i.e. selecting a supplier) that promotes fair and open competition and also protects the events organisation from fraud. It commonly involves all the processes from preparation of contracts through to the invoicing and receipt of payment, and often concentrates on researching the supplier, value analysis, detailed contract specifications and the agreement of financial processes.

The selection of suppliers via a tendering process is outlined in Figure 4.5.

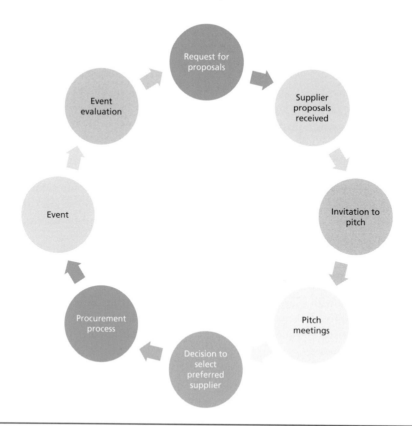

Figure 4.5 Supplier tendering process

4.7 Event logistics

The term 'logistics' is used to describe the movement of products and resources. Events management draws heavily on management logistics theory in order to understand how to manage the flow of goods, resources and information effectively. However, much of this theory relates to supplying the product to the customer – event logistics, by necessity, must consider a logistical approach that brings the customer to the product (the product cannot go to the customer; the customer must come to the product).

At first glance, event logistics can seem incredibly daunting – there is so much to plan and organise that it can feel like an impossible task. To simplify the process, it is sensible to reduce the number of logistical considerations. It is useful to consider two broad areas of event logistics – the customer and the venue/site (see Figure 4.6). (In the past, event academics have talked of a third area – the product – but this is usually defined as the entire event, and is therefore confusing.)

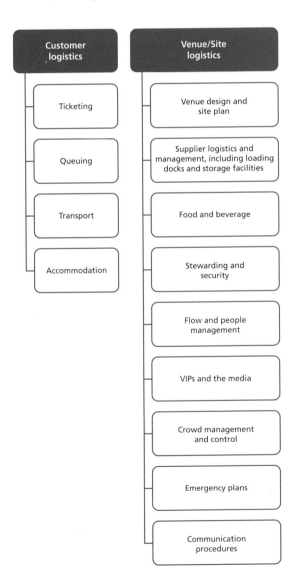

Figure 4.6 Event logistics

Events can be seen as a large jigsaw puzzle, with all the elements needing to be slotted together to complete the picture – it is the role of logistics to ensure that these elements all fit and are brought together at the right moment.

4.7.1 Venue/site logistics

Event venues or sites can vary enormously. Corporate events taking place in a five-star hotel have very different on-site logistical requirements from those of a festival taking place in a desert in the middle of Arizona. The event logistics manager must therefore think carefully about their specific venue and the logistical requirements of their choice. Some of the key considerations can be seen in Figure 4.7, and each will be discussed in more detail throughout this section. It is important to stress the individual nature of every event and the fact that these individual aspects will result in very different logistical requirements.

4.7.1.1 Venue design

Much of the information in this section is adapted from *The Event Safety Guide* (HSE 1999).

GENERAL PRINCIPLE OF VENUE/SITE DESIGN

The guiding principle for the design of venues or sites is to provide an arena where the audience can enjoy the entertainment in a safe and comfortable atmosphere. The venue has to be suitable for the event's needs and also for the needs and wants of the audience.

The choice of a venue is one of the hardest and most important aspects of an event – it is often easy to get enthusiastic about a fantastic venue and forget that the audience's enjoyment is key. Questions such as those in the list below should be paramount in any venue or site decisions:

Venue/site design

Supplier logistics and management

Food and beverage

Stewarding and security

Flow and people management

VIPs

Crowd management and crowd control

Communication

Health and safety and emergency procedures

Figure 4.7 The key areas of venue logistics

- Will the audience like the venue?
- Do they have a clear sight of the stage?
- Can they find the location easily?
- Are the transport links adequate?
- What about the catering and general service?
- How large is the site, and how easy is it to navigate?
- What facilities are available?

SITE SUITABILITY ASSESSMENT

Once a potential site or venue has been identified, it is essential to visit it to assess suitability well before the event. In order to assess the suitability effectively, the event manager must have a proposed capacity in mind, have some ideas of the concept and theme, and have an idea of the programme – what you want to happen and when. This provisional plan will need to be flexible to work with the venue, but the more detail you have, the easier the site assessment will be.

Three crucial areas should be considered on the first visit to a new venue or site:

1 Available space for audiences and temporary structures – stages, marquees and so on.
2 Backstage facilities – how much room will the crew have? Do you want back or front projection? Is there room for performers? Crew equipment? Crew areas?
3 Parking/camping, rendezvous points and transport.

This visit allows the event manager to determine what facilities are available. Event managers should check such facilities as rooms and layouts, location and access, ground conditions, traffic routes, first-aid provision, toilets, waste-disposal areas, power, water, gas and electrical supplies, fire exits, stages, barriers, exits and entrance areas, hospitality areas, sight lines and so on.

Once the visit is completed, it is usual to produce a pre-design appraisal of the site. The final design will depend on the nature of the entertainment, location, size and duration of the event. It will also need to take account of the geographical, topographical and environmental infrastructure. This appraisal of the site visit will typically cover:

- proposed occupant capacity
- artist profile
- audience profile
- duration and timing of event
- venue evaluation
- alcohol availability
- audience: seated or standing?
- audience movement between facilities/entertainment
- single stage/multiple-arena complex, etc. (HSE 1999)

4.7.1.2 Site plans

Once the event design is in place, the event manager can begin to put together the site plan. Such plans are the primary means of ensuring communication is flowing and that the various managers (stage manager, lighting manager, production manager and so on) working on an event understand the key elements. Their main purpose is to indicate the proposed areas to be used by the event and the locations of various activities within the event site or venue. These plans are also key tools for communicating logistical requirements – they should, if produced correctly, alleviate the need for explanation and highlight key areas of concern.

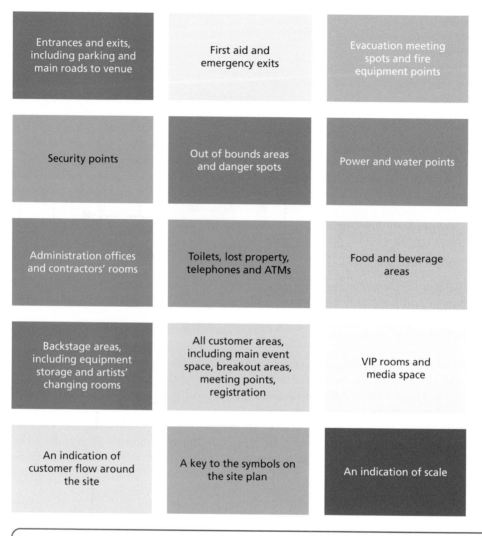

Figure 4.8 Contents of a site plan

Figure 4.8 provides a list of what should be included in a site plan. It should be noted that these plans need to be far more detailed than the venue or site maps that are given to the customer. The final site plan will often not be ready until the day of the event set-up, when all ticketing and entertainment have been finalised.

Figure 4.9 shows a site plan for the University of Greenwich. The Greenwich campus is a World Heritage Site, with a stunning location on the banks of the Thames in London and classical buildings designed by Sir Christopher Wren. It is an ideal venue for academic conferences, celebratory meals, public lectures and fundraising events, and it has a wide range of rooms and facilities, making it important that event organisers, suppliers and attendees can all navigate the site easily. The site plan details the layout of the venue and allows event organisers to get a visual feel for the layout; it also directs suppliers to the right part of the campus and helps attendees arrive in the right place.

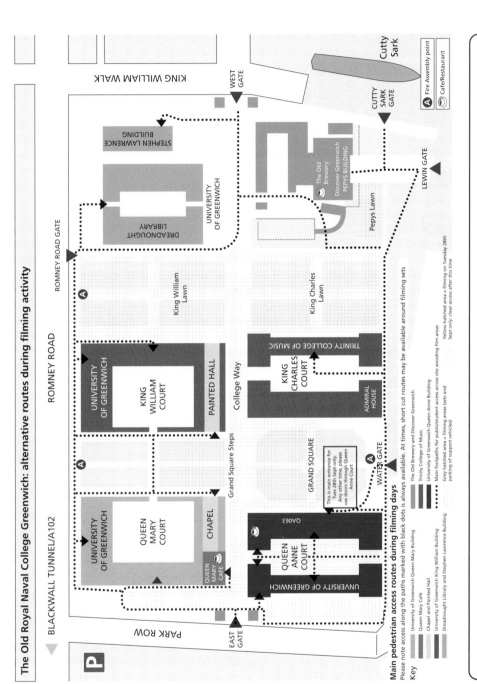

The Old Royal Naval College Greenwich: alternative routes during filming activity

BLACKWALL TUNNEL/A102   **ROMNEY ROAD**   **ROMNEY ROAD GATE**

PARK ROW

KING WILLIAM WALK

Main pedestrian access routes during filming days

Please note access along the paths marked with black dots is always available. At times, short cut routes may be available around filming sets

Key

University of Greenwich Queen Mary Building
Queen Mary Cafe
Chapel and Painted Hall
University of Greenwich King William Building
Dreadnought Library and Stephen Lawrence Building

The Old Brewery and Discover Greenwich
Trinity College of Music
University of Greenwich Queen Anne Building
Main footpaths for public/student access across site avoiding film areas
Grey hatched area = filming areas (lets and parking of support vehicles)

Yellow hatched area = filming on Tuesday 28th Sept in film areas

Grey only: clear access after this time

Ⓐ Fire Assembly point

Ⓒ Cafe/Restaurant

This is main entrance for Tues 28th Sept only. Any other time, please use doors through Queen Anne Court

Figure 4.9 Example site plan: the University of Greenwich

4.7.1.3 Supplier logistics and management

The main thrust of logistics is the flow of equipment, product and people around the venue and to the places where they need to be, when they need to be there.

Therefore, one of the key areas that needs to be considered is the coordination of all the event suppliers – how and when they will reach the site, and how they will move around the venue, must be planned carefully. It is the logistics manager's responsibility to do this. Ensuring that your suppliers know how to find the site and where and when they need to be available is essential, so each supplier will require a detailed briefing. This can be a very complex process. For example, a conference for a hundred delegates may require the coordination of a caterer; an audio-visual organisation; lighting and stage set production companies; room dressers to create a specific theme; furniture-hire companies; drinks suppliers; entertainment; and a cleaning company. Each of these organisations will have their own set of requirements and their own timelines for set-up. They will also require specific access (often through loading docks) and a large amount of storage space for equipment.

4.7.1.4 Food and beverage

The provision of food and beverages should be an important part of the logistics plan, with ample time built in to ensure that the catering is provided properly. Caterers at an event have very specific logistical requirements that will vary depending on the size of the event and the type of venue used. A large trade show may involve twenty different catering suppliers – each caterer must be on site, set up and equipped with the necessary facilities in good time before the show opens. They will usually need access to running water and waste disposal, refrigeration and gas supply/electrical power points, and will have lots of equipment and a large amount of perishable goods. Moreover, they will have strict times for how long they need to set up, and how long they need to be on site before the event opens. All of these issues will need to be taken into account when drawing up the logistics plan.

4.7.1.5 Stewarding and security

One of the key security issues for the logistics manager is ensuring that the right people have access to specific areas during set up, at the event itself and during the shut-down process. This can be managed by giving suppliers or VIP guests laminated badges (for example, a creative event producer who works closely with the event manager, the audio-visual team and the entertainment will probably need an 'Access All Areas' badge). Colour-coded wristbands can also be used, acting in the same way as badges to control the movement of staff and suppliers. It is the responsibility of the logistics manager to issue these control methods (badges or wristbands), to ensure that every supplier and staff member has the correct access level.

4.7.1.6 Flow and people management

Events of any scale feature a large amount of movement in the venue or on site. Suppliers will move around with their equipment, sponsors and exhibitors will move around with their resources, and customers will move around once the event starts. This movement of people around the event venue or site is known as the 'flow', and the people who move around are often referred to as 'event traffic'.

The flow of event traffic grows more complex as the event grows in size. A small networking dinner for fifty can be fairly straightforward, with only the caterers and the venue staff to consider during set-up, and with the flow from the kitchens to the dining room being uncomplicated

CASE STUDY 4.1

Lake of Stars Festival

Location: Malawi
Date: each September
Event type: non-profit music festival
Attendees: 3300

The Lake of Stars Festival in Mangochi, Malawi, is an award-winning festival that aims to promote Malawian arts and tourism through international inter-action and exposure. In 2010, it featured ninety artists from a variety of art forms and exposed over 200 million people to Malawi through media coverage. It is the country's number-one tourist event. In 2010, 100-plus local people were employed and 3000-plus people attended the festival. Such an event requires robust security and crowd management measures.

In order to deliver a safe and secure event, the festival organisers employ a UK security firm to ensure the efficient deployment of four separate security providers plus a large detachment of Malawian police officers. Oliver Gardiner, managing director of Vespasian, has been head of security for the festival for two years.

Edwina Fitzpatrick, assistant production manager of the festival commented, 'Working on Lake of Stars is no easy task, both physically and professionally, but Ollie's intuitive ability to constantly re-evaluate systems, procedures and to manage security situations in a foreign country with a lack of resources, trained staff and an absence of large event production demonstrates his considerable skills.' She went on to explain that the key roles for Vespasian personnel included working alongside and training Malawian police officers and private security firms in crowd control/event security. This required the management of large teams whose first language was not English, whilst observing Malawi's social etiquette and culture.

Sources: http://www.vespasiansecurity.co.uk; http://www.lakeofstars.org

(in the right venue). However, a festival with a vast number of venues within a single site will have hundreds of suppliers (including caterers, audio-visual suppliers, lighting engineers, staging set producers, entertainment, VIP guests, security personnel, gate, fence and crush barrier builders, water and electrical engineers, first-aid operatives, toilet suppliers, vendors, media, waste removal and equipment transporters). All of these suppliers need to be controlled and need to be able to flow around the site without inhibiting other suppliers during the set-up and shut-down processes.

Once the event has started, the need to move people around the site does not lessen – in fact, the flow of event traffic becomes even harder to manage as suppliers often still need to move equipment around but will now also have to contend with customers. An experienced logistics manager will consider where the customers will be at all times, and will ensure that the rest of the event traffic flows around them. So they may suggest that suppliers cannot move equipment during peak times – such as arrival, coffee breaks or lunch sessions – or they may ensure that the supplier traffic is flowing in a different direction to the customer flow.

The Burning Man Festival – held in the Nevada Desert each August – has encountered problems with event traffic moving around the same site as event customers. In 2003, a woman was killed when she fell under the wheels of an 'art car'. In the same year, a truck carrying 30,000 pounds of ice rolled over and injured a person (*New York Times* 2003). These examples highlight the importance of considering the entire flow of event traffic prior to the event as part of the overall event plan.

4.7.1.7 VIPs

Another element that can cause problems for the logistics manager relates to dealing with VIPs and the media. It is important that the flow of VIPs around the venue or site is managed effectively and professionally. Event VIPs might be special guests for any number of reasons: they could be supporting the event financially, performers, or celebrities who will add value to the brand. Ensuring that these guests are able to reach the VIP areas and the entertainment arena easily is essential, as is moving them around the site efficiently. Getting a performer from one stage to the next in plenty of time and then back to the VIP area without them experiencing congestion or being exposed to too many customers will help to ensure they take a favourable view of the event.

4.7.1.8 Crowd management and crowd control

Management of the customer base should be a priority for anyone concerned with operational planning of events – from a logistics point of view, the customer base is a crowd. Priority should be given to planning proper operating procedures, as the impacts of not managing a crowd correctly can be incredibly damaging and sometimes even tragic. For example, at the German Love Parade in 2010, police attempted to stop people reaching the parade area, which led to a stampede and the death of nineteen people (BBC 2010). Unfortunately, there are a number of similar examples, all of which highlight the importance of a thorough understanding of the issues relating to crowd management and control, and of the need for a robust strategy at every event, no matter how small or large.

It is important to distinguish between the techniques of crowd *management* and crowd *control*: the former is concerned with moving the crowd effectively, whereas the latter is a reactive process relating to the steps that are taken once a crowd (or part of a crowd) has started to behave unexpectedly, often in a disorderly or dangerous manner (Abbott and Geddie 2001).

It is essential that event managers have a basic understanding of a crowd's basic sociological behaviour. Much has been written on this (see, for example, numerous journal articles in the *Journal of Events Management*, Berlonghi (1995), Fruin (2002), Abbott and Abbott (2000), the HSE (2000) guide *Managing Crowds Safely*, as well as online resources, such as those provided by the International Centre for Crowd Management and Security Studies (http://www.crowdsafetymanagement.co.uk) and consultants (http://www.crowddynamics.com)).

The main aim for logistics managers is that they have practical measures in place for an effective crowd management plan. Abbott and Abbott (2000) suggest that areas such as communication, signage, ushering and security, alcohol distribution and on-site legal counselling all need to be considered. Managers must also have carefully thought-through crowd control procedures in case the crowd loses control. For an in-depth analysis of crowd control plans and advice on how to formulate them, it is recommended that students read Abbott and Abbott (2000).

Crowd management is covered in more detail in Chapter 8.

4.7.1.9 Communication

Communication between staff is a key logistical concern. From an operational point of view, all staff members and suppliers need to be able to communicate quickly and effectively; finding the right solution to facilitate this is therefore essential. For small events, this can be as straightforward as mobile-phone usage. However, for larger events, this can be impractical, expensive and difficult to manage – particularly as the event manager may want to communicate the same message to more than one other person at a time. In such circumstances, the use of hand-held, two-way radio transmitters is useful. For complex events, several radio channels may well be in operation, with security operating on one, suppliers and contractors on another, and event staff on a third. The employment of runners who can physically take messages from one area to another is another common, and useful, communication technique.

It is recommended that a communications plan is devised prior to the event. Typically, this will include full contact details of all staff members and suppliers and fax, pager and radio call IDs, extension and mobile phone numbers, as well as where each person will be stationed during set-up, event time and shut-down. Communication planning should also take into account emergency situations, should be part of the overall project management plan, and should be included in the risk assessment (Bowdin *et al.* 2010).

4.7.1.10 Health and safety and emergency procedures

Event operations and the logistical planning for an event must include emergency procedures, which can range from evacuation procedures and the amount of first aid on site through to major-incident or disaster planning. Each event will need its own specific procedures, but the basic requirements are outlined in Figure 4.10.

It should be noted that much of the health and safety and emergency procedural planning will take place during the production of the risk assessment documents. It is imperative that these issues are taken seriously, as events can be shut down very quickly if the relevant authorities perceive health and safety or emergency procedures are inadequate. More detail on risk assessment is provided in Chapter 8.

4.7.2 Customer logistics

An event's customers are usually perceived as those who pay for it, although, of course, many events (particularly culturally focused and local community events) are free. The customer is therefore better defined as someone who is attending an event.

Each event will need a different logistics plan that caters to the needs of its specific customer base. For instance, the transportation, ticketing and accommodation plans for the Burning Man Festival, which attracts customers from around the globe, will need to be vastly different from those for a community festival, such as a Holi Festival in India, whose customers all come from within a five-mile radius. The key areas for consideration in customer logistics are shown in Figure 4.11, and are discussed in detail in the following sections.

4.7.2.1 Ticketing

The distribution, collection and security requirements relating to ticketing should be a key concern for the event manager. From a customer's perspective, the process of purchasing, receiving and using tickets is often the first impression they will have of the event, and it marks the start of a relationship between the customer and the organiser. It is therefore vital that this impression is a good one.

First aid planning
- Where will it be located?
- How many first aiders are there?
- Is there a need for further medical assistance, such as medical representatives or ambulance provision?
- Are all staff briefed so that they can contact or locate medical assistance quickly?

Major-incident planning
- Defined by the Health and Safety Executive in the UK as one 'that requires the implementation of special arrangements by one or more of the emergency services, the NHS or local authority' (HSE 1999: 32). Advice should be sought from relevant authorities to ensure that the event organisers have plans in place for these major incidents. In the UK, a useful document is *The Event Safety Guide* (HSE 1999).

Evacuation processes
- These are informed by the emergency planning document and should cover evacuation procedures at different points of the event (when customers arrive, during the different event stages and as customers leave).

Figure 4.10 Key features of health, safety and emergency planning

| Ticketing | Transport | Queuing | Accommodation |

Figure 4.11 The key areas of customer logistics

From a logistical perspective, whilst not all events have an entrance fee, ticketing should always be a consideration, as it enables the organiser to control customer numbers and monitor the flow of guests throughout the event.

A key issue to consider is how much of the ticket sale allocation will be pre-event. Ticketing is usually an essential part of the cash flow – event finance tends to be unbalanced, with the majority of costs happening before the event takes place (see Chapter 6 for an in-depth look at event finance). Revenue generated by advance ticket sales therefore often covers expenses that need settling before the event date (Cherubini *et al.* 2007).

As well as helping the cash flow, selling tickets prior to the event allows the organiser to know exactly how many customers will be attending, which enables them to plan operationally in terms of food, beverages, staffing and so on.

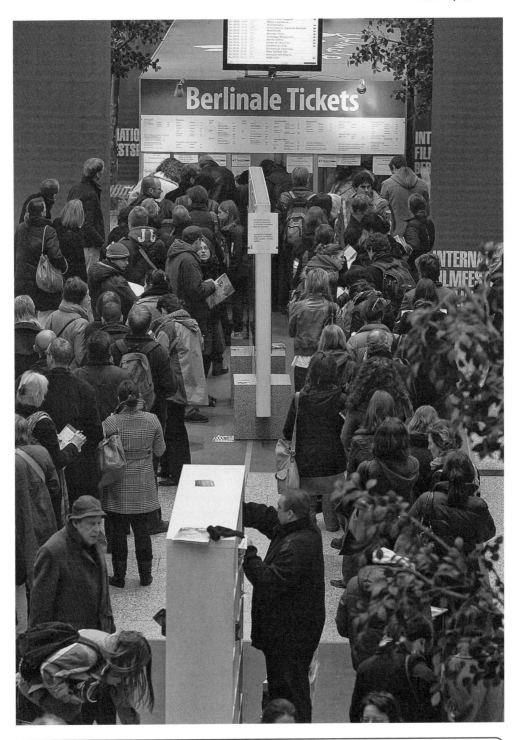

Image 4.2 Berlin prepares for 59th Berlinale Film Festival
Source: Sean Gallup / Getty Images

Increasingly, events tickets are being issued electronically, with barcodes or Quick Response (QR) codes that can be scanned by security staff equipped with hand-held scanners. The eLearning Guild used QR codes in this way for the DevLearn08 conference and reported positive results (Corbin Ball Associates 2011). This method increases the speed of entry and reduces the risk of fraudulent tickets. It also saves the organiser printing and mailing costs.

Another recent development that often utilises QR coding technology is sending tickets to mobile phones – known as mobile ticketing. This process allows customers to order, pay for, obtain and validate tickets via their mobile phones. The most common method of mobile ticketing involves customers receiving their tickets in an SMS after texting a code to the organisers. The price of the ticket can either be added to their next mobile-phone bill or debited from a previously set-up account. These mobile tickets are then visually inspected or scanned at the entrance to the event, thereby reducing production and distribution costs and increasing customer convenience.

With the increasing use of phones that support applications, it is expected that these tickets will become the main form of ticketing at future events. However, it should be noted that such tickets create a revenue issue for event organisers because mobile-phone operators often insist on a large percentage of the overall ticket price.

4.7.2.2 Transport

It is a common misconception among event managers that the way in which customers travel to the event is outside of their control and therefore not their concern. In fact, the way that customers are transported to an event is an important part of the overall logistics planning process. Bowdin *et al.* (2010) describe transport to the site as the customers' first physical commitment to an event.

From a logistical point of view, it is essential to establish *when* customers will arrive at an event. Event managers use two words to describe the arrival of customers: *dump* refers to customers all arriving at around the same time (for a music gig or a conference, for example); and *trickle* refers to customers arriving at different periods throughout the event (as they do at an exhibition or trade show). It is essential that those responsible for the logistics plan understand when their customers will arrive so that plans to accommodate them can be drafted.

How customers will reach an event is a key question and one that is usually considered fully during the planning stages. Below are some of the questions that should be asked of the venue, from a logistics point of view:

- Does the venue have good transport links?
- How reliable are the transport links?
- Are there likely to be problems with the transport – strikes, engineering works and so on?
- Is the venue near to major transport hubs, such as train stations and airports?
- Will travel to the venue represent an additional cost for the customer?
- If so, will this additional cost make the overall event proposal less attractive to the target market?

When considering major and mega-events (such as the Commonwealth Games or Glastonbury), transportation logistics become particularly important. As Bowdin *et al.* (2010) point out, permission must be gained from local councils, highways agencies or police, and road closures often need to be arranged as part of the logistics planning. Ensuring that roads are clear, that there is sufficient signage to direct traffic, that one-way systems are in place and so on will enable suppliers and customers to arrive and depart quickly and with minimum disruption to the local area. It is especially important to consider the transportation logistics for events that take place in usually quiet, tranquil areas, as disrupting the local community can cause repercussions for the event organisers, including pressure not to return in the future.

4.7.2.3 Queuing

Once the ticketing method has been decided, and the guests have arrived on site, the logistics manager must consider how the guests will present their tickets for inspection in order to gain entry to the event. This will involve some form of queuing – and as this is often the customer's first physical impression of an event, it is one of the key aspects for the logistics manager to consider.

There are many techniques for managing queues, as well as a vast array of literature covering all aspects of queuing, from waiting times to physical management, much of which is too detailed to discuss here. (See, for example, Oakes and North (2008), Shelby *et al.* (1989), Jenner (2010) and the excellent work carried out by the International Centre for Crowd Management and Security Studies (http://www.crowdsafetymanagement.co.uk.))

This section will touch on the three major techniques for queue management. It should be noted that we are concentrating on entrance and ticketing queues but there are similar issues and techniques for queuing once inside the event. Gaining access to toilets, catering, showers, activity booths, exhibition stands and so on usually involves queuing and therefore demands some attention to ensure that it is managed effectively.

PHYSICAL QUEUING

The most common form of queue management is the physical queue. The logistics manager must ensure that queues are designed to make the wait as pleasant as possible. Queues should be kept simple for customers, with waiting times kept to a minimum and protection from the weather in place (rain and hot sun are two important issues here). The right number of personnel should be on hand to deal with the queues and the waiting times should be signalled as often as possible to manage customer expectations.

There are several strategies that help to achieve a pleasant queue environment, including:

- *Queue capacity*: expanding the queue capacity allows more customers to join. This can be done by increasing the lane size or the length of the queue, or (more usually) by designing a line that zigzags. This shape allows for a larger number of customers to queue in a smaller area and also ensures that customers cannot perceive the true length of a particularly long queue.
- *Queue entertainment*: TV screens, music or entertainers can be used to distract customers from the length of their wait.
- *Signage* that indicates the length of the queue is advisable.
- *Secondary queues*: VIP queues or fast-track queues for guests who have paid a premium are becoming ever more popular at events.

Once inside, customers will be faced with queues for the toilets, food, beverages and merchandise, all of which need to be given the same level of consideration as the entrance/ticket queue, as they often have the largest impact on a customer's event experience.

VIRTUAL QUEUING

All queuing systems have problems – the main one being that the customer must arrive ahead of time and wait in line. A recent development in managing queues has sought to alleviate this through the use of virtual queues. This technique allows the customer to enter a virtual queue via their mobile phone or the internet, and await an alert that tells them when they are nearing the front of the line. They can then make their way to the event, greatly reducing their physical queuing time at the entrance. This technique seems to increase the patience of customers and ensures that there are fewer no-shows.

Exit strategies

Techniques that ensure the safe exit of customers from an event also include elements of queuing theory. For example, staggered leaving, as operated at most football grounds (one set of fans waits in the ground until the other set of fans have left the venue and the surrounding area), ensures the safety of the customers. Stadium music gigs often empty VIP rooms first, while those standing are usually the last to leave the arena. And festivals must consider exit strategies if they are to avoid chaos – thousands of vehicles all leaving a remote area at the same time can result in long queues and extremely frustrated customers. Fruin (1984) discusses time-based control techniques, such as metering (a strategy used to control the rate of arrivals and degree of crowding at a known pedestrian bottleneck) and processing rates (the capacity and the time taken to move through or towards certain areas at the event). These strategies, when implemented properly, will help to prevent critical crowd accumulation.

4.7.2.4 Accommodation

Many events must consider customer accommodation. These are usually events that span several days or continue late into the evening, making travel home difficult or unnecessary. Examples include corporate team-building weekends and cricket Test matches. When dealing with accommodation, it is essential that the logistics manager considers the time taken to travel to the site and the efficiency of transportation links, as well as whether the available accommodation matches the needs and expectations of the customers.

4.7.3 Logistics planning folder

It is advisable to create a logistics planning folder (sometimes known as an event manual) that can be consulted when on site. These are frequently now contained on netbooks or tablet computers, so that they can be updated easily and so that the information is available to a large number of users simultaneously. The contents of a planning folder are shown in Figure 4.12, with details of each section given below.

- Contact list, including full contact details of all contractors and suppliers, entertainment details and sponsors' and exhibitors' details. These should be up-to-date and include mobile-phone numbers.
- Venue or site plan – several spare copies should be made.
- Project management plan. This could be presented as a critical path, a timeline or a Gantt chart. It is essentially a checklist of everything that has been done and everything that needs doing.
- Production schedule. This is a detailed schedule of all activities during the day(s) of the event.
- Contracts signed with audio-visual suppliers, entertainment suppliers, sponsors and venues will help to resolve any on-site disagreements quickly.

Figure 4.12 Contents of a planning folder

4.7.4 Event shut-down

The event manager's job does not end as soon as the customers have left. Rather, it continues right through the process of breaking down all the equipment and removing all signs of the event from the site or venue. This process is known variously as the event shut-down, the site phase-out or the event breakdown, and it is as important a part of the logistical planning as the set-up and staging of an event.

Smaller events may require hardly any shut-down. It may just be a case of ensuring that the venue is clear of debris and customers have not left behind any personal items. Conversely, events on a larger scale require a complex and thoughtfully put-together shut-down schedule that coordinates all suppliers and works to strict timelines. The shut-down for large events will include the breaking down and removal of all equipment; the final dealings with the entertainment, including payment; cleaning and removal of staging areas; and any outstanding financial transactions. Finally, all sponsors, exhibitors, staff and contractors must be thanked and left with positive thoughts of this event and encouragement about the next event.

Once all of this has been completed and the site is clear, the event manager's shut-down will continue for several weeks back in the office. Figure 4.13 shows the processes involved in the total shut-down of an event. The key point is that operational processes should be assessed and evaluated against original plans to examine their effectiveness. Lessons will always be learned from this process and it is essential that it takes place within a few weeks of the event, whilst memories are still clear.

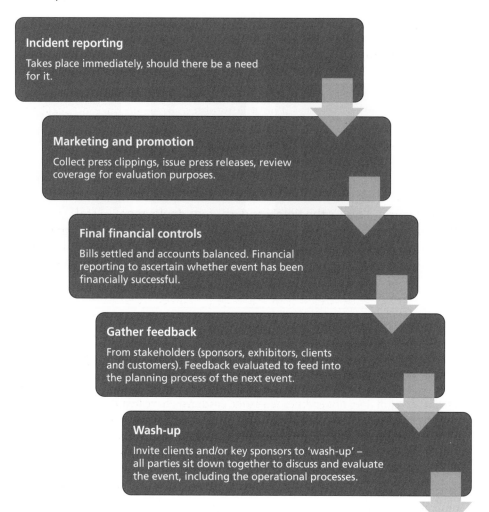

Incident reporting

Takes place immediately, should there be a need for it.

Marketing and promotion

Collect press clippings, issue press releases, review coverage for evaluation purposes.

Final financial controls

Bills settled and accounts balanced. Financial reporting to ascertain whether event has been financially successful.

Gather feedback

From stakeholders (sponsors, exhibitors, clients and customers). Feedback evaluated to feed into the planning process of the next event.

Wash-up

Invite clients and/or key sponsors to 'wash-up' – all parties sit down together to discuss and evaluate the event, including the operational processes.

Figure 4.13 The event shut-down process

Industry voice

Oliver Gardiner, managing director, Vespasian Security

The typical day of an event crowd manager

Depending on the type and duration of the event, the demands placed upon the crowd manager can vary each day. Invariably, each day begins with an early start, with accommodation either on or very close to the event site. Many of our teams are present on site on a twenty-four-hour basis and I prefer to be as close as possible in case a significant issue arises. Once on site, my first port of call is our night manager/supervisor to receive a brief regarding any incidents they may have faced.

My next stop is the production office and a face-to-face discussion with our client. During this informal meeting we will agree and/or confirm the times throughout the day when we will hold timetabled meetings, including with all members of the emergency services and relevant stakeholders.

Events are fast moving but the planning for them is methodical and often slow. Part of my role during each event is continually to reassess how the day is progressing in relation to the crowd management plan and try to pre-empt possible issues.

The next crucial stage is the timely and efficient deployment of staff throughout the site in preparation for the gates being opened. Our logistics team sign all staff in, ensure that all SIA staff are carrying their licences correctly, issue personal protective equipment, issue two-way radios and event-specific briefing sheets. My role as crowd manager is important but I must also remember that we are a service provider dealing with a large and diverse workforce. The teams that we deploy are our product and so our logistics staff are there to ensure all Vespasian staff have all the support they need to do the best job possible.

Depending on the timings of the event, the first meeting with the Event Liaison Team (ELT) could occur before or after staff deployment. This meeting will cover all aspects of the event that day and any outside factors that could affect the project – for example, weather forecast or transport infrastructure problems. This is the first opportunity that all agencies have to brief the collective group regarding any and all issues. Plans often remain the same as on paper but these meetings are the chance to tweak them where necessary to respond to emerging issues around the site.

Once the deployment of staff and initial ELT meetings have been attended, my next stop is our radio control room to update the supervisor there on any change of plans that will occur due to decisions taken by the ELT. This is often done as part of a wider supervisors' meeting. All of our supervisors and section managers will be in attendance and all relevant aspects of the day will be discussed. The supervisors will then disseminate all information down to their individual teams.

Once the teams and supervisors have been placed in their work locations, the next step is to take a walk around the site with the head of production or the safety officer. This is to make sure that the site is ready to open. All teams are asked to call into control and report any issue causing a barrier to opening the site. Once we are satisfied that the site is ready and safe, we ask for radio silence and notify the gate supervisors to allow the public entry to the site.

The three main phases of crowd management are ingress (entering), circulation and egress (leaving). Once the crowd have begun to enter, our supervisors monitor and report back to control on a regular basis. My focus switches to maintaining the site in the circulation phase of the day; this includes front-of-stage pit barrier teams, response teams, the efficiency of the radio control room and monitoring the emergency evacuation routes. The majority of the day is represented by the circulation phase. During this period, I regularly walk the site and drop in on supervisors and the control room, as well as reporting any relevant issues back to the ELT. Several incidents may be occurring at any given moment. These could range from lost children to a crowd collapse. Many incidents have set procedures in place to help to manage them, but some challenges come out of the blue and pose a problem that you have not encountered before. This is the point when I rely on the training and experience of those around me to help me manage and respond to the issues at hand.

Before the headline act or main attraction of the event appears, I again make my way to the ELT to meet with all agencies. The subject of this meeting is the forthcoming egress of the crowd and how any changes in the course of the day have affected the plan. Either during the meeting or just afterwards I ask the radio controller to call all egress gates and confirm that they are clear and ready for egress. This enables us to catch any structural problems with the gates and get them fixed before the end of the event.

The supervisor in charge of the stage is in close contact with the stage production manager and updates the radio control room regarding the number of songs left until the end of the performance. Once the artist has left the stage, the radio controller calls for radio silence on all radios unless the message is urgent. I attempt to get to a vantage point to view the egress or a CCTV control room that has cameras to cover the egressing crowd. Depending on the flow and the density of the crowd, using my supervisors and their teams, we guide sections of the crowd to different gates to reduce the pressure in certain areas.

After the main body of the crowd has left the front-of-stage area, we organise our staff into a long unbroken line stretching across the arena. This line then moves slowly towards the exit gates with the staff politely ushering people towards the exits.

Post-event, I meet again with the production team and the ELT to review the day and discuss how it could be improved. I then return to a meeting with my senior supervisors and we discuss the day, too. I encourage all those attending the Vespasian team meetings to be as open and forthright as possible in their thoughts and opinions of the event and the operating systems. This results in great ideas being put forward and has helped me change our systems for the better.

4.8 Summary

This chapter has highlighted the importance of events operations. Throughout the chapter, it has been made clear that every event is different and individually complex, so there is no set formula for operations. The legislation relating to health, safety and risk changes regularly and it is important that event managers keep abreast of the current legalities and regulations.

The chapter has also focused on two key operational aspects of events: the consideration of legalities, regulations, licences, permits and contracts involved when managing an event; and event logistics, including logistical planning for customers and on site at venues.

The planning of event operations to decide which resources, skills and equipment will be required is an essential part of the events management process and needs to be considered fully within the context of both the event planning process and health, safety and risk analysis.

Further reading

Allen, J., Harris, R., Jago, L. K. and Veal, A. J (eds) (2000) *Events beyond 2000: Setting the Agenda, Proceedings of the Conference on Evaluation, Research and Education, Sydney July 2000*, Sydney: Australian Centre for Event Management, University of Technology. Includes useful papers on event operations, including the Abbott and Abbott paper on crowd management and control. These proceedings also cover many fundamental issues for events management studies and are thoroughly recommended.

Bentley, R. (2008) Corporate Manslaughter Law: No Place to Hide, *Personnel Today*, 17 March [online]. Available at: http://www.personneltoday.com/articles/2008/03/17/44774/corporate-manslaughter-law-no-place-to-hide.html. Accessed 28 December 2010. An interesting article that offers a useful checklist for event managers operating within the regulations of the Corporate Manslaughter and Corporate Homicide Act 2007.

Tum, J., Norton, P. and Wright, J. N. (2006) *Management of Event Operations*, Oxford: Elsevier. An incredibly detailed view of the management of event operations, useful for those who need to look in depth at a specific operational aspect. The book is particularly strong on operational techniques, such as forecasting and gap analysis. Tum *et al.* also provide a useful overview of the supply chain management of event operations. It should be noted, however, that the event operations management model proposed in this book is very complex and may well include too much under one 'umbrella' term.

Chapter 5

Managing the event human resource

Contents

5.1 Aims

By the end of this chapter, students will be able:

- To analyse the human resource challenges of managing events.
- To explain the process of event recruitment and selection.
- To appreciate the complexities of managing event employees and volunteers.
- To discuss methods of event employee learning and development.

5.2 Introduction

This chapter provides a general overview of the human resource management practices and processes used in the events industry as they relate to the effective staffing, training, management and motivation of employees and volunteers. This is particularly challenging for event managers, often because of an event's vastness and the disjointed and 'pulsating' nature of its temporary organisation. Much of the mainstream human resource management literature covers conventional, more permanent organisations, so it generally fails to provide event managers and students with the necessary understanding of the topic in relation to the practical challenges of their industry.

5.3 The event human resource challenge

The human resource for an event behaves differently from that in other organisations, so the planning and management of people who make up the workforce at an event differ, too. This important distinction is not fully considered by Shone and Parry's (2010) view of a more monolithic, hierarchical events organisation, which recognises the need for the management of staffing priorities depending on the mission, goals, culture of the event organisation, as well as the event's size, required volunteer/professional staff mix, scheduling tasks, roles and expertise. Bowdin *et al.* (2010) and Getz (2007) also confine their scope to a broader discussion of personnel planning, recruitment, training and general human motivation as applied to the workforce. When considering human resource management (HRM) in the events industry in light of Chapter 2's discussion of project management, the limited value of such generic management theories becomes clear. Because event organisations tend to be 'project-led' rather than functional, they do not practise HRM in the same way as permanent organisations. This is because project-led event organisations respond to the requirements of each individual event they undertake, making traditional functional structures and their associated processes less helpful when assessing how to staff events and manage workers effectively.

As also discussed in Chapter 2, events as projects often require managers to navigate the difficulties posed by stakeholder requirements, tight timelines and deadlines, limited resources and ongoing and constant change. Events also tend to have 'pulsating organisations' (Toffler 1990), causing the processes and practices explained here to be constantly revised in line with this fluctuating event environment.

As is often the case in the business world, the terminology applied to event staffing has altered significantly in recent years, in line with its increasing complexity. Twenty years ago, a practitioner or student would have referred to the staffing of an event as a function of 'personnel management', rather than using the current preferred term – 'human resource management'.

Walton (1999) suggests this change resulted from the increased complexity facing HR professionals. There has been an accompanying change in expectations of how employees might perform in organisations, as well as varying expectations of what people hope to derive from work itself.

Study activity

To what extent do you consider a move from 'personnel' to 'human resource' management to be due to the emergence of new ways of thinking and working? How does this relate to the events industry? To what extent do you think a change in terminology might simply be due to a desire to increase the importance of the staffing role? What problems do you think might be associated with considering workers simply as a 'resource'?

5.3.1 Event personnel

Goldblatt (2010) treats the event workforce mainly as a resource, based on the notion that events are primarily staffed by volunteers and that the primary focus of 'events leadership' is to source sufficient numbers of volunteers from various groups within a local community. This early perspective seeks to address the difficulty of obtaining large enough numbers of people to work on events. However, it fails to emphasise that events are constituted of people who are effectively producers of the event experience, and therefore play a much more important role than simply a resource which should be acquired in sufficient numbers.

Thus, Van der Wagen (2007: 5) views events as 'a new context for human resource management'. She argues that people are not just an essential resource for an event, but a key success factor. Building on this important point, events as gatherings of people are conceived, designed and delivered by people, for people. They decide the all-important raison d'être of the event (Brown and James 2004), which is crucial to an event's authenticity. As discussed in Chapter 2, if an event's designer wishes attendees to be either immersed or absorbed in a particular experience, event staff will be essential to achieving this. Such an important role will often be key to an event's successful staging and the ultimate expression of its planned legacy.

In more recent years, due to the increasing importance of strategy within organisations, managers have increasingly focused on strategic HRM (see Walton 1999). Human resource strategy is concerned with the philosophy of an organisation, rather than just its processes and its people. This view is important to event managers, given the strategic nature of most events and the way they are managed by ad hoc organisational structures which are often formed, revised and disbanded according to present need.

Berridge (2007) focuses on the memorable 'wow' factors of designed events, and thereby stresses the important element of interactions, which, though 'artificially' designed, are engaged in by an event's staff and its attendees. Booms and Bitner's earlier work (Booms and Bitner 1981; Bitner 1993) recognised that the traditional '4Ps' marketing mix – product, price, place and promotion – was inadequate for service industry use. Therefore, such industries, including the events industry, should consider the additional components of people, process and physical evidence in order that their offerings might be effectively managed. This view emphasised the essential and complementary role the human resource plays in the design and production of an event experience for attendees. The role of personnel forms one of the main elements of the

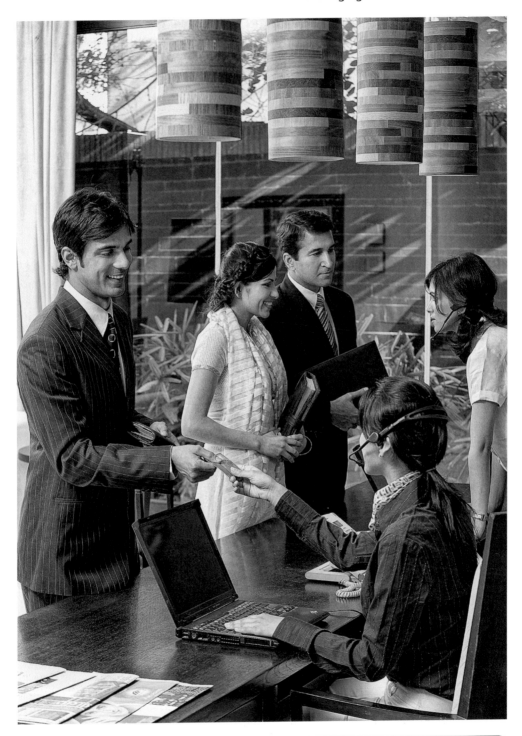

Image 5.1 Customer service is a key feature of the experiencescape
Source: Alex Mares-Manton / Getty Images

delivery of service within the experiencescape (see Chapter 3). The extent to which other, related event elements – such as communication and the flow of activities – play their parts should not be underestimated, and these are actioned by the event workforce. Even the staging elements, which consist of the remainder of the holistic experiencescape, are mostly delivered by these all-important people.

5.3.2 Understanding event professionalism

This recognition of the importance of hiring people with the right skills and attributes became crucial to the fast-commercialising events industry. Since the 1980s, the age-old tradition of events (see Chapter 1) has become an industry in its own right, and has required increasing numbers of skilled professionals.

5.3.3 Establishing the desirable attributes of event personnel

With the increasing demand for suitably useful event personnel have come various attempts by the industry and academic institutions to define and categorise the desirable attributes of such workers in terms of competences. As the learned capacity to do certain activities (and, some would argue, excel at them), the required competences of event staff will vary, in part, according to the requirements of the particular event in question. At the end of this chapter, an industry professional shares some of her experiences about establishing desirable event employee attributes with event operations managers.

5.4 Finding the right people

The task of HR planning for an event involves predicting gaps between the activities that will take place throughout the event cycle and the suitably competent people and teams required to complete those activities successfully. 'Recruitment' relates to attracting sufficient numbers of competent candidates for a position, whereas 'selection' refers to the processes used to appoint a person to that position. This process can be illustrated as follows:

- State specific event need.
- Use appropriate recruitment and selection methods.
- Match suitable applicant to job.
- Review recruitment and selection processes and modify as required.

Needless to say, the flexibility of the event, of the task in question and of the applicant will all greatly influence the ease of 'fit' between the person and the job. However, the consequences of errors made during this process can impact more heavily on the event organisation than they would in other, more day-to-day, functional organisations because of the time-sensitive nature of the event cycle and the 'once-and-for-all' nature of the offering. Events cannot simply be repeated or refunds offered if shortfalls occur in the delivery process due to the wrong people being hired.

Another basic consideration is the building of a large supply of labour with ongoing availability for future events. Such a strategy can greatly reduce costs in the form of recruitment advertising, interviewing and other hiring expenses. Also, the costs of inducting and training new employees can be reduced if workers remain with a particular events organisation across multiple or repeat events.

Loyal event recruits can also promote improved quality of work task delivery, such as improved safety and customer service, as well as better teamwork due to familiarity with the culture of the organisation, expected standards of performance and the events market as a whole.

5.4.1 Recruiting

For every event, there is a need to attract, screen and select adequately qualified workers through either a formal or an informal recruitment process, which involves:

- determining the vacancies
- sourcing strategy
- preparing and publishing information
- processing and measuring applications
- notifying applicants. (Tyson and York 2000: 106–107)

Due to the sheer scale of many events, it is common practice for event organisations to use recruitment intermediaries to assist with what can often be a resource-intensive and specialised activity (see Case Study 5.1).

CASE STUDY 5.1

Event Recruitment, Australia

Event Recruitment is a specialist events industry recruitment consultancy based in Sydney, Australia. It director, John Hackett, worked in marketing and event coordination in the corporate sector before establishing his career in the recruitment industry. He has over twenty-five years' recruitment consulting experience both within Australia and overseas, and ran his own recruitment consultancy for seven years before taking over Event Recruitment in 2005.

Event Recruitment is a specialist consultancy which offers a distinctive and highly targeted service to organisations across the meetings and events industry, encompassing events management agencies, corporate, government, association and non-profit entities, commercial conference and exhibition organisers.

With an extensive and expanding database of talented events management professionals, Event Recruitment can quickly and effectively respond to employers' needs through sourcing and recruiting experienced and capable candidates available for contract, temporary or permanent work.

Event Recruitment was borne out of a need to fill a void in the rapidly growing events industry. The company has made significant contributions to the ongoing growth and success of organisations in the industry. Its website states:

> Whilst there are hundreds of recruitment agencies, none specialise nor have the networks and first-hand knowledge of this unique industry that we do. Our knowledge of the events industry comes from both years of working

within the industry and recruiting for it. This means we have a unique insight and understanding of your needs.

The company's executives are also active members of the events industry. With an emphasis on building business relationships, they are members of Meeting and Events Australia, regularly write for industry journals, survey the market to identify industry and salary trends and regularly talk to decision-makers in the industry about the issues they are facing and to candidates seeking guidance and support as they navigate the next step in their event careers.

Source: http://www.eventrecruitment.com.au/

Study activity

1   What do you consider to be the advantages and disadvantages of using a recruiting company such as Event Recruitment to staff events?
2   Find a local, specialist events recruiter.
3   Research its website:

- What are the company's main target markets?
- What other activities does it seem to be involved in, other than recruitment?
- What professional experience does it seem to have?

Whether the event organisers use recruitment agencies or manage this process in-house, it is important that effective procedures and processes are formulated, possibly for each individual event, in order to ensure that the most suitable candidates are matched with the planned jobs. Ineffective recruitment may lead to significant shortfalls in performance; and in the events industry, as the cliché states, 'You are only as good as your last event', so failure is much more difficult to rectify than in many other industries.

Recruitment and selection methods should attract sufficient numbers of suitable applicants and should be fair in relation to the candidates' chances of being selected. According to Pilbeam and Corbridge (2006: 137), recruitment and selection involves:

1   Attraction of suitable candidates.
2   Reduction of unsuitable candidates.
3   Selection of suitable candidates.
4   Transition of a successful candidate to an effective employee.

Almost every company will face problems when trying to carry out these activities – such as a shortage of qualified candidates and issues relating to the organisation's macro environment.

However, because of the temporal nature of the events industry, geographical movement, the complexity of stakeholder relationships and fluctuations in environmental factors (including media coverage), the challenge of recruiting suitable staff is even greater for the events organiser.

5.4.2 Designing event jobs

Prior to beginning the process of recruitment, the event planner should complete an in-depth job analysis to assess the positions that need to be filled. This will include collection of information about the tasks that must be completed before, during and following event delivery. Obviously, the more rigid and less changeable the event concept and plan are, the simpler this task will be. Any changes will require subsequent revision, perhaps including the addition of cost buffers to timelines and budgets.

The end result of the job analysis will be a list of job descriptions, which group the various tasks coherently, and job specifications, which clarify the specific competences of the candidates who will be recruited for these jobs.

5.4.3 Clarifying job designs and descriptions

A job description will need to include the following key information:

- Job/role title.
- The event-related tasks and activities included in the job. These will be linked to the objectives of the role. Performance indicators can also be stipulated here.
- Levels of responsibility and any departmental affiliations within the event organisation, as well as the name of the line manager for the position.
- Pay scale.

5.4.4 Establishing applicant suitability

Once the parameters of the job have been established, attention can turn to what is required of those who might fill the position, including:

- Formal educational qualifications, event-related certifications (such as first aid), criminal record checks, health and safety certifications and so on, as required by the event and its predicted target markets.
- Competences, including skills, knowledge and prior experience.
- Any physical characteristics demanded by the role, such as heavy-lifting capabilities.

Each of these may be expressed in terms of 'essential' (minimum) and 'desirable' requirements to avoid misunderstandings during the selection phase, and to ensure that the event hires the best individuals for the various posts. Many events are vast undertakings in which many people perform a great variety of different roles, so there will inevitably be considerable differences between them in terms of abilities and competences. As Boxhall and Purcell (2008: 176) observe: 'Thus, as we move up from low-complexity work (such as routine clerical work) to jobs where greater ambiguity is involved in decision making, differences in skills and judgement become more pronounced and are more consequential for the organisation.' This means that, as event tasks become more complex, there is a need to find employees who possess a wide range of skills. An event producer, for example, may possess high levels of innovation and creativity, yet these talents matter little if she is unable to communicate her ideas effectively. Obviously, the ideal candidate will be creative *and* an effective communicator.

However, it is important not to set required competence, skill, attribute and qualification levels too high. Nor should physical or skill requirements discriminate against applicants with disabilities, unless these are essential for the job to be performed successfully. There is a discussion of some of the pertinent legislation relating to this issue later in this chapter. Many event organisations provide on-the-job training or certifications, but these can prove costly and take so long to complete that it is often impossible to hire workers who do not already have them.

Study activity

1 For events local to you, what are the legal requirements regulating employees? Consider the certifications you would be expected to possess in order to work in your country.
2 What are your country's main disability discrimination laws? Provide examples of steps an event manager might take in order to make event jobs more accessible to physically and mentally challenged applicants.

5.4.5 Communicating event vacancies

Potential event employees are attracted through numerous methods, including basic advertising, word-of-mouth referral and formal recruitment sources. Recently, there has been a significant shift in recruitment media. In the UK, for example, while daily newspapers have declined in both relevance and popularity, there has been substantial growth in internet-based advertising, job search engines and online recruitment agencies. Web 2.0, including such social networking sites as Facebook and Twitter, has also had an increasingly significant role to play. This has created both challenges and opportunities for event recruiters, as applicants are no longer passive in the application process, but rather engage in two-way, adaptable messages, often in 'real time'. For example, many Facebook groups have been formed specifically to publicise paid and voluntary employment vacancies in the domestic and international events industry.

Though often free or advertising-supported, such online vehicles sometimes charge a commission for referral, which can lead to event organisations paying a variety of charges – from an almost negligible 'click-through' fee to substantially larger commissions for recruitment of high-level executives. It should be noted that the legal framework governing such media is changing fast in order to bring it more in line with laws governing offline practices, and this should be monitored closely to avoid litigation.

More traditional agencies for event recruitment include job centres, industry fairs, schools, colleges and universities. More will be discussed about specific strategies for the ongoing recruitment of event volunteers later in this chapter.

5.4.6 Screening

Following the receipt of applications via the sources discussed in the previous section, a process of screening should be applied to eliminate unsuitable applicants and reduce the numbers of less suitable candidates in favour of those who more closely match or even exceed the particulars of the planned job specification. It should be remembered that this part of the selection process involves subjectivity on the part of those responsible for selection. Whilst subjectivity can never be wholly avoided, screening and elimination measures should be as clear and as valid as possible. A variety of laws and ethical practices regulate these HR activities, and these will be discussed later in this chapter.

There must be mutual trust and respect between employer and applicant, as a psychological contract is formed between the two parties which is based on their expectations of one another as well as assumptions and inferences derived from their mutual interactions, in addition to any formal communication and legal contracts. Certainly, many premature breakdowns in formal contractual relationships between employers and employees can be traced back to this less formal, yet often more important, psychological contract.

Study activity

What are your likely expectations of your employer? Which of these can be classified as comprising the 'psychological contract' between the two parties? List these and discuss ways in which you think event organisations can improve their management of employee expectations from the very start of the employer–employee relationship.

5.4.7 Selecting

As the applicant moves through a transition towards becoming an employee, the recruiter will attempt to use the selection procedure to predict on-the-job performance. To this end, the events manager may employ a number of valid measurement tools to assess a candidate's suitability. However, this can be problematic as there is no real capacity for a trial period of employment in the events industry, as events are invariably time-constrained. Each event also varies considerably from the previous one.

Torrington *et al.* (2009: 171) suggest that selection methods should be chosen on the basis of a combination of the following factors:

- selection criteria for the post to be filled
- acceptability and appropriateness of the methods
- abilities of the staff involved in selection
- administrative ease
- time factors
- accuracy
- cost.

Because of the people-centred nature of events work, those involved in the selection process are likely to favour face-to-face contact – ideally in a one-to-one interview – with an applicant in order to gain an accurate impression of their interpersonal skills. Such meetings allow the interviewer to make an assessment of the candidate's suitability and to present a realistic job preview. However, time, cost and other resource constraints usually make wholesale use of this method unfeasible, particularly for larger events. So most event managers are obliged to use alternative methods in the selection process:

- application forms
- telephone or webcam interviews
- aptitude tests
- group interviews and problem-solving exercises, business games, competitions and so on
- work sampling, including written work, business plans, portfolios and presentations
- references.

Several of these will usually be used in combination, depending on the type of event in question. References are especially important, with many event specialists relying on the recommendations of credible referees, such as university teaching staff and the applicant's previous employers.

5.5 The challenges in practice to the events industry

Certainly, the process discussed thus far is widely accepted and practised, and it finds application in the international events industry. However, many event managers will no doubt take issue with much of the time, detail and documentation requirements implied here. This will mainly be due to the usual time and resource limitations commonly associated with events. It will also reflect the transitory and temporal nature of events, discussed earlier in this chapter. Indeed, there would appear to be little benefit in mapping out job descriptions and the qualities and qualifications of the people required to perform them if one event differs widely from the next. Most event roles maintain a large degree of consistency across different events, but the processes already described sometimes need to be altered due to rapid changes in event organisations and the different events they manage.

5.6 Formulating and conducting event induction and acculturation

5.6.1 Induction

Whilst traditional new-employee induction is intended to promote effective adjustment and integration of the new employee into his or her new workplace, in the events industry it involves much more. Though it was formerly assumed that induction was a first-day familiarisation tour, in the events industry it begins at interview and continues to the end of the worker's involvement with the event, or with longer engagements until the employer and employee have reached a mutual understanding of their relationship. A distinction also needs to be drawn between the employee's induction to the event organisation and their induction to the current event. The weight given to these two components depends on the type of event, the stage at which the employee joins and the type and expected duration of their role.

In events, new-employee induction is crucial: it can safeguard lives and ensure the health and welfare of customers, colleagues and the employees themselves, primarily because of the intrinsic dangers associated with many event sites and venues. (See Chapter 8 for more information on this.) Walton (1999) explores 'virtual induction', in which companies post important familiarisation and training materials on their websites and intranets for consultation by new and existing employees. Such sites provide vital event information relating to company policies and procedures, employee duties, site plans and so on. This supplements the usual induction process, which informs the new employee of the procedural and legal guidelines they must follow and gives them an opportunity to ask questions. In many events, the overall concept will be explained in relation to the employee's specific role. Event organisers will often pair new workers with more experienced employees in order to familiarise them with an event.

5.6.2 Organisational culture and events

During this induction phase, the employee will gain an impression about various cultural norms they will be expected to observe during their time working on the event. Edgar Schein (2010: 7) observes: 'Cultural forces are powerful because they operate outside of our awareness. We need to understand them not only because of their power but also because they help to explain many of our puzzling and frustrating experiences in social and organisational life.'

The organisational culture of an events company gives each of its events a specific 'personality'. According to Schein (2010), organisational culture mainly consist of the factors outlined in Table 5.1.

Table 5.1 The factors comprising organisational culture

Beliefs and assumptions

What does the organisation do?

What business(es) is it in?

What does it seek to achieve in the future?

Who are its stakeholders?

Values

What do its stakeholders want from the business?

What are the standards of behaviour of the people associated with the organisation?

How do the personal and professional values of the people align with those of the organisation?

How does the organisation view 'progress'?

Norms

How do the people associated with the organisation commonly:

- behave
- interact
- communicate
- implement/react to change?

To what extent do these norms match corporate guidelines and expectations?

What is the relationship between the groups in the organisation, the national cultural groups, the organisational culture and the corporate culture?

Signs

Organisations often display outward indications of how they work, such as employee uniforms or visible price or service promises. How do such outward signs relate to or contradict the above factors?

It is important to understand the organisation's culture because, whenever a new employee joins, they will very quickly reach their own conclusion about it, based on their assessment of the above factors. Event customers do the same thing. Overall, this will greatly influence the actions and reactions that these groups have towards the organisation and each other. This contributes to the input/output relationships identified in Figure 5.1.

So far, this discussion has mainly focused on organisational aspects in general. Obviously, the debate becomes far more complicated when the combined influences of other types of culture found in an organisation are also considered. It should be remembered that there are various cultures within work groups. For example, members of a banquet service staff team are likely to have their own sets of assumptions, values, norms and signs, which may differ from those of the parent organisation and/or the event. If groups have different cultures, this might lead to conflict between them. When national cultures and ethnic cultures are also thrown into the mix, alongside group cultures, the culture of the event itself and the corporate culture of the parent organisation, the HRM implications for the event manager can be daunting.

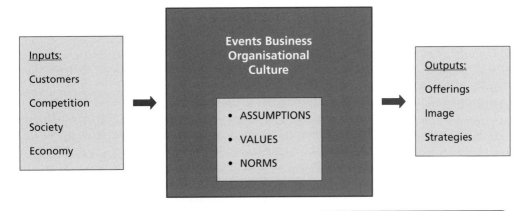

Figure 5.1 How organisational culture works in the events organisation
Source: Adapted from Schein 2010

Study activity

Each year, Gartner sends a team of events staff to the Cannes Film Festival. Answer the following questions:

1 Which different categories of culture would an event manager need to consider during this event?
2 What types of problem or challenge may arise as a result?
3 What steps can be taken to minimise their effects.
4 Specifically, what areas of training could be provided for new employees in relation to these cultural forces?

5.6.3 Team building

Goldblatt (2010) discusses the problems of leading and managing event teams, particularly from an outsourcing perspective. Many event managers – especially those who are new to the profession – are keen to outsource the more 'mundane' tasks, such as cleaning, while retaining direct control over the more creative aspects, such as design and production. However, more experienced event managers understand that the success of an event often depends upon the effective delivery of 'wow' factors that require a level of expertise that is rarely found within the skill set of the general organisational team. There are other factors in play which also contribute to this perspective, including legal and safety restrictions, and the required capital and talent investment. Factors such as talent are often not found within most general events management organisations, so they may need to be found elsewhere for use in particular events. The construction, management and leadership of event teams, particularly in the context of the foregoing discussion relating to group culture, can prove challenging for any event manager. (For a wider discussion of events leadership and organisation structure see Chapter 2.)

Some event organisations take a psychological approach to the construction of teams. Widely available psychometric tests can be used to assess the personality traits of individuals, and these can be utilised as early as the selection stage of the HRM process. Whether event managers favour this option will mainly depend on their own experiences in respect to trying to predict future employee performance.

In a team-building context, the most effective approach will be taken depending on the planned purpose of the team in question. Event teams can provide basic event delivery, such as customer service or various staging provisions. Others might be responsible for relatively complex, problem-solving activities. The psychological characteristics, skill sets and competences of employees performing these roles will vary according to their specific planned context.

The combination of the above characteristics of individuals within the team should also be considered. Pfeffer (1998) found teams to be much more effective than individuals at organisational problem-solving. In the context of creative design, the more diverse the team, the longer the decision-making process, but the more effective the final result. According to the Gorge Group study (1994), excellence in team problem-solving performance was based on the creation of synergy between members, the building of commitment towards a common goal, the fostering of independence, constructive debates and mutual concern and respect for each other.

It should also be stressed that teams in the events industry are increasingly virtual in nature, particularly in vast, multinational parent companies. Information technology now makes it possible for events specialists in the field to enlist the support of members of a virtual 'back office', many of whom they may never meet face to face.

5.7 Developing effective communication with event workers

Boxall and Purcell (2008) focus on management of the 'employee voice' in organisational decision-making through the promotion of employee involvement strategies. This approach is influenced in the events industry by the involvement of trade unions and professional associations, whose scope and power vary widely, depending on the country concerned. More discussion of the role played by trade unions appears at the end of this chapter.

According to the Gorge Group (1994), effective communication requires the organisation to:

- develop shared understanding proactively
- focus on the needs of others and predict their questions
- clarify points outside of meetings.

When the company parent is multinational, care must be taken to avoid the use of jargon and slang in order to minimise misunderstanding. Managers should disseminate messages via their audience's preferred media and style. And attention should be paid to using appropriate levels of formality.

5.8 Event employee learning and development

The event organisation will be required to facilitate various degrees and types of employee development in order to maximise performance. Whilst leading writers in events management (e.g. Bowdin *et al.* 2010) consider this in the context of more general employee training, it should be stressed that the specialised field of HRM has continued to view these activities more as the facilitation and promotion of cultures and processes which allow employees to learn. Formal training programmes certainly have a part to play in increasing the effectiveness of event employees, particularly in mandatory, operational management areas, such as safety. However the ability of many firms to differentiate themselves from their competitors often depends on their ability to become learning organisations in which personnel are encouraged to learn and improve continually and are supported with the resources to do so. Indeed, the London 2012 Olympic Games volunteering programme, whilst a vehicle for the achievement of much of the initial social legacy portion of the bid, primarily encourages volunteering by promising that volunteers will gain skills during their activities in the lead-up to and during the Games.

5.8.1 Reflective practice

Kolb's 'learning cycle' can be applied to the events industry as shown in Figure 5.2. This adapted model is an ideal starting point for the development of the learning events organisation as it focuses on problem-solving.

Events industry HR specialists, whilst following the general approach outlined above, will be required to conduct a formal, organisational programme of learning and training. Torrington *et al.* (2009) propose the following four main areas:

1   Identify development need.
2   Design development activity.
3   Carry out development.
4. Evaluate development.

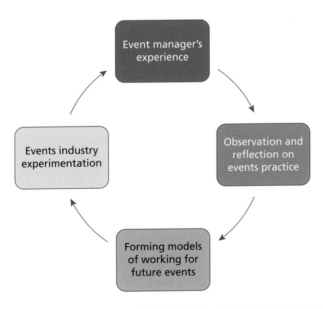

Figure 5.2 Kolb's learning cycle
Source: Adapted from Kolb 1984

These four areas constitute the 'people development strategy' of the organisation, within the wider context of the business strategy, in relation to the business environment.

The identification of the development need will take place via various formal and informal systems. As Bowdin *et al.* (2010) point out, this can be linked to the appraisal systems of the organisation, although this approach will not be practical for most event organisations, which have many members of staff who are temporary and short term. Certainly, on-site employee observations that identify shortfalls between customer expectations and their perceptions of the service provided are useful.

Designing and carrying out the development activity will involve the planned use of methods of learning and development, which may include items in the following list, also developed from Torrington *et al.* (2009):

● off-job methods, such as education and training courses
● on-job learning methods, such as coaching, mentoring, peer relationships, self-development individually or in groups
● e-learning methods.

Evaluation of learning is likely to be continual and will rely on the accurate assessment of behavioural or attitudinal changes in line with the initial objectives set following the needs analysis. There are also employee-centred assessment methods, such as self-administered questionnaires, which are designed to measure the satisfaction derived from the learning process.

5.9 Motivating, maximising performance and retaining employees

Motivation of employees is a vast topic, an in-depth analysis of which is outside of the scope of this chapter. However, there are some useful models which can prove helpful to understanding this important subject.

Tyson and York (2000: 11) define motivation as 'an inner force that impels human beings to behave in a variety of ways'. By revisiting Maslow's 'hierarchy of needs' motivation model (reviewed briefly in Chapter 1 in relation to general event attendees' motivation), it can be seen employees' motivation results from unfulfilled human needs. Maslow's hierarchy of needs (1943) explained the range of human needs and suggested a human tendency to pursue the satisfaction of needs in a hierarchical order towards self-actualisation. Fourteen years later, Festinger's (1957) 'Theory of Cognitive Dissonance' stated that such dissatisfaction will result in psychological discomfort which the individual will seek to overcome. However, in the context of Maslow's hierarchy, the modifying theory is Herzberg's 'Two Factor Theory', which demonstrates that event employees are likely to view aspects of work differently according to whether the latter are:

● motivators arising from intrinsic aspects of the job itself (e.g. challenging work, recognition, responsibility) that give positive satisfaction; or
● hygiene factors (e.g. status, job security, salary and fringe benefits) that are extrinsic to the work itself and do not give positive satisfaction, although dissatisfaction results from their absence. (Hackman and Oldham 1976)

To overcome the simplifications of Maslow's and Herzberg's theories, Vroom's 'Valency Expectancy Theory' proposed that the degree of effort an employee would exert to satisfy a need depended directly on the expectation that their effort would achieve their predicted goals. This is expressed as:

Force (F) = Valency (V) × Expectancy (E)

In order to supplement the above models' contributions to the wider understanding of employee motivation in an events context, more research has been conducted into the motivation of a particularly important group of event workers: volunteers.

5.9.1 Event volunteers and motivation

Many events succeed because of the efforts of a pool of willing and often repeat volunteers. However, as Bladen (2009) found, little research has been conducted into the motivation of this crucial human resource. McCurley and Lynch (1998) emphasise the non-event volunteer's commitment to the advancement of a cause or organisation. Others (e.g. Bowdin *et al.* 2010; Van der Wagen 2007) have discussed various approaches to understanding volunteer motivation, mainly based on generic, human resource motivation theories, which, in the absence of supporting research, do not provide practical explanations for event volunteers' motivation. Event-specific studies (e.g. Elstad 2003; Coyne and Coyne 2001; Cuskelly *et al.* 2006) have tended to focus on smaller, repeat events.

It is recognised that repeat volunteering will be based, to some extent, on the volunteers' favourable evaluation of their initial experiences. This is particularly crucial because, as Bowdin

Image 5.2 Beijing Olympics volunteers
Source: ChinaFotoPress / Getty Images

et al. (2010) state, event organisations that use large numbers of volunteers tend to recruit far more than are needed and then shed the unsuitable ones. If practised by repeat-event organisers, this process could jeopardise the sustainable future of such events. Additionally, we propose that future researchers examine attitudinal factors as potential predictors of volunteers' future behaviour. The general literature (e.g. Flashman and Quick 1985; Cuskelly *et al.* 2006) tends to link event volunteers' motivation to altruism, which generally refers to an individual's desire to benefit others with little expectation of personal reward. However, while altruisim seems to be an important motivating factor in initial volunteer attraction, it seems less significant in repeat volunteering. We suggest that the reported increasing tendency of repeat volunteers to volunteer only for short periods might be considered in terms of egoism – that is, the self-interested desire to benefit oneself. This is supported by Stebbins (1996), who found that core – or 'career' – volunteers were not altruistic. They continued volunteering due to the intrinsic rewards associated with the volunteering experience itself.

> ### Study activity
>
> Have you ever volunteered for an event? What were your reasons for doing so? Were they mostly based upon altruism or egoism? Why?

5.10 Remunerating staff

Remuneration relates to the total benefit to a member of staff; it therefore includes more than simply 'pay' for a job done. The events industry provides tangible benefits in the form of money paid to workers, though most volunteers can expect little or no payment for their services, aside, perhaps, from reimbursement for expenses, such as travel to the venue. Event managers need to consider their chosen reward strategy for remunerating employees carefully. Certainly, if staff motivation depends on rewards, then the reward package must be sufficiently substantial to attract applicants and retain them once they become employees. However, this can be costly because of the vast numbers of staff needed by many events; there is therefore a danger, if too much is spent on reward packages, that the whole event might become unsustainable.

There is still much debate about the roles of and rewards granted to volunteers. Many volunteers tend to be students, who view their participation in events as work experience with a view to future employment. However, there is an ethical question relating to whether such students should be expected to work for free as a standard part of their training while the organising company profits from their efforts.

When setting payment levels, employers must consider the market rate for that type of employment. There are minimum-wage requirements in the UK, the USA and Australia, as well as other considerations when setting pay levels. For instance, in many countries, it is routine to consult trade unions, although this is unusual in the UK events industry. Most countries also have legislation in place which guarantees workers equal pay for the same role, regardless of gender. Nevertheless, there are still fairly frequent reports of gender discrimination on pay in the UK, US and Australian events industries. Companies found guilty of such infringements often face substantial penalties.

Other types of payment for work done, such as bonuses and commissions, are uncommon in the events industry.

Which trade unions represent event workers in your country? What are their general approaches to pay negotiation and strike action? Would you join a trade union? Why?

CASE STUDY 5.2

Jet Set Sports

Recognised globally for the quality, character and scope of its corporate hospitality management services, Jet Set Sports has been officially involved with the Olympic Games since 1984. The company's website defines its business with the strapline 'Creating a corporate hospitality experience that reflects the excellence of the Olympic Games'.

Founded in 1975 by travel and hospitality executive Sead Dizdarevic, Jet Set Sports was created to focus on the 1984 Olympic Winter Games in his native Sarajevo. Motivated by a desire to introduce new corporate clients and sports organisations to his home country, Dizdarevic fashioned a unique Olympic Games hospitality programme. Since then, he has continually sought to refine and improve his corporate hospitality services by linking them more directly with the sports marketing objectives of his corporate clients. To serve their needs, he has transformed his company to suit the specific demands of each Olympiad: building and reconstructing hotels and restaurants when necessary; taking over the management of hotels, apartments and condominiums; establishing relationships with the finest restaurants and corporate hospitality venues; chartering jets and cruise ships; and cultivating relationships with an invaluable network of more than two dozen National Olympic Committees and the National Governing Bodies of various sports.

Since 2000, Jet Set Sports has been a sponsor of the US Olympic Team. Additionally, it was the Official Hospitality Services Provider of the 2010 Vancouver Winter Olympics, the Official Hospitality Operator of the 2008 Beijing Olympics, and an Official Sponsor of the 2006 Torino Winter Olympics, the 2004 Athens Olympics and the 2002 Salt Lake City Winter Olympics. It has also been named Authorised Distributor of London 2012 Hospitality in partnership with the London Organising Committee and plans to be involved in the Sochi Winter Olympics in Russia in 2014. These partnerships represent a natural culmination of the incredible growth and accomplishment of the world's leading provider of Olympic Games hospitality.

Since 1984, the scope of Jet Set Sport's operations has expanded markedly. In Beijing in 2008, it hosted over 70,000 guests – the largest number in its twenty-five-year history – in the best hotels and finest restaurants the city had to offer (3,200-plus rooms and 200,000 meals); operated and maintained its largest pool of vehicles to date (320-plus); and had its largest team of highly skilled staff members (1,500), all accredited by the Beijing Organising Committee. These members of staff left nothing to chance: they delivered the seamless, five-star programmes with which their long-standing clients have become accustomed.

Jet Set Sports donates thousands of complimentary event tickets to its Olympic Games volunteers, Olympic Aid and numerous other non-profit organisations. In addition, it has provided complimentary tickets to, and otherwise aided, underprivileged youth, Paralympics athletes, art and culture programmes and community-based organisations in every Olympic Games host city for which the company has provided hospitality services.

HR focus

Jet Set Sports is legendary for its enthusiastic and hard-working staff. They are committed to ensuring that their local staff and supporting management team are passionate about the Olympics and Paralympics, are highly knowledgeable about the host city, and have the skills to provide hospitality experiences that will leave a lasting impression on all those who partake in them.

Establishing a host city-based team for each Olympics and Paralympic requires more than just a financial and professional investment. It requires dedicated resources, a considerable amount of time, and a strong commitment from each team member. It is not just a matter of securing and deploying staff. Instead, it involves a complex understanding of the host city and country, the local education sector and employment market, the hospitality, hotel, travel and tourism and events sector's goals and challenges, as well as the role and goals of the Olympics Organising Committee.

Whilst an organisation could recruit a large team and train each person to perform their individual role(s), Jet Set Sports understands what it means to bring together a workforce that is not only trained for each person's specific job function but contemplates the bigger picture. As a company, it builds a strong understanding of the current education and job markets and then ensures that the training and experience they provide support the hospitality industry at large, and the people who make up that industry.

This model played a fundamental role in Jet Set Sports' pre-Games and Games-time operations in Beijing, and it has now become a strong legacy for Jet Set Sports' staffing programme in the host cities of Olympic and Paralympic Games.

Study activity

1 Explain how the international characteristics and mission of Jet Set Sports blend with the values of the Olympic movement.

2 Using Case Study 5.2 and the Industry Voice section, discuss some of the challenges facing a company such as Jet Set Sports in managing event human resources.

3 Consider your current curriculum vitae or employment résumé. What changes could you make to the way you present yourself to such a company to make yourself more employable?

4 Practise writing a covering letter to Jet Set Sports, or another company of your choice, in which you introduce yourself and explain why you would be an asset to the company.

5 Imagine you have been called for an interview. Write down some questions you are likely to be asked by the interviewer and your possible responses.

Industry voice

Tracie Carlsund, Jet Set Sports

There is an incessant buzz in my ear; it won't go away. I suddenly realise it is my phone vibrating under my pillow. A glance at the clock shows 2.30 a.m.

Sliding my earpiece into my ear, I hear loud music, celebratory cheers and a highly energised client manager on the phone: 'Hi there, my client wants to hold a VIP dinner party tomorrow night, in addition to the planned itinerary of going-to events, sightseeing, lunch and dinner for the rest of the guests. Is it possible to get some additional staff to assist for the evening?'

At this point I am up, pulling my spreadsheets off the side-table, pen in hand, and through bleary eyes scanning the next day's staff allocations. I then shoot off, in rapid fire, a series of questions, all of which I need answers for now, to ensure we can: a) find staff who are the best fit for the dinner/client; b) find staff who are not allocated to a client and/or task; and c) have the correct information for communication.

'OK, how many, what time and where will you need people? What positions/skills do you need? Any languages required? What are the responsibilities of these staff members? Company uniform or client "look"? Briefing and training for party? Who is point of contact?' Following the answers, we confirm the ongoing communication plans to keep everyone involved. Another glance at the clock, 3.00 a.m. Deep breath, this day has begun. Fifteen more to go.

If you had said to me as little as five years ago that I would be moving to cities who will host some of the biggest multinational events in the world, building, training and deploying teams of up to 2000 front-line hospitality and operational staff and event professionals, and taking calls at 2, 3, 4 a.m. to solve challenges, I think I would have been in awe and shock at the suggestion. However, here I am as a staffing director in my third country in three years, with a corporate hospitality company whose sole purpose is to provide outstanding, five-star hospitality experiences for their clients and guests.

To get to this point, I have taken a pathway that has forked left and right, but always with a focus on my own and others' development of skills, knowledge and experience that can be transferable to any position, career or lifestyle in a cross-cultural context. This has meant I have taken opportunities to live and work in six different countries, some developed, others developing, some with English, some without, some with cultures that are similar to mine and some that are not. While not a lifestyle or career choice for some, over time I have developed a strategy for the process and this is also reflected in my day-to-day core business of staffing operations.

Pre-arrival in a new city, research aplenty is conducted. Employment markets, education markets, housing markets, culture and language, hospitality, tourism and travel, events, hotels and trade. What is happening? What are the trends? What are the gaps? What are the laws? How much do people earn? How much does it cost to live? How do you function in the city: transportation, sightseeing, history, culture, language, customer service, banking (the list continues)? How does this impact on me personally and how does this impact on recruiting staff for events?

On arrival, it is a question of taking the research and investigating the 'real life' of the city. Does the research stand up to what I have found in the real world? Once the research and 'live' check are conducted, it is time to build a plan for developing a team. The teams are complex and require a significant amount of planning, recruiting, training and considered allocation before finally deploying for the event.

To make it easier for us to build teams in any city and culture and for any event, I have developed a set of key behaviours/attitudes/soft skills (these terms are often interchangeable) that we look for as inherent in all our staff, ready to develop further during training: passion for customer service and for getting the best out of the experience for their clients/guests; the ability to lead and be led in the team; fearless resolution to take on the challenges and see them resolved; desire to get in and get the job done through flexibility and adaptability; prepared for and able to manage change in a fast-paced, quickly changing, high-pressure environment over a sustained period of time; and, finally, ready to be an ambassador for themselves, their place of study or employment, our company, their clients, the event they are working at, and the host city and host nation.

It is as a result of the above staff dynamics, research and planning, recruiting, training and effective deployment that I am able to handle the 2.00 a.m. calls from a rather frantic client manager. I follow my strategy of research: establish the challenge; plan – look for a solution; recruit – find staff that meet the requirements; train – ascertain knowledge and educate about the task at hand; deploy – put the solution into action through communication and collaboration.

The ultimate outcome: a successful event with clients and their guests wanting to attend again; staff members who have had the experience of a lifetime and have grown both personally and professionally; and, for myself, the satisfaction of an event completed with an outstanding team, knowing we have contributed a strong legacy of skilled and experienced staff to the host city event and hospitality industry, and that each staff member will have friends and memories that will last a lifetime.

5.11 Summary

This chapter has analysed the human resource challenges of managing events. It should be noted that there are significant differences between management of the human resource associated with events and the management of ordinary employees in other industries due to the temporal, project structure of event organisation. Therefore, the process of event recruitment and selection also tends to differ significantly from that found in other businesses, and these differences are compounded as the scale and duration of the event being managed increase. Also, the complexities of managing event employees and volunteers relate closely to the pulsating nature of the organisation and therefore require constant review throughout the event cycle, so that short-term changes can be made in response to the usual fluctuations in customer attendance and the various transitions through the stages of the event cycle. Through employee retention methods, employee learning and development can be facilitated in conjunction with the strategic requirements of the event and its organisers.

Further reading

Cuskelly, G., Hoye, R. and Auld, C. (2006) *Working with Volunteers in Sport: Theory and Practice*, London: Routledge. Focused on sporting events, this book gives a thorough introduction to volunteering in events, including useful references to the research in the field.

Schein, E. (2010) *Organizational Culture and Leadership*, San Francisco: Wiley. This book is a good overall introduction to this important topic.

Van der Wagen, L. (2007) *Human Resource Management for Events: Managing the Event Workforce*, Oxford: Elsevier. A thoughtful and practical overview of HR in events, this book has the added advantage of being thoroughly events related.

Chapter 6

Event finance

Robert Wilson

Robert Wilson is a Principal Lecturer in Sport Business Management at Sheffield Hallam University, UK. His subject specialisms are financial reporting, management accounting and economic decision-making in the sports and leisure industry, and his main research interests are in the financing of professional team sports and the economics of major events.

Contents

6.1 Aims

At the end of this chapter, students will be able:

- To appreciate why financial skills are an important part of the event manager's portfolio of skills.
- To understand the key financial terminology that is often applied to events.
- To understand the meaning of budgeting in operational, tactical and strategic event management contexts.
- To analyse budgeted against actual performance using recognised evaluation techniques.
- To understand sources of funding and how to secure such funding.
- To monitor and evaluate an event's financial performance effectively.

6.2 Introduction

This chapter examines the importance of event finance and places it in a context that should be easily understandable for any event manager to apply to their event, whether that event is a major undertaking, like the Olympic Games, a local community fare or farmers' market. For all events, it is essential that the overall governance is underpinned by sound financial management. Without needing to be a fully qualified accountant or having specific training in finance, all event managers should be able to answer two fundamental questions. First, is the selling price higher than the cost? In other words, will the event bring in more money than it pays out? Or, is the event going to make a profit? If you are managing a small community, not-for-profit event, it is simple to modify this question (because it is still important) to: is the event operating within the resources allocated to it? If the answer is 'no', then the event will struggle.

The second question all events must answer is: can this event continue? In financial terms, this question relates to the event's ability to pay its creditors (people to whom it owes money for goods and services). Many events will never take place due to an inability to meet these obligations because they have not considered cash flow and run out of money to pay creditors before the event can generate revenue. Being unable to meet these obligations is not uncommon, and this is the reason why you see businesses going bankrupt today. Event managers must ensure that they can pay their bills as they fall due and understand how to negotiate payment dates that fit in with income streams. Moreover, the sustainability of events is an increasingly important component of an event plan, and you will need to demonstrate how you can generate the income to meet your expenses.

Before we start, however, it is important to establish some ground rules: put simply, finance is not just about numbers; and you do not have to be a skilled mathematician to understand finance or to manage money. Instead, you need to understand the guiding rules and principles that help compile and structure a set of financial documents. As students or managers who work within the event industry, it is important that you appreciate the importance of financial management and responsibility and that you can communicate key financial information to both the internal and external stakeholders. These skills – coupled with those you have considered already and will consider later in this book – will enable you to set up, run and manage successful events.

A successful event cannot happen without sufficient financial support and, by definition, financial management. The most significant, and perhaps most routine, error when committing to an event is to do so without securing the necessary financing (or funding) at a very early stage. This can be a concern for any event manager from beginning to end, and ultimately causes the event to be presented in a less than satisfactory way, which hinders success and event sustainability planning.

Many event managers shy away from managing money and financial performance because they are scared of the associated terminology. They will often focus on 'sexier' components – such as marketing and volunteer training – rather than managing the basic functions of financial control. Financial viability of an event should be the key issue of any event planning process, and if the expenses far outweigh the income streams, then managers should not be afraid to abort the whole event. If they are not prepared to do so, they compromise the future of similar events, acquire a poor image for their own organisation, and reduce the opportunities for bidding groups to bring other events to the region.

Unfortunately, the events industry has lagged behind other business sectors from a financial management point of view. For the most part, event marketing, planning and strategy have dominated event management education, which has led to a growing maturity in such areas. By contrast, financial management has often been overlooked, anecdotally because individuals claim to have some sort of fear of numbers. There are still many event managers and graduates with event management degrees who struggle to understand even the basics of a budget or cash-flow statement, let alone have the confidence to make informed judgements on the financial health of their event. However, as Wilson and Joyce (2008) point out, every organisation – ranging from multi-million-pound operations through to small, local, voluntary sports events – need to manage money and make routine financial decisions. Therefore, if organisations have to do it, the chances are that successful managers will have to understand, communicate and use financial information, too.

6.3 Financial terminology

Understanding the nature and application of finance is often a question of understanding the terminology used by financial experts. Demystifying this terminology is the first step in managing finance effectively, as it will help you to understand what things mean and why they are important.

Essentially, there are two types of accounts: financial and management. Depending on the nature of a user's information needs (something that is explored in more detail later in the chapter), the style of the accounts and financial documents may be quite different. From the section above, you should have noticed that financial information can look two ways. When looking backwards – into the past – it is normal to examine financial accounts as they are prepared for external use and are based on historical information; they are also required by law. A set of financial accounts will, for example, illustrate the past financial position and financial performance of an organisation.

> **Financial accounting** is the term used to describe the system for recording historical financial transactions and presenting this information in summary form.

However, should a manager wish to be more proactive and examine future trends and issues, then they will need to examine more forward-looking (future) accounting information. Such information will not be found in financial accounts. Hence, there are management accounts: that is, accounts that look forward and are based on providing information for managers to help with the planning, decision-making and control of organisations. Unlike financial accounts, management accounts are not a statutory requirement. It is important that managers understand the distinction between the two types of accounts, as they dictate where they should look for information. These two types also structure the remainder of this chapter. Financial accounting and reporting are beyond the scope of this chapter, as we are examining the tools that you can use to manage event finance. Consequently, we will focus on management accounting and how to plan, make decisions and control event finance.

> **Management accounting** is the term used to describe more forward-looking financial data for planning, decision-making and control purposes.

In reality, event managers should appreciate that they will plan their operations, consider the implications of their decisions and control their organisation in such a way that they reach (in most cases) their organisation's objectives. In order to plan and make effective decisions, a manager will have to adopt the principles of good management accounting – for example, budgeting, break-even analysis and cash-flow forecasting – some of which will be explored towards the end of this chapter.

Before we continue, it is worth outlining more key terms that you may encounter when moving through the following sections:

- income statement or profit and loss account – a summary of financial performance and therefore actual income and expenditure over a period of time;
- balance sheet – a snapshot of a company's financial position at a specific point in time;
- cash flow – a forecast of funds coming in and out, presented over a period of time;
- assets – those things of value that a company owns, such as buildings, equipment and vehicles;
- debtor – an individual or organisation that owes the company money or service, such as someone to whom you have lent money;
- liabilities – the opposite of assets, such as a credit card company;
- creditor – an individual or organisation to which you owe money or service;
- depreciation – the decrease in value of assets over time; for instance, a computer will be worth less after it has been used.

6.4 Financial planning and control

The concept behind financial management is not the simplistic idea that you need to manage profit, but, more importantly, how to monitor, evaluate and control the income and expenditure for an event. It is vital for event managers to understand the changing values of the events industry and recognise that a large number of events are provided to achieve social objectives, which operate at a loss and will therefore normally require a government or local authority subsidy to function. This does not mean, however, that proper financial planning and controls are unimportant. It is vital that event managers have an understanding of the costs of the products and services that they offer in order to operate as effective business entities, either to generate profits or ensure that taxpayers' money is not wasted on frivolous plans or ideas.

Many events rely on funding from national, regional or local government, grants from quangos (such as Sport England or the Arts Council), sponsorship or flexible credit terms from suppliers. However, using money from a third party is normally based on the simple assumption that the organisation's future returns will be sufficient to cover the borrowing or meet other objectives. Problems can occur when organisations fail to meet their financial obligations. Consequently, an organisation's ability to pay its debts as they fall due is usually the difference between financial success and financial failure. If event managers are to make effective plans and decisions, they need to control their organisations' finances.

Exercising sound financial planning and control is of fundamental importance in running a successful event. A lack of knowledge regarding the cost of the event will lead to almost certain failure. It is essential to plan, budget and monitor finances throughout the planning and execution of an event to avoid any implications with cost variation or changing economic conditions.

Before an event progresses too far into the planning process, it is essential to assess its financial viability. This will mean setting out a financial plan to balance the cost of running the event against any existing funds and prospective income. Several draft budgets may need to be compiled before producing the final version. Initially, the budget will be based on estimates, but it is important to confirm actual figures as soon as possible to keep the budget on track and to exercise something resembling financial responsibility (Running Sports 2007).

If the decision is made to go ahead with an event, this will be managerial and therefore rather subjective. However, such a decision can be informed by a thorough understanding of the finances involved and the ability of the event to meet its financial obligations. What is more, the decision that determines whether an event is financially viable will ensure that effort (and money) is not wasted. Earlier chapters have stressed the importance of project management and event design and production, and these stages are indeed vital for the operational success of an event. But they will yield success only if sufficient financial resources are available for them to be implemented.

CASE STUDY 6.1

The Cultural Olympiad

Location: Sheffield, UK
Event type: cultural event
Attendees: approximately 10,000

Background

Spread over four years, the Cultural Olympiad is designed to give everyone in the UK a chance to be part of London 2012 and to inspire creativity across all forms of culture, especially among young people. More than 975 events were staged across the UK – ranging from sports to art, and from dance to exhibitions – with 21 of them held in Sheffield. Each event featured a special challenge, and gave visitors the chance to try something new or take an existing skill to a new level. More than 2000 people took part in the Sheffield events, with highlights including:

- Sheffield Try-Athlon – three types of Olympic-inspired street entertainment happening across the city centre over three days, including the city's five torch-bearing Olympians.
- 2012-Metre Swimming Challenge, which saw dozens of participants at pools all over Sheffield swim a total of 2012 metres.
- 2012 Together – a national event featuring the Concord Youth Marching Band that involved 2012 musicians marching and playing at the same time at different locations all over the UK.

Sheffield has also used exhibitions such as 'Extraordinary Moves' – a project developed by Sheffield Hallam University's Centre for Sport and Exercise Science, Huddersfield-based Chol Theatre and independent artists – to challenge perceptions of disability through an exploration of human movement. Its main aim is to utilise emerging technologies to enhance human abilities. Extraordinary Moves brings together young people, communities and artists to provide different ways to think about, experience and interpret the concept of disability in relation to competitive and expressive movement. As part of the IMOVE programme, Extraordinary Moves is at the heart of Yorkshire's cultural ambitions leading up to 2012. The project will create and present installations, new writing, exhibitions, documentary photography, performances and debate across Yorkshire and beyond.

The 2011 event

In 2011, along with the rest of the UK, Sheffield participated in Open Weekend – the celebration of one year to go to the opening of the Olympic Games in London 2012. A variety of events took place across the city over the weekend of 22–24 July, with the central one occurring on Tudor Square and titled '2012 By Any Means'. This featured a fifty-metre athletics track surrounded by activity stalls and installations from creative organisations. Members of the public were challenged to come along and get from one end of the track to the other using any means or in any guise – with particular emphasis given to sports, physical activity, movement and creativity. All abilities were encouraged to participate, including those accompanied by companions, in wheelchairs, with guide dogs and so on. People turned up with many weird and wonderful forms of transport – from skis to broomsticks – and in all manner of fancy dress – from flamenco dresses to diving suits. The more creative, the better!

The Sheffield Steering Group commissioned local artists and arts organisations to engage people and help them take part in the challenge. These artists brought equipment and materials so that participants could make their own costumes or make/borrow forms of transport to get around the track. As well as laps taking place throughout the day, creative workshop sessions run by professional arts practitioners combined creativity and physical activity – for example, dance workshops. The event was designed to allow people to be playful and lose their inhibitions and to encourage movement through creative activity, with each participant's lap of the track going towards a final distance covered through out the course of the day, with the aim of totalling 297 kilometres – the distance between Tudor Square and Marshgate Lane, Stratford, the site of the Olympic Stadium.

This event, like most community-based events, had to generate funding through grants, local authority support and payments in kind. It also relied heavily on a volunteer workforce. A bid to Arts Council England for £10,000 was successful, and this amount was almost matched by Sheffield City Council. Moreover, the track was provided free of charge, and Sheffield Hallam University supplied volunteers and event evaluation. A summary of the full event budget can be found in Table 6.1.

Table 6.1 2012 By Any Means budget

INCOME

City Council Budget	£9,000.00
Arts Council Award	£10,000.00
Running Track	£12,000.00
SHU Student support	£1,200.00
Tudor Square	£1,200.00
City Council Officer Time inc event management	£1,200.00
Other earned income	£—
TOTAL INCOME	**£34,600.00**

EXPENDITURE

Artist Commissions x 6	£7,000.00
Confirmed commission	£1,000.00
FMTV	£2,000.00
Museums Sheffield Tent	£—
SHU Xpod	£—
Face Painting	£200.00
Staging/PA/Generator/Engineer	£500.00
Host fee	£250.00

Market Stall hire x 10	£400.00
Site Dressing	£600.00
Furniture (tables/chairs)	£300.00
Expenses/Water/Tape	£50.00
First Aid	£200.00
Lost Children support	£200.00
Signage	£50.00
Print	£750.00
Project & Event Management Fee	£5,000.00
Contingency	£500.00
Tudor Square hire (in kind)	£1,200.00
City Council Officer time (in kind)	£1,200.00
SHU Student Support (in kind)	£1,200.00
Running Track	£12,000.00
TOTAL EXPENDITURE	£34,600.00
TOTAL INCOME	£34,600.00
TOTAL EXPENDITURE	£34,600.00
BALANCE	£—

Some of the activity on the day reflected the culture (including the food) of international athletes who will be resident in the city during 2012 due to the international training camps that Sheffield will host. For instance, Sheffield residents and visitors were able to sample Brazilian Capoeira and Carnival skills; American line dancing and food; and Serbian music. Athletes and Paralympians were invited and grants of between one and two thousand pounds were made to a series of arts organisations to enable their participation. These groups collected stories about people and movement, ran digital art workshops, delivered circus skills or performances, showcased the talent of groups of young people with disabilities and so on.

Sheffield arts trusts were asked to contribute ideas and activities on the day. For example, Sheffield Theatres and Museums Sheffield and the Central Library hosted a variety of arts events and activities. Sheffield Hallam University's Extraordinary Moves Pod was available, as was the IMOVE Extraordinary Moves Pod.

The 'journey' down the athletics track was documented with time-lapse photography and relayed live on to a screen in Tudor Square. This footage was subsequently turned into an animation that showed each participant's contribution. The whole square was dressed and festooned with Olympic branded materials and had a very different feel to activity elsewhere in the city, where the annual Tramlines Festival was running on the same weekend.

Image 6.1 An athlete taking part in a special performance of Martin Creed's work *No. 850* at Tate Britain to mark the start of Open Weekend, celebrating the launch of the Cultural Olympiad in London
Source: Matt Cardy / Getty Images

6.5 Users of event finance information

Financial information is useful to a wide variety of stakeholders. These will often span several sectors and each will have a slightly different need for the information. For example, the board of directors of Intercontinental Hotels Group will want to see how much profit they have made from trading activities and see how each arm of the business is performing so that they can make future investment decisions and consider returns to shareholders. Sheffield City Council will want to know how much subsidy they have to provide in order to keep all of their leisure services running across the city, so that their council-taxpayers get value for money. The chairperson of the Cheltenham Swimming and Water Polo Club will want to ensure that enough money is being received through subscriptions and funding to cover running costs.

Who do you think are the most important audiences for financial information: (a) in a private commercial organisation; (b) in a local authority event team; and (c) in a voluntary event organisation?

Generally, information relating to the finance of an organisation is of interest to its owners, managers, trade contacts (for example, suppliers), providers of finance (for example, banks and funding bodies), employees and customers. All of these groups of people need to be sure that the organisation is strong, can pay its bills, make a profit if it is commercial, and remain in business. An indicative list of users and their areas of interest is illustrated in Table 6.2.

Table 6.2 Users of financial information and their information needs

User groups	Areas of interest
Event managers	Managers require financial information so that they can make present and future plans for the event and see how effective their decisions have been.
Trade contacts (e.g. suppliers)	Suppliers and other trade contacts need to know if they are going to be paid on time by the event organiser.
Providers of private finance (e.g. banks and so on)	Banks and other lenders of finance need to ensure that any loans and interest payments are going to be made on time before they lend money and during the repayment period.
Providers of public finance (e.g. government agencies, quangos and so on)	Funding bodies will want to ensure that their funds are being used for the appropriate purpose and that those funds are helping to meet their performance objectives.
Tax authorities	The tax authorities require information about the profits/surplus of the event so that they can work out how much tax the organisation owes. They also need details for VAT and employees' income tax.
Employees/volunteers	Organisations' employees and volunteers often wish to know whether their jobs are safe and that they are going to be paid on time or that the event is likely to go ahead.
Spectators	It is normal for spectators to know if goods/services purchased are going to be delivered/provided.

6.6 Budgeting and events

Budgeting is a subject area with origins in the field of management accounting as it helps management plan, make decisions and exercise control. It can be shown to be part of the overall planning process for a business by defining it as 'the overall plan of a business expressed in financial terms'. These plans might involve trying to achieve a predetermined level of financial performance, such as a specified profit over the course of a year, or having sufficient cash resources to be able to replace the equipment in a gym. Organisational business planning can be summarised as an analysis of four key questions:

1   Where are we now?
2   How did we get here?
3   Where are we going?
4   How shall we get there?

To illustrate the link between general business planning and budgeting, the question 'Where are we now?' can be modified to 'Where are we now *in financial terms?*' Similarly, the question 'Where are we going?' can be modified to 'Where are we going *in financial terms?*' To diagnose where a business *is* in financial terms requires the ability to be able to 'read' an income statement (or profit and loss account), a balance sheet and a cash-flow statement. To predict where a business is going is difficult (just like any attempt to predict the future), but techniques such as compiling an expected income statement (profit and loss account), balance sheet and cash flow can help to focus attention on the business essentials. Furthermore, the process of planning ahead using budgets can help to test whether what you wish to achieve and the accompanying financial consequences are compatible (or 'internally consistent'). The concept of internal consistency will be covered in the next section, but we should conclude this section by clarifying that the meaning of budgeting is *the overall plan of a business expressed in financial terms.*

6.7 Budgeting as a logically sequenced planning process

A key point about budgeting is that it is an ongoing process rather than a time-limited, one-off event. The actual mechanics of drawing up the numbers involved in a budget are but a small part of the overall budgeting process. By bearing in mind that budgeting is designed to help an organisation with planning, decision-making and control, it is possible to appreciate that budgeting is a continuous part of business life. This point can be reinforced by viewing budgeting as steps in a logically sequenced planning process, as shown in Figure 6.1.

Below, each of these nine stages of budgeting are explained.

6.7.1 Define your business objectives

The first question to ask when dealing with financial business planning is: 'In monetary terms, what are we trying to achieve?' Of course, most sane businesspeople would not answer, 'Make a loss.' Losses are made in business, but it is inconceivable to imagine that managers set out deliberately to lose money. Losses normally occur when there is a mismatch between what was planned and what happened in reality. Organisational objectives will vary according to the nature of the business. A community sports club which exists for the benefit of the members may desire nothing more than to break even or to make a small surplus to maintain its existing

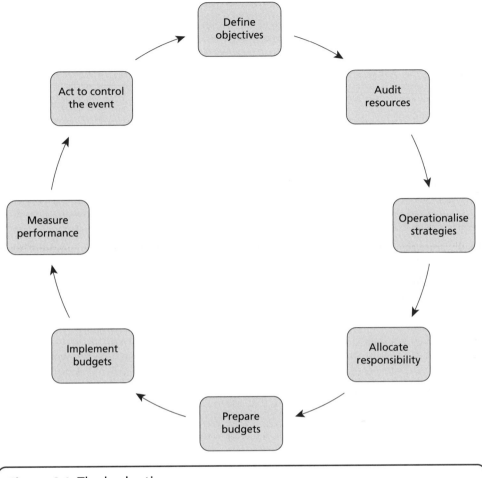

facilities. A more complex organisation, such as a professional football team, needs to balance the requirements of producing a successful team on the pitch (utility maximisation) with the requirements of being a commercial franchise (profit maximisation). Whatever the objectives of an organisation, they need to have certain qualities that enable them to be measured. These qualities are contained within the 'MASTER' mnemonic.

- Measurable – e.g. a profit of £3 million in the financial year, or simply to break even.
- Achievable – the organisation must have the capability to attain its objectives; capability means staff, other resources, and competitive advantage.
- Specific – objectives must be specific: e.g. '£3 million profit', not 'to do well this year'.
- Time limited – objectives must have a stated date for achievement.
- Ends related – objectives must relate to achieving outputs (ends) rather than describing means (how).
- Ranked – ideally, objectives should be ranked in order of priority.

An example of an objective meeting the MASTER mnemonic might be:

Our first priority is to achieve a net profit of £3 million in the financial year 6 April 2012 to 5 April 2013. This target is considered to be attainable as the organisation has increased its capacity and the market is expanding.

6.7.2 Audit resources

The audit of resources is a 'reality check' on the objectives. Its purpose is to ensure that the objectives and the resources required to achieve them are internally consistent. As an example, Sheffield United need around 15,000 spectators per home match to break even. With a stadium capacity of nearly 31,000, it is clear that 15,000 people can be accommodated at a home match, as long as they can be attracted to the match in the first place.

Where there is a discrepancy between the objectives and the resources available to achieve them, two courses of action are possible. First, the objectives can be changed so that they are compatible with the resources. Second, the gap between the resources available and the resources required can form the basis for prioritising capital investment, such as increasing the capacity of a stadium or identifying training and development needs to ensure that staff have the skills to deliver what is required of them.

6.7.3 Operationalise strategies

Having defined what you want to achieve and confirmed that you have the resources to deliver the objectives, the budgeting process evolves to consider the day-to-day tactics to be used to meet the objectives. In small-scale events these might include the marketing plans, funding requirements, customer care protocols and opening hours. If organisational objectives can be regarded as *what* we wish to achieve, then operational strategies can be regarded as *how* we plan to achieve the objectives. Thus, a football club aiming for average match-day turnover of £300,000 might set out to achieve it via operational strategies for spectators, corporate hospitality customers, programme sales, half-time draw tickets, catering and beverage sales, merchandising sales and car parking.

6.7.4 Allocate responsibility

Successful achievement of objectives does not happen by chance, nor as a result of a mechanical exercise. Events management is primarily a service industry and the most important people in determining the extent to which objectives are met are an organisation's staff. In order for people to see where their contributions fit into an organisation's overall plan, they need to have agreed responsibility for particular areas of work. Agreed responsibility is particularly important in situations where staff can be rewarded, or indeed punished, on the basis of their performance. Remember that this could be particularly difficult when managing volunteers. For example, a volunteer responsible for the health and safety of an event could be assessed on the basis of the event running smoothly and without incident. If it is known and clearly stated 'who is going to do what and by when', then there is the basis for a meaningful comparison of actual performance compared with planned or expected performance.

6.7.5 Preparation of budgets

It is worth noting that the actual preparation of budgets does not occur until the mid-point of the budgeting process. This is important because it makes the point that budgeting is not an isolated process and is integral to overall business planning. When preparing a budget there are two important considerations: namely, *how much* income or expenditure; and *when* the income or expenditure will occur. To illustrate the point, if a major festival is expecting 52,000 admissions at an average price of £25, then the answer to 'How much income will be generated?' is £1,300,000. However, it is unlikely that a festival will average 13,000 admissions per day for four days. There will be peak times, such as during the weekend, and off-peak times, such on a Thursday, when people are at work. Thus, in order to make sure that the appropriate level of resource (for example, staff) is in the right place at the right time, it will be necessary to plan the predicted level of activity on a day-by-day basis. Doing such an exercise will enable event managers to plan ahead for situations where expenditure is greater than income and there is insufficient cash to meet the shortfall. Having identified situations requiring management attention, strategies can be put in place to deal with them, such as negotiating an overdraft facility at the bank, rescheduling expenditure on capital items, or simply not paying creditors on time. The important point of note is that the process of budgeting identifies potential problems in advance of them happening so that pre-emptive action can be taken.

It is unlikely that at the first time of asking the figures produced in the preparation of budgets will deliver the outcomes required. Therefore, managers may be asked to revise their budgets in such a way that the desired outcome is achieved. In practice, there are five ways in which a budget can be revised:

1   Increase revenue and keep costs constant. This could be achieved by increasing prices, increasing throughput, or a combination of the two. The key assumption here is that any increase in price will not be offset by a reduction in demand.
2   Decrease expenditure and keep income constant. This could be achieved by making savings on non-essential expenditure or reducing the quality of the service on offer (for example, fewer staff on duty).
3   Increase income *and* decrease costs, as 1 and 2, above, are not necessarily mutually exclusive.
4   Alter the financial outcome required. It may be impossible to bring the required outcomes and the budget into line by using 1, 2 and 3, above. Therefore, rather than alter income and expenditure, management may decide to alter the financial outcome required. This approach can work both positively and negatively. If staff provide managers with a budget that exceeds the required bottom line, and the assumptions underpinning the budget are correct, then it would make sense to increase the overall budget target accordingly. A much more likely scenario is that the targeted outcome cannot be met by revisions to income and expenditure, so managers decide to settle for a reduced financial outcome: for example, an annual profit of £2.9 million rather than £3 million.
5   Change the overall business objectives. It may well be the case that it is impossible to arrive at an acceptable solution to a budget using steps 1–4, above. Under these conditions it may be that the required outcomes and the organisation's capabilities are incompatible. The only remaining alternative is to change the organisation's objectives. As an example, private contractors managing local authority events are often required to meet social as well as financial objectives. On occasion, pursuit of these differing aims may be mutually incompatible in the sense that programming activities for priority groups at certain times prevents revenue maximisation. Every use of resources has an opportunity cost: that is, the price of the best alternative foregone. Thus, in order to make the budget balance, it may be that some priorities which are no doubt desirable and equitable have to be sacrificed to the cause of wider business interests. For this reason, it is important that, where possible, objectives are ranked (see 'R' in the MASTER mnemonic above).

The significance of preparing a budget, comparing it with business objectives and taking corrective action where appropriate indicates the importance of achieving internal consistency. Using the budgeting model described thus far ensures that what an organisation wishes to achieve in overall terms and the financial consequences of doing so are consistent. If potential problems can be identified at the planning (input) stage, pre-emptive action can be taken by drawing up plans to deal with adverse circumstances. Clearly, this approach has a greater chance of success and is more desirable than trying to deal with situations reactively as they materialise without prior warning. The process of modelling the financial consequences of various scenarios until an acceptable outcome is achieved is known as an 'iterative' approach; or, in less scientific terms, 'trial and error'.

6.7.6 Approval of budgets

Once an acceptable match has been achieved between an organisation's business objectives and the financial consequences of those objectives, a line needs to be drawn under the preparation of budgets stage. The point at which this line is drawn is at the approval of budgets stage, which effectively puts an end to the various iterations of the budget and leads to the formal adoption of the budget the organisation wishes to pursue. It is recognised good practice for the approval of a budget to be formalised in the minutes of a board or committee meeting. Furthermore, budgets should be approved in advance of the financial period to which they relate. The wider significance of a budget being formally approved is that those who have compiled it and those whose performance will in part be judged by it know exactly what their responsibilities are. This, in turn, has two benefits. First, if you know what is expected of you, then evaluation of performance can be objective rather than subjective. Second, expectation generates accountability, which, in turn, gives managers the focus to concentrate on those things that are important in terms of meeting the organisation's objectives.

6.7.7 Implementation of budgets

As a logical consequence of a budget being approved, it can be implemented with effect from the date to which it applies. For example, if an organisation's financial year operates from 1 April to 31 March, then it would be a reasonable expectation for the budget to be approved by the committee or board by the end of February, at the latest. A less than ideal situation would be an organisation entering a financial period without an approved budget, which would be the managerial equivalent of a boat sailing without a rudder. However, for one-off events, it may be necessary to write up and implement budgets outside of normal financial periods so that they reflect the demands of the event itself.

6.7.8 Measurement of performance

To reinforce the notion of budgeting being integral to overall business planning, it is vital to realise that the budgeting process does not end once the preparation and implementation phases are over. Once the budget is operational, it is essential that periodically (at least monthly, or weekly, in some cases), a check is made of how the organisation is actually performing, compared with how it planned to perform. One of the greatest motivators in life is feedback, and the same is true in budgeting. Management accountants use the mnemonic CARROT as a way of categorising the features of good-quality information for feedback purposes. Each component of CARROT is explained below:

- Concise – Information fed back to managers needs to be to the point.
- Accurate – Feedback is used for planning, decision-making and control purposes, so it follows that feedback should be error free.
- Reliable – Similar to 'Accurate', the same results of an actual versus budget comparison should be obtained if different people carried out the analysis: that is, the source information is robust.
- Relevant – Different levels of management require different levels of information; therefore, feedback should be presented in terms that are relevant to the intended recipient.
- Objective – Feedback should be concerned with verifiable factual evidence and not with individual interpretation of findings.
- Timely – There is a trade-off between timeliness and accuracy, but feedback should always be received in sufficient time for it to be of value in terms of planning, decision-making and control purposes.

Measurement of performance is not an end in itself and is valuable as an exercise only if it is used to add value to the process of management in an organisation.

6.7.9 Taking action to control the event

If we accept that rational decisions require information that meets the requirements of the CARROT mnemonic, the final stage of the budgeting process is to use the information to inform the direction of the organisation. It is highly unlikely that there will be a perfect match between budget and actual comparisons, so the first decision to make is whether overall variance is within a tolerable range. If variances are tolerable, then significant changes in policy will be unlikely. By contrast, if variances are considered to be so significant that the organisation is 'out of control' (in financial terms), then proactive management action may be needed. On a positive note, if performance is considerably ahead of target, it may be prudent to revise targets upwards. If, however, actual versus budget comparisons reveal a significant shortfall in performance, then corrective action may be needed. Such action might include extra marketing to increase sales, reducing price to stimulate sales, improving the quality of sales to boost repeat business, or, more predictably, cutting costs to try to maintain profit margins.

In concluding this section, it is worth making three points relating to the assertion that budgeting is a logically sequenced planning process.

Budgeting is a process designed to help managers make sensible decisions about running their organisations. It helps to inform decisions, but clearly budgeting is not a decision-making process in itself. Compiling a budget is an iterative process. It is unlikely that the first draft of a budget will produce an acceptable result. Various scenarios will be modelled and differing assumptions will be tested until an acceptable solution is found. Figure 6.1 is a simple model of an ideal process; in practice, the numerous iterations will result in a more complicated picture. However, the basic point is that each step of the model is a reality check on the previous step, which is designed to ensure that an organisation's overall plans and the financial consequences of those plans are internally consistent.

Although Figure 6.1 implies a step-by-step approach to compiling a budget, in reality some steps are seamless. For example, defining your objectives (step 1), conducting and audit of resources (step 2) and devising operational strategies (step 3) are likely to be interrelated and to occur simultaneously.

6.8 Common methods of budgeting

In this section, 'methods of budgeting' refers to budgeting processes and behavioural aspects of budgeting. In terms of budgeting processes, there are two common ways in which budgets tend to be compiled. The most frequently used is 'continuation' budgeting (or business as usual); the other, 'zero-based budgeting' (ZBB), is somewhat rarer. Continuation budgeting refers to situations whereby the business objectives of an organisation do not change significantly from one financial period to the next. Under these circumstances, it makes perfect sense to continue with essentially the same business objectives and hence the same approach to budgeting. An example of a continuation budget might be a voluntary swimming club's open meet whose main aim is to break even and provide a service to the members. You should note here that these types of budgets will rarely be used for one-off events, but they may be considered for events that occur as part of an annual calendar of activity. If the club's basic operations lead to a situation whereby the selling price is higher than the cost, then apart from increasing spectator tickets and secondary spending prices to keep up with inflation, there is no point wasting time and resources on a more complicated approach to the event's finances.

Continuation budgeting is also referred to as 'incremental' or 'decremental' budgeting. The former refers to a situation whereby an organisation increases its income and expenditure, usually by the rate of inflation, in order to pursue its existing policies. The latter refers to a situation whereby an organisation agrees either a standstill level of funding (a cut, in real terms) or an absolute decrease in funding. When faced with a decremental budget, managers are faced with the problem of deciding whether to pursue existing policies with fewer resources; to reduce funding to all policies by the same relative amount ('the equal misery' approach); or to cut funding to some activities in order to preserve the more highly ranked priorities (see 'R' in the MASTER mnemonic). An example of a simple continuation budget for a swimming club's open meet is shown in Table 6.3.

The basic assumptions in Table 6.3 are that the club will pursue the same policies from one year to the next and will increase income and expenditure by the rate of inflation (in this case 3 per cent). Thus, all that has happened to the numbers in the budget is that they have increased by 3 per cent. There are some advantages and disadvantages to using continuation budgeting, which are outlined below.

6.8.1 Advantages of continuation budgeting

- Continuation budgeting is intuitively simple and easy to understand.
- It is an effective use of resources if business objectives, infrastructure and strategies have remained unchanged.
- It is quick and easy to update figures and budget templates that are readily to hand.
- It requires fewer staff resources and therefore costs less than zero-based budgeting.

6.8.2 Disadvantages of continuation budgeting

- The overall rate of inflation within a country does not necessarily equal the rate of inflation within a particular industry; therefore, using the headline inflation figure to increase budgets is somewhat crude.
- Continuation budgeting does not encourage growth in real terms. In Table 6.3, the net position is that the business stands still. Businesses need to grow in real terms to remain competitive and to have the resources to maintain their operating infrastructure.

Table 6.3 Open swimming meet continuation budget

INCOME	This year (£)	Inflation	Next year (£)
Spectator Tickets	1,450	3%	1,494
Other Ticket Sales	250	3%	258
Sponsorship	1,700	3%	1,751
Catering	220	3%	227
Merchandising	130	3%	134
Total Income	3,750	3%	3,863
EXPENDITURE			
Voulunteer Kit	700	3%	721
Pool Hire	2,500	3%	2,575
Marketing Activities	136	3%	140
Administration	342	3%	352
Total Expenditure	3,678	3%	3,788
PROFIT / (LOSS)	72	3%	74

- Changes may be occurring within the market place which demand a response, such as the application of internet technology and e-marketing. By not taking advantage of business opportunities as they present themselves, standing still may actually be going backwards, relative to your competitors.
- There is a danger that if income and expenditure budgets are not challenged occasionally, then targets are 'soft' rather than a fair test of an organisation's capabilities. Managers can build 'slack' (unnecessary expenditure) into budgets which can be 'rewarded' when budgets for the next year are confirmed without detailed scrutiny.

Study activity

What are the benefits and drawbacks of using a continuation budget for an annual music festival?

> **Budget** – the business or overall plan of an organisation expressed in financial terms.
>
> **Cash budget** – an analysis of how the cash available to an organisation is expected to change over a given period of time.
>
> **Continuation budgeting** – budgets compiled on the basis of no change in policies or priorities: business as usual.
>
> **Variance** – the difference between actual performance and planned performance.
>
> **Zero-based budgeting** – a method of budgeting which starts with the priorities of an organisation and allocates resources to those priorities according to their order of importance.

Although continuation budgeting is by far the most commonly used budgeting technique in all industries (not just events), if an organisation is facing a fundamental change to its operating circumstances or if you are planning a one-off or new event, a more analytical approach may be needed. Rather than starting with last year's budget (or one that you have found elsewhere) and updating it, the zero-based budget starts with a blank piece of paper and challenges every item of income and expenditure. Some zero-based budgeting questions might be:

1   What is the purpose of this expenditure?
2   On what will this expenditure be made exactly?
3   What are the quantifiable benefits of this expenditure?
4   What are the alternatives to this proposed expenditure?
5   What would be the outcome of cutting this expenditure completely?

In order for funds to be allocated to a given item of expenditure, a robust defence would have to be made for the expenditure through the five questions listed above. If some expenditure was not defendable, then it might be cut and be reallocated to more deserving areas of an organisation's activities. As an example, consider the case of the large festival we considered earlier. As part of its agreement with volunteers, it runs its own laundry to wash and iron volunteers' kit. The laundry will make use of staff, space, equipment, energy and consumables – all of which cost money. Furthermore, in the long run, equipment will need to be replaced and service contracts will have to be in place in case machinery breaks down. If commercial laundry facilities that matched the quality of service provided in-house at a cheaper price were available locally, then, in addition to saving money, the club could use the released staff, space and other resources on more important business objectives. Alternatively, it may be even more cost effective simply to buy additional kit and benefit from discounted prices. Clearly, using the zero-based approach would be a more rigorous way of questioning existing business practices than simply accepting that the club has always provided an in-house laundry and will continue to do so.

The purpose of zero-based budgeting is the allocation of resources in a systematic manner which is consistent with an organisation's wider business objectives. It makes an implicit assumption that people within an organisation act rationally and prioritise business objectives rather than personal agendas. Sometimes, this can be a very ambitious assumption. Compared with continuation budgeting, zero-based budgeting is resource intensive and therefore can be wasteful if there has been no significant change in business objectives and operating procedures. It is therefore dangerous to make sweeping generalisations about one budgeting process being better than another. As in many instances of using applied management techniques, the best methods to use are those that are most appropriate to the circumstances faced by an organisation. Therefore, if a business is stable, with no major changes on the horizon, continuation budgeting might be the best method to use. By contrast, if a business requires a major strategic overhaul, or if you are planning a new or larger event, then zero-based budgeting might be more advisable. Like many things in life, compromise can help to keep most of the people happy for most of the time. So a business could use continuation budgeting most of the time, but once every three or five years a zero-based approach could be used to challenge the status quo and reallocate resources to where they are most needed.

Study activity

What are the benefits and drawbacks of using a zero-based budget for an annual music festival?

In addition to being familiar with methods of budgeting, such as continuation and zero-based approaches, it is important to realise the human dimension of budgeting. Event management is a people business and ultimately the extent to which business objectives are realised depends on the extent of staff motivation towards meeting targets. One of the great de-motivators in life is having targets imposed on you from above (top-down), without consultation. Equally, for management, there is nothing more depressing than letting staff set their own budgets and finding out that these so-called 'bottom-up' budgets do not deliver the organisation's overall business objectives. The compromise approach is for a participatory budgeting style whereby all staff whose performance will in part be judged by meeting the budget have some influence in the compilation of the figures by which they will be judged. There are no hard and fast rules about when to use top-down, bottom-up or participatory methods. Good managers need to have a broad range of skills and techniques in their managerial toolboxes. Furthermore, these skills and techniques should be used in a context-sensitive manner, contingent upon the particular circumstances of the business and its operating environment.

6.9 Applying budgeting to worked examples

Event organisers should report a summary of their financial transactions in two, or sometimes three, standard formats:

- the income statement (previously called the profit and loss account, or the income and expenditure statement in the case of non-profit organisations);
- the balance sheet (if the event is running through an established company); and
- the cash-flow statement.

The income statement is a measure of an organisation's financial performance; the balance sheet is a measure of financial position; and the cash-flow statement illustrates how the cash available to an organisation has changed over a given period of time. In financial terms, the answers to the questions 'Where are we now?' and 'Where are we going?' can be seen by constructing an income statement, balance sheet and cash-flow statement to show the change between the starting point and the end point. In this section, examples of the income statement and the cash-flow statement are modelled, and issues relating to them are discussed. (Should you wish to read about the balance sheet, you should follow up some of the additional activities at the end of this chapter.)

6.9.1 The income statement

Table 6.4 reproduces the first two columns from Table 6.3, above, and shows how a swimming club might produce a summary of its income statement for its event. The key message emerging from Table 6.4 is that the club is planning to make a surplus (profit) of £72 during the year (or event).

The problem with Table 6.4 is that a year is a long time, and it is unlikely that income and expenditure will occur at the same rate throughout the year. Indeed, as this statement reflects the event, it is likely that it reflects only the final position and the budget does not tell you when profits or losses will occur. Many events are seasonal and will have peaks and troughs in terms of their level of activity. This, in turn, has implications for other areas of management, such as staff scheduling and cash-flow management. If the data in Table 6.4 were to be allocated over twelve months on the basis of when such income and expenditure were predicted to occur, the monthly budget would appear like the example shown in Table 6.5. Remember that this is a

---

Table 6.4 An income statement

INCOME	This year (£)
Spectator Tickets	1,450
Other Ticket Sales	250
Sponsorship	1,700
Catering	220
Merchandising	130
Total Income	3,750
EXPENDITURE	
Volunteer Kit	700
Pool Hire	2,500
Marketing Activities	136
Administration	342
Total Expenditure	3,678
PROFIT / (LOSS)	72

Table 6.5 Swimming meet budget sub-analysed by month (£)

INCOME	Aug	Sept	Oct	Nov	Dec	Jan	Feb	March	April	May	June	July	Total
Spectator Tickets	0	0	0	0	0	0	0	0	1,450	0	0	0	1,450
Other Ticket Sales	0	0	0	0	0	0	0	0	250	0	0	0	250
Sponsorship	0	0	0	0	0	0	1,700	0	0	0	0	0	1,700
Catering	0	0	0	0	0	0	0	0	220	0	0	0	220
Merchandising	0	0	0	0	0	0	0	0	130	0	0	0	130
Total Income	0	0	0	0	0	0	1,700	0	2,050	0	0	0	3,750

EXPENDITURE	Aug	Sept	Oct	Nov	Dec	Jan	Feb	March	April	May	June	July	Total
Volunteer Kit	0	0	0	0	0	0	0	700	0	0	0	0	700
Pool Hire	0	0	0	0	0	0	0	0	0	2500	0	0	2,500
Marketing Activities	0	0	0	136	0	0	0	0	0	0	0	0	136
Administration	0	0	100	100	42	0	0	100	0	0	0	0	342
Total Expenditure	0	0	100	236	42	0	0	800	0	2,500	0	0	3,678
PROFIT / (LOSS)	0	0	-100	-236	-42	0	1,700	-800	2,050	-2,500	0	0	72
Cumulative	0	0	-100	-336	-378	-378	1,322	522	2,572	72	72	72	

157

relatively small swimming event and you may well have to include much more data – the principles are the same, though.

Two important points emerge from Table 6.5. First, simply by looking at the profit or loss per month, it is clear that the event's position in the calendar is a factor in the event's financial fortunes. Income is received from sponsors in February and again during the event in April in the form of spectator ticket sales and other ticket sales, while expenditure exceeds income in October, November and December, and again in March and May. This negative cash position must be managed. Second, a simple table of figures is not particularly helpful to somebody reading the budget. It would be much more helpful if the numbers were explained by a series of notes, such as the examples given below.

- Income: Spectator ticket sales will occur in April and we expect 580 spectators to purchase tickets at an average price of £2.50 (total = £1,450). (Last year, 500 sales @ £2.50 = £1,250.)
- Expenditure: Pool hire costs are based on a discounted rate and are paid in May, after the event has taken place. Costs are £2,500. (Last year, pool hire was £3,700.)

In practice, it would be expected that all items of income and expenditure would be qualified by a written explanation. By providing a brief written commentary to the key figures and assumptions that underpin the budget, it is possible for those people who look at it to have a much clearer idea of the organisation's plans. If the club planned to make a profit of £72 (financial performance), then it follows that the club's overall financial position would increase by £72.

For most sports managers, budgeting tends to start and end with a budgeted income statement, sub-analysed on a monthly basis (as in Table 6.5). This is a perfectly acceptable level of skill for most event managers. However, those who wish to have full responsibility for all aspects of an organisation's financial performance must also be able to produce and act upon budgeted income statements (balance sheets) and cash-flow statements.

In the next section, the review of budgeting concludes with an example of measuring actual performance against budget.

6.10 Comparing actual and budgeted performance

The ultimate purpose of budgeting is to assist managers in the planning, decision-making and control of a business. To achieve this aim, periodic comparison of actual performance compared with planned or budgeted performance is required. Table 6.6 is an example of how such a comparison might be presented to the managers of an organisation. The columns in this table are explained below.

- 'Actual' income and expenditure refers to entries made to an organisation's accounting system which are supportable by documentary evidence, such as invoices, receipts, staff time sheets and so on. 'Actual' figures are drawn from the financial accounting systems and can be supported by an audit trail of evidence.
- 'Incurred' (or 'committed') expenditure refers to expenditure which relates to the financial period in question that we know has been made, but has not been billed for, as yet. This sort of data can be picked up from such documentation as purchase order forms. When producing timely budget reports, it is sometimes not possible to wait until all of the paperwork relating to expenditure in a period has been received. Thus, in order to reflect a more realistic picture of events, the 'Incurred' column is used to log known expenditure

Table 6.6 Actual versus budget comparison

INCOME (£)	Actual	Incurred	Total	Budget	Variance	Direction	Note
Spectator Tickets	1,450		1,450	1,350	100	F	1
Other Ticket Sales	250		250	0	250	F	
Sponsorship	1,700		1,700	1,800	−100	U	2
Catering	220		220	200	20	F	
Merchandising	130		130	100	30	F	
Total Income	3,750	0	3,750	3,450	300	F	3
EXPENDITURE (£)							
Voulunteer Kit	700		700	600	100	U	4
Pool Hire	2,500	0	2,500	3,000	−500	F	5
Marketing Activities	136		136	140	−4	F	
Administration	342	50	392	400	−8	F	
Total Expenditure	3,678	50	3,728	4,140	−412	F	
PROFIT / (LOSS)	72	−50	22	−690	712	F	6

that is not formally in the books of account. This column tends to be used only for expenditure; it would be unusual to have incurred income.
- 'Total' is simply the sum of the 'Actual' and the 'Incurred' columns.
- 'Budget' refers to the approved budget for a given financial period.
- 'Variance' is the difference between the 'Total' column and the 'Budget' column.
- 'Direction' is a reference to whether the variance on any given line of the budget is favourable (F) or unfavourable (U). One characteristic of good information is that it is relevant to the intended recipient. For non-finance specialists, spelling out whether a variance is favourable or unfavourable is a helpful aid to understanding the underlying meaning of the figures.
- 'Note' is a cross-reference to a written qualitative explanation of a variance. Numbers in isolation do not explain a variance, so it is sometimes useful for a written explanation to accompany some of the more significant variances.

To illustrate how qualitative explanations can help to explain the meaning of variances, presented below are examples of the notes that might have accompanied the actual versus budget comparison in Table 6.6. Note how these notes are written in the form of a report and can be cross-referenced easily to Table 6.6.

EVENT BUDGET REPORT
To: Swimming Committee
From: Event Manager
Date: 10 September 2011
Re: Actual versus Budget Notes

- Note 1: Spectator Ticket Sales – Spectator ticket sales (580 at £2.50) were 40 ahead of target (540 at £2.50). More spectator ticket sales have been achieved by encouraging people who attended the event in the past to return this year.
- Note 2: Sponsorship – Following the renegotiation of last year's agreements with our club's partners, we were able to secure £1,700 in sponsorship (£100 below our target). This unfavourable result was due to one company having to reduce its involvement due to market pressures.
- Note 3: Total Income – Total income is £300 ahead of target following strong spectator ticket sales. However, it is not all net gain (see Note 6, below).
- Note 4: Volunteer Kit – The increase in event size necessitated an increase in the number of volunteers and therefore an overspend of £100 against budget. Our club policy is to reward these volunteers for their time with an event T-shirt, and we purchased twenty additional items at a cost of £5 per item.
- Note 5: Pool Hire – Pool hire costs were £500 below budget due to an improved discount from the facility. We have reached an agreement to pay this set fee for the next five years.
- Note 6: The Bottom Line – The event had been due to record a loss of £690 following an agreement at the last Annual General Meeting. However, strong ticket sales and a significant reduction in pool hire costs (due to the five-year agreement) mean that the event has made a small surplus of £72. This surplus will be reinvested into the swimming club to provide support to transportation costs for away galas.

Signed
Event Manager

Any chairperson/director reading the above report would be able to grasp the basic point that the event performed ahead of budget and had secured future discounts for the benefit of the club. At this stage, the actual versus budget comparison would be noted and no action would need to be taken, other than to congratulate and encourage those responsible for delivering the better-than-anticipated performance.

Study activity

Why is it important to compare budgets with actual performance, and how frequently should a manager do this for: (a) small events; (b) annual events; and (c) major events?

6.11 Summary

The purpose of this chapter has been to demonstrate the importance of financial management within an events management context. While any detailed analysis was beyond the scope of the chapter, provision has been made to equip managers with the necessary skills to communicate, in basic terms, the financial sustainability of an event. The cyclical process of planning, decision-making and control, coupled with the analytical techniques that can be applied to management accounting information, should enhance the toolbox of skills that any event manager should possess. The importance of this process should not be underestimated in both profit and not-for-profit events, regardless of size or stature.

The main objective of all events should be to operate within their own resources so that they can be sustainable and so that people can appreciate their value. The tools identified in this chapter, including budgeting, should help this process. Furthermore, using financial and management accounting information as two sides of the same coin – which is rarely acknowledged – will help provide managers with the discipline and confidence to plan, make effective decisions and exercise financial control.

The income statement, balance sheet and cash-flow statement equip managers with information that can determine the financial performance and position of an organisation and demonstrate the difference between profit and the typically scarce resource of cash. In addition, it can be determined whether the event should be held and whether you or your competitors can pay their debts as they fall due.

It has not been possible to cover all event finance information and budgetary techniques here. However, you should have grasped the idea that financial management is important enough to be considered an integral part of any event. Other skills are required to come up with a marketing campaign or a training and development plan, but only those who understand finance can establish whether they are financially viable, worthwhile or even necessary. The best way to ensure that you develop the full range of financial management skills is to achieve a thorough understanding of the theoretical concepts involved and some tangible experience of event finance in practice.

Further reading

For guidance on recording and reporting financial information, and for more detail on performing a thorough financial health analysis, see:

Wilson, R. (2011) *Managing Sport Finance*, Abingdon: Routledge.
Wilson, R. and Joyce, J. (2008) *Finance for Sport and Leisure Managers: An Introduction*, Abingdon: Routledge.

For more information on general event funding and financial planning see:

Masterman, G. (2009) Financial Planning and Control, in *Strategic Sport Event Management*, London: Butterworth-Heinemann.
Phoenix, F. and Wilson, R. (2009) Managing Events, in K. Bill (ed.) *Sport Management*, Exeter: Learning Matters.
Watt, D. C. (1998) Funding, in *Event Management in Leisure and Tourism*, Harlow: Longman.

A general view of accounting in leisure is given in:

Owen, G. (1994) *Accounting for Hospitality, Tourism and Leisure*, London: Pitman Publishing.

Chapter 7

Event marketing

Contents

7.1 Aims

By the end of this chapter, students will be able:

- To describe practical event market analysis methods and considerations and explain marketing planning components.
- To explain basic customer-focused event marketing terminology and the role of new media in event marketing.
- To evaluate the relevance of event marketing as an effective relationship-building tool.
- To describe the role of event sponsorship and understand the process of attracting suitable event sponsors.
- To explain the process of managing the sponsorship process and sponsor relationships and current issues facing event managers in relations to sponsorship.

7.2 Introduction

There have been significant challenges for the development of effective event marketing analysis, planning, implementation and control methods. This chapter will attempt to highlight the crucial and changing role of the sponsor in modern events, where connection is made between the development of the relevance of the media to modern events, the scope for communication of sponsorship messages to specific audiences and the significant cost recovery potential to event managers. In addition to the advantages of sponsorship to events, some of the main challenges facing this important activity will be explored.

It is important to understand what marketing can bring to the discipline of events management and to be clear about what 'event marketing' means. (Event experience is an important part of event marketing, and this has already been covered in Chapter 3.) Event marketing is: 'the process by which event managers and marketers gain an understanding of their potential consumers' characteristics and needs in order to produce, price, promote and distribute an event experience that meets these needs and the objectives of the special event' (Bowdin *et al.* 2011: 367). Bowdin *et al.*'s definition emphasises the fact that events should be seen as 'special' and that each event merits its own distinct marketing plan. However, this definition does not emphasise the need to build up longer-term relationships with event consumers. Marketing should certainly not be seen as a bolt-on activity, nor viewed as merely the creative part of the event planning process. Perhaps an all too familiar view is that marketing commences once the event has been booked and the starting date set; but in this instance, what many event managers understand to be marketing is actually advertising. In fact, advertising is only part of the marketing process. Marketing must be viewed as a discipline that is important *before* the event takes place and as one that is used *during* the event and *after* it has finished. It is also the responsibility of everyone involved with the running of the event, not just of the marketing department or team. Certainly, it is important to make it clear to everybody involved in an event that customer satisfaction should be at the heart of everything that event organisers do.

The event attendee looks for a 'lifestyle experience' (Allen *et al.* 2011) and something that they will remember as interesting, memorable and exciting. This is sometimes known as the '3Es' of event marketing – entertainment, excitement and enterprise (Hoyle, 2002). The event attendee wants to be entertained by the event, anticipates feeling some excitement as a result of the element of celebration at the event, and expects event organisers to innovate or show enterprise.

Event marketing

Event marketers should differentiate between events that target consumers – B2C – and those that are aimed at business or trades – B2B – as these groups may have different motivations for attending. In B2C, the event attendee is a private consumer who is attending for personal motives, such as to see a favourite musician or to attend a festival. B2B customers are more likely to attend principally for business reasons, such as those who visit the Nuremberg Toy Fair (see below). The task of the event marketer becomes more complex when some events attract both business customers and private customers who are interested in the theme of the event. For instance, the model train section of a toy fair attracts professional buyers as well as hundreds of enthusiasts who are keen to see the latest developments in their hobby.

7.3 Event marketing planning

The most effective way for an event manager to coordinate the marketing activities for their event is to develop them within a marketing plan. The key purpose of the marketing plan is to identify the current situation in which event organisers find themselves and then to map out a path for the events management team to follow. As in any plan, the event marketing team should then undertake the necessary evaluation to see if they have achieved their goals. Using McDonald's established marketing plan (see Figure 7.1), these main areas of marketing planning are:

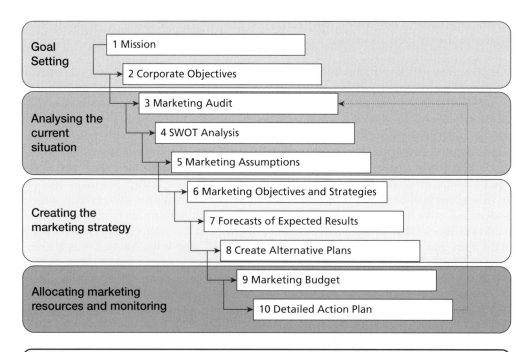

Figure 7.1 McDonald's marketing planning process
Source: Adapted from McDonald and Wilson 2011

- To set goals.
- To analyse the current situation.
- To create the marketing strategy.
- To allocate marketing resources and to monitor or evaluate the plan.

It is critical that the people responsible for marketing an event are clear about the goals that need to be set for it. The event's mission, or that of the events management organisation, should remind the staff working on it exactly what its purpose is. The mission of a corporate event organiser might merely entail becoming a key player in its market. The award-winning event company Mike Burton sets out to 'exceed expectations' and to 'live up to promises', and this mission seems to have served it well for the past thirty years. The simplest mission statements are often the most effective to communicate to an events team. Setting corporate objectives are also targets that the event organisers can use to guide the direction of their business. These might entail being the most recognised brand in the sector within five years, or to have the highest satisfaction levels of volunteers in the industry.

After setting the mission statement, the next stage is to analyse the current situation of the event through the use of market research. This looks at the capabilities of the organisers and how they are positioned in the market, and evaluates their marketing strengths. The main tool in this exercise, as shown in Figure 7.2, is a SWOT analysis. The 'internal analysis' shows the strengths (S) and weaknesses (W) of the organisation, while the 'external analysis' illustrates those factors which present the greatest opportunities (O) – such as market data which show increased attendances at music events – and threats (T) – such as the introduction of new safety legislation that might demand increased expenditure.

The next stage is to set marketing objectives in quantifiable terms – for example, using research data to show why people attend an event – which are used to clarify what the marketing team has to achieve. These might specify the levels of customer satisfaction or enjoyment expected at an event, or the level of awareness resulting from marketing activities. A typical example of a marketing objective might be to receive positive feedback about the event from

	Strengths	Weaknesses
Internal	1 Established longer than competitors' events 2 Strong brand image 3 High levels of customer feedback 4 High customer loyalty	1 Low volunteer retention 2 Low use of web-based applications
	Opportunities	Threats
External	1 To set up an additional event in a new venue 2 To sell more tickets to overseas visitors 3 To increase sponsorship revenue	1 New safety regulations for events 2 Leading competitor has grown more than current industry average 3 Key target group has reduced spending power

Figure 7.2 SWOT analysis

more than 75 per cent of all attendees, or to achieve 40 per cent of sales from previous event attendees. Once the marketing objectives have been identified and the budget determined, a detailed action plan will list exactly what needs to be done, by whom and when.

7.3.1 Expectations of event attendees

As the event market becomes more competitive, and more events take place, it is critical to understand the demands and expectations of attendees. To what extent has the organiser considered the concept of entertainment inertia, and that a percentage of their target group might choose not to attend because their diary is already full with other events? Can this potential consumer justify giving up time and money to attend another event (Wakefield 2007)? Is this a very important event in the lives of those attending, with a reputation for delivering enjoyment or excitement?

An attendee's expectation of an event is unlikely to be based solely on the experience of the performer or enjoyment of the event theme. Level of service, or service quality, is also important. The issue of service quality is well established, and researchers such as O'Neill and Wakefield have shown links between service quality and customer satisfaction, even though many of these event experiences are also considered to be 'intangible' and therefore hard to measure (O'Neill et al. 1999). Event managers are increasingly turning to SERVQUAL customer service software, which considers people's expectations of service and measures this against their experience of service delivery. However, one can assume that there is a level of expectation of quality of service for most event attendees. In some cases, just asking the question, 'How easy is it for people to get to my event?' might help the organiser to identify factors which could affect attendance (Wakefield 2007). While factors such as availability of parking space, ease of access, refreshments, toilets, signage and the helpfulness of event staff might not be considered crucial, it is a straightforward exercise to gauge attendees' attitudes to these points through a carefully constructed questionnaire (O'Neill et al. 1999).

7.3.2 Market research for events

The main aim of conducting market research is to try to reduce the risk of running an unsuccessful event and to help meet the objectives of the event organisers (Goldblatt 2011). Without doubt, the main research tool used in event research is the questionnaire. A well-constructed and -tested questionnaire allows a sample of people to give important feedback about all aspects of the event, and it can be the basis for producing meaningful research data to help guide decision-making. The questionnaire should not be seen as the only tool in the armoury of the market researcher, but it does have a significant role to play in events management. For the event manager, engaging in market research should become an important part of their role. Published market research reports for the events industry are limited, but there is nothing to stop event organisers building up their own market research data. This will not only help organisers make more informed decisions about events but will be an important aid in attracting sponsorship.

Event managers can also use market research to help them predict the likely attendance at a new event. Using the Market Breakdown Calculator (MBC) is a good way to estimate the likely demand for an event by using market research, and it allows the event manager to input some of their own experience and knowledge of that particular event market. In Table 7.1 the MBC shows how to measure the likely attendance at a wedding fair, which is targeted predominantly at brides-to-be. It is expected that most of the attendees will be female; will live within fifty kilometres of the venue; will be aged between eighteen and thirty-five; will have had the

Table 7.1 Using the Market Breakdown Calculator to calculate likely attendance at a wedding fair

Source: Holden and Wilde 2007

Variable	% Value	Population	Source of information
Population within 50km of event venue	100%	1,000,000	National statistics
Females	51%	510,000	National statistics
Females 18–35	30%	153,000	National statistics
Females 18–35 not married but in a relationship	40%	61,200	National statistics
ABC1 – Middle Class	65%	39,780	Marketing pocket book
Number of people likely to react to adverts (adverts shown four times)	20%	7,956	Advertising industry averages
Actual number who will follow up this interest	40%	3,182	Industry experience
Likely to bring two other people	× 2	6,364 visitors	

opportunity to see four adverts promoting the event; will have been in a relationship for more than six months; will be in one of the higher socio-economic groups; and will probably bring at least one other person with them.

Using this method, the overall population of the targeted area is calculated and the key criteria for the target group are established. Then, by a process of elimination, those who are unlikely to attend are subtracted. This initial calculation shows that there are likely to be 3,182 in the target group, each of whom should bring one other person to the event, making a segment size of 6,364 visitors. Of course, this is only one of the likely target groups, and the process can be repeated for other segments, with calculations revised when new research data become available. Market research data can be used in the MBC and while many of the calculations are only estimates, the outcomes are better than complete guesswork. Using a spreadsheet means that the variables can be quickly changed. If there is another wedding fair running simultaneously in the area, then the event organisers must try to calculate what impact such competition will have on their event.

7.3.2.1 Observation as a research method

Attending an event and taking notes about customer behaviour or their interaction with the event is another way of researching events. This is often called 'participant observation'. To use this research technique, rather than asking attendees about their experiences, researchers attend an event as if they themselves were attendees, record their observations of attendees' behaviour, and then listen for comments made by participants that might give further insight into their views of the event. However, it is important to be aware of the ethical guidelines concerning this type of research, and researchers should not do anything that might impact on people's enjoyment of the event or research in such a way that might endanger those attending or participating.

Researchers who attended the Coca-Cola Masters Surfing Event in Australia as observers were able to capture important information about the event experience. When supported by formal feedback through a questionnaire, this gave a more accurate impression of attendees' levels of satisfaction (O'Neill *et al.* 1999).

7.3.2.2 Secondary research

The key starting point for research data about the events market is published or secondary data in journal or book form. In some countries, this data might be available for free through such institutions as business libraries. Industry bodies might also produce annual reports on the events industry, and this data can be key in helping to develop marketing plans. Typical secondary reports for the events industry are Mintel's *Ticketing Purchase Process: Sports Events and Concerts in the USA* (available at http://www.oxygen.mintel.com) and Key Note's *Exhibitions and Conferences 2011* (available at http://www.keynote.co.uk).

7.3.3 Stakeholders

While consumers are the most important group for an event manager, there are other key people to consider – stakeholders. (These people will be covered in more detail in Chapter 9.) An event stakeholder is any group or individual with influence over the running of an event or someone who might be affected by the event. Allen *et al.* (2011) refer to the most important stakeholders as 'key players'. The event manager should consider what each of these stakeholders is seeking to gain from the event.

The importance of stakeholder groups varies from event to event, but many, such as the Planning Department at the local council, are important groups for a number of events as they are often required to grant permission before an event can take place. The key to successful stakeholder analysis is not only to identify the most important groups but to manage communication with them and consider which messages are sent to them. This is illustrated in Table 7.2, where some key stakeholders are identified. This list is not exhaustive and serves only to demonstrate how many important stakeholders there are. This table can be adapted to any number of events and new stakeholder groups can be introduced. The local bank, for example, is important to help the event organiser secure funding to cope with the high levels of investment needed to launch the event, but it helps the bank management to make their decision when they see how much publicity the event is receiving and how much it is likely to impact on the local economy and community. Event sponsors are also key stakeholders. These will be covered later in this chapter.

Study activity

Using the structure in Table 7.2, choose five stakeholder groups (one of which must be attendees) for a new three-day music festival that will take place on the outskirts of your town. At this event, 3000 people are expecting to see 10 bands, with around 1500 of the attendees arriving by car, and as many as 2000 camping in a nearby field.

Stakeholder groups	Most appropriate means of communication	Current links with stakeholder (key people or groups)
Local government Planning Department	Written report to the Planning Department and a meeting to discuss the impact of the event in the chosen area	Planning Director Head of Planning Department Director of Cultural and Sporting Events
Governing body for the event	Letter Meetings Report of previous event	Supported by an association – International Festivals and Events Association (IFEA)
Local community	Local newspapers Radio stations Local television station Leaflets, letters and brochures Newsletters	Community leaders representing particular areas of town Police team responsible for local community
The media	Events management journals Local newspapers Local TV Websites	Journalists in each publication with responsibility for events; specifically named correspondents Radio and TV news departments

Table 7.2 Event stakeholders

7.3.4 Segmenting the events market and why people attend

While it might be assumed that people are attending an event for the same reason, research shows that attendees often have different motivations and come from a range of backgrounds (Fink *et al.* 2002). How many people are attending an event for the first time, perhaps out of curiosity or as a result of promotional initiatives, and how many are regular attendees? By applying the principles of market segmentation, event managers can divide their attendees into clearly identifiable groups, ideally starting with their motivation for attendance. Capturing data about the social group, age and marital status is basic demographic information, but this is a useful starting point for segmenting events. Kahle *et al.* (1996) looked at the reasons why people attend sporting events, but some of these reasons probably apply to other types of event, too. If event managers are able to identify specific segments and their motivations for attending, then it should be possible to send tailored messages to each of these groups.

Kahle *et al.* (1996) discovered that fans attend sporting events because they enjoy the camaraderie of attending with like-minded people, and they sometimes feel obligated to attend as a result of a history of attending. It seems plausible that such reasons will motivate people

169

to attend music or arts events, too. Some of the people who attend an event may well do so just because they like to go to a variety of events – they like to spend time with friends and enjoy the excitement of the build-up and the unpredictability. This is a significant segment, so it is important to capture their contact details.

Kim and Chalip (2004) developed a conceptual model to identify why people attend events. Their research focused on 'push factors', such as age, gender, education, income and previous attendance at events, and linked these to 'mediating factors', such as the attraction of the event and interest in the event. They found that the perceived risk of attending and financial constraints impacted on intention to attend.

Research will often show important reasons why people attend events and help event managers to make more informed decisions about their events. Nicholson and Pearce (2001) looked at the Wildfoods Festival, which incorporated four different events, and found that the most important factor for attendance was because attendees were specifically interested in one of the activities on offer, such as food and wine tasting.

In many cases, attendees might just come along in order to meet new people. A feature of many developed countries is the mobility of labour, with people taking jobs away from the place where they grew up. Single people will therefore attend events on their own or as part of organised groups as a way of enriching their social lives (Melnick 1993).

7.3.5 Event objectives

Many events have set capacities for attendees and participants. Goal-setting for an event with a stadium capacity of 50,000 people is relatively straightforward and just a matter of working out who these 50,000 people will be. Many event managers use customer relationship management (CRM) databases to manage lists of existing customers. This also includes such areas as loyalty cards for event attendees to encourage attendance at future events. Football clubs in England and NFL franchises in the United States often have huge databases, sometimes containing details of more than 400,000 contacts, and these can be important starting points in helping them sell out their venues.

A simple objective might be to achieve a 70 per cent level of satisfaction with the event, which can be measured by a survey of a sample of those who attended. An event organiser should be careful not to assume that most people who attended were happy if they have no evidence to back up this opinion.

7.3.6 Event marketing mix

The next stage of the event marketing plan – the marketing strategy phase in McDonald's marketing plan structure – is to consider the elements of the marketing mix and break them down into discrete components. For event marketing, these components are usually broken down into Booms and Bitner's '7Ps': product, place, price, promotion, people, process and physical evidence, although some researchers use only five categories (Hoyle 2002). The latter include the make-up of the event product and the range of activities built into the event; the place or location which is most appropriate to deliver the right event experience; the pricing levels which represent value for money for those attending while maximising revenue; the promotion or publicity that can be generated in the media to help publicise and make stakeholders aware of the event; and knowing how to position the event in the minds of potential attendees so that they might consider attending it again in the future.

Events also have different characteristics, such as intangibility, inseparability, variability and perishability (Blythe 2009). Research by Lovelock and Gummerson (2004) found that most

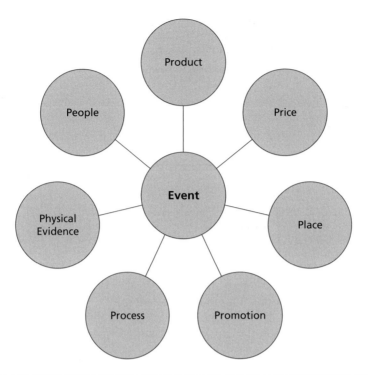

Figure 7.3 Event marketing mix
Source: Adapted from Booms and Bitner 1981

writers on services marketing referred to the four characteristics of intangibility, heterogeneity, inseparability and perishability. An event is not a physical product – it is intangible – so it is difficult to promote without an understanding of the event experience that appeals to attendees. Booms and Bitner (1981) suggest that the event attendee therefore requires some physical evidence of their event experience. One way of addressing the issue of intangibility is to provide merchandising, such as T-shirts at music events, which act as tangible reminders of the event. The event itself is produced and consumed at the same time, so these are inseparable, which means that planning the event experience is also critical. The event production is variable, as the experience of the attendee at music festival or show is not guaranteed, and in a sporting event the outcome is uncertain. Finally, most events are perishable, because empty seats cannot be sold and potential revenue is lost once they have begun.

7.3.6.1 Event attributes and branding
Developing a recognisable brand and improving brand image are critical for event planners. These should not be seen as separate activities but as parts of the overall marketing plan. Blythe (2009) suggests that a consumer receives the following benefits from a brand:

- self-image
- quality
- cost

- expected performance
- differentiation from competing brands.

Consumers of prestigious events have an expected level of performance and quality, which are usually differentiated from competing events, where its cost reflects the status of the event and the event helps to improve aspects of their self-image. The physical evidence of the brand comes in the form of the brand name and logo, which are often an attendee's first view of the event in publicity material, so event organisers should invest in the outward appearance of these to items.

7.3.6.2 Event pricing and break-even analysis

Pricing strategies should reflect the objectives of an event organiser and should offer the potential customer value for money, while also taking the pricing of competitor events into consideration. An important starting point for price setting is to establish the break-even point. This is the point at which all the costs of the event are matched by the total revenue. If the total cost of the event is £10,000, and the typical cost of a ticket is £10, the break-even point is the sale of 1000 tickets. Hitting this target as early as possible will allow the event manager to relax, at least a little. (See Chapter 4 for more on ticketing.)

The week-long Docklands Comedy Festival in London, which attracts a number of well-known celebrities, is free to attend, as it is entirely financed by the sponsorship of large banks that are based in the area. This is also the case for the Nuremberg Classic Music Party in the Park, a biannual classical music concert that is free to enter for over 10,000 people because it is entirely financed by local businesses.

7.3.6.3 Demand-oriented pricing

Demand-oriented pricing takes into account the various market segments which are attracted to events, allowing the attendee more options to purchase. This requires a more sophisticated approach to pricing and a better understanding of how people buy. The different levels of price might reflect the position of the seats at the event or built-in extras, such as free gifts, discounted refreshments, free car parking and free event literature. Event marketers should always try to add value when they review their pricing, rather than take the riskier option of discounting. Price reductions serve to devalue the event and can ultimately lead to a fall in total revenue, presenting the event manager with the task of investing more money to try to generate new attendees to make up for the resulting shortfall in revenue.

This approach to adding value is also referred to as 'upgrading' (Wakefield 2007). The customer who paid £30 for a ticket to last year's event might be happy to pay £35 this year if they get a better seat, a free drink in the bar and a 20 per cent discount voucher to purchase merchandise. More importantly, this represents another sale to an existing customer and possibly increases their loyalty to the event. Increasingly, consumers expect to be able to purchase tickets online, so these should be made available, but again with added value. Online ticketing is a quicker way of generating extra sales without the cost of employing ticket sellers, and for certain groups of event attendees this is their preferred purchasing method. Moreover, setting up online payment is a relatively straightforward procedure for event organisers (Holden 2008).

7.3.6.4 All-inclusive pricing

This is sometimes referred to as a 'package price'. It offers the event attendee added value while maintaining revenue levels. For some people, the ticket price might be set at an acceptable level, but they might still be dissuaded attending if they think they will not be able to buy affordable, good-quality food at the event. Such people's concerns might be alleviated with the offer of an all-inclusive ticket.

7.3.7 Event distribution channels

'Place' is where the event experience is delivered and also where the distribution of tickets takes place (Blythe 2009). This includes websites, which are now an essential support tool for most events. The main functions of an event website are to remind people about the event experience, to facilitate the sale of merchandise and to make it easier to purchase tickets. For loyal event attendees, the website should manage their expectations and keep them up-to-date with news and developments about the event, performing the role of an online newspaper or magazine, or replacing the products that event managers use to publicise their events. The event manager can also use social media networks and e-mail to disseminate information to potential customers.

7.3.8 Event promotion

A perceptual map is an important technique in the positioning of an event. It requires an understanding of how consumers view events, and also takes into account their attitudes to competitors' events.

In Figure 7.4 the hypothetical Premier Arts Festival (PAF) is positioned using eight variables, which represent the attendee's view of the event experience and also take into account the views of competitors' events. The data needed for this analysis can be provided by questionnaires. In Figure 7.4 the PAF ranks lower on all-inclusive tickets and its range of additional services than

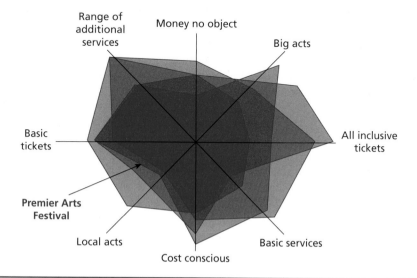

Figure 7.4 Perceptual map for an arts festival

Wedding Magazine

- Readership = 200,000 adults monthly
- Coverage (of ABC1 females) = 60.000 monthly)
- = 1% of total UK population of AB females

- Our campaign runs for six months/editions
- Max reach (assuming no duplication) = 360,000
- Max frequency (assuming all duplicated) = 6 OTS

Figure 7.5 Measuring the impact of adverts

all of its competitors. These results show the event marketer areas where improvements need to be made.

Advertising represents additional cost for an event marketer, so it is essential to understand what impact this has and how its effectiveness can be measured, in order that realistic targets might be set. In Figure 7.5 the impact of placing an advert for a wedding fair in a wedding magazine is evaluated. The advert is placed every month for six months. The target group of 60,000 women therefore have six opportunities to see (OTS) the advert, making a total maximum reach of 360,000, assuming that nobody sees the advert more than once. If only 5 per cent of this group do anything as a result of seeing the advert, then this represents 18,000 people. If the total cost of six adverts is £36,000, then the cost of reaching each of these people is £2. Similar calculations can be used for other forms of advertising, but the most important consideration is that advertising does not have the impact that novice event managers often expect it to have.

CASE STUDY 7.1

Convention of the National Soccer Coaches Association (NSCAA)

Location: Philadelphia, USA
Attendance: 8500

The NSCAA national convention is one of the biggest events in the soccer (football, to the rest of the world) calendar. It has been held for more than sixty years. Such is the scale and importance of the event that the dates are already set for the next ten years. It has 8500 visitors (out of a total of 26,000 registered football coaches), many of whom are actively coaching football teams and are therefore in regular contact with around 500,000 football players. The convention attracts 300 companies, predominantly from the USA, who hire around 700 booths, which has increased yearly over the past ten years. The organisers' aim is to provide an environment where those attending can have fun, excitement and learning opportunities, which involves attracting the most appropriate exhibitors. They create the perfect platform for attendees to observe coaching classes and to mix with important people from the world of football coaching. Usually, at least three high-profile soccer coaches or administrators are recruited to put on shows.

The number of overseas visitors to the convention is increasing, as the rest of the football world starts to wake up to the size of the youth football market in the USA. Trade exhibitors can demonstrate the latest in coaching equipment, footwear and clothing, technological innovations, as well as additional services, such as financial services, insurance and travel. Recent exciting changes include Major League Soccer's (MLS) Superdraft, where young players are given the opportunity to have trials with MLS teams.

The NSCAA generates additional revenue by selling advertising space in its publications. The *Soccer Journal* is sent to all 26,000 members and an online magazine called *The Technical Area* is e-mailed twice a week to members. Advertisers can also purchase mailing lists which allow them to target all members, providing the NSCAA with additional revenue. Exhibitors are also encouraged to join the corporate membership programme, which offers additional benefits and the chance to network with current members, such as Adidas.

Away from the daytime convention, the NSCAA attracts sponsors to host evening activities at clubs and restaurants, with partners including hotels, restaurants and bars. Rooms are provided for NSCAA committee meetings, and awards ceremonies are hosted to recognise achievement in football coaching.

The convention is usually held during the second or third week in January – in the middle of the traditional break for most clubs based in the north of the USA – which helps to ensure high attendance figures. With increasing numbers of participants, exhibitors and attendees, the convention looks set to continue its growth and enhance its reputation as an important part of the US football market.

Study activity

As the event director for the NSCAA, suggest five or six marketing objectives that you would set for next year's convention.

7.3.9 E-marketing and internet marketing

It is important to clarify the meaning of the terms 'e-marketing' and 'internet marketing', as they are often used interchangeably. According to Chaffey *et al.* (2006: 252), internet marketing is 'achieving marketing objectives through applying digital technologies', which include websites, e-mail, wireless or mobile, and digital television. E-marketing refers to all of these too, but also to 'digital customer data and electronic customer relationship management systems'.

The fast pace of development in e-marketing and web-based technologies continues to present ever more opportunities and threats to event marketers. However, whenever an event manager decides to use any of these new applications, they must do so because they see it as a means of improving the overall consumer experience, not just because it is administratively more efficient or a lower-cost option than traditional methods. The challenge for the event marketer is to use these applications to improve overall marketing performance without creating distance from customers (Holden 2008).

The areas that event managers should focus on when developing their e-marketing plan are as follows:

- Information strategy – knowing what information the customer needs and providing it.
- Production/delivery strategy – knowing how the product or service (including information) can reach the customer, despite their dealing with the marketing team from a distance.
- Organisational strategy – what needs to happen in the business to enable everything else to happen for the customer.
- Assessment strategy – a way of monitoring success and failure.
- Marketing strategy – focusing on customers to steer all of the above in the direction the company needs to follow to achieve its aim. (adapted from Holden 2008)

Managers must ensure that the information needs of attendees are identified, and must then focus on the production and delivery of the event so that customer needs are satisfied. It is also vital to ensure that the whole event team is aware of the benefits of these applications and that evaluation techniques are used to assess the success or failure of the event. The final component is to build e-marketing activities into the overall marketing plan.

The World Wide Web (WWW) enables users of the internet to share information in the form of text, pictures or sounds, and it is a perfect vehicle through which event managers may communicate with key stakeholders (De Pelsmacker *et al.* 2010). For many international event attendees, the internet is usually their first point of contact when seeking information, so it is important for the event organisers to present their event in a professional manner. Web-based applications have built-in measurement tools, such as Google Analytics™, which show how many people have visited a website, the amount of time that each visitor spends on a web page, and if any of the site visitors have requested further information or purchased anything. When a website is visited and the contents of a banner advert are accessed, this is called the 'click-through', so the 'clickthrough rate' is the proportion of website visitors who click on an advert (Chaffey *et al.* 2006).

Google Analytics™ has several other useful features, too:

- Advanced segmentation – This enables the event manager to segment their visitors by region, by number of visits to the site, by revenue generated per customer, and so on.
- Analytics intelligence – Here, any significant changes in data are noted and automatically pointed out to the site manager.
- Custom reports – All data on Google Analytics™ can be used to produce reports which present data in a more professional format.

- Advanced analysis tools – Extra tools enable the analysis of data using multiple dimensions and features that filter data. (http://www.googlenalytics.com)

If an event website is used to sell advertising space, payment will usually be based on how many people clickthrough the advertiser's banner advert. It is important for the event manager to ensure that their website appears near the top of search engines, such as Google, a process called 'search engine optimisation'. Clearly, more organisations are now using web technology, as the number of adverts that appear online is growing by as much as 20 per cent per annum, perhaps encouraged by the built-in feedback that web technology provides (De Pelsmacker *et al.* 2010). Selling sponsorship on the event website is also possible, with the rate paid based on the number of visitors to the site, the time spent on the site and any data that show the type of visitors to the site.

Ever more event managers are now organising online, or virtual, events. One company in Australia – Online Events – specialises in this and has a growing number of people registering for its events. It hosts corporate events and conferences that can be broadcast to several countries simultaneously via the web (see http://www.onlineevents.com.au/). Increasingly, event managers are also using Facebook's 'Events' pages to encourage their attendees and supporters to post information and to inform followers about the next event (see Chapter 15 for more on social networking websites).

Study activity

How might social networking sites, such as Facebook, be used to support the activities of an event's marketing manager? You should focus principally on promotion, pricing, brand image and working with stakeholders.

As the vice-president of the Phoenix Suns NBA basketball team stated at the Sports Marketing Association Annual Conference in 2005, 'I sometimes think that the internet was invented for our business.' The fact is that the internet helps event managers to sell and distribute their tickets and provide information to stakeholder groups. Web-based applications are still evolving but they are already essential tools for event managers (Holden 2008). Consumers now expect events to have their own websites or pages, and increasing numbers of people are purchasing tickets online. For instance, when the O2 Arena in London announced that 20,000 tickets were available for a Tina Turner concert, they sold out online in less than an hour, with many bought by overseas customers. In total, sales were over £1 million. The Olympic Delivery Authority (ODA) sold the majority of its tickets for the London Olympics online in special auctions, with 1.3 million people applying for only 30,000 tickets that were available for the men's 100-metre final alone (Topping *et al.* 2011). Efficient ticketing systems not only benefit customers but enable the event manager to process money from ticket sales more effectively.

7.4 Event sponsorship

The events business provides some of the best examples of how sponsorship works, with some of the biggest sponsorship deals linked to major events. According to BDS (2010), sponsorship is: 'a business relationship between a provider of funds, resources or services and an individual,

Image 7.1 Virgin Racing media launch
Source: Jeff J. Mitchell / Getty Images

event or organisation which offers in return rights and association that may be used for commercial advantage in return for the sponsorship investment'.

As more companies research their sponsorship activities, they forge better relationships with their sponsors. Some sponsorship managers have changed their job titles to 'relationship manager' or 'partnership manager', to demonstrate the increased importance of their role. The practice of sponsoring events is well established. For instance, car manufacturers frequently supported early motor races by providing cars, expert mechanics or tyres at reduced cost because their association with the event helped promote their core business to participants and spectators.

As the events market grows, so event managers must learn about the increasing cost-recovery possibilities that sponsorship presents. While sponsorship is a key function for some companies, the fact remains that the majority have not thought to use it as a marketing tool because they have not been approached by event managers.

7.4.1 Attracting sponsors

The first consideration for event managers who are looking to secure sponsorship is to ask how much money they might secure. Clearly, their goal is to try to get as much as possible in order to make the event more viable and ultimately more successful. The value of any sponsorship deal is subject to the following:

- How much coverage will the event receive in the media (press, radio, television, web)?
- Who will be taking part in the event?

- Who will attend the event?
- What, in particular (value), might the sponsor gain by supporting this event?
- What help could be provided to make the partnership a success, such as the number of staff who might be allocated to look after the sponsor at the event?

Finding the answers to these questions will depend on securing data from events through market research. Some of this data will be generated by the event organiser's own activities, while the rest might be found in secondary sources.

Increasingly, sponsors are interested in reaching people by electronic media, and an event organiser who is able to provide a list of contact details for attendees might stand a better chance of securing a deal. Perhaps one of the most important target groups for sponsorship is the media itself, with radio stations likely to be the most cooperative (Skinner and Rukavina 2003). Inviting media partners to be sponsors, even if this is only sponsorship in kind, means that they are much more likely to promote the event. This is invaluable in helping to raise the profile of an event and making it a more attractive proposition for other potential sponsors.

Media coverage is almost certainly the biggest driver of sponsorship deals for events, because it delivers a much bigger potential audience for the sponsor. While perhaps 100,000 people might attend an event and see the names of sponsors on billboards, the television audience – numbering in the millions, sometimes across many countries – has a much greater chance of increasing awareness of the sponsor's brand. For instance, the Guinness Rugby World Cup was shown in around 150 countries to a combined television audience of around three billion (Rines 2002), and this level of exposure is obviously of interest to major sponsors. However, even without media coverage, and for any size of event, an understanding of how the event audience might be attractive to the sponsor can help to maximise the value of the sponsorship deal.

There are different levels of sponsorship, with the most important being title sponsorship. Here, the sponsor's name is inserted before the event title, such as the Pedigree Chum United Kingdom Dog Show. Other levels of sponsorship enable more sponsorship partners to be recruited. In addition to the main title sponsor, different sponsors might be secured for specific parts of the event. These will receive less coverage and fewer benefits. Finally, minor sponsors might provide catering and refreshments.

An event organiser should always ask the question, 'What can I do for my sponsor(s)?', not 'What can the sponsor(s) do for me?' The organiser of a relatively new music festival is likely to view their 5000 customers simply as lovers of music, and perhaps as passionate supporters of the event, but these people will have other interests and leisure activities, and they will consume many other products and services. A well-maintained database might highlight that they are predominantly middle class and that they are interested in travel and holidays. These event attendees would therefore be of great interest to a travel company that sells adventure holidays. A mail-out to these music lovers – as an official sponsor of their music festival, with an enclosed discount voucher – might easily generate fifty leads. If the company subsequently managed to sell just five holidays as a result, that would probably more than recoup the money it paid in sponsorship. Of course, this promotion would also increase awareness of the sponsor's core business and might well lead to future enquiries, making it even more financially beneficial. If the event organiser were to provide a hospitality package for the holiday company, enabling it to introduce some of its best clients to one of the bands, this would add even more value to the deal.

7.4.2 Developing the event sponsorship plan

Securing sponsorship for an event starts with a sponsorship plan to highlight what the event can offer a sponsor and the likely cost of the deal. A useful starting point is to produce a list of the costs of the event to see where it might be better to secure sponsorship in kind. Hiring a hall to put on the event might eat into the budget, so securing a sponsorship in kind deal with an organisation that has use of a hall would be a good idea. Another example is Lucozade's sponsorship in kind of the London Marathon. The company provides the thousands of drinks that are handed out to runners during this gruelling event.

It is crucial to research potential sponsors. This type of investigation should uncover important information that will enable the event manager to find areas of mutual interest, but it might also prevent potentially embarrassing associations. As the number of sponsorship deals increases, more companies are starting to issue guidelines on what they expect from a sponsorship deal (Stotlar 2005). These guidelines usually show that a company has experience in the sponsorship market, so they are very useful for any event organiser who is in the process of drafting sponsorship proposals.

> ### Study activity
>
> List the key factors that you would need to present to a drinks company if you wanted them to sponsor a musical event that will attract an audience of 5000 people, mainly female and between the ages of eighteen and thirty. What would you expect the level of sponsorship to be for your event?

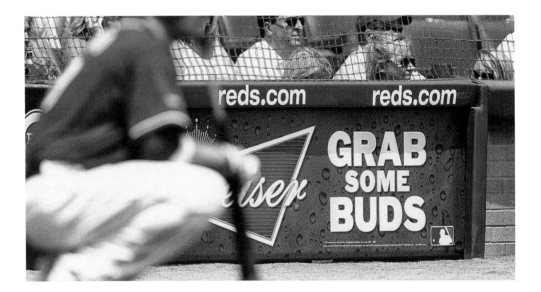

Image 7.2 Budweiser advertisements at a baseball game
Source: John Grieshop / Getty Images

7.4.3 Setting event sponsorship objectives

Having researched potential sponsors, the event manager can start to develop appropriate objectives for the proposed plan, which will outline the benefits of the sponsorship deal. In many cases, the person dealing with the proposal in the sponsor's organisation will not be the ultimate decision-maker, so providing them with a clear list of potential benefits should make their job of convincing their boss to approve the deal that much easier.

Sponsorship objectives must be realistic, and where possible should be measurable. For instance, if the aim is to raise awareness of the sponsor's name, a pre-event survey will show what current awareness levels are, and then subsequent surveys can be carried out during and after the event to provide evidence of the sponsorship's effectiveness.

Some potential sponsorship objectives are:

- To increase awareness levels of a company's products/services (Rines 2002).
- To demonstrate new or improved products to clients in an exclusive environment (Rines 2002; Skinner and Rukavina 2003).
- To improve the company's image (Sneath *et al.* 2005).
- To incentivise the workforce (Rines 2002; Stotlar 2005).
- To motivate/recruit/retain the workforce (Rines 2002; Skinner and Rukavina 2003).
- To develop better working relationships with distributors (Rines 2002).
- To improve relationships with the press (Rines 2002).
- To increase global exposure (Stotlar 2005).
- To increase sales (via product sampling (Stotlar 2005).

More than one of these can be achieved in one deal. Perhaps the most popular objective is to increase levels of awareness of the sponsor's brand, but sponsors increasingly expect more than just this (Rines 2002).

Attendees are more likely to view a company more favourably as a result of the latter's sponsorship of an event. For instance, as many as 57 per cent of attendees said that their opinion of a motor manufacturer had improved after a six-day charitable event in the USA that attracted over 750,000 spectators (Sneath *et al.* 2005). Increasingly, evaluation services are being offered by specialist agencies, such as Sport und Markt, a German agency that is expanding throughout Europe.

7.4.4 Preparing the sponsorship proposal

In order to inform new potential sponsors what they might gain from sponsoring an event, the management team must draw up a sponsorship proposal. This will communicate to the potential sponsor the precise benefits of sponsoring the event and how much cash or sponsorship in kind they will be expected to provide. It should also explain why they will achieve a much better return on their investment through sponsorship than they would from traditional advertising or sales promotions (Solomon 2002). A survey in the United States showed that around 55 per cent of all new sponsorship deals were secured as a result of a cold call to a potential sponsor (IEG Survey 2001, cited in Stotlar 2005). Ideally, a sponsorship proposal should cover the following areas (adapted from Solomon 2002):

- Exclusivity – Proposed sponsor to be the only one from their product category.
- Television – Specify the minimum amount of TV coverage for the sponsor.
- Signage – State how many signs the sponsor will be allowed to place at the event.

- Entertainment – Indicate how many hospitality options and free tickets are included in the deal.
- Display/merchandise – Indicate which merchandise options are available to the sponsor.
- Promotions/public relations – List the sponsor's access to event promotions and PR activities.
- Advertising – Detail how the sponsor's logo will be used in event advertising.
- Cost – How much the deal is worth and when the money should be paid.

These categories are the minimum that a potential sponsor will require; they should be comprehensive enough to protect both the sponsor and the event organiser; and they will form the basis of the sponsorship contract. A sponsor will pay more for an event with media coverage, so a guarantee of a minimum level of media exposure might need to be specified. Increasingly, sponsors insert clauses into their contracts which specify minimum levels of media coverage. Therefore, the amount of space which will be in view of the media must be included, particularly if the names of other sponsors are going to appear in view at the same time. The total number of entry tickets to be included as part of the deal must be clarified to enable the sponsor to plan exactly who will benefit from them. Increasingly, sponsors expect to be able to hand out publicity about their company, and in some cases give out samples, so the proposal must state exactly what they will be entitled to do. Using the sponsor's name in any advertising, promotion or public relations activities must be considered, as the sponsor will gain more value from the deal in this way.

When the drinks company Allied Domecq sponsored the Royal Shakespeare Company in 1995, its aim was to improve its image by linking with such a high-profile and prestigious company. It was also able to put on a special event in New York, where it entertained key stakeholders, including diplomats and politicians. This helped the company to develop better relationships with its stakeholders but in a more relaxed and stimulating environment, while showing that it had a working relationship with one of the most celebrated arts organisations in the world (Skinner and Rukavina 2003).

7.4.5 Creative sponsorship strategies

The events sponsorship market is expected to grow at around 3 per cent annually (Mintel 2009), creating many new opportunities for event managers. Some of the biggest sponsorship deals are now struck over naming rights of venues. For instance, the Sheffield Events Arena was recently sponsored by a local radio station and is now called the Hallam FM Arena.

Increasingly, though, companies are looking to develop more innovative sponsorship strategies. When the National Westminster Bank sponsored cricket in England, it used a corporate social responsibility strategy to try to position its brand at the heart of the community. It designed a 'Cricket Community' road show which invited local children to try cricket for the first time, with research showing 85 per cent of people thought that it had encouraged more children to take up sports. The amount of publicity that these events generated was important, but the fact that the bank was involved in such an important project also helped to change the perception of some of its stakeholders.

It is important to manage relationships with sponsors. Early sponsorship deals were secured as a result of personal preferences within the sponsoring company, rather than for commercial reasons. When a local engineering firm sponsored an annual music festival, it was often as a result of a decision made by a director of the company who wished to support his partner's favourite event, rather than for sound commercial reasons. Of course, an engineering firm might receive considerable benefits by sponsoring such an event, but such an investment needs to be made as a result of effective research.

Many successful sponsorship deals now involve 'activation' – an amount of money which a sponsoring company invests above its initial sponsorship payment. According to Performance Research, after making a £1 million sponsorship payment, a company might find it beneficial to invest another £3 million to promote and support their sponsorship of an event (cited in Stotlar 2005: 38).

Companies are increasingly turning to sponsorship agents to help them find the best match. Fiona Green, a sponsorship consultant with over twenty years' experience in the field, brokers deals between companies and potential sponsors. When representing an organisation that is interested in sponsorship, she compiles a list of events and compares these with the potential sponsor's objectives. She then contacts the managers of the most appropriate events to see if a deal can be struck. (See the 'Industry Voice' section below.)

7.4.6 Evaluating event sponsorship

Evaluating the effectiveness of sponsorship shows sponsors that their main objectives have been met, and hopefully exceeded. However, a budget for these activities must be agreed in advance. For larger sponsors, these services are usually provided as part of a comprehensive package by companies like the International Events Group (IEG). Smaller sponsors might also contract out some of their evaluation, but increasingly they carry out their own research as part of their overall market research activities.

One of the most important techniques for assessing the impact of a sponsor's activities is to measure the amount of publicity generated, as is highlighted in Table 7.3. The most frequently used measurement is the advertising equivalency of publicity (AEP). The exposure of the sponsor's brand on television is measured against the cost of buying the same amount of time in a TV advert. If, for example, Euronics sponsors the Ideal Homes Exhibition, which is then featured on television, the amount of time that the sponsor's name appears is recorded. According to the International Events Group (IEG), this is based on the amount of time that the brand name appears in shot as long as it is at least 75 per cent visible (Lagae 2005). If the brand name appears in a prime-time television show for thirty seconds, then the AEP is the same as a thirty-second advertising slot during that programme. If the cost of placing a thirty-second advert is £40,000, then the AEP is £40,000. If this appears in five different countries, then calculations must be made for each of those markets. Similarly, if the brand name appears in a half-page story in a magazine, and the cost of a half-page advert is £5000, then the AEP is £5000. Clearly, the simple appearance of a brand name does not have the same impact as an advert, but it is a recognised form of measurement. Keeping cuttings from press articles and presenting them to the potential sponsor is one way of showing them how they will benefit from event sponsorship.

Other evaluation techniques include interviewing important stakeholders, such as participants, to test their view of the sponsorship and their attitude to the brand. For larger groups, a survey will also provide important feedback. Sponsorship packages which direct participants to a website can be measured by the number of visitors to that website and the degree of movement around it.

When Guinness sponsored the Rugby World Cup in 1999, one of its principal objectives was to create a consistent global identity, which it believed sponsorship could deliver more cost-effectively than advertising. The cost of advertising in all countries exposed to the event was much higher than creating similar levels of exposure through sponsorship (Rines 2002).

Table 7.3 Sponsorship evaluation techniques

Aims of sponsoring events	Techniques for measuring the impact of sponsorship
To increase awareness levels of product/service and company (Rines 2002)	Survey to measure percentage recall of the sponsor's involvement with the event, based on prompted brand awareness
	Media exposure measurement based on time on television and radio and the number of column inches in publications
To demonstrate new products or improved products to clients in an exclusive environment (Rines 2002; Skinner and Rukavina 2003)	Feedback from participants or attendees to gain their views about new products shown
To improve company image	Collect of press cuttings and record number of mentions and the audience or readership of the media where cuttings appear
To incentivise the workforce (Rines 2002; Stotlar 2005)	Staff attitude survey or interviews about proposed sponsorship
To motivate, recruit/retain the workforce (Rines 2002; Skinner and Rukavina 2003)	Staff survey and interviews as part of appraisal
To develop better working relationships with distributors (Rines 2002)	Formal and informal feedback from distributors who attend the event
	Measure the increase in sales, or sales leads, as a result of sponsoring the event
To involve the local community	Interview key stakeholders Survey local community
To create a global identity (Rines 2002)	Measure the impact of media coverage on a global basis

Study activity

What are the main threats that an event manager will face when trying to secure sponsorship for the first time?

7.4.7 Building loyalty and sponsor networks

Even though the sponsorship market is growing, unfortunately, for event managers, sponsors do not always continue to sponsor the same event. If the principal aim of the deal was to increase awareness of the brand and this has been achieved, a sponsor might choose another marketing communications activity that will help to generate new sales leads. Others do not renew their deals if the sponsorship has not delivered the expected benefits. Event managers must take this into consideration and develop effective working relationships with their sponsors. As a minimum, they should produce an annual report with feedback about the impact of the sponsorship deal, and collaborate with the sponsor throughout the year.

Other, more innovative ideas are to hold a party for the sponsor to celebrate the relationship and to give gifts, such as signed photographs or other tangible mementos of the event (Skinner and Rukavina 2003). It is also important, if possible, to sign long-term agreements with sponsors, or to renew contracts if the partnership has been beneficial. In some cases, encouraging staff and participants to buy the sponsor's products is a simple way of rewarding the sponsor for their investment.

7.4.8 Ethical and legal considerations in event sponsorship

Event organisers are under increasing pressure not to associate with controversial sponsors. When tobacco companies were banned from advertising on television in the 1970s, they turned to the sponsorship of major events, predominantly sporting, in an attempt to ensure that their brand names received continued media exposure. But now, while Formula One teams are still sponsored by tobacco companies, they are not allowed to show the sponsor's name or logo when they compete in France (Stotlar 2005). This legislation also extends to the large fleets of vehicles that are used to transport team equipment from event to event. There is also increasing pressure on event organisers not to work with sponsors from the booming online betting industry, and there has even been some discussion about accepting sponsorship from fast-food companies. While these companies are not yet affected by legislation, it is important to monitor current opinion and to be clear about how this type of sponsorship impacts on brand image.

Event organisers should also be aware of ethical considerations when choosing their sponsors. While a local school might be happy to receive £20,000 to help in the staging of its annual swimming gala, is it acceptable for a local fast-food outlet to sponsor the event, given the current problem of childhood obesity? It is sometimes difficult to find the right answers to such questions, especially when large sums of money are involved, but the event organiser should always be aware of the danger of negative publicity.

Ambush marketing represents a threat to sponsorship agreements, and event managers must be prepared to protect the interests of their sponsors. An ambush marketer creates marketing communications at or near an event to convince stakeholders that they are an official sponsor, even though they are not. So an organiser must take steps to prevent attendees displaying the brand names of non-sponsoring organisations. Event personnel might be instructed to confiscate any non-sponsor branded items, to stop them from being filmed by television cameras or photographed by the press inside the venue. This created a stir at the World Cup in Germany in 2006, when Dutch football supporters were instructed to remove branded dungarees that had been handed out by a non-sponsor, leaving the fans to watch the match in just their underpants.

A few years later, the major computer game manufacturer Nintendo chose not to attend the Nuremberg International Toy Fair, but it ambushed the event by driving a mobile promotional van through the centre of the city during the week of the event.

CASE STUDY 7.2

Nuremberg International Toy Fair: embracing new technology

Venue: Nuremberg, Germany
Type of event: trade fair
Attendance: 75,000 trade visitors and 2700 exhibitors

When Dr Angela Merkel, Chancellor of the Federal Republic of Germany, agrees to open the sixtieth Nuremberg International Toy Fair (ITFN), it is clear that this event is an important contributor to the German economy. Nuremberg is the 'Toy Fair City', and it has a history of toy-making dating back to the thirteenth century.

When visitors land at Nuremberg airport during the week of the fair, the centre of the luggage carousel is filled with large models of popular toys provided by one of the many sponsors of the fair. As soon as they pass through the airport doors, they are greeted by representatives of the ITFN, who make sure that they know exactly how to get to their hotel accommodation and to the fair itself. Hotels tend to be filled to capacity during the week of the fair, and shops and restaurants are packed – all providing a great boost to Nuremberg's local economy.

The ITFN takes place in the impressive, council-funded *Messe* (Exhibition Centre) on the outskirts of the city. This centre is a purpose-built, versatile venue that is capable of hosting a range of events, and it enjoys excellent transport links with Nuremberg and surrounding towns. It comprises about fifteen separate halls, as well as bars, shops, restaurants, a business centre and childcare facilities.

The fair receives more than 75,000 trade visitors from 115 different countries, and hosts 2700 exhibitors from 59 countries – making it one of the biggest toy fairs in the world. Some of the stands are small and hired by new organisations, while others are huge, occupied by multinational companies and staffed by as many as fifty people. On display at any one time are around one million products, with some 70,000 of them new, in a display area of 160,000 square metres. While the event lasts for only one week, the management and marketing run all year round.

The aim of the organisers is to use pricing to maximise their revenue, while encouraging repeat attendance and developing new business. Prices are therefore usually based on the number of square metres that a stand occupies, with additional prices charged for extra services, such as telecoms access and administrative services. There is flexibility in pricing in order to incentivise new attendees, as new product innovations attract visitors. While the fair is aimed primarily at the toy trade and key stakeholders in the industry, a day pass – costing only twenty euros – allows other people to attend and provides additional revenue. Such visitors can take advantage of reduced rail fares to the venue, on account of the fair's sponsorship deal with Deutsche Bahn.

As many as 60 per cent of visitors book for the following year, and the organisers employ agents in key overseas markets to help them sell exhibition spaces on a commission basis, ensuring worldwide coverage. The organisers have also set up a subsidiary company called World of Toys to extend the toy fair brand and to manage other fairs around the world.

The ITFN provides an important service for the toy industry by allowing companies to exhibit their goods and services to key stakeholder groups, and it gives exhibitors an opportunity to catch up with many of their clients in one location. Many of the exhibitors are frequent attendees at the ITFN, and promotional offers encourage them to book early for the following year. Regular adverts are placed in toy trade magazines, but it is the database of contacts that supports the direct marketing efforts of the fair's organisers. Exhibitors travel from around the world, so direct advertising, using mail-shots and e-mail, has proved to be the most cost-effective marketing strategy. In order to test the effectiveness of their communications, the organisers monitor traffic to their website and capture the details of people who download information.

The ITFN is not just a place to demonstrate toys and games. It is an important event in the world toy market. Exhibitors learn about trends in the Toy Business Forum, where leading industry experts advise attendees about the latest public relations and marketing initiatives or about new ways to present products in shops or online.

Another important stakeholder is the media, and a database of magazines, newspapers, journalists, radio and television contacts is used to guarantee that the show will receive the widest possible media coverage. In 2009, the fair's organisers were contacted by 2589 journalists from 39 different countries. A monthly newsletter is published in ten different languages, helping to position the show as an important part of the world toy industry. Nor does the promotion stop once the event has begun, as the organisers produce a daily *Toy Fair* newspaper – available in hard copy and online – during the week of the show. All the important information relating to the fair is also provided on free software.

The organisers categorise attendees according to size of company, size of stand and type of product (there are ten different categories of toys and games, ranging from models and educational toys to high-tech products). New exhibitors form a separate category and are given extra support during the show.

As a predominantly business-to-business (B2B) event, the ITFN generates considerable income for the city, and its partnerships and sponsorship deals reflect this. The list of key partners includes Nuremberg City Council, the Nuremberg Tourism Congress, local chambers of commerce and business associations. These partnerships lead to extra events, such as the Toy Fair Cocktail 2010, where bars and restaurants compete to produce the best cocktail during the week of the fair. They are important to the continued success of the event, so the organisers plan to improve their relationships with key stakeholders in the city in the future.

Industry voice

Fiona Green, sponsorship consultant

 I have worked in the sponsorship industry for over twenty years, with brands including Coca-Cola, Adidas, Visa, Mastercard and Anheuser-Busch. My career has primarily been within football, working with FIFA and UEFA, but has also included tennis, cricket, sailing and athletics events, in the UK and internationally.

Sponsorship expenditure on events has risen considerably over the past five years. This is mainly due to the fact that we understand sponsorship and how it works much more now, and we know that it is a powerful and cost-effective tool, which encourages potential sponsors to invest. Advertising is also less effective at communicating messages as viewers are more able to 'block' the message, whereas sponsorship is able to deliver messages 'subliminally'.

Event sponsors can use sponsorship to create a competitive advantage that will give them a way of setting themselves apart and give their customers a reason to buy more of their products or services. Most event sponsors insist on 'exclusivity' to prevent competitors' products from being associated with the same event. They can also gain brand exposure, so it is important to know how many people are likely to be exposed to their brand if they sponsor an event. Building on this, brand association is very important and sponsors need demographic details of those who are likely to see the event. Rolex, for example, target individuals with a high disposable income and will want to be associated with an event that helps them to maintain or enhance their brand image. More sponsors seek unique access to the event and the 'money-can't-buy' opportunity, such as a visit behind the scenes. Many want to be able to offer hospitality to key stakeholder groups, such as their staff or customers. In some cases the event sponsor looks to gain 'one-to-one' communications with event attendees, so access to the event database of customers might encourage sponsors to pay more for the deal.

The events management team should consider all of these points when trying to attract potential sponsors. The event manager should also have in mind a realistic sponsorship figure, and should be able to show what the likely returns will be for the sponsor. Carrying out research into the potential sponsor's company will indicate that the event manager is taking into consideration the likely benefits of the deal. The sponsor should also know that the event will be able to take place without sponsorship.

It is helpful to set objectives, as the sponsor will always look for the best deal with the least outlay. The event manager should consider what impact the sponsorship will have on improving brand awareness and how it can motivate their staff. They also need to ensure that extra costs are covered, such as unique access to the event and extra accommodation for hospitality guests.

Increasingly, new technology has affected both the sponsors and the events seeking sponsorship. E-mail campaigns are used more, as is website advertising. Technology has allowed messages to be delivered quickly across geographic boundaries. In some cases, event attendees will have their photograph taken at an event and then e-mail it to their friends with the message: 'Look what I am doing at this event courtesy of Coca-Cola/Kodak/Ford, etc.'

If sponsors are mainly concerned with brand awareness, then media coverage is usually vitally important: the more coverage that can be guaranteed, the higher the value of the sponsorship deal. However, this is not the case at some prestigious events – such as polo – that do not receive media coverage.

As the understanding of sponsorship has developed, sponsorship proposals or requests have also had to change. The proposal should be of interest to the potential sponsor and should hold their interest over the length of the deal. If the event will be shown on the internet and used in mobile video clips, then the sponsorship proposal should mention this.

Evaluating the success of the event sponsorship is critical. However, not all factors are 'tangible', which makes them harder to measure. Ideally, such factors should be linked to the objectives set earlier. Furthermore, when sponsorship is part of a successful integrated campaign, it can be difficult to assess the relative contributions made by advertising and sponsorship.

I would encourage anybody to seek employment in this area, as it is a fascinating and constantly evolving industry. Those who are looking to work in the industry should research the companies involved and approach them directly. They will have a much better chance of getting an interview if they show an understanding and passion for the business.

7.5 Summary

To gain an understanding of what event consumers require from an event experience, it is necessary to investigate what role the event plays in their lives, and which emotions are associated with that experience. Events are about lifestyle, excitement and escapism from day-to-day life; they must be memorable and an important ingredient in the lives of attendees. This requires a new approach to research and marketing planning to ensure that organisers cater for both consumers and key stakeholders who can contribute to the success of the event. Event managers must ensure that research is at the heart of everything they do when planning an event. They must work hard to develop the event's brand image and must be willing to improve factors that impact on service quality. More attention needs to be paid to pricing and promotion, as well as to new technologies that can improve overall customer satisfaction.

Growing numbers of event managers are now dependent on sponsors for funding, so they must find ways to improve relationships with these companies. An ability to attract sponsorship might well be the difference between success and failure, so more resources must be devoted to sponsorship evaluation and innovative sponsorship strategies that will make potential sponsors even more keen to invest in events.

Further reading

Fink, J. S., Trail, G. T. and Anderson D. E. (2002), Environmental Factors Associated with Spectator Attendance and Sport Consumption Behaviour: Gender and Team Differences, *Sport Marketing Quarterly*, 11: 8–19. This important article explores sports fans' consumption during sporting events and features the previously under-researched area of female attendance at events.

Holden, P. R. (2008) *Virtually Free Marketing*, London: A & C Black. This is an important textbook that covers the important issues relating to social media, an increasingly crucial area in events management.

O'Neill, M., Getz, D. and Carlsen, J. (1999) Evaluation of Service Quality at Events: The 1998 Coca-Cola Masters Surfing Event at Margaret River, Western Australia, *Managing Service Quality*, 9 (3): 156–165. This is one of the first articles to consider the importance of service quality as part of an overall marketing plan in events management, with clear suggestions for future research in this area.

Chapter 8

Event health, safety and risk management

Contents

8.1 Aims

By the end of this chapter, students will be able:

- To understand key health, safety and risk management terminology.
- To evaluate the health, safety and risk legal and moral obligations associated with managing events.
- To explain the process of risk management at events.
- To analyse in detail three of the key risks associated with events.

8.2 Introduction

Within the events industry, the perception of health, safety and risk issues is changing fast. In the past, there has been a tendency to view health and safety issues as 'red-tape' bureaucracy that merely ticks regulatory boxes whilst creating extra work for the already stressed event manager.

However, over the past ten years, the importance of health, safety and risk has been highlighted through many high-profile event disasters that could, conceivably, have been prevented if correct health, safety and risk procedures were in place. These issues have been covered extensively in the media and have resulted in governments and industry bodies seeking to regulate against future problems by increasing legislation.

The difficulty of balancing health and safety requirements with the provision of exciting events is becoming a significant challenge as laws and regulations grow at the same speed as innovations and experience opportunities. The industry strives to juggle both aspects, driven by the desire to put on a good but safe show. As the UK event management industry bodies AEO, BECA and EVA (2002: 9) suggest: 'There is no great mystery in managing Health and Safety onsite, but there is a skill in managing it well – especially whilst retaining the all-important WOW! factor.'

There are three elements to managing health and safety matters correctly: first, the management of health, safety and risk prevents or reduces accidents and near misses on site; second, correct management prevents litigation, claims, fines, imprisonment and bad press for the event organisation; and third, risk assessment and health and safety compliance are often legal requirements.

8.2.1 Guiding principles

For industry professionals, the essential principle to understand is that health, safety and risk management is a key part of event planning. It should be factored in from the very start of the process and should be considered during every part of the planning process.

There are four key principles relating to health and safety that every event organiser should bear in mind. These are summarised in Figure 8.1.

8.2.2 Impacts of health, safety and risk-related incidents

Health, safety and risk-related incidents at events can have wide-ranging and often disastrous impacts. Without proper attention to health, safety and risk management, event organisers expose their audience, their colleagues and their contractors to injury and loss of life.

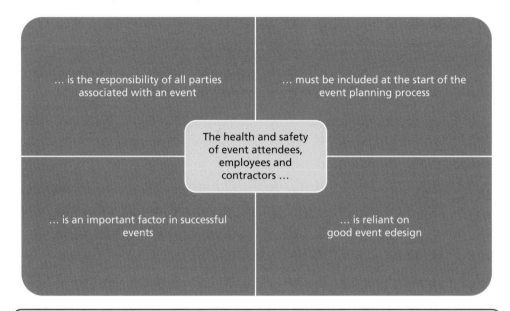

... is the responsibility of all parties associated with an event

... must be included at the start of the event planning process

The health and safety of event attendees, employees and contractors ...

... is an important factor in successful events

... is reliant on good event edesign

Figure 8.1 The importance of health and safety at events

A small-scale incident, such as a person tripping and falling, can result in a loss of event focus as the audience is distracted by the incident. This loss of focus will affect the audience's perceptions of the event and may result in issues with stakeholders, who will be unhappy with the shift in focus, away from their key messages. Such small-scale incidents can therefore impact on the future effectiveness of an event, so their importance should not be dismissed.

However, it is the large-scale incidents that will cause the most problems for the event organisation. It is important to remember that these health, safety and risk-related incidents can also have devastating and ruinous results. The media may report the incident, resulting in negative publicity, changes in the local mood towards the event and a shift in worldwide perceptions. One example of this was the 2010 tragedy at the Love Parade in Germany, which resulted in nineteen deaths, worldwide negative publicity and the eventual dissolution of the event. (For news reviews and footage of this disaster, see the YouTube sources list at the end of the book.)

Another large-scale event disaster occurred when the *Marchioness* leisure boat sank in 1989. The boat was hosting a private party with 131 people on board when it collided with a large dredger. The pleasure boat sank almost immediately and fifty-one people drowned. According to Hartley (2002), the long-awaited public inquiry blamed almost everyone involved, including the Department of Transport, the captains of both vessels, the companies that managed them and the police. This inquiry eventually led to the Department of Transport carrying out a comprehensive Formal Safety Assessment of River Thames passenger vessels (later extended to all operating environments for domestic passenger ships in the UK), which covered every aspect of their safety, including 'their encounter risk with large ships and bridges, fire risk, stability, subdivision, freeboard, visibility, life saving appliances, means of escape, manning, passenger numbers, trading areas and safety management' (Maritime and Coastguard Agency 2005: 1).

8.2.3 Key areas of health, safety and risk for the average event

This textbook demonstrates that every event is unique and needs particular attention and consideration. However, it is useful to note some key areas of event planning that need a particular focus from a health, safety and risk perspective. These can range from significant aspects of event planning – venue and site design – to circumstantial issues, such as refreshments and sanitation (HSE 1999).

Some of the key areas for event organisers to consider can be summarised as:

- control of hazardous substances
- communication procedures
- crowd management
- electrical installations and lighting, including special effects and pyrotechnics
- facilities for people with special needs
- fire safety
- food, drink and water
- noise and vibration
- major incident (emergency) planning
- medical, ambulance and first-aid management
- performers, TV and media
- sanitary and waste facilities and management
- structures and barriers
- transport management
- venue and site design and management. (List adapted from HSE 1999: 3)

Later in this chapter, three specific risks of particular interest to event managers will be discussed in detail.

As well as the individual areas that need health, safety and risk management, it is important that event organisers consider the event phases and the safety implications for each. These phases can be represented as the build-up (pre-planning); load-in (set-up of the event); show (the event itself); load-out (dismantling equipment); and breakdown (dismantling the venue or the final processes of leaving the venue, as appropriate). These phases and the safety implications for each can be seen in Figure 8.2.

Figure 8.2 Event safety phases

8.2.4 Legal requirements

The regulations, laws and legislation that event organisers are required to adhere to vary from country to country, but it is always essential that organisers understand their legal obligations.

Bear in mind that an event organiser must understand the laws and regulations in both the country where their organisation is based *and* the country where the event will take place – often, there are marked differences between the two. It is essential that anyone involved in event management is clear on the legal responsibility that they have in relation to compliance with health and safety legislation because, in the majority of cases, this responsibility will rest with the event organiser (HSE 1999: 167).

Legal issues are the foundation of all elements of event planning. The importance of operating within the rules set by government and local authorities must never be underestimated. Readers should consult the Event Operations chapter (Chapter 4), which covers legal issues relating to duty of care, responsibilities of event organisers, contract law and so on.

8.3 Health and safety legislation

Health and safety legislation changes continually, and it is often difficult to keep up to date with the latest amendments and additions to laws and regulations. It is essential, however, that event managers do so. Figure 8.3 gives some useful links to resources that contain the latest health and safety regulations around the world.

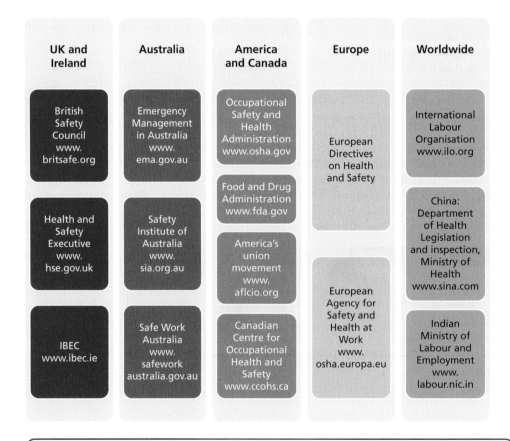

Figure 8.3 International resources for health and safety legislation

8.3.1 Regulations, licences and permits

Many of the myriad licences, permits and regulations that events operate within and around are related to health and safety. As already noted, these will differ from one country to the next, but they all tend to have similar requirements. It is essential that the event manager checks these in detail at the start of the planning process. It is the responsibility of the event company to ensure they have researched the relevant requirements and that they are in compliance with them.

Many of the regulations, licences and permits relate to environmental issues (such as noise control); licences for temporary or personal activity; licences for premises; fire regulations; ambulance, medical and police provision; highways and traffic control; and general workplace health and safety. In the UK, guides issued by organisations such as the Association of Events Organisers (AEO), the Association of Event Venues (AEV) and the Event Supplier and Services Association (ESSA) are key resources. In particular, *The Guide to Managing Health and Safety at Exhibitions and Events* (AEO, BECA and EVA 2002) and the AEO, AEV and ESSA *E-Guide* (2010) should be read by event managers. The Emergency Management in Australia is a useful tool for event managers operating there, and other countries have similar resources which are equally easy to find. The AEO, BECA and EVA (2002: A1) guide lists UK regulations that need to be considered during the build-up, show and breakdown phases of an exhibition (these can be related directly to all other events; similar regulations exist in other countries):

- Health and Safety at Work etc. Act, 1974
- Management of Health and Safety at Work Regulations 1999
- Workplace (Health, Safety and Welfare) Regulations 1992
- Personal Protective Equipment at Work Regulations 1992
- Provision and Use of Work Equipment Regulations 1998
- Lifting Operations and Lifting Equipment Regulations (LOLER) 1998
- Manual Handling Operations Regulations 1992
- Fire Precautions (Workplace) Regulations 1997, as amended 1999
- Health and Safety (First Aid) Regulations 1981
- Reporting of Injuries, Diseases and Dangerous Occurrences Regulations (RIDDOR) 1995
- Electricity at Work Regulations 1998/EVA Regulations for Stand Electrical Installations
- Health and Safety (Signs and Signals) Regulations 1996
- Noise at Work Regulations 1989
- Building Regulations
- Building Standards (Scotland) Regulations
- Environmental Protection Act 1990/Environment Act 1995.

Additional codes of practice and guides to consider include:

- The Licensing Act 2003
- Guide to Fire Precautions in Existing Places of Entertainment and Like Premises 1990
- *Event Safety Guide* (a guide to health, safety and welfare at music and similar events which is due to be revised in 2012)
- NOEA's Code of Practice for Outdoor Events
- Temporary De-mountable Structures Guidance on Design Procurement and Use 1999
- Specific local authority regulations (your venue will be able to advise you about these)
- Health and Safety in Construction – HSE Publications HS(G)150.

This list is not exhaustive, but it demonstrates the large number of issues that the event manager needs to consider at the start of every event. It should be noted that there is concern that the sheer volume of health and safety regulations is strangling some sectors of the industry – in particular small-scale local community and cultural events. For instance, organisers of local street parties often find the myriad rules, regulations and legalities intimidating. They fear that they might face the cost of acquiring licences and permits, and worry about navigating the legal system, so it is hardly surprising that they frequently come to the conclusion that it is not worth the effort.

The UK has a long history of street parties, including those held on VE Day in 1945 and on the occasion of Queen Elizabeth's coronation in 1953. However, such parties have declined in recent years, largely because of the significant increase in local council regulations relating to health and safety. In response to this, in 2009 an initiative called 'The Big Lunch' aimed to reignite interest in street parties. The organisers of the Eden Project launched this new scheme with the aim of getting as many people as possible to have lunch with their neighbours, encouraging acts of community spirit, engagement and fun (Big Lunch 2011). They use the internet as a resource for local communities to try to make the organisation of a local street party as simple as possible. The website provides details about the type of insurance required, and tells communities how and when to approach their councils. It advises organisers to hold their events in private or community gardens to avoid the need for road closures, and gives guidance on whether there is a need for risk assessments and health and safety certificates. This

Image 8.1 The Royal Wedding, 2011 – street parties and celebrations are held throughout the UK
Source: David Levenson / Getty Images

advice falls in line with the industry view that local community events should be kept simple: small, private parties and local community events do not need risk assessments and certificates, but if anyone can attend or if tickets are sold, the other processes and requirements outlined in this chapter may come into play. In 2011, over a million people took part in the Big Lunch. (For further information on the Big Lunch, see the YouTube sources.)

8.3.2 Health and Safety at Work etc. (HSW) Act 1974

This is the primary piece of legislation for health, safety and welfare of people at work within the UK and is an example of national legislation that affects the events industry. In Australia and the USA, similar legislation is in the form of the Occupational Safety and Health Acts. If there is no such legislation in the country where the event manager is operating, it is suggested that they follow the procedures and requirements outlined in the HSW in order to develop their own code of practice.

The HSW sets out general principles of managing health and safety at work, and enables the creation of requirements through such regulations as the Control of Substances Hazardous to Health Regulations 2002 (COSHH) and the Management of Health and Safety at Work Regulations 1999 (MHSW). It therefore explains the general duties that employers have to employees and members of the public, and the duties that employees have to themselves and to each other.

In the UK, this is the most important legislation to which the events industry must adhere. It makes it mandatory for all employees to conduct a risk assessment of their work activity (Upton 2008). It is therefore essential that each event manager and company has a grasp on the document and its key points. Specialist legal support should be sought, if necessary, and students working or living in other countries should be familiar with their own key pieces of legislation.

8.3.3 The Management of Health and Safety at Work Regulations (MHSW) 1999

The Management of Health and Safety at Work Regulations 1999 generally make employers' legal obligations with respect to health and safety much more explicit. Like the HSW, they apply to every work activity: 'The MHSW regulations have been put in place in order that you take care of all those you work in conjunction with – employees, contractors, clients or customers. The aim of the regulations is to reduce damage by assessing all potential risks and to create action plans for emergencies' (HSE 2003: 2). The regulations require employers to review risk assessments periodically, to ensure that they are familiar with hazards and risks in the workplace, to improve safety procedures at every opportunity, and to ensure work is organised and training is offered (HSE 2003).

8.3.4 Corporate manslaughter law

Legally, the event organisation often has responsibility for the safety of its employees. In the UK, this is covered by the Corporate Manslaughter and Corporate Homicide Act 2007. Event organisers operating in other countries should check their own laws on corporate responsibility in detail. These laws specify that adequate safety practices and procedures must be in place, and they allow for conviction if it can be proved beyond reasonable doubt that a company was homicidally reckless about risk (Slapper 2007). During events, this applies to accidental death of both employees and attendees.

In 2008, there was a stampede of 2000 people at the launch of a sale event at a Wal-Mart store in America, and an employee was trampled to death. The employee's family sued Wal-Mart in a wrongful-death lawsuit which claimed that the company had engaged in specific marketing and advertising techniques specifically to attract a large crowd and create an environment of frenzy and mayhem. In America, a wrongful-death case alleges that a person was killed as a result of another's negligence or other form of liability. The lawsuit was settled when Wal-Mart agreed to improve its crowd control for its day-after-Thanksgiving events, and 'the world's largest retailer also agreed to set up a $400,000 victim's compensation fund, donate $1.5 million to the community and provide 50 jobs annually to high school students in the area' (Robideaux 2009; see also the YouTube sources).

Study activity

For non-UK students

Find the relevant corporate responsibility law or act for your country and make a note of its exact name. Now do the same for control of hazardous substances and safety at work legislation. Finally, identify the governing body for health and safety and note any other specific health and safety regulations for your country.

For UK students

What are the major differences between the Health and Safety at Work etc. Act 1974 and the Management of Health and Safety at Work Regulations 1999? Discuss your findings with another student.

8.4 Health and safety management

The information and advice in this section is based on *The Event Safety Guide* (HSE 1999) – essential reading for all events management students and organisers.

8.4.1 Key elements of successful health and safety management

As we have seen, legislation and regulation of health and safety have become paramount to the successful and safe delivery of any event. Once the event concept is developed, but *before the event manager proceeds any further*, it is essential that they turn their full attention to the management of health and safety before, during and after the event. This process begins with the creation of a health and safety policy.

AEO, BECA and EVA (2002: A2) advise the following procedures for the creation of a health and safety policy (they are concerned chiefly with exhibitions, but their advice is relevant industry wide):

> Your policy and arrangements for managing Health and Safety on-site at your exhibition must be written down formally. Your Health and Safety Policy should be broken down into three major sections:

1 The policy statement
2 Organisation of the health and safety
3 The arrangements for the management of health and safety

This demonstrates to an enforcement officer that you have considered and made provision for the safety and welfare of people within the exhibition.

It is a legal requirement that employers with five or more employees produce a written health and safety policy. Once the policy has been created, the event manager must ensure that it is put into practice. This involves the dissemination of the relevant parts of the policy to all relevant stakeholders, including all staff, the local authorities and government, suppliers, the venue and the customers. Once these stakeholders have been briefed, the event manager must monitor the ongoing delivery and performance of the health and safety policy and ensure that all aspects of it are implemented correctly, efficiently and within all legal requirements and available guidelines. The last part of the management of any health and safety policy happens after the event has finished. At this point, the policy should be fully reviewed and audited, in order to assess its performance and management. The importance of this should not be under-estimated. If the health and safety policy is not managed effectively, then the event manager and their organisation may be held liable for any accidents or issues that arose during the event.

8.4.2 Responsibilities

In order to be clear on the importance of ensuring health and safety policies and procedures are in place, it is useful to have an understanding of the responsibilities of both the employee and the employer/event organisation.

8.4.2.1 Employer

An event employer must consult employees or a health and safety representative on (among other things) any changes that affect health and safety at work; the information to be given on the likely risks and dangers arising from event work and the measures to reduce or eliminate these risks; what to do when dealing with a risk; and health and safety planning.

General employer duties also include: making the workplace safe; ensuring machinery is safe; and giving the necessary information, instruction, training and supervision for health and safety. In particular, an employer must assess the risks to health and safety and make arrange-ments for implementing the health and safety measures identified as being necessary by the assessment. They must also appoint a competent person to assist with health and safety respon-sibilities, and consult the safety representative about this appointment; cooperate on health and safety with other employers sharing the same workplace; set up emergency procedures; provide adequate first-aid facilities; and ensure that the workplace satisfies health, safety and welfare requirements (HSE 1999).

8.4.2.2 Employee

It is important to note that event employees' health, safety and welfare at work are protected by law in most countries. However, an employee also has a responsibility to look after themselves and others around them. This responsibility includes the need to identify potential issues and recognise problems within the health and safety provision. These problems can be small, such as identifying a loose panel on a stage set and informing someone so that it does not cause injury. Or they can be large, such as noticing that the planned layout for crowd flow may cause a crush and ensuring the relevant amendments to the plan are carried out. At the very least, if there is a problem, event employees should discuss it with their employer or safety representative, if there is one.

8.5 Risk management

Risk management involves an organisation or employer looking at risks in the workplace and implementing policies and procedures to minimise them. It is not solely concerned with health and safety. In fact, risks can arise in any area of the business, including financial, business planning and strategies, employee relations and sales and marketing. In events, the management of risk will therefore relate to the overall event strategy, with organisers required to carry out several other forms of risk management based on specific issues, such as finances and return on investment, marketing and PR, sponsorship/ticket revenue strategy, and environmental impact.

In particular, risks are now frequently assessed in terms of the Triple Bottom Line (TBL), which refers to the social, economic and environmental aspects of activities. These aspects are usually assessed in the evaluation of an event to determine the outcome for various stakeholders (Hede 2007), and it is becoming increasingly common to include them in a risk assessment which reviews external risks to the event. In other words, a TBL risk assessment will ask questions relating to the social, economic and environmental risks and impacts associated with the event, will assess how these risks affect the wider public, and will gauge the extent to which the event organisation is accountable for them. (A TBL approach to risk management is also often related to sustainability, which is covered extensively in Chapter 14.)

Another key aspect of risk management is that risk is not solely a negative concept. A good risk management strategy will highlight opportunities as well as potential problems. Risk management theory has moved away from the idea that the process is about crisis management. Instead, it is now widely agreed that the identification of risk can lead to greater understanding of a company's relationships, working practices, decision-making processes and overall output. It is therefore important for the event manager to understand the fundamental purpose of risk management and how it should be used across the events business.

However, the major focus for an event manager when considering risk management in an event context is the consideration of specific risks that usually relate to operational issues. Allen et al. (2008: 588) define risk as 'the likelihood of the special event or festival not fulfilling its objective', and from hereon this chapter will focus on the operational risks that might result in such an eventuality.

8.6 Risk assessment

A risk assessment focuses on risks that really matter and pinpoints the (usually straightforward) solutions to ensure that risks are controlled. Risk assessments protect workers and businesses and ensure compliance with the law. As the Health and Safety Executive (2011: 1) points out, 'The law does not expect you to eliminate all risk, but you are required to protect people as far as "reasonably practicable."' Carrying out a risk assessment is an absolute necessity for all event managers, even when the legislation does not require one.

An event risk assessment is an examination of elements that could cause harm to people. In other words, it is the identification of things that could go wrong (Tum et al. 2006). Every event will have many elements of risk: for instance, bad weather can create havoc at an outdoor event; overcrowding of one area can cause a crush; heavy consumption of alcohol may result in behavioural problems; a loose piece of wire may cause a trip; and so on. Every event should therefore have a risk assessment which enables the organisers to gauge whether they have taken adequate precautions to prevent harm to employees, visitors and suppliers. Organisers are legally required to assess the risks in the workplace and implement a plan to control those risks (HSE 2011).

As Tarlow (2002) points out, risk assessment is not only a way of identifying potential risks and attempting to eliminate or reduce them – it should also form the basis for contingency plans and emergency procedures.

8.6.1 Definitions

There are several key words that event industry professionals use when referring to health, safety and risk. It is important that the definitions of these words are clear and properly understood.

- *Hazard* – Anything which has the potential to cause harm to people. This could be a dangerous property of an item or a substance, a condition, a situation or an activity.
- *Risk* – The likelihood that the harm from a hazard is realised and the extent of it. In a risk assessment, risk should reflect both the likelihood that harm will occur and the severity of it.
- *Risk assessment* – The formal assessment of the relevant hazards and the potential severity of the outcome.
- *Risk control* – Methods employed to reduce risk to acceptable levels.

8.6.2 Carrying out an event risk assessment

A risk assessment should identify the period of time for which it will remain valid. It should take account of the views of employees and safety representatives and should follow the five steps outlined by the Health and Safety Executive (shown in Figure 8.4). Broadly, in an event

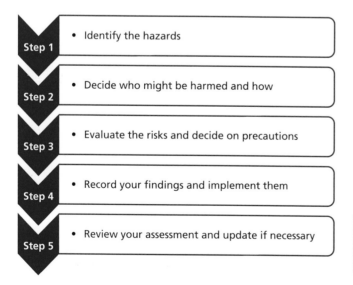

Step 1 • Identify the hazards

Step 2 • Decide who might be harmed and how

Step 3 • Evaluate the risks and decide on precautions

Step 4 • Record your findings and implement them

Step 5 • Review your assessment and update if necessary

Figure 8.4 Five steps to risk assessment
Source: HSE 2011

context, these steps equate to identifying and assessing hazards and implementing preventative measures.

The record should be retrievable for use by the employer in reviews and for safety representatives, other employee representatives and visiting inspectors (HSE 2003). A risk assessment template can be seen in Table 8.1. Included are some typical examples of potential hazards to illustrate how to complete the form.

Risk assessments should not be overcomplicated. Often, the risks are well known, and appropriate control measures are easy to apply. An event manager usually does not need to be a health and safety expert to complete a risk assessment – they simply need to have a good understanding of what is involved. However, larger and more complex events may require some expert help. A variety of risk assessment organisations can assist here, while local authorities and governing bodies are often able to advise, too.

Table 8.1 A sample risk assessment document

EVENT DETAILS

EVENT NAME

EVENT DETAILS	Location	Date	Running times	Expected audience numbers
DURATION	Site build	Live event	Break	
PERSONNEL	Organiser	Venue contact	Sponsors/ exhibitors	Audio-visual suppliers
	Entertainment/ Artist	Staging/set designers	Catering	Other suppliers
RISK ASSESSMENT	Completed by	Signature	Date	

IDENTIFICATION OF HAZARDS

What is the hazard?	*Who might be harmed and how?*	*Existing measures to control risk*	*Level*	*Further action required*	*Responsibility*
Slippery floor	Staff and visitors might slip on wet floor left by caterers or caused by spillages in food hall.	General good housekeeping. Suppliers and cleaners briefed thoroughly to mop floors.	Low	Food hall monitored every 30 minutes by nominated personnel.	Event manager

What is the hazard?	Who might be harmed and how?	Existing measures to control risk	Level	Further action required	Responsibility
		regularly, and immediately after a spillage.			
Transportation around site	Movement of vehicles around event site requires transport to use the same pathways as pedestrians. Accidents may occur.	Some designated roads for vehicles. Pathways clearly signposted for pedestrians. Routes positioned to enable easy access to work areas.	High	Separation of pedestrians from transport pathways by fencing.	Site manager/event manager
Risk of verbal or physical abuse	Unhappy visitors may abuse staff, entertainment or artists.	Managers on hand to intervene and security to be called if necessary.	Low	N/A	Event manager/ HR manager/ supplier managers
Manual handling of boxes, event material and equipment	During set-up and breakdown of event, staff may be at risk of injury.	Porters employed to do most movement of materials. Materials as far as possible to be delivered to the correct room/building to avoid second handling.	Low	Staff will not set up on their own – always working in pairs. Trolleys provided to transport material.	Operations manager
Fire evacuation of main room/ building	All	Staff briefed on fire evacuation procedures. Fire evacuation procedures explained to	High	Ensure that all staff running event have received information and training on	Operations manager

What is the hazard?	Who might be harmed and how?	Existing measures to control risk	Level	Further action required	Responsibility
		student staff when they first arrive on site for the event. Basic fire evacuation procedures explained to visitors during the introductory talk.		fire evacuation procedures (usually given during induction).	

As Shone and Parry (2010) point out, however, the risk that is inherent in much of events management is not chiefly related to safety. It often relates to whether suppliers will provide their services, whether the audience will turn up, or whether the marketing will deliver the expected results. Such risk factors, often identified during the screening process, do not need to be included in the risk assessment document. However, contingency plans should be in place as part of the overall event plan.

Study activity

Think of the last event you attended and, using the information from the sections above:

- Describe five potential hazards at the event and the level of risk they represented to attendees, employees and/or contractors.
- Suggest which controls could be introduced to ensure that these risks are reduced to acceptable levels.
- Link the risks you have identified to the relevant legislation.

8.7 Specific event risks

Event organisations are usually concerned with a number of particular risks. It is important to note, however, that the three specific event risks listed here by no means comprise an exhaustive list. Event organisations will certainly need to consider many more issues when compiling a risk assessment. These include the use of volunteers, communication procedures, emergency planning (including medical, ambulance and first-aid management), environmental impacts, recording and reporting of incidents, smoking, the protection of children and facilities for special needs. Of course, each event is unique and therefore demands a particular and individual risk assessment process.

8.7.1 Alcohol and drugs management

The management of alcohol, drugs and smoking makes up an important aspect of the control systems that need to be implemented in order to maintain a safe and comfortable atmosphere at an event. These elements are highly unpredictable, which means they represent a risk, so they should be managed as such. Many events have been cancelled or fined due to problems caused through the provision of alcohol or illegal drug-taking in the audience. Sometimes, even the threat of such activities is enough to disrupt an event. For instance, in 2010, the district administration in southern Goa revoked a 'no-objection' certificate that had been granted to a music festival that was due to take place on Agonda Beach, citing concerns over potential drug-dealing. (See YouTube sources.)

For many events, provision of alcohol is part of the organisational plan. Different types of events will, of course, involve different levels of consumption. A weekend musical festival with a primary target audience of eighteen–twenty-five-year-olds will probably need to think carefully about the management of the likely heavy consumption of alcohol, whereas a classical music concert in a park will probably be dealing with much lower consumption. Nevertheless, both events demand consideration and planning.

It is important to note that alcohol is defined as food under the law, so its provision must meet the relevant food safety legislation, regulations and codes of practice. In order to ensure that the provision of alcohol is kept within legal, and safe, limits, Bowdin et al. (2010) suggest implementing alcohol risk management procedures that include limiting ticket sales, closing hotels early, increasing security and roping-off certan areas. In addition, the following prevention strategies should be employed:

- Ensure that security are well trained and correctly briefed.
- Ensure that no under-eighteens are served.
- Serving staff should be fully trained to refuse service, recommend soft drinks and slow down service, if necessary.
- Use a drink ticketing system.
- Provide adequate access to food.
- Implement crowd management procedures.

The risk of drugs at events has increased steadily in line with the proliferation of drugs in society generally. In the UK, much of the current anti-drug legislation and many of the drug policies have their roots in attempts to regulate the illegal raves that were prevalent in the 1980s (Lenton et al. 1997). Whilst this particular cultural moment has passed, there is still a strong correlation between dance events and drug use. Students interested in how drug use impacts upon events will find much of interest in research that centres on rave culture and dance events (a good starting point is the aforementioned article by Lenton et al.).

It is important to note that many drugs are illegal, so the prevention of drug-taking should be paramount to event organisers. Strategies for searching guests, refusing entry and involving the police, where appropriate, are essential. However, most events with a profile audience who may be open to the use of drugs now operate a controlled drug policy, which, as well as putting into place prevention strategies, ensures that harm-reduction measures are in place. Lenton et al. (1997) suggest three main strategies to minimise the drug-related harm suffered by youngsters at dance

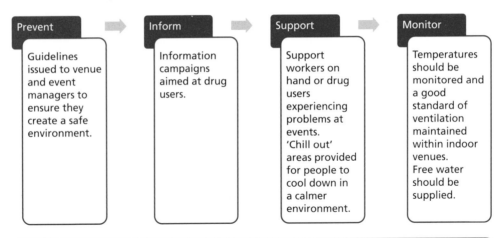

Figure 8.5 Drug control strategies to minimise potential drug-related harm

events: information campaigns; guidelines issued to nightclub owners and/or rave promoters; and the employment of outreach workers. Figure 8.5 incorporates these strategies alongside other practical solutions to provide a robust drug control policy that should minimise harm.

8.7.2 Fire safety

Uncontrolled fire at events can cause problems that range from minor injury or property damage to panic, stampedes and death. Fire prevention and evacuation procedures are therefore essential parts of the risk assessment process.

In 2003, the heavy-metal band Great White started a fire with their stage pyrotechnics. These pyrotechnics ignited the highly flammable soundproofing in the club where the band was performing, and ninety-six people died as a result. The band's tour manager, Daniel Biechele, pleaded guilty to 100 counts of involuntary manslaughter and spent four years in prison. One of the club's owners received a similar sentence, while the other received a ten-year suspended sentence, three years' probation and 500 hours' community service. In 2008 it was reported that a total of $175 million had been offered to the victims' families by various defendants (*USA Today* 2008; Challis 2009).

Events are subject to fire prevention regulations. In the UK, this is covered by the Regulatory Reform (Fire Safety) Order 2005. Event managers need to ensure that they understand the fire regulations and requirements of whichever country is hosting their event. These regulations usually establish minimum requirements that will provide a reasonable degree of safety from fire in buildings or other structures. They cover such areas as the number and functionality of fire exits, the storage of flammable liquid, the extinguisher or sprinkler systems, and the use of open flames and cooking devices (Silvers 2004). They also outline the regulations relating to safe capacity of spaces and evacuation procedures.

In order to understand the provision of fire safety, it is essential that event organisations follow these general principles:

- People can walk unaided to safety; particular provision should be in place for those less able to walk unaided and for disabled visitors.

- The route out of the venue should be clearly recognisable and accessible no matter where the fire breaks out.
- When fire breaks out, people often try to leave the way they entered. Where this is not possible (perhaps because the fire has broken out there or smoke is causing visibility issues), people should be able to find an alternative route to safety (HSE 1999: 22).
- Stewards and staff must be trained to usher people to safety. There is often resistance from guests who have underestimated the risk and do not want to use another exit.

Large-scale events or those involving pyrotechnics or other designed elements that present a fire hazard will require a site inspection by a fire warden or fire marshal. The event manager will be present during this inspection, and they might be asked to install extra fire extinguishers or fire exit signs. Equipment may need to be moved and venues may be required to install sprinkler systems (Silvers 2004) or to make provision for extra fire wardens on site during the event.

Finally, whilst it is much less likely that people will be trapped by fire at an outdoor event, the risks should still be managed and controlled as they are for indoor events. Fire warning systems are required for outdoor structures, such as marquees, campsites should have fire watchtowers, and campers should be provided with safety advice.

8.7.3 Managing crowds safely

As Abbott and Abbott (2000) suggest, crowd management and crowd control are two distinct but interrelated concepts. The former relates to the facilitation and movement of crowds during the normal circumstances of an event, whilst the latter relates to the steps that must be taken when a crowd starts to behave unexpectedly. Therefore, crowd management is proactive, whilst crowd control is reactive. Crowd management is carefully planned and implemented via the risk management and risk assessment processes prior to an event, and 'a well-conceived crowd management plan hopefully will eliminate the need for extensive crowd control' (Abbott and Geddie 2001: 269).

Before discussing crowd management in detail, it is worth hearing the opinion of a key industry voice on this important and complex issue.

Industry voice

Oliver Gardiner, managing director, Vespian Security

Within my role as a crowd manager and head of event security, I must take into consideration the expectations and motivation of all those attending and organising an event. When a customer, contractor, organiser or artist attends an event, they expect to be safe, treated fairly and with respect, that they will enjoy themselves and that they will have access to help and assistance, if required. These expectations encapsulate many aspects of an event site and its organisation – from toilets, queuing, pricing and crowd safety to medical assistance, conditions underfoot and entertainment programming.

Great crowd management and security are about a friendly, customer-focused approach and an accurate understanding of the event and audience demographic that is attracted to it. Depending on the demographic, the expectations of the crowd at different events could be poles apart, as would be the solutions to managing those crowds correctly. If insufficient numbers of security and crowd management staff are placed in certain locations, crime and disorder, or a crowd safety incident, could go unnoticed, resulting in complaints, poor press on social networking sites, minor or serious injuries, or even death. The importance of a safely managed event, where everyone is able to return home safely with themselves and their belongings intact, must not be underestimated.

No two days are ever the same, and no two events are ever identical. An important part of the modern crowd manager's roles and responsibilities is to be able to adapt plans and systems at a moment's notice to achieve the end goal, no matter what the situation may be.

8.7.3.1 Key issues of crowd management

CROWD ANALYSIS

The most important of aspect of crowd management involves making an accurate estimate of the number of attendees (Bowdin *et al.* 2010; Silvers 2004). When doing this, event managers need to bear in mind the capacity of the venue, and they should be able to forecast expected turnout. This forecast should be based on several factors: attendance in previous years, numbers who visit similar events, proposed level of publicity, number of advanced ticket sales, and so

Image 8.2 The Glastonbury Festival, 2011
Source: Tabatha Fireman / Getty Images

on. Allowance should always be made for much larger numbers turning up on the day, especially for events that are not based solely on advanced ticket sales.

At the end of the 1990s, the Glastonbury Festival suffered a few years of over-attendance, and these additional attendees (who gained entry without tickets) caused numerous safety problems. These problems became so severe that the festival was prosecuted in 2000 for having too many people on site, and the local authority felt that it could no longer issue a public entertainment licence. The following year, the festival took a year off to review the situation and its organisers devised workable solutions that complied with safety regulations, allowed proper crowd management and did not impact on Glastonbury's core philosophy and creativity. They set up a Licensing Working Group and liaised closely with industry experts, the police and the local authorities to implement various highly effective measures. (See Glastonbury Festivals 2002, a report that is strongly recommended for students interested in crowd management and crowd safety. A shorter discussion of the festival's crowd management techniques can be found in Glastonbury Festivals 2011.)

Event managers need to have a good understanding of the type of event they are staging and how their audience might react. However, this is not as simple as deciding that a concert for 70,000 young adults will need detailed crowd management plans whereas a classical music event for 15,000 middle-aged adults will not. Whilst it is true that the majority of crowd-related disasters happen at rock concerts and sporting events, anywhere with a large number of attendees is susceptible. A loss of crowd control can occur in the most unlikely places, as the Wal-Mart stampede tragically proved in 2008. Similarly, religious festivals often suffer crowd-related tragedies. For instance, 147 people worshippers died in a crush in a Hindu temple in 2008 (BBC 2008); and more than 450 people died in a stampede at a water festival in Cambodia two years later (Sky News 2010). There have also been many serious incidents during the Muslim Hajj: in 1990, 1400 pilgrims died in a stampede in a pedestrian tunnel; in 1994, 270 people were crushed to death; in 1997, 350 people died in a fire; in 1998, 180 pilgrims died in a crush; in 2004, stampedes resulted in the deaths of 250 people; and in 2006, at least 362 people died in a similar fashion (Al-Bab.com 2011; BBC 2001; and see Case Study 8.1).

Abbott and Geddie (2001) also highlight the importance of circumstances that may trigger crowd problems. Their list includes: cancellation, no-shows, congestion, lack of parking, the use of special effects, and the presence of obscene or violent performing acts. Other factors, such as weather, noise levels and the presence of rival groups, should be carefully considered in the crowd risk management process.

CROWD BEHAVIOUR

It is important to have an understanding of the type of attendee the event will attract. A rock concert that encourages dancing and generally boisterous behaviour will have a very different crowd management plan from that of a toy exhibition, which will attract mainly families. The Health and Safety Executive (HSE 2000) therefore advises that it is important to know the age range and social mix of attendees, which will allow event managers to anticipate likely behaviour and make appropriate arrangements for it.

Unforeseen circumstances can interfere with the management of a crowd, so the event manager must pay close attention to the actions and mood of the crowd. It is important to note, as Silvers (2004) does, that many of the worst disasters involving crowds have occurred at events with a large number of attendees. Most deaths in crowds result from suffocation. As the crowd loses control, its members crush together or collapse, and victims are unable to breathe:

> Crowd forces can reach levels that are almost impossible to resist or control. Virtually all crowd deaths are due to compressive asphyxia and not the 'trampling' reported by

the news media. Evidence of bent steel railings after several fatal crowd incidents show that forces of more than 4500 N (1000 lbs) occurred.

(Crowd Dynamics 2011)

No two crowds are the same, so it is difficult to predict how one will behave in unexpected circumstances, but event managers should still have an understanding of a crowd's basic sociological behaviour and how it might react. For further information on this topic, see numerous relevant articles in the journal *Events Management*, Abbott and Abbott (2000), Abbott and Geddie (2001), the HSE's *Managing Crowds Safely* (2000) and Crowd Dynamics (2011).

Silvers (2004) provides a useful list of definitions to explain potential reactions of a crowd in unforeseen circumstances:

- *Crowd crush* – The crowd is compressed into ever-smaller areas due to an absence of a portal or escape, and this compression quickly becomes critical. An example was the Hillsborough Stadium disaster in 1989 (see YouTube sources).
- *Crowd collapse* – Individuals at the front of a crowd fall over, and those behind consequently lose their balance and fall on top.
- *Crowd craze* – This is rarer than other crowd reactions and typically occurs when the crowd rushes or pushes forward, towards an individual or a desired object.
- *Crowd panic* – The frenzied desire to escape a real or perceived danger. Panicking crowds often trample those who have fallen and are lying on the escape route. In the aforementioned Cambodian water festival disaster, the crowd seems to have panicked because of rumours that people were being electrocuted and that the bridge on which they were standing was starting to collapse (see YouTube sources).
- *Crowd surge* – This often occurs at concerts. In the 2009 Mawazine Festival in Morocco, the 70,000-plus crowd surged forward to see singer Abdelaziz Stati. This resulted in at least eleven deaths and forty injuries.

The general principles are that the event manager must know their crowd and must have the right precautionary (and often calming) measures in place before the event starts. These measures can range from ensuring the visibility of security staff and personnel to removing audience members who are displaying inappropriate or unruly behavior. Obviously, they will need to be appropriate to the type of event and audience.

8.7.3.2 Crowd control planning

In order to implement a successful crowd management plan, event managers also need to assess the factors that make up a crowd control plan. This will consist of the steps and procedures that should be taken once a crowd has lost control, and it will outline the measures that should be implemented at different stages of the event (Abbott and Geddie 2001).

Abbott and Geddle (2001) suggest that there are three stages in a crowd control plan – pre-crisis, crisis and post-crisis. During the pre-crisis stage, the event manager will consider certain preventative tactics to avoid crowd control problems (such as staff training, facilities management and the use of a control centre to aid communication). A crowd-related risk assessment will be produced at this stage. To help with this, the event manager should consider what might go wrong, who might be harmed and what the best response would be (see Table 8.2).

The second stage – the crisis stage – begins when the preventative measures fail. During this stage, practical crowd control measures, such as clear evacuation procedures and calm

> ## Table 8.2 Crowd management risk assessment checklist

Are the numbers controlled and predictable?

Are visitors likely to be familiar with the venue?

What are the characteristics of the predicted crowd – age/gender/family structure?

Is the event likely to generate high emotions?

How will performers affect this?

Might there be aggressive behaviour/drug/alcohol use?

Are gatecrashers likely?

---

personnel, are essential – as is a proactive response before the situation escalates. For instance, overcrowding should be dealt with before the crowd starts to panic.

The final stage – the post-crisis stage – involves the review and evaluation of the strategy after the event. A full review should be completed by the organiser to ascertain whether security and personnel all responded effectively and efficiently, and to identify key issues or problems that may arise again in the future.

CASE STUDY 8.1

Crowd safety: the Hajj

Muslims consider pilgrimage to the holy city of Mecca, Saudi Arabia – known as the Hajj – as the most significant demonstration of their faith and unity. In December 2008, as the world's largest annual pilgrimage, the Hajj attracted two and a half million people.

The pilgrimage traditionally ends with the 'Stoning of the Devil' ceremony at Mina. As all pilgrims endeavour to attend this part of the festival, all pass through a small area, which has caused major crowd safety implications. Most people try to cast their stones after the lunchtime prayers, which has resulted in fatal stampedes in the past. The most recent, in 2006, led to the deaths of 362 people. After this tragedy, the Saudi Arabian government took steps to manage crowds at this crucial point in order to reduce the risk of future fatalities. Their plan included the construction of a further two levels, resulting in a total of three balconies from which pilgrims could throw their stones, enabling freer and faster passage. Tens of thousands of personnel were hired to promote safety and provide stewarding and safety-related services to attendees. Hundreds of closed-circuit television cameras were installed along the route to monitor crowd movement, allowing the timely correction of bottlenecks of pilgrims as soon as they arose, and to enable stewards to clear groups of people as they gathered.

In addition to improving safety at the 'Stoning of the Devil' ceremony, the organisers have focused on the health of attendees. Over forty ambulances are now on hand to attend to victims of heatstroke, those experiencing breathing problems due to overcrowding and poor ventilation, and those who have been hit by rebounding stones. Cooling equipment has been installed inside the galleries on each balcony to maintain air circulation and reduce the temperature.

These modern measures, designed to reduce the risk of death and injury, were implemented in order to bring one of the world's oldest festivals into line with both health, safety and welfare legislation and the progressive practices of the modern, international events industry. Impressively, the organisers have achieved this without losing the essence of a creative and exciting event.

Source: CNN, 9 December 2008

Study activity

The 'Stoning of the Devil' ceremony requires the organisers of the Hajj to balance religion, culture, tradition and safety. In pairs, discuss what you think the organisers' priorities should be and pinpoint five of the key challenges they face in managing this crowd.

Industry voice

Jessica Templeton, University of Greenwich

 I run the Events Department at the University of Greenwich. We have three sites in the south-east of England, including the main campus in Greenwich, London. The university hosts a large number of conferences, public lectures, weddings, summer schools and other events.

As the events are held on the campus, my team needs to give careful consideration to the environment. It is our responsibility to ensure the safety of the event guests. However, we must also consider the safety and welfare of tourists, students and staff who attend the site every day. The Greenwich campus is a very busy tourist attraction, attracting many visitors on a daily basis – especially in the summer. So, although we don't need to worry about students during the summer break, we have a completely different set of people to consider.

The university arranges or hosts a wide range of visits and on- and off-campus activities involving children and young people. Examples of these are work-experience placements, children's university, sports clubs and language schools using university facilities, and nursery and play schemes. A lot of health and safety legislation refers specifically to the protection of children and young people when involved with work activities. As such, we have developed a code of practice that sets out the general arrangements, and certain prohibitions, to be followed to ensure that children are safe if they are on university premises or affected by university activities. The code applies to staff, students, visitors and contractors.

When the university is arranging an event, it is usually the responsibility of the head of school or office making the arrangements to ensure that the legal requirements are met and that best practice is followed. When we are hosting an event or activity, the prime responsibility for the safety of guests usually rests with the client, but we are required to ensure the premises and any equipment or services that we provide are safe. This means we have to work very closely with the clients to ensure all arrangements meet the necessary requirements. We also need to consider the insurance arrangements and ensure that the university's policies cover all the necessary visitors, employees and guests.

We haven't had any major health and safety issues at our events – largely because we take it so seriously in the first place. We are required by law and by university regulations to carry out a risk assessment for every event we hold. These assessments cover a wide variety of hazards, including any special needs, such as disabilities and dietary restrictions; assessing suitability of areas; equipment (including protective equipment); waste and spillage; transportation around the site; fire evacuation and overcrowding. We consider different areas within the university as high or low risk – reception areas, restaurants, libraries, computing areas and single-occupancy offices would normally be regarded as low-risk areas as they have hazards similar to the domestic environment.

My team uses a checklist, called the 'Health and Safety Event Evaluation', which runs to two pages. It asks them to do things like ensure they know what audio-visual equipment the client will need and hire it from a reputable source; consider storage plans; implement emergency plans for fire evacuation and first aid; organise waste disposal; and print up briefing sheets for visitors. We always hold briefing sessions for all the staff involved in the event delivery to ensure that all the health and safety issues are covered. Then, at the end of every event, we hold a debriefing session with all the event staff to identify what worked well and what could be improved next time. During this session, we make a note of all these items so that any necessary improvements can be included in the risk assessment, planning and arrangements for next time.

As my team facilitates events, we don't have a large remit for event design – the concept is often developed by our clients. In terms of what we can and can't do within the venue, we are restricted by the nature of our buildings –

the Greenwich campus is protected by various laws and regulations (including the UK government's listed buildings legislation). This means that there are many things that we would love to do but can't. For instance, we can't attach anything to the walls, which limits the sort of stage sets we can use.

Because of the nature of our venues, we need to keep abreast of the changing regulations, laws and licences required to run events. We do this by checking regularly for updates on the relevant legislation, ensuring we look at best practice of relevant bodies, and seeking advice from our colleagues at the university or within the Greenwich Foundation when we aren't sure of the most recent policies.

The other two venues are not protected in the same way, but they have their own issues. University policy is that teaching must be priortised, so my department has to fit the events we are responsible for around a very busy teaching timetable – juggling the needs of the students with the needs of the clients is sometimes a full-time job!

So, as well as the health and safety issues, we have lots of other things to think about. It can get quite complex and my team always needs to be on the ball and thinking about what can and can't be done. Our clients give us very positive feedback on the event delivery and event experience – and, whilst it is difficult at times, I think we manage to juggle the creativity of events with the incredibly important considerations of health and safety.

8.8 Summary

This chapter has demonstrated the centrality of health, safety and risk issues in the event planning process. The guiding principle is that health, safety and risk management should be built into the planning process from the very start. The health, safety and welfare of event attendees, employees and contractors are the responsibility of all parties associated with events and should be paramount in all decision-making.

Health and safety is governed by much legislation and regulation, and event managers need to be confident that they understand the myriad licences, permits and regulations required to stage an event (no matter what size) and that they are operating within the relevant laws. Professional advice should be sought if there is any doubt.

This chapter has also focused on the management of health and safety, particularly on the design of an event to ensure that hazards and risks are minimised. Without due care and attention to the management of health and safety, and the assessment of potential risks, event organisers expose themselves to potential claims, fines and even criminal prosecution, should things go wrong. And when things go wrong at events, they often do so with catastrophic results. Identifying what may be a hazard, and the likelihood of that hazard causing problems for the staff or attendees, is therefore an essential part of the risk management process. The risks associated with event management are wide ranging and atypical – every event is unique and should be assessed as such. This chapter has outlined the key risks and has looked at some of them in more detail, but a successful event manager will understand that the information presented here is far from exhaustive.

Whilst health, safety and risk management can cause some restrictions to event design, the experience will not be compromised if it is handled skilfully. Consequently, the delivered event will be both excellent and safe.

Further reading

AEO, BECA and EVA (2002) *The Guide to Managing Health and Safety at Exhibitions and Events: 'The Red Book'* (2nd edn), Berkhamstead: AEO, BECA and EVA. This guide, produced by the industry's principal trade associations, provides only part of the information required to implement health and safety procedures both pre-show and on site at exhibitions or events in the UK. It mainly deals with the responsibilities of four parties: venue owner, organiser, exhibitor, and contractor. It is also essential to refer to all the statutory regulations (and the specific venue and local authority regulations), especially the Management of Health and Safety at Work Regulations 1999.

Berlonghi, A. E. (1995) Understanding and Planning for Different Spectator Crowds, *Safety Science*, 18: 239–247. This paper provides summaries of different factors for distinguishing and assessing crowds within the context of special event planning. It relates the practicalities of events management to academic theories.

Health and Safety Executive (1999) *The Event Safety Guide*, Norwich: HSE. An essential guide to health, safety and risk management for event organisers. The book has a UK focus, but it can be used as a starting point for key areas of consideration for event organisers around the world. The aim of the book is to enable organisers, local authorities, emergency services and the Health and Safety Executive to work together to improve safety. It provides advice that focuses largely on music events, but many chapters can be applied to a variety of other events. It was written in conjunction with industry professionals and offers advice on broad safety topics, such as venue and site design, fire procedures and major incident planning. It also offers advice on specific issues, such as transport, barriers, electrics, refreshments, merchandising, amusements, attractions, sanitation, noise, vibration and so on. It is due to be revised in 2012.

Silvers, J. (2004) *Professional Event Coordination*, New Jersey: John Wiley & Sons. A very practical look at events management, with clear and sound advice on aspects of risk assessment, the identification of hazards, the provision of security, the emergency services and communication procedures. Recommended for those new to events management in practice.

Worksafe Victoria (2006) *Crowd Control at Venues and Events: A Practical Occupational Health and Safety Guide*, Melbourne: State Government Victoria. A useful forty-four-page guide that will help both crowd control agencies and host employers (venues and events) to fulfil their responsibilities in relation to the Occupational Health and Safety Act 2004. It identifies common safety problems and suggests solutions to ensure crowd control is conducted as safely as possible. Finally, it provides numerous recommendations and tools to ensure the health, safety and welfare of crowd control staff as well as other staff and patrons.

Chapter 9

Sporting events

Contents

9.1 Aims

By the end of this chapter, students will be able:

- To review the development of the sports industry to its present role.
- To understand the processes involved in sports event business management.
- To discuss the challenges posed by current issues affecting sports events.
- To understand the legacies of particular sports events.

9.2 Introduction

This chapter will highlight the specific nature of sports events and their major contribution to the development of events management as a worldwide industry. The issues of political influence, legacies, economic impact and how to bid for sporting events will also be discussed, as will the extent to which the event manager can prepare to deal with these. The motivation of attendees, the development of sponsorship and the role of television in sporting events will be reviewed. Particular practical emphasis will be placed on the management of participants, event safety in relation to challenges of crowd behaviour, and management of such issues as violence, racism, drugs and alcohol.

The history of sporting events is unclear, as the first events began more than 2000 years ago. There is evidence of these occurring in ancient Greece, China and Egypt, with the first Olympic Games held in 776 BC (Masterman 2009). The first modern Olympics took place in Athens, Greece, in 1896. Football – now perhaps the biggest global sport – was first played in its current format in Sheffield in 1860, when Sheffield FC, the oldest football club in the world, met Sheffield Hallam FC, the second-oldest club in the world, at Sandygate Lane, the oldest football stadium in the world. They competed for the Youden Trophy, sponsored by Thomas Youden, a local theatre owner, at a cost of £2 (equivalent to £170 today; Sheffield Hallam FC website).

That first football game in Sheffield exhibited some of the key components of a modern sporting event. The sport of football was given a set of rules by the Sheffield FA, which enabled competition to take place within a clearly laid-out formula. Each team or participant had the opportunity to win a prize – donated by a benefactor or sponsor – and they were overseen by a referee. Spectators either paid to watch or were invited to attend, hospitality and catering were laid on for them, and the media – at this stage simply the local newspaper – was present to record the event. In the following years, as the number of teams grew, so did the competition, the number of spectators and the revenue from the sale of refreshments.

9.3 Overview of the sports industry

The scale of sporting events varies from the small local event, attracting only a handful of competitors and maybe no spectators at all, to the mega-event that is open to billions of people around the globe. As illustrated in Table 9.1, sporting events vary in terms of number of participants, total media coverage, value of sponsorship deals, total running costs, management type and the distance travelled by the participants. However, all of these events, whether a one-day local wrestling competition or a one-month international basketball tournament, usually feature an individual or team winner, some form of prize, and arbitration of the event. In all events, it is the spirit of sport and taking part that are the most important factors, and, as

Masterman (2009: 3) points out, there is 'wider significance to society than just the staging of a sporting event'. Such are the growth and increasing value of the sporting events industry that more political intervention and political comment in the future are almost inevitable. Governments have long used sporting events to make political statements, such as the US government boycotting the Moscow Olympics, and many people are prepared to stake their political and personal reputations on bidding for lucrative sporting events. Thirty years ago, a mega-event might generate a few million pounds in revenue, but now the bidding process alone can easily stretch into the tens of millions. This has led to accusations of bribery and corruption being levelled at both those who wish to host events and members of awarding committees.

All of this illustrates that the sporting events industry is a fast-growing and lucrative business. Sporting events management is a relatively new academic research area, with very few books covering the topic. Somewhat more academic journal articles have been written on the subject, but most of these focus on the US sporting events industry.

The sports industry has boomed over the last thirty years. In the United States, the overall sports market – which includes participation in sports, taking part in events and attending as a spectator – was estimated at between $44 billion and $73 billion in 2005 (Humphreys and Humphreys 2008). This not only establishes sports as an important contributor to the general economy in terms of employment and revenue generated but suggests that sports, and sporting events, impact on the lives of a significant number of people. A key turning point in this development of sports as a profitable business was the 1984 Olympic Games in Los Angeles – the first modern Games not to incur a huge loss for the host city. Profits were achieved through the greater involvement of sponsors, lucrative broadcasting contracts and other outside investment. All of this was in stark contrast to the Montreal Olympics in 1976, which incurred such huge losses that the city government was still paying off the debt thirty years later.

There is frequent discussion about European football leagues and the fact that just a handful of teams in most countries win the majority of the league titles and cup competitions, and that these leagues and cups are not competitive for most teams as they lack outcome uncertainty. American sporting events organisers take this problem very seriously, to such an extent that they have devised a system to overcome it. In order to maintain competitive leagues and retain the interest of all fans throughout the season, the National Football League (NFL) manages professional teams' recruitment of new players by ensuring that the best college players sign for the teams that finished lowest in the divisions. This 'draft pick' was introduced in an attempt to ensure that all teams are competitive and have a chance of winning at least their regional division (Cousens *et al.* 2001).

9.3.1 The impact of sporting events

Considerable emphasis is now placed on sporting events' impact and legacy. These topics will be covered in more detail in Chapter 14, but their importance in the sporting events industry merits further attention here. Sport England, a key governing body for the development of sports in England, has produced several reports which consider the impact of sporting events on the wider community.

9.3.1.1 The social impact of sporting events

There are a number of ways in which a sporting event can impact on a local community, either positively or negatively. The key negative impact is inconvenience for local residents (Small 2007), with specific problems including increased traffic congestion, extra people in the area during the event and the possibility of crowd disorder or even hooliganism. These have been

Table 9.1 Typology of sporting events

Size of event	Characteristics of the event
Local	For example, school sports day
	Restricted to local entrants
	Usually well established
	Small-scale sponsorship and local media coverage
	Costs are usually covered by entrants and donations of facilities made by the local community
Regional	For example, regional baseball tournament
	Restricted to counties or states
	Usually linked to a regional sports organisation
	Sponsorship usually offered by a sponsor with direct interest in sports
	Media coverage might (occasionally) include television
	Most costs are covered by entrants and/or their sports team
National	For example, national ice-skating championships
	Open to all clubs/individuals based in one country
	Organised by a national sports body and financed by the entrants
	Sponsorship linked to a recognised national brand
	More media coverage than a regional event
International	For example, Berlin Marathon
	Open to a number of countries but cost to entrant determines the level of international involvement
	Majority of participants come from host country and nearest neighbours
	Organisers mainly part time, with support from volunteers
	More media interest but still mainly national media coverage
Global event (mega-event)	For example, Olympic Games
	Participants travel from many countries, so most cover considerable distances
	Organising committees are usually full time or on long contracts, with high volunteer involvement
	Sponsorship is high due to increased media coverage on a global basis
	Revenue-generating opportunities are considerable

issues for decades, but recently more individuals and communities have started to argue that the benefits of hosting sporting events outweigh the negative aspects. The following example illustrates this change in attitude.

In the 1970s, Sheffield United Football Club applied to its local council to redevelop part of its ground. The proposal included building a hotel, expanding leisure facilities, increasing the overall capacity of the stadium, and introducing new corporate hospitality viewing areas. These extensive plans were rejected by the city council, which ruled that an increase in traffic and numbers of people attending the stadium would affect the quality of life of local residents. The latter were already unhappy about the disruption caused by sporting events in the area, which numbered only about twenty-five each year. Thirty years later, the football club submitted much-revised plans, but with the same aim of developing the stadium to include more facilities. This time, they have been accepted, and it is hoped that the development will regenerate what has now become a rundown area of the city. It will certainly create much-needed jobs for a local community with high unemployment. The current stadium already has a hotel and several office suites that are rented out to local companies, and these have created jobs and have generally improved the local environment.

Obviously, objections from the local community can seriously threaten the success of a sporting event. The London Olympics have drawn fierce opposition from the residents of Greenwich – an important stakeholder group – who feel that the equestrian events – which are to be held in their Royal Park – will cause disruption for at least six months before the main event in August 2012 and that the park will be closed during this time. This is a far from unusual reaction. While governments generally promote the positive social impacts of major sporting events, local residents are still often sceptical (Preuss and Solberg 2006).

Some sporting event organisers attempt to overcome such opposition by claiming that local residents will have the opportunity to meet people from other countries and other cultural backgrounds, and that the event will benefit other local cultural activities. For instance, a car-racing event in Florida was promoted as a sports tourism event, because it was expected that attendees would stay on after the race and take part in local cultural activities. However, research found that most people who attended the main event did not take part in other events in the area, so there was no significant social benefit (Pennington-Gray and Holdnak 2002).

9.3.1.2 The economic impact of sporting events

The economic impact of a sporting event is usually a key part of the bidding process for staging it. Barget and Gouguet (2007) estimated the net social benefit of hosting a prestigious new tennis tournament in France. After deducting all of the costs associated with the tournament, and measuring the reactions of local people, the net social benefit was €215,000 (£195,000). There are two schools of thought, and much debate, among sports economists and event planners about the economic impact of sporting events. For instance, some researchers have highlighted 'time switchers' – people who are displaced when an event takes place in a major location (Preuss 2005). If an event takes place in Barcelona in August and attracts many visitors, other people who would normally visit the city in the summer might well avoid it because they have no interest in the sporting event. Their revenue is 'displaced' for that year, and they may never return in the future, either. Event planners often ignore this consequence of hosting a sports event. They are more likely to make a calculation based solely on the number of visitors to their event multiplied by the average amount of money that those people will spend when they are in the city. To that can be added the jobs created by building the new facilities, such as the Olympic Village in London, which will be used to provide housing for local people after the event, and regeneration of what is deemed to be a deprived area. However, those opposing the event might well suggest that the government should build houses and regenerate the area anyway, as part of their general responsibility to the community, without the need for an Olympic Games.

In sum, then, a city will usually gain some social and economic benefits from hosting a sporting event. However, there will almost certainly be costs, too, and these should always be considered when planning an event.

9.3.2 Sporting event legacies

The legacy of a sporting event is now one of the key criteria for sporting events bids, and it is frequently discussed by politicians and the media. Barcelona gained improved transport links and benefited from other regeneration projects as a direct result of hosting of the 1992 Olympics. However, the Olympic Stadium itself now stands empty. It was handed over to the football club Español after the Games, but they have now moved to their own purpose-built stadium, a fact that has been largely overlooked by sports marketing academics. The future of the London's Olympic Stadium has been the subject of much legal wrangling and challenges in the courts, with several rival football clubs bidding to make the stadium their new permanent home. At the time of writing, the stadium's ultimate fate remained uncertain. Manchester City Football Club's move into the city's Commonwealth Games Stadium was less problematic and ranks as one of the more successful conversions of a mega-event stadium after a games.

Study activity

What potential advantages and disadvantages must be considered by cities that wish to host high-cost sporting events?

9.3.3 Bidding to host sporting events

In the previous sections, dealing with the impact and legacy of sporting events, reference was made to the potential social and economic benefits of hosting a sporting event, as well as the influence of local and national governments. There is now increasing competition to host such events, with governments from all over the world putting in bids. The competition is so fierce for events such as the Olympics, the European Football Championships and the FIFA World Cup that several million pounds have to be invested in the bidding process alone. New bidding procedures have emerged in an attempt to guarantee fairness in the selection of hosts, and therefore bidding teams should pay more attention to making successful bids.

Countries now set up organising committees to prepare complex bids for high-profile events, while multi-venue events – such as the FIFA World Cup – also generate strong *internal* competition between cities who want to host some of the games. This means that sports clubs and their local authorities now invest heavily in trying to become a designated host venue. When the Football Association (FA) in London coordinated its bid to host the World Cup in 2018 or 2022, fifteen potential host cities tendered bids to host matches, meaning that three were likely to be unsuccessful if England were awarded the competition. These were complex bids requiring teams of experienced people from football clubs, sporting associations, local councils, area development agencies, industry figureheads and sponsors, each of whom spent up to six months working on the project. (For further information, see the FA website.)

Of course, the vast majority of bids for sporting events end in failure for the bidding committee (Emery 2002: 317), meaning that deprived areas are not regenerated and the region does not gain a reputation as a major sporting venue. As a result of the high failure rate of bids, any sporting events people who have been involved in successful bids are highly sought after and rewarded, not only in their host countries but overseas. For instance, Mike Lee was part of the successful bid teams for both the 2012 and 2016 Olympics, and then helped Qatar secure the 2022 World Cup (see *Guardian* website).

Given the increase in the number of bids to host sporting events, bidding teams need to look closely at the factors that contribute to a winning bid, and need to incorporate these elements, where possible, in their own bid. Of course, it could be argued that the bidding process varies according to the sporting event, but a review of the literature suggests that a number of factors are universally helpful to all bids. Recent successful bids have hired well-known personalities in an attempt to influence the key stakeholders that make up the team which awards the event. For instance, the British government recruited footballer David Beckham to lobby individual members of the International Olympic Committee (IOC) during the 2012 bidding process. Gold medal-winners Dame Kelly Holmes and Sir Steve Redgrave were also part of the lobbying group, but Beckham was the key weapon. Prime Minister Tony Blair introduced him to individual IOC members who had not yet decided how they would vote, and many of these men and women were said to have been 'star struck' in Beckham's presence. With the final vote so close, Beckham's influence may well have secured the Olympics for London.

In a survey of 135 people from 21 countries who had been involved in bidding for a variety of 'hallmark' sporting events, 8 key factors for success were identified (Westerbeek *et al.* 2002; see Table 9.2). These provide a useful starting point for any group that is interested in compiling a bid for a sporting event.

A bidding host city or sporting body must address all of these issues when making a presentation. They comprise a checklist for the bidders but also for the committees charged with choosing the successful applicant. While the cost of facilities is not necessarily the most important factor, it is becoming harder for countries without a strong infrastructure to be successful in bids, as the costs of providing the necessary facilities are unlikely to be covered by sponsorship revenues and government grants. The typical cost of a new stadium for a mega-event can easily reach £750 million, but some of this outlay can be recouped if it is handed over to a new owner or tenant once the event has finished. This also has the benefit of making the venue available for future bids for other events.

While this research was conducted into bidding for mega-events, those wishing to host smaller events can learn from it, too. The principal reason for staging a sporting event should be to promote and develop sport, so this should always be stressed in a bid. This could help to secure the support of local politicians who wish to promote healthy lifestyles among the community. In turn, this might persuade other key stakeholders to offer their support or funding. Any potential benefits to the local economy should also be calculated and presented to stakeholders, as should any research which indicates that the local community is in favour of the event.

9.3.4 Venue design

If a bid has been successful, the first thing to consider is the design or development of the stadium (or stadiums) where the events will take place. Over the last ten years, greater emphasis than ever before has been placed on venue design. The economic viability of a stadium has become a key factor in this design process, with owners keen to ensure that their investment continues to generate revenue on a regular basis.

Table 9.2 Key success factors when compiling a bid for a sporting event
Source: Adapted from Westerbeek *et al.* 2002

Success factors	Issues to address
Accountability	To what extent does the bid represent the views of the community whose tax revenues will be spent on the event, and how strong is the reputation of the bidder in this sport?
Political support	Are the key decision-makers in the sporting bodies, local council, local government and national government known?
	Does the event promise to leave a legacy for the bid city?
Relationship marketing	Are there enough people with influence in their sport, or established event managers, who can influence key stakeholders?
Ability	What evidence is there to show that the bidder can successfully manage this type of event? Experience counts.
Infrastructure	Where will all the spectators, competitors and employees stay during the event, and how good are the arrangements for transporting them to and from the venues?
Bid team composition	Can a bid team be assembled that represents the sport and will be able to deal comfortably with important decision-makers?
Communication and exposure	How well known is the potential host city and does it have a reputation for hosting events?
Existing facilities	Given the escalating costs of providing new facilities for events, are there existing facilities that can be utilised for the event?

Table 9.3 provides some examples of recently built or redeveloped sports stadiums that now operate as multi-purpose event arenas. These innovative approaches have generated considerable additional revenue for the stadiums' owners. Charlton Athletic and Leyton Orient secured public funds for their redevelopment projects by incorporating a school and a health centre, respectively, in their new facilities. Portsmouth Football Club has ambitious plans to build hundreds of new apartments on regenerated land next to the site of its new stadium, which will then be sold to part-finance the development of the new ground. And the New York Yankees' new stadium is another wonderful example of a multi-purpose stadium. With 1.3 million square feet, it can cater for a range of non-sporting events that generate additional revenue on an almost daily basis.

Table 9.3 Features of new and developed sports stadiums

Club or organisation	Country	Extra features at venue
Arizona Diamondbacks	USA	Replaceable stadium floor to cater for events that cannot take place on grass or astroturf
Wembley Stadium	England	Sliding roof to reduce the impact of inclement weather
Sapporo Stadium	Japan	Sliding roof and interchangeable floors to suit different sporting events
Emirates Stadium	England	Assisted housing for local people employed in key services, conference facilities and museum
Phoenix Suns	USA	Nightclub, café and shops
Leyton Orient Football Club	England	Apartment blocks in corners of the stadium, medical centre and training facility shared with local community
Sheffield United Football Club	England	Offices that can be converted into hospitality areas on match days, car parks used for the city's Park and Ride scheme, new hotel and conference facilities
Charlton Athletic Football Club	England	School/college that converts to hospitality area for events, including gym and crèche
New York Yankees	USA	Extra space for non-sporting major events, including conference facilities and hospitality

Study activity

You have been asked to design a new 30,000-seat sports stadium and incorporate as many features as possible that will help the owners to maximise customer experience and increase revenue-generating opportunities. Assuming that an average ticket costs £20 and that a sold-out venue will therefore generate around £600,000, list the additional features that you intend to introduce in your design, and say how much they will contribute to turnover. For example, if you incorporate a coffee bar that serves around 1000 people a week and generates an average of £2 per person, that makes a weekly turnover of £2000, or about £104,000 a year. Outline the potential advantages and disadvantages for each of your design features.

CASE STUDY 9.1

Baseball in Cuba

Location: Cuba
Event type: sporting event
Attendees: up to 30,000

In this case study, look for the differences between hosting sporting events in a developed market when compared to doing so in a politically controlled country, such as Cuba. What are the main differences and what changes should the organisers of Cuban baseball make?

Cuban sports receive little or no help or investment from outside sources. In the country's National Baseball League, the teams play around 100 games per season, frequently travelling long distances, but the players are amateur and receive no salaries, apart from small contributions to their food, accommodation and clothing costs. Nevertheless, Cuba still produces very high-quality players, most of whom will only ever play in their own country. They share a love of baseball with the fans, which makes for very exciting sporting events. Many fans still revel in their country's last victory over the United States in the World Baseball Final, where the Cuban players defeated some of the highest-paid sportsmen in the world.

Big games are televised, and at first glance they could easily be from the United States. However, on closer inspection, there is no evidence of any sponsors, no in-field advertising boards and no commercials during breaks in play. In fact, the only evidence of any commercial involvement might be the brand name Siemens, worn on a Real Madrid shirt by a fan in the stands, no doubt a gift from an exiled family member. Some grounds do have hoardings that resemble advertising boards, but most simply read 'Viva La Revolución' ('Long Live the Revolution') or 'Hasta La Victoria Siempre' ('Always the Victory') – slogans from the revolutionary days of the late 1950s.

Baseball in Cuba is now one of the few remaining examples of a major sport that does not benefit (or suffer) from commercial involvement and broadcasting fees. It is a fascinating relic of how most sporting events used to be.

9.4 Managing the sporting event: managing participants

The role of the participant in sporting events is sometimes taken for granted, yet in an increasingly competitive sporting event environment, there is increasingly strong competition for future competitors.

At the Regensburg Marathon in Bavaria, Germany, many of the publicity stands are occupied by promoters of other marathons, such as Munich and Berlin, who are keen to sign up participants for their rival events. A keen German runner might have the choice of six different marathons in his region in a single year. Sporting event participants should therefore be treated in a way that makes them want to return and take part in future events, so there is a need to manage their experience and convince them to participate again. In other words, while it is important to cater to the needs of the media, spectators and sponsors, participants should certainly never be neglected. Below is a list of the factors that an event management team needs to take into consideration when managing participants:

- Develop a player-friendly event so that participants have a positive experience. They are more likely to come to the next event if they enjoy themselves.
- Think about the timing of the event and how this fits into the participants' timetables. Avoid clashing with a competitor's event.
- Consider whether the family and friends of the participant should be looked after, particularly if they are supported by a large number of people. The latter might be asked their opinion of the event and could well be influential.
- Organise a player-friendly party either at the beginning or at the end of the event. This will add to the experience of the participant and will influence how they view the event.
- Can they be given souvenirs or gifts, or at the very least photographs, as reminders of the event?
- Use contracts to protect the event and the participant. These can have incentives and bonuses built into them, and help clear up misunderstandings. They might also have a clause that allows the event manager to withdraw a competitor should their behaviour away from the sport have a detrimental impact on the event. (Adapted from Cousens *et al.* 2001)

9.4.1 Managing participants' drugs and alcohol consumption

The first attempt to address the problem of drug use in sports came in 1967, with the founding of the Olympic Committee Medical Commission, which was established after rumours of drug-taking in the Olympic Games (Beckett and Cowan 1979).

One of the biggest issues facing sporting event organisers today is the high percentage of athletes who take medicine or supplements prior to competing. In a survey carried out for the 2004 Olympics, 75 per cent of the athletes admitted taking supplements or medicines three days before competition, with as many as 20 per cent of these competitors taking five or more supplements (Ambrose 2004: 502).

The English FA has taken the lead in attacking the use of drugs to enhance sporting performance (in a sport where drug-taking is not considered to be a serious problem) by introducing random drug testing in mobile units for its affiliated players.

Alcohol abuse is much easier to identify, and many sports clubs now carry out random tests on players to see if they are under the influence of alcohol.

9.4.2 Safety at sporting events

While most sporting events proceed without complications, they are potentially very dangerous places for both attendees and employees. It is the duty of the event manager to ensure that everyone at the event remains safe.

For many people, the sporting event provides an escape from the monotony of day-to-day life and an opportunity to get excited by their favourite team or athlete. Some relish the chance to let off steam by shouting, cheering and singing. In such an environment, passions can run high and lead to catastrophe.

Recent disasters at sporting events are etched in the memories of those who attended. In 1985, around fifty people died in the Heysel Stadium, Belgium – a stadium that was due to be rebuilt as it was deemed unsuitable for modern sporting events. Just a couple of weeks earlier, fifty-five people had died in a stadium fire in Bradford, England. Then, in 1989, ninety-six people were crushed to death at Hillsborough in Sheffield (Dickie 1995). After this tragedy, the British government commissioned the Taylor Inquiry to look into stadium safety. Its final report recommended that all major stadiums should be all-seater and issued a host of other safety guidelines. Many of these were followed, with all clubs in the top two divisions of English football replacing their terraces with seats. However, similar reforms have not been implemented elsewhere. As late as 2009, many supporters died at a stadium in the Ivory Coast when a wall collapsed on top of them. This occurred despite FIFA devoting much time and energy towards improving safety at football grounds. Its guidelines are helpful in the management of both large- and small-scale football matches, and they should also be considered by organisers of other sporting events (see the FIFA website).

Another safety concern at sporting events is the threat of terrorist attack. Most organisers now manage this very carefully and efficiently inside the stadium, but terrorists are constantly developing their strategies in response. Recently, both the Togo football team and the Sri Lankan cricket team have been attacked en route to matches, illustrating the importance of protecting competitors outside as well as inside the venue.

Study activity

Look at FIFA's safety guidelines (on the FIFA website) and suggest which of these regulations might also be useful in a basketball or athletics event. Pick the five most important regulations.

9.4.3 Crowd management

One of FIFA's guidelines on stadium safety states that 'the match organiser must take all reasonable measures to ensure that the consumption of alcohol does not interfere with the spectators' safe enjoyment of the match' (FIFA website). Nevertheless, in a survey of football supporters in Scotland, it was found that around 20 per cent of all casualties recorded at matches were related to excessive drinking (Crawford *et al.* 2001).

Of course, the problem of alcohol consumption at sporting events is not restricted to football in Scotland. It presents a serious dilemma for the majority of sporting event managers, particularly as sponsorship revenue may well come from major brewers. For instance, InBev has signed a six-year sponsorship deal with the NFL that is reputed to be worth around $1.2 billion. To counteract criticism of such links with brewers, some sporting event organisers have introduced alcohol-free areas in an attempt to isolate any drink-related problems that might arise.

9.4.4 Violence and racism at sporting events

While the majority of sporting events take place without any spectator violence, organisers must always be sensitive to the threat of it. As far back as 1910, Swedish fans invaded the pitch to attack opposition players (Andersson 2001), and since then there have been numerous examples of violence at football matches throughout Europe, although the number of incidents has fallen significantly over the past ten years. There are still serious problems at football matches in Argentina, where the *Barras Bravas*, the name given to hooligan gangs, are responsible for vicious assaults on rival fans (Duke and Crolley 1994). Such is the level of violence that the Argentinian government has frequently suspended the football league in order to penalise the clubs, who otherwise seem to have little interest in rectifying the problem. While many event organisers will argue that hooliganism is a societal problem rather than a sporting problem, they need to be aware that people often cite violence at football matches as a reason for not attending any live sporting events.

Another recurring problem at some sporting events is racism. Black footballers have been subjected to racist chants and taunts from opposition supporters, especially in Eastern Europe and, more recently, Spain. Nor is this problem confined to football in Europe. Tennis players Serena and Venus Williams suffered racist abuse at the Indian Wells Tournament, California, in 2001. As a result, they refused to play in the event for the next two years – a boycott that had a significant impact on the success of the tournament (Spencer 2004).

Many clubs and organisations are taking positive steps to tackle this issue through anti-racism campaigns. The 'Kick It Out' campaign was English football's attempt to convince fans to reject racism and the racist groups that have long tried to recruit new members at matches. Meanwhile, Atlético Madrid has specifically encouraged immigrants from South America to support the club, thereby broadening the ethnic mix of its fan base. It is estimated that up to 500,000 people have arrived in Madrid from South America in the past few years, and a television advertising campaign has urged these new arrivals not only to come along to Atlético's matches but to integrate with the wider community.

CASE STUDY 9.2

Football in an Argentinian chocolate box

Location: Buenos Aires, Argentina
Event type: sporting event
Attendees: 40,000 (cut from 60,000 to comply with safety requirements)

This case study highlights the dilemma faced by modern sports teams looking to redevelop their stadiums. Old stadiums are iconic for fans who are reluctant to see any changes. But the lack of change means that their clubs might become less competitive in the global market place. The clubs themselves can see the advantages of new facilities, but in a country like Argentina, where the 'spectacle' is a big part of the game, how can they develop new stadiums and retain the cherished atmosphere of match day?

As the players and officials walk out onto the pitch, the noise that greets them, the sea of tickertape and the smell of burning fire-crackers resemble the opening ceremony of a major sporting event. So much paper is blown onto the pitch that the club has had to invest in hand-held blowers to clear the playing surface before the game can even start. The first time that somebody enters this atmosphere, the hairs on the back of their neck stand up. The fans' band can be heard above the noise that is generated by tens of thousands of fanatical supporters.

At first glance, *La Bombonera* (The Chocolate Box) Stadium seems to be modern, but on closer inspection it looks tired, and it visibly shakes as the supporters jump up and down on the old concrete terraces. The club needs a new stadium, possibly in a new part of town, but the opposition from supporters and the local community is slowing down the process. The local people have a deep attachment to their club, with many painting or decorating their houses in the blue and yellow of Boca Juniors. Even though many are not able to buy tickets to games, they still clearly identify with the club. *La Bombonera* is located right in the heart of the Barrio Boca, the home of *El Caminito*, where the Argentine Tango was invented, but also one of the poorest parts of town.

The attraction of Boca goes far beyond the local barrio and extends to the rest of Argentina and indeed the whole of South America. Boca attracts the support of as many as 40 per cent of all Argentinian football fans. As the club's marketing director, Orlando Salvestrini, points out, 'We know that we need a new modern stadium but if we build it too big and can't fill it, then the stadium will lose a considerable amount of its atmosphere, or its "carnival", which sets it apart from the football stadia of other countries.' Such is the atmosphere generated by the crowd that attendees find themselves watching the hardcore fans and their routines – from playing music in the band to waving flags and launching firecrackers – rather than the match. Their most famous supporter is Diego Armando Maradona, himself a sporting superstar, whose presence whips the crowd into even more of a frenzy. The club's *Superclásico* derby match with main rivals River Plate always attracts a considerable amount of attention. Gavin Hamilton suggests that the big derby game between Glasgow Rangers and Glasgow Celtic is like watching a kindergarten match when compared with the *Superclásico* .

The club's directors fear that the supporters will turn against Boca if they try to find a new ground away from the current stadium. Besides, they would need to build a modern stadium to generate additional revenue streams, and that would cost at least £300 million. Orlando Salvestrini was impressed by the facilities at Arsenal and Manchester United when he visited England, but he knows that Boca does not have the resources to build a comparable stadium. The club is a members' club, or *socios*, and as such it cannot sell shares in the business to help raise finance. Individuals are not allowed to own clubs in Argentina, as they do in England and the USA, which makes it difficult to raise the finance needed to develop facilities.

Salvestrini is doing all he can to overcome this problem. He has set up *Boca Crece*, a separate company that manages the Boca brand. It sells all of the club's merchandise and negotiates sponsorship deals and television rights, and its efforts have made Boca by far the biggest club in Argentina, accounting for in excess of 60 per cent of all football merchandise sold in the country. In 2005, Boca's centenary dinner was attended by around 3000 people, and such is the popularity of the club that it arranged for the Boca torch, similar to the Olympic torch, to tour Argentina before parading it in *La Bombonera* on the night of the centenary itself.

The new Boca Juniors Hotel in Buenos Aires, the club's fleet of taxis, its bars, its museum and even its own cemetery illustrate how important the club is to its fans, but it faces some difficult times if it remains in the ramshackle *La Bombonera* while its competitors around the world move to ever-larger and more impressive stadiums.

Sources: Hamilton 2004; Wilde 2009

Image 9.1 Boca Juniors' stadium, Argentina
Source: AFP/Stringer / Getty Images

9.5 Sporting events marketing

Sporting events marketing attempts to unravel what motivates people to attend sports fixtures, matches and tournaments. While there are examples of research into sporting event attendees dating back to the 1970s and 1980s, it was only during the late 1990s that the first specialist publications in sports marketing started to appear. This fact always surprises people in the sports industry, who assume that this is a well-established and thoroughly researched subject. Perhaps 90 per cent of all research papers on sports marketing focus on US sports, such as baseball, American football, ice hockey and basketball, and they look at collegiate as well as professional events. NASCAR, arguably the most popular motor sport in the United States, also features regularly in publications. This should come as no surprise, as the NASCAR merchandising market is vast, generating a staggering $2 billion each year (Lowry 2004, cited in Amato *et al.* 2005). The Sports Marketing Association (SMA) was launched in the United States in 2002, in recognition of the growing importance of sports marketing among practitioners and as an academic subject.

The main difference between the marketing of normal goods and services and the marketing of sporting events is that the outcome of the latter is uncertain, meaning that the attendee could view it as either the best or the worst event ever. However, the focus remains the same, with the aim of the organiser being to satisfy a range of customers in the expectation that satisfied customers will choose to return in the future. A sports event marketer must therefore identify the service needs of attendees, understand those needs, and continue to satisfy them. As well as customers who pay to attend the event, the organiser must be aware of their relationship with other stakeholders, such as sponsors and broadcasters who pay to televise it.

In trying to understand why people attend sporting events, factors influencing attendees can be broken down into three broad categories: front room, back room and circumstantial, as shown in Table 9.4 (Tomlinson *et al.* 1995). Using these various factors, researchers attempted to gauge the attitudes of sports fans attending events. It is important to consider all of the reasons why people attend such events in order to satisfy their needs and requirements. While it is assumed that the main reason for attending an event is love of the sport, Table 9.4 shows that many other factors also influence attendance. This table therefore provides a useful checklist for sporting event organisers. When Tomlinson *et al.* (1995) carried out their research, they found that back-room factors had the largest negative impact on attendance.

Image 9.2 Argentina winning the Football World Cup, 1978
Source: Bob Thomas / Getty Images

> **Table 9.4** The factors that affect attendance at a sporting event
> Source: Adapted from Tomlinson *et al.* 2005

Front room	Back room	Circumstantial
Does the general atmosphere appeal to the attendee?	Is there a tradition of going to games?	Are they attending with family or friends?
Are the right food and drinks available?	Is it an evening game? (May have different atmosphere to a daytime game)	Are they interested in live sporting action?
Is the venue clean?	How easy is it to get to the stadium?	Do they prefer to attend at certain times of the season?
Is the stadium well designed?	What is the parking like?	Does the team have a chance of winning?
Is there any pre-match entertainment?	Is the game live on television?	Has the team played well recently?
Is there off-field entertainment?	Will star players be appearing?	Are there other games on television?
How will the other fans behave?	Is there community support for the team?	Are there other sports teams near by?
Is there a band?	Are there facilities for children?	Is the weather good for this event?
How good are the seats?	What is the transport like for the event?	Has the team won a high percentage of their games?
		Is this game a special event?
		Is the opposing team successful?

While seeing their team win is important for sporting events customers, the other factors are equally important – and perhaps even more important – to compensate for the team losing. A typical example is the quality and value of the food and drink that are available. Clearly, with attendances of over 50,000 people, and at an average of around £4 per head in additional expenditure, the potential revenue from refreshments alone can be as much as £200,000.

One of the key challenges for sporting event marketers is to ensure that customers receive high levels of service and that the issue of queuing is taken seriously. Research undertaken in the United States has found that service quality, the physical environment and waiting times all affect attendees' enjoyment of the event (Hightower *et al.* 2002). At the very least, then, sporting event managers should look for innovative ways to reduce queuing times for attendees. For instance, upgraded tickets could include food and drink in the purchase price, and these items could then be delivered to the attendee's seat during the event. Consequently, that attendee would not have to waste time queuing for food, and the queue would be shorter for those who did not choose to buy the upgraded ticket.

Tomlinson *et al.*'s research (1995) challenges the traditional view that fans' motivation to attend is based primarily on the performance of their team. Other researchers, such as Wakefield and Sloan (1995), also challenge this view, suggesting that people are motivated by the experience of the event, being with similar people and pure escapism. This area is still ripe for research, and sporting event organisers will certainly benefit from an increased understanding of why people attend their events.

Fan festivals and events prior to the start of an event are innovative ways to attract more attendees. For instance, the Women's United States Soccer Association held an interactive fan festival – 'Soccer Sensation' – in which fans were able to meet players and take part in soccer activities (Jowdy and McDonald 2003). The main objectives of this type of 'experiential branding' are to raise customer awareness and to improve relationships between players and supporters. On this occasion, the event also raised cash through sponsorship, which meant it was able to sell tickets for future matches at discounted prices.

Study activity

To what extent does the televising of sporting events affect attendance at live sporting events?

9.5.1 Types of attendees at sporting events

The crowds at sporting events are often made up of groups of similar people, and a sporting event organiser should be able to identify these distinct groups using the principles of market segmentation. Most of these people will insist that they are unique individuals and do not resemble any of their fellow attendees, but research has shown that that is rarely the case.

As can be seen in Table 9.5, there are four broad categories of sports attendee: the most devoted, who attend frequently; the moderates, who attend an average number of games; the less frequent, who attend occasionally; and the 'new fans', who are relatively recent attendees at sporting events. All of these fans might claim to be loyal, but they consume sporting events differently, so attempts to communicate with them should be different, too. This basic level of segmentation is a starting point for developing marketing strategies. For instance, those fans who attend only three or four games each season, out of a possible twenty-five, might be encouraged to attend just two more games each year. Meanwhile, those who already attend every game could be offered the opportunity to upgrade their tickets. Different marketing techniques might then be devised to increase the attendance of those who usually watch events from private hospitality boxes, the increasingly important family market, and the growing number of female sports fans. Compiling a database of attendees will help the sports event organiser to categorise them much more accurately, and will therefore enhance the efficiency of their marketing initiatives.

Table 9.5 Classification of sports fans by frequency of attendance

Type of fan	Author/researcher
Most loyal: high or vested, devoted, fanatical, dysfunctional, frequent, season-ticket holders, hard core, old, genuine, traditional	Branscombe and Wann 1991, Sutton et al. 1997, Hunt et al. 1999, Arnett and Laverie 2000, Tapp and Clowes 2002, Rodriguez et al. 2003, Malcolm et al. 2002, Amato et al. 2005, Stewart et al., 2003
Fans showing average support: medium or focused, local, enthusiast, moderately frequent attendance	Branscombe and Wann 1991, Sutton et al. 1997, Hunt et al. 1999, Arnett and Laverie 2000, Rodriguez et al. 2003
Occasional fans: low or social, temporary, casual, infrequent, sporadic spectator	Branscombe and Wann 1991, Sutton et al. 1997, Hunt et al. 1999, Tapp and Clowes 2002, Amato et al. 2005, Arnett and Laverie 2000, Rodriguez et al. 2003
New fans: usually watch major teams/stars, corporate, temporary	Redhead 1997, King 1997, Giulianotti 2002, Sandvoss 2003, Rodriguez et al. 2003, Tanaka 2004, Stewart et al. 2003, Hunt et al. 1999, Crespo et al. 2003

Study activity

How does an economic downturn affect the running of a major sporting event, such as the Olympic Games?

CASE STUDY 9.3

Phoenix Suns go dancing

Location: Phoenix, Arizona, USA
Event type: basketball
Attendees: 19,000

This case study demonstrates some of the principles of effective marketing based on a clear understanding of the types of people who attend sporting events. The

Phoenix Suns are continually innovating to ensure that their fans retain their interest in the club, which motivates them to attend more often. One of these innovations has been to incorporate a nightclub in the stadium. This makes commercial sense, but it also enhances attendees' overall event experience.

The Phoenix Suns are similar to many of the other clubs that compete in one of the most popular sports in the world. Basketball is hugely popular in Latvia, Croatia, Russia, China and Greece, but all of these markets are dwarfed by that of the USA. Here, the broadcasting rights alone are in the region of $1 billion a year. If anyone doubts that the Phoenix Suns take their business very seriously, they should look at the number of people who make up their marketing department. It is unlikely that these industrious people will be able to grow their business to the same extent as the NBA has over the past fifteen years, but they are always looking to enhance consumer experience and improve loyalty to the club, even though they have not enjoyed any major success for a number of years.

The most important principle for the Phoenix Suns is to make going to the game an important part of the lives of their fans. The club's approach to pricing means that it is possible to pay around $1000 for a court-side seat, but a number of tickets are also available at just $10 for fans on low incomes. Of course, there are plenty of other pricing options between these two extremes, with special tickets available for children, families, students and groups. At the top end of the scale, the club offers an executive ticket with valet parking, an exclusive refreshments area, and the best seats in the house. Other packages offer better value or extra refreshments areas for fans who want to upgrade their tickets. In response to the huge demand for court-side seats, the club has introduced second and third rows at lower prices, which has enabled more fans to get close to the action.

The club has also embraced new technology. It introduced bar-coded tickets that could be downloaded via the internet and printed at home when other clubs still forced fans to make special journeys to the stadium just to pick up their tickets. The marketing team regularly consults its customer database to look for patterns of attendance, and then sends out ticket offers to those fans who are attending less frequently than others. As most of this communication is now done through e-mail, costs are much lower than they used to be when using the traditional postal system, and the success of such mail-outs can be easily measured.

There is a very heavy emphasis on selling merchandised goods carrying club's logo, which is important to fan groups as it allows them to identify more closely with the Suns. Of course, this is also another major revenue generator for the club.

NBA clubs, including the Suns, are now looking to promote themselves and their sport overseas, and part of this campaign has involved playing some games in other countries. A recent NBA game that was hosted by the O2 Arena in London generated in excess of $2 million.

There is much to be learned from the success of the Phoenix Suns and its commercial activities. Of course, not all of their fans go on to the in-house nightclub once the game has finished, but it has certainly proved an attractive option for many of those who want to celebrate a victory or drown their sorrows after a defeat. Either way, the club is happy to accommodate them.

Source: Phoenix Suns website

Study activity

Choose a sport, such as football, American football or cricket, and identify six key market segments that you think a club should target. You should indicate what percentage of the total supporter base each segment might represent.

Industry voice

Steve Sutherland, sports marketing and events consultant, formerly marketing manager of the Football League, assistant to the chief executive of Charlton Athletic Football Club

 Steve Sutherland has witnessed dramatic changes in the sports industry over the last twenty-five years and he has been involved in many major events. Now, in his new role as a sports marketing consultant, he is advising Greenwich Borough Council as it prepares to host a number of high-profile events in the 2012 Olympics.

Steve recognises the extent to which new technology has changed the events industry:

It seems incredible now, but my first experiences in events were in the pre-internet days when Twitter and Facebook were still some twenty years away. These were the days when not many football clubs or other sports clubs had computer databases. Information on supporters or businesses was kept in paper form in flip-files, and database marketing was no more sophisticated than sending letters to supporters once a year about renewing season tickets. When I was given a car phone in 1991, it felt very high tech.

I'm very proud of the fact that the very first club to launch a club-branded credit card was Charlton Athletic, when I did a deal with a company called Transnational Financial Services in 1990. Now all clubs have exactly the same product.

Steve was also involved in some of the first TV deals when he was marketing executive at the Football League, just before the Premier League was launched: 'At that time, the collective deal for four football divisions was a mere eleven million pounds and the sponsorship deal with Barclays was just two million.'

The events industry changed dramatically after the Taylor Inquiry issued its report on the Hillsborough tragedy, as Steve recalls:

> This effectively forced football clubs to invest in their stadiums to make them safer and more customer oriented, and there were major developments in the modernisation of professional football. Football clubs, which formed part of a multi-million-pound events industry, were also forced to review crowd safety and policing. Faced with mounting police bills, football clubs like Charlton Athletic started to train their own stewards. In fact, Charlton is still a leader in steward training courses and has advised other clubs.

Steve is currently one of the leading authorities on sports and corporate social responsibility (CSR). He advises companies on how to invest in community-based sporting events and still works closely with the Charlton Athletic Community Trust (see the CACT website):

> Football clubs are now extremely sophisticated with regards to their marketing practices, with the result that sponsors and advertisers still flock to become involved in the sport. Clubs now play a significant part in their local communities, recognising that the iconic status of the football club can be a force for good, and the more enlightened ones even recognise that community marketing also boosts interest in the club and attendances on match days.

Steve was also behind the pioneering Valley Express service, an initiative that was copied by other event organisers. As he points out:

> Finding a parking space at the Valley, home of Charlton Athletic Football Club, was problematic and impacted on local residents, so we set up the Valley Express, a subsidised bus service that picked up fans within a seventy-mile radius of London. With 3000 fans on these buses, about 15 per cent of a typical gate, traffic congestion was greatly reduced at the venue.

Steve feels that the events industry has much to gain from becoming more involved with community projects:

> From my time at Charlton Athletic and at the British Amateur Boxing Association, where I was also a CSR consultant, I have noticed that working with children in deprived areas helps get them off the streets and into

gyms, which in turn helps to teach them about respect and discipline. There is an opportunity for the sporting events and the wider events industry to get involved with CSR programmes, as the power of a tracksuit over a suit or a uniform cannot be overstated.

Steve is also clear about the positive effect of hosting regular sporting events in a local community, such as Charlton:

Without a doubt, if the football club is thriving, then the local economy will be too. Charlton Athletic is a significant local employer, not just full-time staff but large numbers of match-day staff in catering, security and maintenance, and each week many thousands of people flock to the area and frequent the local bars, restaurants and shops.

Charlton was also one of the first football clubs to develop strategic partnerships with other organisations in order to increase income:

For a stadium to survive, it is vital to develop facilities and work in partnership in order to generate non-event revenue. We formed a strategic alliance with Greenwich Leisure Limited and grant funding enabled us to build a gym in the West Stand. We then obtained a European grant to operate classes, and a full-time college was set up at the club. For a stadium to thrive, it has to be used every day of the week, and whether that's for hospitality, seminars, presentations, product launches, classrooms or medical matters, strategic alliances are vital in achieving this. The latest project is a new drop-in medical centre, built with grant funding from Greenwich NHS.

Finally, Steve offers advice to people who would like to work in the sporting events industry:

Football clubs do advertise key positions, so relevant qualifications are important. But most jobs in football go to people who are known to the club. So I would recommend volunteering or becoming a match-day worker in security or catering, or even taking a level-one coaching course and getting work as a part-time coach in the community department.

9.6 Summary

This chapter has highlighted the significant growth in the sporting events industry, in terms of participation, media attention, overall revenue generation and the importance of staging events to local and national governments. Consideration has been given to the impact of sporting events and the legacies left by some of them, as well as the process involved in making a successful bid for an event. Politicians' involvement and influence have also been discussed, as has the relationship between sports and politics.

The chapter has shown that sporting event arenas have changed significantly over the past twenty years to meet higher consumer expectations and to compete with other events. More emphasis is beginning to be placed on comfort and additional services, both for fans and for those using the facilities when the main sporting event is not taking place. Examples of good practice in stadium design have been given, as have suggestions for how sporting event managers might incorporate these into their future plans. We have seen that significant improvements have been made in customer care and event safety in recent years, but also that crowd violence may still pose problems for event organisers. Managing the experience of participants has also been identified as an important consideration for staging events in a more competitive sporting event market. Finally, we have highlighted the need for more research into why people attend sporting events. What remains clear is that the sporting events industry is vibrant, with increasing revenues, rising attendances and ever-expanding television viewing figures.

Further reading

Emery, P. R. (2002) Bidding to Host a Major Sports Event: The Local Organising Committee Perspective, *International Journal of Public Sector Management*, 15 (4): 316–355. An article that provides insight into the bidding process for major sporting events and offers a useful framework for those who want to find out more about the subject.

Masterman, G. (2009) *Strategic Sports Management* (Olympic edn), Oxford: Butterworth-Heinemann. This is the leading book on sporting events management from a European perspective, with particular reference to the management of the Beijing Olympics in 2008.

Tomlinson, M., Buttle, F. and Moores, B. (1995) The Fan as Customer: Customer Services in Sports Marketing, *Journal of Hospitality and Leisure Marketing*, 3 (1): 19–36. This article, one of the first to focus on customer service in the sporting events industry, used research to identify the most important service factors from a spectator's perspective.

Mega-events

Contents

10.1 Aims

By the end of this chapter, students will be able:

- To define and categorise mega-events.
- To analyse individual mega-events across different periods of their existence.
- To evaluate the relationship between mega-events and urban regeneration.
- To evaluate the relationship between mega-events and tourism.

10.2 Introduction

Mega-events, like the Olympic Games and the World Expos, have become increasingly important in the global economy as governments compete to bring them to their cities to catalyse economic, social and cultural change. These events attract attendances in the millions and the largest of them command television audiences that number in the billions. This chapter is intended to introduce the concept of the mega-event and to highlight key challenges in successfully managing this diverse group of events. A definition and typology of mega-events will be given which shows that the 'mega' category can relate to audience size, economic impact, visitor numbers and/or socio-cultural significance. Emphasis will be placed on understanding the pre-, during- and post-event periods and the relationships between mega-events, tourism and urban regeneration.

10.3 Defining mega-events

The term 'mega-event' refers to those events that take place for a global media audience and/or that have significant, long-term impacts on economies and societies.

For the purposes of distinguishing between different kinds of events and for moving on to think about how these events are planned and delivered, we can place mega-events on a scale of large events, depending on their socio-economic and media impacts.

Mega-events are distinguished by the immense scale of their audiences and their social and economic impacts, as shown in Figure 10.1. Included in the total audience are both large numbers of attendees at the 'live' event and even larger numbers of people who watch the event via various media, especially television. Increasingly, these media audiences are being extended and developed through the use of streaming media and media archives. While 3.4 million people watched the matches of the 2006 FIFA World Cup in Germany live, the cumulative television audience was 26.3 billion (FIFA 2007).

Events on this scale are infrequent but usually periodical. The Summer and Winter Olympic Games, for example, take place on four-yearly cycles. The World Expo, a global cultural fair, moves between countries on a five-yearly basis, and the most recent one attracted 64.59 million visitors over a six-month period, with an Expo-record 835,832 visitors on its busiest day (see Case Study 10.1).

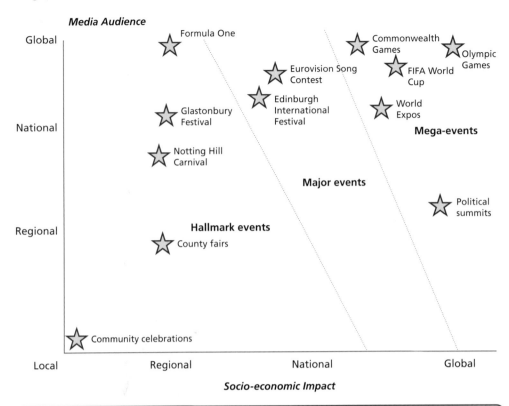

Figure 10.1 Media and socio-economic scales of large events

CASE STUDY 10.1

The Shanghai World Expo 2010

Location: Shanghai, China
Event type: mega-event
Attendees: 64,590,000

The World Expo in Shanghai ran for 184 days, from 1 May until 31 October 2010. The event was themed with the concept 'Better City, Better Life' and aimed to attract 70 million visitors to an exposition of urban life and forms. Up to 400,000 visitors per day were anticipated by the organisers, including 4 million overseas visitors, who made use of a new airport that was constructed specifically for the purpose. Two hundred countries were represented at the Expo, with many hosting 'pavilions' within the event site that showcased national architecture.

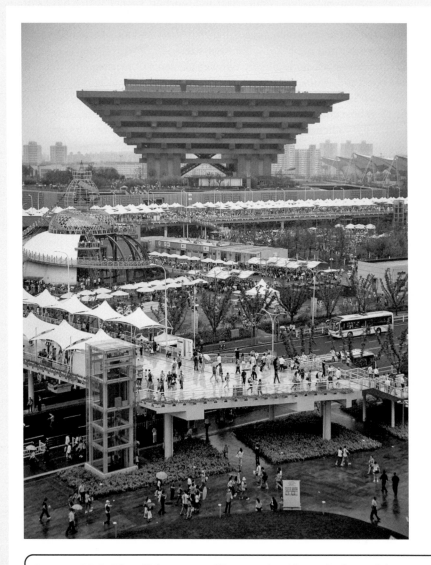

Image 10.1 The Chinese pavilion at the Shanghai World Expo 2010
Source: Win Initiative / Getty Images

An area of 5.28 square kilometres was developed to host the Expo within Shanghai, and the event boasted more than 20,000 planned conferences, events and exhibitions over the 184 days. The estimated budget for this mega-event was £2.8 billion.

Roche (2000: 1) defines mega-events by referring to their significance and appeal, describing them as 'large-scale cultural (including commercial and sporting) events, which have a dramatic character, mass popular appeal and international significance'. Roberts (2004) emphasises the stand-alone character of mega-events, suggesting that they are out-of-the-ordinary events, discontinuous in character and remarkable for their size.

Discontinuity and drama are undoubtedly two key elements of mega-events that help us to understand their appeal and significance. However, these are relative concepts that vary between locations and cultures. Events such as the Glastonbury Festival, an annual UK music festival, stand out within their host communities as dramatic and a break from the normal routine, but Glastonbury's 2009 TV audience of just 16.3 million viewers suggests that it is on a different scale to the most recent Olympic celebrations in Beijing 2008, which attracted an estimated worldwide audience of 3.6 billion. Getz (2007: 25; emphasis added) incorporates this relativity into his definition of the mega-event, explaining that they are 'those that yield extraordinarily high levels of tourism, media coverage, prestige, or economic impact *for the host community, venue or organisation*'.

Within the category of mega-events, three major kinds can be identified that are characterised by their audience and/or significance at the global level: cultural, political and sporting mega-events.

10.3.1 Cultural mega-events

These mega-events focus on the development and/or promotion of regional or national culture. Typically, they involve the designation of an area or region as the event hub for a specific period of time and include a wide programme of cultural events across a variety of cultural forms. Examples include the Eurovision Song Contest, which involves a series of regional and national events and finally a single international event, and the European Capital of Culture programme.

Liverpool was awarded the title of European Capital of Culture in 2008 after winning a competitive bidding process against eleven other European cities. Winning this title helped to secure £4 billion in new investment for the city, and hosting the year-long cultural festival generated £800 milion in revenue from 15 million visitors to cultural events and attractions. It is estimated that the worldwide television audience for the opening event was 300 million (Liverpool08 2009). Istanbul won the Capital of Culture bid for 2010. The organisers announced the following aims, which illustrate the diverse expectations of mega-event impacts:

- From 2006 onwards the name of Istanbul will be associated with culture and the arts all over the world.
- As Turkey moves ahead with the process of its candidacy for the European Union, the projects that will be realised will demonstrate that Istanbul, the symbol of the country, has been interacting with European culture for hundreds of years.
- The city's cultural heritage will be managed in a sustainable manner and it will become even more of a magnet than ever.
- Istanbul will achieve lasting gains in the fields of urban renewal, urban living and environmental and social development.
- New museums will be established to protect and display our cultural assets and historical buildings will be renovated, given new roles, and opened to the public.
- People of Istanbul will embrace new artistic disciplines. Young, talented people will have the opportunity to become more closely involved in artistic creativity.
- Jobs will be created for a large number of people, ranging from communications to organisation, education, design, management and creative fields.

- Those who come to Istanbul for cultural and artistic projects will visit the city's cultural riches, mosques, churches, palaces and museums.
- Cultural tourism will be invigorated and develop. (Educated, cultured tourists spend three times as much as normal tourists. This means that, as a European Capital of Culture, Istanbul will have a great tourism potential.)
- Many people from the world of culture and the arts, together with members of the print and visual media, will come to Istanbul from Europe and different countries all around the world. This will make a positive contribution to the promotion and branding of Istanbul. Being selected as a European Capital of Culture will give a boost to the city's economic relations with Europe as well as contributing to its cultural relations. With the renovation that will take place, the administrators and administered will join together, hand in hand, sharing their knowledge and experience, to develop a long-term sustainable model for the future.
- Istanbul local residents will be proud of their city as they further discover its beauty. (Istanbul 2010 2011)

10.3.2 Political mega-events

These events have increased in frequency and size with the progress of globalisation since the 1970s. Now, more than ever, political delegations and NGOs from the developed and developing world meet to debate and harmonise policies on global trade, security and the environment. These events, like the World Economic Forum and the parallel World Social Forum, have a global significance that transcends visitor numbers and budgets that would normally be associated with a major event, such as a music festival or sporting contest.

The United Nations Climate Change Conference Copenhagen 2009 (COP15) is an example of this new kind of mega-event. This event brought together 15,000 delegates and 5000 journalists for eleven days in an attempt to reach a new global agreement on the response to climate change. An increasingly common feature of these events is the large number of protesters and demonstrators who attempt to disrupt or influence them. At COP15, around 100,000 protesters took to the streets, provoking a large and costly police response. Despite this, the event made a contribution of around £80 million to the local economy.

Key to understanding the position of COP15 as a mega-event, however, is its political and environmental significance. A total of 193 countries sent delegates, and the event brought together political leaders and decision-makers with global levels of influence. Millions more participated in the event at a distance through protests and demonstrations in other countries, with the aim of influencing the proceedings.

10.3.3 Sporting mega-events

Sporting mega-events are the most commonly analysed type in the events management literature. Tournaments such as the Olympic Games and the FIFA World Cup stand alone in terms of their attendance, media audience and commercial activity. New technologies of communication and digital media have played a part in the development of sporting mega-events as the world's premium media events. Since 1960, the amount paid by US broadcasters for the rights to broadcast from the Summer Olympics has grown from $390,000 for Rome to $894 million for Beijing, and a predicted £1.18 billion for London 2012 (Horne and Manzenreiter 2006). The budget for the Beijing Olympics in 2008 – by far the largest and most visually spectacular games yet seen – reached $40 billion and involved the creation of six new Olympic venues and the reconstruction of a large area of the city.

It is now customary for sporting mega-events to be justified in terms of their funding and public policy impacts by the development of a significant legacy from these events. This legacy will normally include post-games uses for the Olympic venues, improved infrastructure in the host city and an improved destination brand for the city in the international tourism market. Four years after hosting the 2006 Winter Olympics, Torino, in northern Italy, was the country's fourth most visited city, after Rome, Florence and Venice. This was achieved through the development of the local tourism industry during and following the Games period, the use of the Games as a catalyst for urban renewal and the increased media profile of this largely industrial town. This demonstrates the potential power of the Games to rebrand a host city through harnessing the vast investment and media audience that the world's largest mega-events generate.

Study activity

What events in your country would you class as mega-events? What are the impacts of these events at the local, regional and national levels?

10.4 Mega-event periods

Like all events, mega-events have a planning stage and have impacts that extend beyond the life of the event itself. Specifically for mega-events, we can talk about the pre-event period, the event period and the post-event period.

10.4.1 The pre-event period

10.4.1.1 Competitive bidding

The first stage in the pre-event period is when the decision is made to stage a mega-event or, more commonly, to *bid* to stage a mega-event. Of course, some mega-events are intimately linked to particular places (such as Munich's Oktoberfest), but this process usually begins with the event owners – for example, the International Olympic Committee or the International Expositions Bureau – announcing that they will accept submissions from potential hosts. There are then several competitive stages during which the number of potential hosts are reduced until a winner is chosen. The stages include the submission of bid documentation, visits by the event owners and formal presentations. Each city will develop a bid file that will normally include:

- Guarantees from the host city to the event owner.
- A profile of the host city, including:

  - demographic information
  - information on the environment
  - economic information
  - political information.

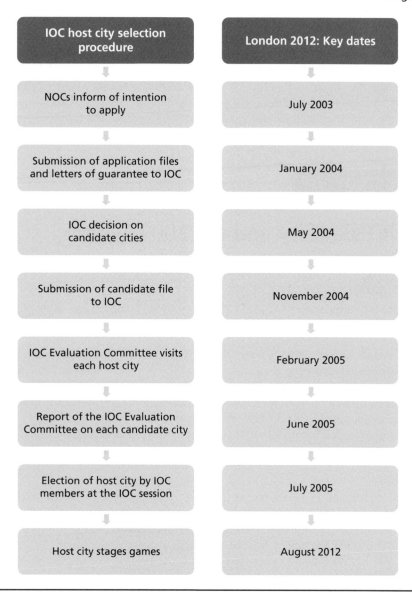

Figure 10.2 The Olympic host city selection process for London 2012
Source: Adapted from Theodoraki 2007

- Plans for the content of the event.
- Plans for facilities, accommodation and transport.
- Plans for associated celebratory and educational events.

The period of competitive bidding will start well in advance of the actual event itself. The level of planning required to stage a mega-event and the resources required to make it a success mean that an eight to ten-year lead-in period is not uncommon for successful Olympic bids (Girginov and Parry 2005). At the start of this period, a Bid Committee will be formed that brings together political figures, Olympic experts, planners, media professionals and a range of stakeholders in the Olympic planning process. This Bid Committee will eventually hand over to an Organising Committee for the Olympic Games (OCOG), which will then be the lead body for the delivery of the Games themselves.

It is not only the Olympic city candidature process that generates a frenzy of bureaucratic activity. The successful bid of Umeå, in Sweden, to become European Capital of Culture in 2014 took ten years from start to finish and involved 350 people and collaborations with six other European cities.

CASE STUDY 10.2

Salt Lake City and the 2002 Winter Olympic Games

Location: Salt Lake City, USA
Event type: mega-event
Attendees: 1,600,000

The awarding of the 2002 Winter Olympic Games to Salt Lake City (SLC) was a controversial chapter in the history of the Olympic movement. In 1995, SLC gained fifty-four votes from a possible eighty-nine in the IOC selection process, a sizeable majority in IOC terms. After an investigation following allegations of bribery and corruption, in 1998 an IOC commission found that the SLC Bid Committee had given nineteen IOC voting members gifts and privileges totalling more than $440,000. However, even removing these nineteen votes would still have left SLC with twenty-one more votes than its nearest rival, Östersund in Sweden.

To investigate the reason for SLC's 'overwhelming victory', Persson (2002) carried out five separate studies into the host selection process for the 2002 Winter Olympic Games and found that the most important aspects of the winning bid, according to the IOC voting members, were, in order of importance:

- Olympic Village
- transportation
- sports arenas
- finances
- telecommunication
- information technology
- media centre.

Also important, but featuring less in the winning bid, were:

- support of the bid in the country
- sports organisation

- security of the games
- city characteristics
- national and regional characteristics
- care of the athletes
- compact Games
- accommodation of all visitors
- programme of the Games
- medical/health service, doping checks.

SLC was measured to have performed best out of the candidate cities at the time by the IOC members, and this finding was confirmed in a post-Games survey three years later.

This is a clear insight into the decision-making processes of the IOC in awarding host city status for the Olympic Games.

10.4.1.2 Resources

A major task facing any city planning to host a mega-event is assembling the required resources to make it a success. It is estimated that the costs of hosting the Athens 2004 Olympic Games rose to $12 billion, far in excess of the possible contribution from the Olympic movement of $4.3 billion. This has serious implications for our understanding of the pre-event period, during which mega-event hosting cities must seek to acquire sufficient resources to produce the event. Although host cities aim to achieve significant benefits and produce a legacy from hosting these events, assembling adequate resources is a key task of the pre-event period. This funding typically comes from two sources: direct public investment, and partnerships with the private sector.

Hosting a mega-event requires large amounts of public investment. From the beginning of the bidding and planning process, the potential host city begins to accrue costs for something which, at this stage, may not even take place. The cost of bidding includes marketing, PR, staffing, premises, travel and lobbying. If a bid is successful, the host city must identify and acquire the land required for developing the mega-event location and begin the long and costly processes of planning and consultation. This is followed by the huge capital investments required in infrastructure development to improve travel networks to cope with visitors and the construction of venues for the event. In addition, the human and organisational capital required to coordinate and manage these processes places a drain on state resources at both the local and the national levels. In the majority of cases, these upfront costs will be met through direct taxation and sometimes a special levy on residents, with the justification that the benefits of hosting the mega-event will outweigh the costs, especially once its legacy is taken into consideration. Politicians and event organisers frequently justify the decision to host a mega-event using the 'public good' argument.

Getz (2007: 330) sets out the three criteria of the 'public good' that have to be satisfied in order to justify the massive public sector commitment to hosting a mega-event:

- Events fit into accepted policy domains (culture, health, economics, etc.).
- Public benefits are substantial (it is worth our while to get involved), inclusive (everyone gains), and can be demonstrated or proved.
- There are rules and accountability for money spent and other actions taken.

Within these three points, the most contentious is the second – demonstrable public benefit. Assuming that the benefits can be anticipated, planned for and measured, then the decision to host a mega-event becomes a matter of performing a simple cost–benefit analysis: will the benefits of hosting the event outweigh, or at least match, the costs of producing it? The assumption that is implicit in all mega-event bids is that they will, but the dispersed and diverse impacts of mega-events make this difficult to assess. Mega-events always have a number of specific effects that occur at different points in the life of the event, as is shown in Figure 10.3.

The problem caused by this distribution of event impacts is that the tangible benefits of hosting a mega-event are predicted to take place during the event itself or after it. (The exception to this is the area of tourism, which will be dealt with in a later section of this chapter.) The very long planning period for mega-events and the huge public resource commitment involved during the pre-event stage can therefore cause significant political difficulties for host cities and governments. (The issue of the public perception of mega-events is addressed below.)

Two categories of partnership are important for understanding the planning and resourcing of mega-events. First, there are the partnerships required between different agencies, departments and companies in the public and private sectors that are involved in delivering the event. Second, there are the partnerships between the event owners and hosts, on the one hand, and private companies, on the other, which take the form of sponsorship arrangements. The most significant sponsorship deals often allow companies to brand themselves as 'official partners'

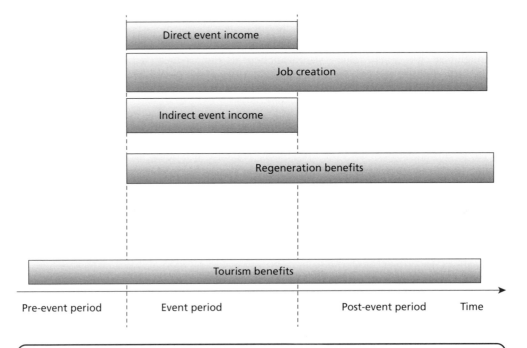

Figure 10.3 The distribution of mega-event impacts over time

of the mega-event. These two types of partnerships can be termed *delivery partnerships* and *commercial partnerships*, and both help to generate the resources needed to stage a mega-event.

Delivery partnerships generate extra resources for a mega-event during the pre-event period in two distinct ways: through planning and construction.

Planning partnerships tend to be embodied in particular organisations or forums. A planning partnership makes use of resources that are dispersed through different public bodies and other organisations. In particular, it brings additional organisational resources, experience and in-kind benefits to the planning of a mega-event, as well as additional human capital in the form of experts and administrative support. An example is PODIUM – the Further and Higher Education Unit for the 2012 Olympic Games. This public body

> functions as a platform on which to build the engagement of the Further and Higher Education sectors with the 2012 Games. The Unit works directly with a number of stake-holders including colleges, universities and the London Organising Committee of the Olympic and Paralympic Games (LOCOG), seconding the Unit's Head into LOCOG's Culture, Ceremonies and Education team for two days per week. Other stakeholders include: London Higher, the Olympic Delivery Authority, Government Departments, Regional Development Agencies, Sector Skills Councils, the Association of Colleges, British University & Colleges Sport, Guild HE and Universities UK.
>
> (PODIUM 2009)

Construction partnerships are typically made between public and private sector bodies, to contract in the experience, capabilities and capital of the private sector to support the con-struction of venues and improvements to infrastructure as well as other capital-intensive projects that would be difficult for the public sector to fund on its own. For example, the $600-million Cape Town Stadium for the 2010 FIFA World Cup in South Africa was constructed by Murray Roberts and WHBO, which were contracted in by the Organising Committee. The project was not directly managed by the state, and the management of the stadium during the event and in the post-event period was handled by a consortium of partners from the private sector with specific stadium-management experience.

Commercial partnerships add capital and commercial support to a mega-event, usually through sponsorship deals that offer a promotional benefit to the event partner. The highest category of these partnerships is that of 'official partner'. Official partners of mega-events are often granted permission to use the event logos and branding materials as part of their own promotional activity.

Liverpool08 had twelve official partners, each making a cash or in-kind contribution to the event. For example, Hill Dickinson LLP was the first official partner announced for Liverpool's Capital of Culture programme, taking on the responsibility for 'all legal and contractual dealings with sponsors, partners, suppliers, event organisers and the myriad of other businesses involved in the multi-year programme building up to 2008 and in the legacy years following' (Hill Dickinson LLP 2009). Virgin Trains paid £2 million for the right to become an official partner of Liverpool08, additionally agreeing to promote the mega-event on its trains and through its services.

Potential sponsorship deals began at £20,000 and were marketed by Liverpool08 as a portfolio of opportunities:

> Depending on the level of investment, companies can get access to a spectrum of Culture Company assets, including:

- intellectual property (logos, designations, 'Look of the Capital of Culture')
- category exclusivity
- corporate use (letterheads, business cards, B2B promotions, website)
- consumer use (TV, radio, print, direct mail, outdoor, website, database use)
- sponsor recognition (banners, advertising, website links)
- tickets and hospitality (complimentary allocation and access to purchase additional)
- event creation and involvement upgrades. (Liverpool08 2008)

10.4.1.3 Public perceptions of mega-events

As mentioned above, the public perception of mega-events is affected by the distribution of event impacts. With the majority of the benefits of hosting a mega-event occurring late in the life of the event itself and often well into the future, beyond the event and into the legacy period, it is not surprising that public reaction to plans to host a mega-event based on predictions of these long-term and often intangible benefits can often be negative or hostile. There is a widespread belief that the 'true' costs of a mega-event are often hidden from the public in order to avoid widespread alarm, an assumption that is supported by facts like the dramatic 300 per cent rise in costs of the Sydney 2000 Olympics in the twelve months before the Games were held (Girginov and Parry 2005).

A key element of the management of mega-events in the pre-event period, then, is the marketing of the event – not to potential event tourists and attendees, but internally, to the population of the host city and country. This internal marketing is a key activity of the bidding team for any mega-event and, once the event has been won, it becomes a significant task for the Organising Committee.

For London 2012, this has involved extensive consultation through roadshow and drop-in events in East London, focusing on the local employment and regeneration benefits of the Games. More widely across the UK, the focus has been on the celebratory aspects of the Games, the increased tourism opportunities they should provide and the increase in sporting participation that they are expected to drive, especially among young people. Research into UK citizens' willingness to pay (WTP – a measure of the amount that individuals think is a reasonable contribution for them to make to the staging of an event) for the 2012 Olympics found that this decreased with distance from London, with Londoners' WTP £22 per annum, Mancunians' £12 per annum and Glaswegians' just £11 per annum (Atkinson et al. 2008). With the vast majority of sporting activities taking place in one area of the country, the Cultural Olympiad programme of events associated with the Games has been promoted as a way of spreading the benefits of hosting the Olympics around the country (Kennell and Macleod 2009).

It is important to note that public perceptions of the decision to host a mega-event are changeable and will be influenced by the actual manifestations or otherwise of benefits associated with the event. Research carried out by Guala (2009: 25) shows that public opinion regarding the Torino 2006 Winter Olympics was representative of that measured for similar events: 'pride and optimism at the beginning, then uncertainties and concerns two or three years before the games . . . then happiness and success during the games and shortly after; one year after the games a more realistic judgement is registered, but always positive about the experience and [the future]'.

10.4.2 The event period

During a mega-event, the organisers will be required to carry out a vast number of functions. The Athens Organising Committee identified fifty-three separate areas of responsibility during the 2004 Olympic Games. Broadly, these functions can be broken down into a number of inter-related areas common to all mega-events (see Figure 10.4). The Beijing Organising Committee

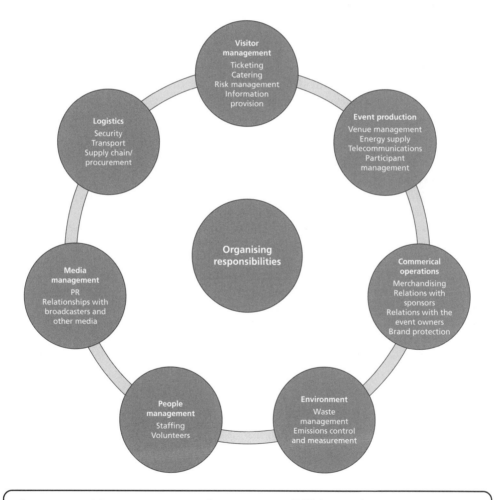

Figure 10.4 Mega-event organisers' responsibilities in the event period

Figure 10.5 The functional structure of the Munich Oktoberfest
Source: Adapted from Shulenkorf 2005

for the Olympic Games (BOCOG) had twenty-five departments, each with a separate management function.

It is not only host cities of the Olympic Games that have to deal with this sort of logistical complexity. Munich's annual Oktoberfest beer festival attracts an average of 7 million visitors over sixteen days each year. There are 700 booths or small stalls and 14 large tents, each capable of holding 10,000 people. Each Oktoberfest contributes approximately $1.4 billion to the regional economy of Munich and Bavaria. To deliver such an annual mega-event successfully, there is a need for a complex functional structure that integrates political oversight, departmental responsibility and management functions (see Figure 10.5).

We look at the management issues associated with all events elsewhere in this book, but it is useful here to look at three areas of management that are of particular significance to mega-events during the event period: volunteers, global media and security.

10.4.2.1 Volunteers

Mega-events make use of volunteers on a huge scale. Without their contributions, mega-events as we have come to understand them could not take place due to the huge investment in human capital that would be required to employ a paid workforce. During Beijing 2008, an estimated 1 million volunteers were involved in producing and managing the Games. The organisers of the 2006 Melbourne Commonwealth Games recognised the important contribution made by volunteers by nominating all 14,500 of them as 'unsung heroes' of the event. Every one was named individually in the official event documentation.

During a mega-event, volunteers can be used in all aspects of staging. These volunteers will be drawn from diverse sections of the population and, although the headline-grabbing volunteer programmes for mega-events publicise opportunities to meet famous people, the majority of volunteer opportunities will be in customer-service or behind-the-scenes roles. Many mega-event hosts seek to link volunteer programmes to skills development and the creation of employment opportunities, both to attract applicants and to contribute to local economic development in the host community. Although it is unrealistic for every volunteer to expect to move directly from the event into paid employment, large-scale, long-term volunteering programmes aim to provide opportunities for citizens to develop their skills and to gain basic qualifications and work experience.

Employment growth is a key element of the justification given by cities for hosting mega-events. Given the huge public investment involved, the success of this is a major factor in influencing public opinion. During the pre-event period of the 1992 Olympic Games in Barcelona, unemployment in the city halved, mainly thanks to the creation of 59,382 jobs that were directly connected to the Games. Immediately after the Games, unemployment rose again by 21,000, before falling back in 1995 (Brunet 2009). The investment generated by hosting the Olympic Games contributed significantly to the strong relative performance of Barcelona's employment market in the legacy period, but the city's experience demonstrates that the employment benefits of hosting a mega-event are not always straightforward or immediate.

This suggests that people must volunteer for reasons other than the hope of gaining direct employment. Indeed, volunteer motivation is a much-researched topic in events management literature. Getz (2007) reviews twelve recent studies and highlights what he judges to be the most important motivating factors:

- altruism
- social benefits
- career benefits
- a sense of challenge
- volunteering as a form of 'serious leisure'
- community pride.

Bladen (2009) conceptualises the motivations of mega-event volunteers within a model of repeat volunteering. This model suggests that first-time or one-off volunteers are motivated primarily by altruism, while repeat volunteers are driven by the quality of the volunteering experience, and career volunteers see the intrinsic benefits of volunteering itself. So there is a progression from altruistic volunteering motivations to egoistic motivations, as shown in Figure 10.6, which implies that different management strategies will be necessary for managing different volunteers successfully. The sheer scale of the volunteer contribution at a mega-event means that event

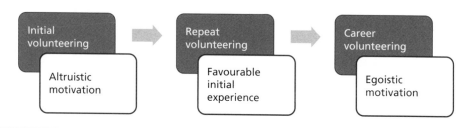

Figure 10.6 Bladen's developmental stages of volunteering
Source: Bladen 2009

managers will be working with large groups of individuals at different points on this motivational journey.

10.4.2.2 Global media

Horne and Manzenreiter (2006) claim that the expansion of mega-events in the twentieth century can be understood only by reference to a 'sports–media–business alliance', based on the development of new communications technologies, the professionalisation and commercialisation of sports and the economic opportunities offered to host cities by successful mega-events. This alliance is encapsulated in the relationship between the Olympics and global media. As Roche (2000) points out, the media audience for other mega-events is dwarfed by that of the Olympic Games; and indeed, for mega-events such as the World Expos, whose aim has always been to showcase global culture, the rise of television and new media has provided increased competition for their natural audiences. In contrast, the growth of visual media has helped to extend and deepen the sporting mega-event audience.

For the Olympic Games, broadcasting rights are sold by territory. In the United States, media companies bid competitively for the right to broadcast the Olympics inside North America. For the 2008 Games, NBC paid $894 million. European rights are sold to a collective entity, the European Broadcast Union, which then re-sells them at the national level. For Beijing 2008, European broadcast rights were sold for $443 million. Broadcast rights account for 53 per cent of total income for the Olympic Games, with sponsorship in second place at 34 per cent,

Table 10.1 US broadcast rights for the Summer Olympic Games
Source: Horne and Manzenreiter 2006

Year	Host city	Network	Amount $m
1960	Rome	CBS	0.39
1964	Tokyo	NBC	1.5
1968	Mexico City	ABC	4.5
1972	Munich	ABC	7.5
1976	Montreal	ABC	25.0
1980	Moscow	NBC	72.0
1984	Los Angeles	ABC	225.0
1988	Seoul	NBC	300.0
1992	Barcelona	NBC	401.0
1996	Atlanta	NBC	546.0
2000	Sydney	NBC	705.0
2004	Athens	NBC	793.0
2008	Beijing	NBC	894.0
2012	London	NBC	1181.0

ticketing at 11 per cent and merchandising at 2 per cent. Table 10.1 shows the growth in broadcast deals for the Olympic Games in the US from 1960 until the present day.

As well as broadcast rights, the media presence at the Olympic Games is managed through the use of an accreditation system. Individual journalists and media organisations are given official permission to report from inside the Games, are granted access to secure areas and are able to use an accredited media centre, which will have been specially constructed and equipped so that journalists can plug directly into global media networks.

The growth of new media and the diffusion of journalism into non-traditional networks, such as blogs and other forms of social media, have complicated the relationship between the organising committees for each Games and the media, and, at a same time when traditional broadcast deals have grown, reporting of the Olympic Games has become less and less controllable. In response to this, the Sydney 2000 Games was the first to include a non-accredited media centre, and this has been repeated in every Games since. These spaces provide facilities for *any* journalist and they are often used by those reporting on the non-sporting aspects of the Games, such as the cultural programme, local-activity and human-interest stories (Garcia and Miah 2004). During Beijing 2008, more than 12,000 journalists used the non-accredited media centre. The incorporation of these reporters provides two main benefits to the organisers of each Games, and to the Olympic movement as a whole. First, it creates a space in which new media realities of citizen journalism and online democracy can be brought into the organisation of the event in a managed way. Second, it helps to legitimise the system of charging for accredited media access to the Games by creating a tiered system of privileged access to athletes, officials and facilities.

10.4.2.3 Security

In order to understand the security implications of hosting a mega-event, it is necessary to examine why events are often targets for acts of terrorism or protests. Tarlow (2002) provides four reasons for why events become targets:

- *Location* – Events are necessarily held close to major transportation routes and population centres.
- *Economic* – Disrupting events can cause significant damage to tourism and other business activity.
- *Media* – The media will already be present on site, leading to increased reporting of any attack.
- *Anonymity* – The presence of large numbers of attendees at an event makes it likely that terrorists can remain anonymous in a crowd.

Mega-events stretch these criteria to their maximum impact, so it is likely that they will continue to be significant targets for terrorism and other forms of political protest.

The most infamous security breach at a mega-event took place at the 1972 Olympic Games in Munich. Palestinian terrorists killed eleven Israeli athletes during the Games and the tragedy was given widespread and instantaneous media coverage thanks to the presence of vast numbers of journalists at the Olympic site. The location of this terrorist attack had been chosen for precisely this high symbolic value.

Post 9/11, mega-event planners are even more conscious of the possibility of a terrorist attack at one of these high-profile, urbanised, global media events. Between the Los Angeles Games in 1984 and the Athens Games in 2004, security costs rose from $79.4 millio to $1.5 billion (Boyle and Haggerty 2009). This is not a uniquely Olympic issue: planning for the FIFA World

Cup in South Africa in 2010 made provision for the use of 40,000 police officers, 50,000 reservists and thousands of private security staff (Giulianotti and Klauser 2009). In 2009, an al-Qaeda plot to attack the Munich Oktoberfest was detected in advance by the security services, leading to the imposition of a 3.7-kilometre no-fly zone around the site and enhanced physical security in 2010.

In common with urban security management generally, attempts to manage the risk of terror are becoming more dispersed and anticipatory, with host cities relying heavily on techniques such as surveillance, behaviour and attendee profiling, as well as the increased use of private security firms. It is likely that one of the legacies of Beijing 2008 for the mega-event field will be its security innovations, including the use of official protest areas and unprecedented levels of monitoring and security clearance that were implemented to reduce the negative impacts of political protest and terror at the event. Although the presence of the Games in China has been hailed by some as helping to create a climate in which limited protest was allowed, in contrast to the pre-Games period in China, these protests were very tightly controlled. It is likely that future Games will follow this model of licensed protest. The 2010 Winter Olympic Games in Vancouver, Canada, saw an unprecedented level of security, with a security budget that rose from an initial estimate of $175 million to more than $1 billion by the end of the event. This money was spent on 17,000 security staff, a network of nearly 1000 CCTV cameras and the establishment of secure zones for channelling both spectators and protesters. A newly formed Vancouver Integrated Security Unit brought together twenty different law-enforcement agencies, armed with semi-automatic weapons, including border police, who carried out spot checks of citizens' immigration and citizenship status during the Games period (Boykoff 2011).

Cultural and sporting mega-events are high profile and require significant political support to take place, which situates them within the political arena. However, political mega-events acquire their significance through their political impact, and this impact also generates significant security concerns in their management. Protests associated with the meeting of the group of twenty industrialised nations (G20) and the World Trade Organisation (WTO) have contributed to the high profiles of these mega-events in the global consciousness and have proved extraordinarily expensive to police. Much of the publicity generated by such gatherings is negative, on account of the often violent security operations that are associated with them. The 2009 meeting of the G20 in London prompted the largest security operation seen in the UK for over a decade, with total security costs estimated at upwards of £10 million for the two-day event.

Study activity

How can mega-event organisers balance security concerns with the need to create exciting, dynamic events? As an attendee at a mega-event, what inconveniences would you be prepared to accept in the name of security and at what point would these deter you from attending?

10.4.3 The post-event period

The post-event period is the longest and most complex to analyse because it has no definitive end point, and because the impacts attributable to mega-events, or claimed by host cities, are numerous. It is therefore necessary to differentiate three separate time-frames within the post-event period (see Figure 10.7).

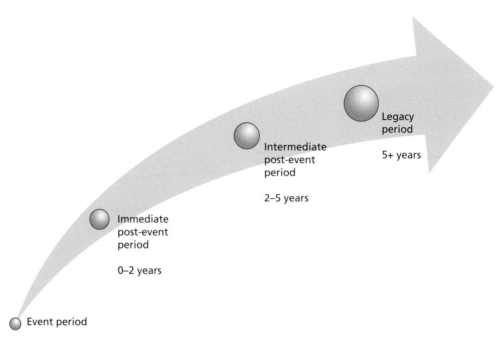

Legacy
period

5+ years

Intermediate
post-event
period

2–5 years

Immediate
post-event
period

0–2 years

Event period

Figure 10.7 The post-event period

Immediately following the mega-event period, a number of short-term effects will occur. These will not necessarily be reliable indicators of the long-term impacts of hosting a mega-event, but they can include: a sudden and dramatic drop in local employment as event-related jobs, and volunteering opportunities, are wound up; problems of over-supply in the tourism market as the increased capacity developed for the event period is no longer needed; and the under-utilisation of expensively constructed mega-event venue and infrastructure projects. These consequences alone can make assessing the impacts of a mega-event problematic in the immediate post-event period. There will also be a period of delay in the winding-up of the event organisation, the processing of statistical information and the movement of capital flows associated with hosting the event, such as sponsorship money, merchandising income and ticket revenue.

The intermediate post-event period is when the impacts of hosting a mega-event can become clear. Within this time-frame, host cities can develop post-event management arrangements for facilities and governance frameworks for former mega-event sites. It is not uncommon for there to be large-scale political changes within a host nation or city during this period, as the post-event period will extend beyond standard political electoral cycles. This will also have an impact on the post-event impacts of a mega-event as the financial, physical and social aspects of the event become part of the political discourse in the host city. Five years after the 2004 Athens Olympics, all but one of the twenty-two Olympic venues were unused, and one of the core venue complexes had become notorious for hosting not prestigious sporting events but large groups of illegal squatters. It is now possible to assess the impacts of the Athens Games accurately, especially in comparison with its successor event in the Olympic calendar – the 2006 Winter Games in Turin – which successfully handed its venues to a management company and has integrated them into its regional and sporting development strategies.

Image 10.2 The empty Athens Olympic complex, seven years after the 2004 Games
Source: Matt Cardy / Getty Images

The legacy period is the most politically charged aspect of the post-event period for a mega-event. Planners and politicians alike view the hosting of a mega-event as a way to fast-track processes of urban development and economic restructuring that would normally take place over much longer time-frames (Andranovich *et al.* 2001). Hosting mega-events now provides a stimulus for the redevelopment of cities, the creation of new urban areas and the diversification of economies. Alongside these instrumental legacies of a mega-event are the intrinsic legacies that hosting high-profile examples of sporting and cultural practices is supposed to deliver: an increase in sports activity within the population, for example, or a rise in cultural participation. Set alongside further socio-economic targets, such as rises in employment, educational achievement and social cohesion, it is worth considering why these mega-events, if they are so beneficial to society, have not become the norm, rather than the exception, in development planning. A look at the history of some of these development goals associated with mega-events shows that these potentially high-impact events are also high risk: for every high-profile success story (such as Barcelona: see Case Study 10.3, below), there is a parallel story of cost overruns, poorly managed legacies and political problems. Issues of event impacts and legacy are dealt with in detail in Chapter 14. The main area in which the long-term benefits of mega-events are anticipated by planners is regeneration.

10.4.4 Mega-events and urban regeneration

As outlined above, many of the positive impacts claimed for hosting mega-events in the legacy period are linked to the concept of urban regeneration. This is a 'comprehensive and integrated vision and action which leads to the resolution of urban problems and which seeks to bring about a lasting improvement in the economic, physical, social and environmental condition of an area that has been subject to change' (Roberts 2000: 17). Mega-events, by virtue of the massive investment they attract and the policy focus that they generate, can provide a major stimulus to regeneration programmes and, in many cases, can become the main element of major regeneration schemes.

Strategies of regeneration have been explicitly employed throughout the UK and Europe since the Second World War as the need for physical reconstruction provided an opportunity for the reconsideration of urban form in response to new economic and social conditions. In the UK, successive governments have produced regeneration and development frameworks that have prioritised different economic sectors, institutional actors and policy outcomes. Table 10.2 summarises the variety of approaches to regeneration that have been adopted in the United Kingdom since the 1950s.

We can see from this historical overview that events have begun to take on a role in regeneration only since the 1980s. This period was one of major economic restructuring in Western economies as industrial production moved globally south and east to areas of lower costs, and the manufacturing bases of many cities were lost. This period of globalisation left many derelict industrial sites in its wake and, with this, a legacy of unemployment, skills loss and social problems. Increasingly, governments in the UK, the US and Europe turned to major projects, such as the hosting of mega-events, as means for regenerating these former industrial areas and addressing their associated cultural, social, political and economic problems.

The contributions that a mega-event can make to regeneration are manifold. Although the tendency is to look to an increase in tourism as the main socio-economic impact of a mega-event, we can identify three strategies of integrating mega-events into urban regeneration, in a development of Evans's (2005) categorisation of cultural regeneration.

10.4.4.1 Mega-event-led regeneration

This strategy places a mega-event at the core of a regeneration strategy, as a catalyst for all other developments in the area. Such schemes use the event to brand the regeneration scheme and to promote its uniqueness and value. An example of a city that has pursued this policy consistently is Barcelona, which used the 1992 Olympics and then the 2004 World Forum of Cultures to drive the regeneration of the city (see Case Study 10.3).

10.4.4.2 Mega-event within regeneration

This category describes regeneration strategies where the event is embedded into a broader regeneration strategy, being only one element amid other, equally important components. An example of this is the role that the 2002 Commonwealth Games played in the regeneration of Manchester in the north-west of England. Although hosting the Games became a major impetus for the deepening and continuation of regeneration in the east of the city, their potential to contribute to existing regeneration policy in the city was identified by planners and politicians at the bidding stage (Carlsen and Taylor 2003). Hosting the Games provided an opportunity to leverage additional external funding into an area that has been undergoing significant regeneration developments since the 1980s (Smith and Fox 2007)

Table 10.2 The evolution of British regeneration policy

Sources: Roberts 2000, Bianchini 1993, McGuigan 1996, Diamond and Liddle 2005, Morgan 2002

Period	1950s	1960s	1970s	1980s	1990s	2000s
Policy type	Reconstruction	Revitalisation	Renewal	Redevelopment	Regeneration	Imagineering
Major strategy and orientation	Post-war reconstruction and extension of older areas and cities, with some suburban growth	Continuation of 1950s themes	Focus on in-situ renewal and neighbourhood schemes; mainly peripheral new developments	Many major high-profile schemes; events begin to be incorporated into regeneration strategies	Move towards more integrated and holistic policy approaches	Flagship projects and mega-events play key roles in regeneration policy
Key actors and stakeholders	National and local government	Greater balance between public and private sectors	Growing role for private sector	Emphasis on private sector and special agencies and quangos	Partnership the dominant approach	Partnership approach continues
Funding	Majority public sector	Majority public sector with growing constraints on private sector	Resource constraints on public sector; greater private sector investment	Private sector dominant, often with public sector funding	Greater balance between public, private and third sector activity	Emphasis on the 'leveraging' of public sector funds to produce large impacts
Social content	Improvement of housing and general living standards	Social and welfare improvement	Community-based action; increase in empowerment	Community self-help, with selective state support	Emphasis on the role of the community	Neighbourhood empowerment and management become key policy concerns

Physical emphasis	Replacement of inner areas and some peripheral development	Continuation of 1950s themes	More extensive renewal of older urban areas	Major schemes of replacement and new developments; growth of flagship schemes	More modest than 1980s; growth of heritage approaches	Urban centre and fringe renewal
Environmental approach	Landscaping and some greening	Selective improvements	Environmental improvement with some innovations	Growth of environmental concern	Broader idea of environmental sustainability introduced	Climate change drives sustainability agenda forward

10.4.4.3 Mega-event added to regeneration

This category describes a situation in which a mega-event becomes an addition to an existing regeneration strategy but is not fully integrated within it. In this category of mega-event planning, the benefits of the event will not be fully leveraged for regeneration purposes. Increasingly, the legacy benefits of hosting a mega-event are viewed as central to successful bidding and to gaining public support for the event, so contemporary events rarely fall into this category. The two most recent Olympic Games to be hosted in the United States, Los Angeles 1984 and Atlanta 1996, can both be identified with this planning style, however. Both host cities emphasised the financial sustainability of their bids, with Los Angeles generating a $200-million profit that was then used to endow a sporting trust, but its Games had no positive impact on the overburdened mass-transit, housing and education sectors of the city. Although contemporary mega-events are less likely to suffer similar criticism, due to the recently developed expectation that all mega-events should contribute to sustainable development, events with poor legacies might fall into this category through bad planning or management. For instance, the Athens 2004 Olympics were poorly integrated into development planning and left the country with a debt of £7 billion (Baim 2009).

Smith (2007) offers ten key principles for the use of events in regeneration:

1 Embed event strategies within wider regeneration programmes.
2 Use the event as a coherent theme and effective stimulus for other regeneration projects.
3 Incorporate regeneration planning into the initial stages of event planning.
4 Promote shared ownership and understanding of the regeneration plans amongst all partners in the event and legacy planning process.
5 Design effective management and functional relationships between event managers and regeneration managers to deliver joint goals.
6 Allocate sufficient human and capital resources throughout the lifetime of an event to achieve its goals.
7 Design event regeneration projects that engage with, and meet the needs of, the most deprived members of a community.
8 Plan for an even geographical distribution of positive impacts across areas targeted for regeneration through an event.
9 Integrate physical and infrastructure developments with social and economic regeneration targets.
10 Ensure community representation from the planning stage onwards in the event management process.

CASE STUDY 10.3

Events and the regeneration of Barcelona

Location: Barcelona, Spain
Event type: mega-event

Barcelona offers a high-profile example of the role that mega-events can play in strategies of urban regeneration. Potential host cities often cite its success to justify their own bids for mega-events, with many of them lauding the 'Barcelona Model' (Balibrea 2001).

Until the 1970s, Barcelona was a major European industrial city, with a large Mediterranean port and manufacturing services for the automobile, pharmaceutical and textiles industries. Global economic restructuring in the 1970s, coupled with the restructuring of the Spanish state in the post-Franco period, led to a series of industrial and economic crises in the city, leaving it in a 'post-industrial' state, with many derelict former industrial spaces and buildings.

In 1991, in response to this period of decline the Mayor of Barcelona, Pasquall Maragall, articulated his vision for a city that would be globally competitive: 'in urban competition, factors like the environment and cultural and education infrastructures count more and more. In a strategic sense we can say that cities are like businesses which compete to attract investments and residents, selling places which are suitable for industry, commerce and all kinds of services' (cited in Balibrea 2001: 213). Maragall oriented the city to a mega-event-led regeneration strategy. In 1986, the city was awarded the 1992 Summer Olympic Games, and this became the key driver of Barcelona's attempts to reinvent itself for the post-industrial era.

The Olympic Village was constructed in the disadvantaged port area of Poblenou and the construction of the Olympic venues and public spaces was integrated into a major physical development programme. This included waterfront developments, a new ring-road for the city, the reclaiming of brownfield sites and the demolition of redundant industrial buildings. The new developments associated with this period of change were polycentric, with the aim of 'Monumentalising the outskirts and revitalising the historic centre' of the city (Balibrea 2001: 212) to produce a more sustainable arrangement of urban form. Tourism development was encouraged through the construction of new hotels as well as rail and airport improvements. Between 1986 and 2000, Barcelona's hotel capacity increased by 300 per cent.

The cost of producing the Games themselves was $1.3 billion, but the associated physical investment totalled $8 billion, demonstrating the contribution made to the development of the city through hosting this mega-event (Brunet 2009).

Alongside these significant physical developments, a process of rebranding and managing the symbolic representation of the city took place during this period

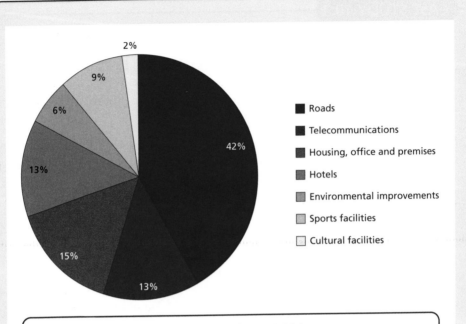

Figure 10.8 Investments in Barcelona, 2004
Source: Brunet 2009

(Garcia 2004). Barcelona's local government seized on the opportunity to promote the city as a leisure and tourism destination, promoting Catalan culture and refurbishing key architectural landmarks, as well as implementing an ambitious cultural development programme, capitalising on the opportunity to reposition itself in the global tourism market. By 2006, Barcelona was voted Europe's most attractive city, and was the continent's fourth most-visited.

In 2004, Barcelona hosted the Universal Forum of Cultures, another global event, in this case under the umbrella of the United Nations. Although this drew only 3.5 million visitors against an expected target of 5 million, and cost $2.3 billion to produce, it provided an opportunity for the city to maintain the mega-event-led strategy of urban regeneration and to continue to develop through event-associated investments in infrastructure and tourism.

Study activity

What steps can mega-event organisers take to win public support for hosting the event when the legacy benefits may not be immediately apparent?

10.5 Mega-event tourism

Mega-event tourism can be defined as tourism activity generated either directly or indirectly by the presence of a mega-event within a location.

The major direct economic driver associated with mega-events, and the most obvious manifestation of their impact in the event period, is tourism. The planned increases in tourism that accompany mega-events are related to the increased exposure that an event location will gain in the three event periods and also the opportunity that a mega-event provides for a host city to reposition itself within the global tourism market place. Forecasts for the Korea International Marine Expo in 2012 predict visitor numbers of 8.9 million (Lee *et al.* 2008), compared to average *national* annual tourist arrivals of just 7 million, clearly indicating the significance of mega-events in the tourism market place.

Tourism that is directly generated will include attendance at the event itself and visits in the pre- and post-event periods that are motivated by a desire to encounter the event in its development or legacy phases. From 2009, it was possible to book excursions and visits to the 2012 Olympic site in London, and this increasingly formed part of tourist itineraries in the British capital in the run-up to the Games.

Indirectly generated tourism activity will be related to the increased media profile of the host city and promotional campaigns mounted by both the city and the host nation to maximise the benefits of this increased global exposure. Typically, these campaigns will include the promotion of other events during the event periods, as well as other destinations in the host nation.

10.5.1 Pre-event period tourists

These tourists have been attracted to the destination due to the increased media coverage of the destination resulting from it becoming a mega-event host. Pre-event tourists may be motivated to experience the planning period of the event – perhaps to visit an event location or to participate in pre-event activities, such as hand-over ceremonies or cultural celebrations.

10.5.2 Event period tourists

Tourism flows in the event period can be positive, negative or neutral. Weed (2008) makes use of Preuss's (2005) nine categories of 'event affected people' to categorise movements of people associated with the mega-event period. These are summarised in Figure 10.9.

This figure shows the complexity of mega-event tourism flows. The scale of the event means that it has implications for understanding the behaviours not only of event tourists directly but of all potential tourists to and from a host city during the event period. In fact, minimising the impacts of negative tourism flows associated with mega-events can be as crucial to the overall economic success of the event as maximising positive flows.

10.5.3 Post-event period tourists

Hosting a mega-event generates both tangible and intangible tourism legacies. The intangible tourism benefits include enhancing or developing the image of the city, and increasing and improving tourism industry skills within the local economy. The tangible benefits for the tourism industry include an increased accommodation supply, improved visitor facilities and transport infrastructure, and new visitor attractions. Many mega-event tourists are cultural tourists who seek new cultural experiences associated with a mega-event; many of these experiences come

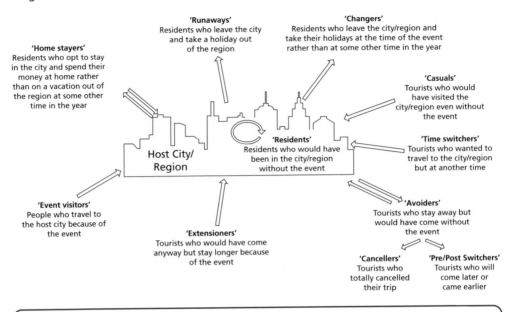

Figure 10.9 Mega-event tourism flows
Source: Weed 2008

after the event thanks to the creation of new districts and cultural facilities. For example, the main attraction at the 2005 World Expo in Aichi, Japan, was life-size reconstruction of a house inhabited by the characters of Miyazaki's animated children's film *My Neighbour Totoro*. This was reopened in 2006 and continues to be the most popular tourism attraction in the destination, having attracted more than a million visitors.

The tangible and intangible tourism benefits of hosting a mega-event can deliver a significant uplift in visitor numbers through enhancing the image of the destination, increasing its media exposure and enhancing the visitor experience.

CASE STUDY 10.4

The tourism impacts of the 2002 FIFA World Cup in South Korea

Location: South Korea
Event type: mega-event
Attendees: 2,700,000

The 2002 FIFA World Cup was hosted jointly by South Korea and Japan. This was the first World Cup to be hosted in Asia, and the first to be hosted by two countries. Each country provided ten stadiums for the event. There were 2.7 million spectators at matches and an estimated global television audience for the final of 1.1 billion (FIFA 2002).

Lee and Taylor (2005) conducted surveys with tourists in the arrivals and departure lounges of three major airports and two seaports in South Korea during the mega-event period. From this research, they developed three categories of tourists who visited the country at this time:

1 Tourists whose main purpose for travelling was to attend the World Cup.
2 Tourists who travelled for reasons indirectly related to the World Cup, such as to enjoy the mega-event festivities.
3 Tourists travelling for reasons not related to the World Cup.

This allowed Lee and Taylor to split tourists into two overall categories – World Cup tourists and ordinary tourists – and to estimate the proportions of each. They asked all respondents to their surveys to provide estimates of their expenditures during their stay in South Korea in terms of accommodation, food and beverages, tours and sightseeing, transportation, shopping, entertainment, game tickets and miscellaneous items.

Their findings indicated that:

- Of all tourists during the event period, 57.7 per cent were there because they were directly or indirectly motivated by the World Cup, with the remainder ordinary tourists. Total World Cup overseas tourist arrivals during the mega-event period were 232,800.
- Per capita tourist spending by World Cup tourists was $2242 – 1.8 times higher than that of ordinary tourists in the same period.
- The total direct expenditure of mega-event tourists during the event period was estimated at $522 million, an amount that 'would not have occurred in the absence of the World Cup' (Lee and Taylor 2005: 599).

Study activity

How can tourism agencies maximise the benefits of positive tourism flows and minimise the impacts of negative tourism flows during a mega-event period?

Industry voice

**Clive Little, director of events and programming, Olympic Park
Legacy Company, London, UK**

Delivering a strategic events programme

 The Legacy Company was established in May 2009 by its founders – the Mayor of London and the British government – as a public sector, not-for-profit company which is responsible for the long-term planning, development, management and maintenance of the Olympic Park and its facilities after the London 2012 Games. The Queen Elizabeth Olympic Park, as it will be known after the Games, will be at the centre of London's growth in the twenty-first century. Its connections, sporting facilities, parkland, waterways and family housing will form a unique mix – building on the best of London's traditions to create a beautiful, active park, embracing East London, its diverse creativity and culture. It will anchor a new city district whilst linking into the surrounding neighbourhoods to promote convergence, regeneration and prosperity in East London.

Unlike the majority of London's major parks, such as Hyde Park and Regent's Park, the future Queen Elizabeth Olympic Park resides in an area of relatively low population density by comparison. These central London parks are, to a much greater extent, self-activating parks, predominantly due to the population that immediately surrounds them but also due to their maturity, high profile and close proximity to major densities of international visitors.

Therefore, the role of events and programming is fundamental to the park's future success, not just in terms of animating the park and ensuring high levels of visitors but also to help ensure that the residential development platforms managed by the Legacy Company reach a peak value, thus maximising the financial return to the public purse. The demand for housing on these development platforms, in and around the park, will have a direct correlation to the events and programming taking place as part of a 'quality-of-life' mix.

In order to fulfil the ambitions for the park and live up to the Legacy Company's aims, as well as public and media expectations, the park needs to deliver an incredibly diverse range of events – from low-level community programming and profile-raising entertainment through to hosting world-class sporting events that build on the legacy aims.

The events and programmes we deliver at the park will be driven by our three key priority themes:

- Building local ownership and showcasing the cultural expression of the East End.
- Encouraging sports and healthy living.
- Attracting regional and international visitors.

Delivering the correct solution needs careful strategic, geographic and logistical consideration that continuously references back to our three priority themes, whilst also consulting, informing and feeding back into numerous planning work streams within the company.

Our planning process can be broken down and simplified to show the key (but not conclusive) elements that need consideration – as follows.

Assess the assets

- Which spaces across the park are suitable for hosting events?
- What are the legacy venues capable of delivering?
- Do we have the correct mix of indoor/outdoor space, especially with regard to seasonality issues?

Research the practicalities

- What limitations might arise due to noise issues (coming from or into the park)?
- Is there a ceiling in terms of total visitor numbers due to crowd control and flow?
- Assess what impact planning and licensing controls might have on the events programme.

Understand the market

- Undertake two major market research pieces, with one looking at the general events market and the other looking specifically at local and community programming.
- Launch a call for 'Expressions of Interest' (EOI) to ascertain what the external appetite is for events and programming at the park, from event organisers, sporting bodies, brands, etc.

Inform the design process

- Recommend ways of adapting or shaping the spaces and venues to ensure we have facilities that work well and efficiently for event organisers.
- Decide what events infrastructure should be facilitated (to add value for third-party hirers/partners).
- Ensure the park and its event spaces work well logistically and spatially.

Build the strategic events programme

- Use the market research and EOI process to inform and shape what the events programme will be.
- Ensure the programme reaches the correct volume, in the correct places at the correct time.

- Shape the programme to have synergy with the physical tone of the park. (The park is sectored into two core zones: the south park – active; and the north park — passive.)
- Ensure the programme offers the best revenue income for the park in order to increase the investment that can be made into local and cultural programming.

Investigate the best delivery methods

How can we deliver the events and programmes whilst reducing the risk to the company? Ensure that the events and programming budget offers best value through:

- Licence agreements/hire to third parties.
- Subsidising when an event delivers strongly in line with our key priority themes.
- Promoting events through the Legacy Company – most applicable to small-scale, high-frequency events or programmes.

By following an ordered planning phase, as outlined above, the events programme and the park can be tuned to ensure the best fit between the two. Comprehensive planning work also gives us a solid set of data and information which can be used to focus energy on spaces and times that might otherwise be neglected.

Delivering the right programming for the park and its users is a hefty challenge but one that would inspire any event manager or programmer. Two hundred and fifty acres of public realm and a set of world-class Olympic venues are incredible assets, and they will offer the ultimate job satisfaction once animated successfully.

10.6 Summary

This chapter has defined and categorised a mega-event as a special kind of large-scale event that delivers global media and/or socio-economic impacts.

The time-frame of the mega-event has been split into three periods. The pre-event period is characterised by huge levels of speculative public investment and the battle to win public approval. The event period itself requires sophisticated organisation and functional apparatus to respond to the complexity of managing one of the world's largest events. Finally, the benefits of perhaps a decade of investment must be leveraged in the post-event period.

Mega-events have the potential to generate massive benefits for host cities and nations, but they can equally encumber both city and state with massive burdens. Embedding mega-events into broader strategies of urban regeneration and tourism development helps to increase the likelihood of positive outcomes whilst reducing the risk of negative impacts.

Further reading

http://www.bie-paris.org. The website of the International Bureau of Expositions, which is responsible for the awarding and regulation of World Expos.

http://www.olympic.org. The website of the International Olympic Committee, which contains archived information on all previous Olympic and Paralympic events.

Weed, M. (2008) *Olympic Tourism*, Oxford: Butterworth-Heinemann. Although this book focuses on Olympic tourism, it contains many models and useful references that will aid understanding of tourism flows associated with all mega-events.

Chapter 11

Events in the public and third sectors

Contents

11.1 Aims

By the end of this chapter, students will be able:

- To analyse the differences between the private, public and third sectors in the events industry.
- To evaluate the particular considerations associated with the planning and delivery of public sector events.
- To evaluate the particular considerations associated with the planning and delivery of events in the third sector.

11.2 Introduction

Definitions of events often rely on management analysis and academic research with a 'for-profit' focus. However, a large proportion of UK events are carried out by and on behalf of the third sector of the economy and the public services. Such events, whilst often high budget and carried out by cash-rich organisations, often do not embody the same characteristics of planning, design and management as their for-profit sector counterparts. Building on the key aspects of events management that are applicable to events in all sectors of the economy, this chapter highlights the particular characteristics of third sector and public sector events and the different nature and style of managing their success.

Getz (2005: 191) identifies three groups of event organisers in each of the private, non-profit and government/partnership groups. However, the recent growth of social enterprise (see below) and changes in the relationship between public and private sectors that are resulting from the economic crisis that began in 2008 with the 'credit crunch' necessitate a redrawing of this model. We can now place organisations that produce events in the three categories that are shown in Figure 11.1.

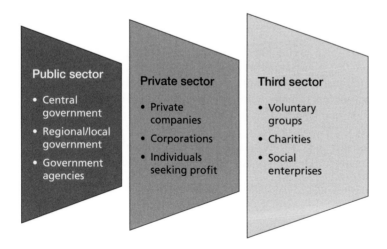

Public sector

- Central government
- Regional/local government
- Government agencies

Private sector

- Private companies
- Corporations
- Individuals seeking profit

Third sector

- Voluntary groups
- Charities
- Social enterprises

Figure 11.1 The three event-producing sectors

The private sector has been the focus of the majority of event management textbooks, dominating the literature with discussions of profitability and revenue management. In this chapter, we will explore events in the public and third sectors, both of which are increasingly using events in order to achieve their social, political and cultural aims.

11.3 The public sector

The public sector refers to those organisations that are either in the direct control of government at the national, regional or local levels, or receive their core funding from public finances. This sector, despite being encouraged to be more businesslike, is fundamentally different from the private sector when it comes to managing events in one major respect: accountability is to local citizens and the electorate rather than shareholders and/or investors (Wood 2009). The main impacts of this are in terms of how public sector organisations justify their involvement in events management and in how the events themselves are evaluated. Although it is tempting to suggest that public sector events will differ fundamentally from events in other sectors in terms of their content and design, recent moves towards greater private and third sector involvement in what have traditionally been areas of public sector monopoly – such as health, education and welfare – have blurred these distinctions.

CASE STUDY 11.1

The role of governments in the events industry

Event name: Scotland: The Perfect Stage
Event category: various
Venue and location: across Scotland
Date: year round
Website: http://www.eventscotland.org/

Event Scotland is the national events agency for Scotland, set up in 2003 to strengthen and promote the country's events industry. It promotes and supports an international and national programme of events, and can supply funding to events and event organisations to help them grow and develop. The agency is funded by the Scottish Parliament, and aims to produce an eight-to-one return on investment by 2020.

In 2009, Event Scotland launched 'Scotland: The Perfect Stage', a national event strategy for the country. This had a visionary mission statement:

> Our 2020 vision for Scotland: Scotland established as the perfect stage for events.
>
> Our mission to deliver this vision: To develop a portfolio for events that delivers impacts and international profile for Scotland.
>
> (Event Scotland 2009: 1)

Study activity

Read through Scotland's national event strategy, available from Event Scotland (2009). Concentrate on Section 4. How far do you agree that events in Scotland can help the government to achieve its political objectives?

There has been a huge recent growth in the use of events by local and regional governments, but concerns have been expressed that these are not always used in a strategic or effective way (Wood 2009). However, despite these concerns, it is clear that events strategy has become a new form of public policy, with the public sector involved in events that range from local, interactive gatherings to mega-events like the Olympic Games. The sections below will look at the strategic role that events can play in the public sector and how these can have the greatest impacts.

We can use the model in Figure 11.2 to categorise the different roles that the public sector plays in the event industry.

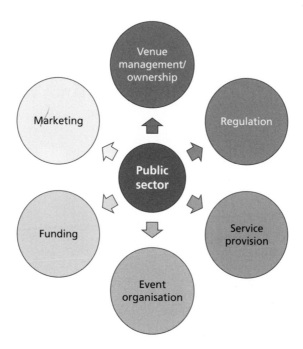

Figure 11.2 The role of the public sector in event management
Source: Adapted from Allen *et al.* 2008: 39–41

11.3.1 Venue management or ownership

In many locations, especially outside regional metropolitan centres, event venues can be publicly owned. Local government is often the owner of theatres, arts centres, community facilities, and parks and streets where events are staged. Public ownership of event venues usually either reflects historical patterns of ownership in an area or is a legacy of public sector investment that has been necessary to develop large event facilities. Increasingly, these venues are operated by specialist event organisations that are able to maximise return on the state's investment through the application of specialist management techniques in promotion, human resources and artist management.

For example, in Nashville, Tennessee, in the United States, the Bridgestone Arena is owned by Davidson County and the Sports Authority of Nashville. The day-to-day management and promotion of the venue have been contracted out to a specialist management company, Powers Management, which has the specialist arena and events management skills required to make a success of this 20,000-capacity venue – the sixth most-visited concert venue in the US (Bridgestone Arena 2011; Nashville Predators 2011).

11.3.2 Regulation

The public sector also has an interest in monitoring and regulating the negative impacts of events, which it does through licensing and the enforcement of statutes on, for example, noise

Image 11.1 Sugarland perform on stage at the 2011 CMT Music Awards at the Bridgestone Arena
Source: Kevin Mazur / Getty Images

pollution. In addition to this, the public sector is able to incentivise or disincentivise particular forms of activity through taxes. This can be done by central government through the manipulation of nationwide taxes, or through changes in local taxation by local government. In 2010, a report by the British Visits and Events Partnerships called on the British government to bring VAT (sales tax) down to a level that would make the country's events industry more competitive with its European rivals (BVEP 2010). Typically, in Europe, sales tax applied to accommodation, facilities management, restaurants and bars is set between zero and 8 per cent, whilst in the UK it has recently been increased to 20 per cent.

11.3.3 Service provision

Using funds raised from taxation, local government will be responsible, to a greater or lesser degree, for the maintenance of public space, transport, utilities provision and the emergency services – all of which must be in place for the smooth running of an event. Liaising with local government departments on these issues is a key aspect of the management of large events and event venues.

11.3.4 Funding

The public sector can make direct and indirect funding contributions to events. Direct funding involves the finance necessary for the production of an event. For example, the UK government supported Create09 – an arts festival that took place across five London boroughs as part of the preparations for hosting the 2012 Olympic and Paralympic Games – through grant awards of £123,000 made by Arts Council England, a government agency. In addition, the London Development Agency invested £195,000 and private sector sponsorship (from the Bank of America) was also raised with a value of £61,000 (Create London 2010: 10–11).

Indirect financial support to the wider events industry is provided through state support for training for events professionals (for example, through higher education programmes) and business support services.

11.3.5 Event organisation

In some cases, public sector organisations are directly responsible for producing events. Although this function is often contracted to specialist event organisers, some celebratory and commemorative events are still delivered directly by public sector bodies. As Pugh and Wood (2004: 61) state, 'the majority of local governments in Britain now have a substantial and varied events programme', but these events are usually supported only by departments with limited, non-specialist resources in terms of staff, funding and time (Wood 2009).

11.3.6 Marketing

Where events receive direct support from the public sector in terms of marketing, this is normally related to destination marketing and tourism promotion. Governments make use of events for destination branding by public sector bodies concerned with inward investment and tourism, as well as, more recently, to support other goals, such as the promotion of social cohesion and civic identity (Raj et al. 2009). Events, especially cultural events and festivals, are becoming key elements in destination marketing (Quinn 2003), and many towns and cities are now building events into their marketing strategies.

The fundamental test of whether the public sector should be involved in events, and whether their involvement has been constructive, is based on the 'public good' argument (Getz 2007). This asks whether the contribution of government to an event will produce benefits for society as a whole or for targeted groups within it. This argument can be tested in the pre-event and post-event phases by asking the following three questions:

1 Does the event fit into the accepted policy domain of government?
2 Are the public benefits significant and inclusive?
3 Is the event managed sustainably in economic, social and environmental terms?

These relatively simple questions often demand complex responses, and local authorities, government agencies and other public bodies sometimes need to recruit external consultants to answer them. For example, in order to develop an events strategy to promote tourism and inward investment, the city of Birmingham in the English Midlands commissioned an external consultancy – Festival and Events International – to develop a strategic framework for events in the city and partnerships with other regional and local bodies. This took four months and involved a national and international benchmarking exercise to establish the extent to which the city's plans to get more involved in events were in the best interests of the public (FEI 2011). In some cases, government-supported events can have negative impacts, such as when the economic failure of the World Student Games in Sheffield in 1991 led to an increase in local taxation (Raj *et al.* 2009).

CASE STUDY 11.2

The relationship of the public sector to the Roskilde Festival

Event name: Roskilde Festival
Event category: cultural
Venue and location: Roskilde, Denmark
Date: every June/July for five days
Attendance: 80,000
Sponsors: Tuborg
Website: http://www.roskilde-festival.dk/uk/

The Roskilde Festival was established in 1971 as an annual festival of rock music on the outskirts of Copenhagen, Denmark. Since then, it has grown into one of the largest annual rock events in Europe. Every year, the festival attracts up to 80,000 visitors, and it is responsible for 20–25 per cent of annual tourism receipts in the Roskilde region.

In 2010, the headline acts were Prince, Gorillaz, Muse and the Prodigy. There are six performance areas in the festival. The smallest, tented space has a capacity of 2000 and the largest, the 'Orange Stage', has a capacity of 90,000. There is an eighty-hectare campsite attached to the festival. A peculiarity of the event is the 'naked run' that takes place every year, in which festival-goers run naked around the boundaries of the site, with one male and one female winner receiving tickets to the following year's event.

The festival is produced by the Roskilde Charitable Foundation, a not-for-profit company with just six full-time employees, but which recruits around 20,000 volunteers to produce the festival each year. Any financial surplus generated by the event is channelled back into cultural and sporting facilities in the region. Since 1992, this has totalled €27 million. Because of the foundation's charitable status, it is not liable for many state taxes and it does not pay sales tax.

The festival generates its own revenues from ticket sales and sponsorship, but it is involved in a number of partnerships with the public sector in areas such as tourism and economic development. The local authority is responsible for licensing the event and for providing policing and transport services. A local university which has developed a specialism in events management now provides training for event staff in crowd control every year, and the regional tourist board has developed a collaborative ticketing arrangement where festival attendees can receive discounted rates in local accommodation and other regional attractions. In 2001, the Roskilde county and municipal councils awarded a €1.5-million grant for the development of 'Musicon Valley', a Silicon Valley-inspired music and technology development, with the aim of building on the success of the festival. This now contains 'Rock City', an entertainment, education and cultural tourism destination.

Sources: Bærenholdt and Haldrup 2006;
Hjalager 2009; Roskilde Festival 2011

Study activity

Read through Case Study 11.2. In what ways does the public sector support the Roskilde Festival? Make a list of the reasons why you think the public sector offers this support. Is such support in the best interests of the public?

11.4 Events in the public sector

Governments can use events to gain control of specific agendas in the public eye, build support for policies and programmes, and deliver on specific policy objectives. National governments take responsibility for major international and political events, occasions of state and national celebrations (Allen *et al.* 2008). Local government has responsibility for place-making, destination-branding, generating inward investment, reducing out-migration and community cohesion, and it makes use of events to fulfil these duties.

Local authorities deliver a wide range of events for their communities, business and visitors, which may include:

- networking events
- conferences
- festivals and other celebratory events
- cultural events
- information and consultation events.

The first four of these are covered in the chapters on corporate and cultural events (Chapters 12 and 13, respectively). However, information and consultation events are specific to the public sector and have specific characteristics that are explored below.

11.4.1 Information and consultation events

These events are used by the public sector to inform the public about new projects or initiatives and to produce a dialogue with citizens that can inform the development of these areas. They can occur on a variety of scales, from small neighbourhood-level meetings to touring information roadshows.

Hiller (2000) emphasises that good public policy development must involve the community in a meaningful and ongoing way. This is especially important in the planning of large and mega-events as, even though the members of the community around an event are often conceived as key beneficiaries of its positive impacts, the idea to stage the event rarely comes from within the community, and the project may face objections and resistance. Hiller shows how far the public sector must go when addressing this community participation deficit through consultation. For the failed South African Cape Town 2004 Olympic bid, the bidding team set up local Olympic steering committees in each area that would be affected by a successful bid, at a neighbourhood level. In addition, bid personnel made hundreds of visits to individual community groups.

Community consultation events can take any one of the four forms illustrated in Figure 11.3.

Figure 11.3 Forms of community consultation events

Information provision events are the most common form of community consultation. Limited forms of interaction are offered, but these events are useful for conveying large amounts of information to a wide audience. They can be repeated and can be mobile, at a low cost. For example, the government of the city of Toronto, Canada, ran three consecutive small events to inform local residents in areas affected by their new 'Tall Buildings Strategy' of the impact that this new planning policy would have on them. These three events took place in community facilities, including a church hall and a gym (City of Toronto 2011)

At public hearings, evidence is presented to the public, along with expert advice, and at the end decisions are taken by a representative body, such as a court or council. An example of this kind of consultation event was the public hearing held on World Water Day 2011 by the Environmental and Sustainable Development Commission of the House of Representatives, in Brasilia, Brazil. The hearing heard evidence from experts on the theme of water conservation and the convening panel then made recommendations to the Brazilian government on the basis of its deliberations (UNESCO 2011).

In consensus-building events, the public are brought into the decision-making process and can influence the outcome of the decision. For example, in 2010, Sport England, the governing body for sports in England, staged this type of consultation in twenty-three locations. Each one involved face-to-face discussions and an online survey. The aim of these events was to develop a consensus view on the future governance and support of athletics. Sport England stated that, 'The consultation roadshows had an additional aim. They weren't just about influencing England Athletics in the delivery of its core activities; they were also aiming to help clubs and volunteers themselves to share their own ideas for action and change' (Sport England 2011).

In a citizens' jury, selected members of the public are asked to represent the views of the community as part of the decision-making process. These have been used more widely in the United States and Germany than elsewhere (Carson 2001), but they are being utilised increasingly in a range of contexts as a cost-effective way of gauging public opinion. An example of this form of consultation met in 2002 in Baltimore, USA, with the support of the United States Environmental Protection Agency, to examine policy responses to the threat of climate change to the Atlantic coast of the USA (Jefferson Centre 2002).

Communities are often also consulted in ways that do not make use of the interactive possibilities offered by events, such as through postal, telephone or web surveys.

11.4.2 The impacts of public sector events

Public sector events share sets of outcomes with all other forms of events (see Shone and Parry 2010), but these have particular implications in the public sector due to governments' responsibilities towards, and accountability to, their citizens (see Figure 11.4)

11.4.2.1 Economic implications of public sector events

Any event can have either positive or negative impacts. However, a private sector event normally has a direct economic impact – one way or the other – only on the event company that produces it. By contrast, a public sector event can have significant economic consequences, sometimes for many years after the event has taken place. In the case of small-scale events, these economic implications may be limited to individual departments or public bodies, but with large and mega-events, the consequences can be much more significant, sometimes affecting national economies and the future delivery of public services. Among the potential negative impacts of a mega-event are consumer price and land price inflation, tax increases, the mismanagement of funds and the costs associated with corruption.

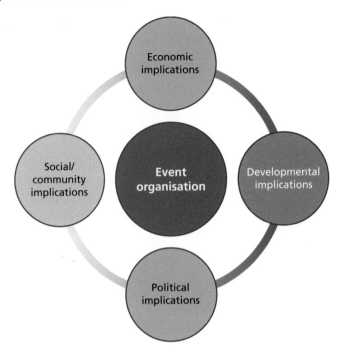

Figure 11.4 Aspects of public sector events

11.4.2.2 Developmental implications of public sector events

The public sector will normally be engaged in the development of particular locations when it supports or delivers events, ideally guided by the principles of sustainable development. However, although developmental goals – such as poverty reduction, educational attainment and public health improvements – often form part of the bid for hosting an event, there is growing scepticism in the literature about whether such developmental targets can ever be achieved in practice (Maenning and du Plessis 2009).

11.4.2.3 Political implications of public sector events

Staging or financing events to support a particular policy or political agenda can work in favour of the public sector or against it, depending on the success or failure of the event. In addition, a non-political event can have political implications if it is seen not to have produced good value for money in terms of public investment or to have caused controversy that reflects badly on the political decision to back it. Especially for major and mega-events, hosting always has political implications when there is public sector involvement.

Barker *et al.* (2001) analysed the impacts of hosting the America's Cup, a sailing competition and the oldest sporting trophy competition in the world, in Auckland, New Zealand. There were high expectations of the potential positive impacts of this event, to such an extent that the government appointed a minister to maximise them. The event was judged to have improved international trade relations, to have increased the potential of the country to attract overseas investment, and to have enhanced New Zealand's international image and reputation, which would strengthen its bids for future major events.

11.4.2.4 Social/community implications of public sector events

Many events are produced or supported by the public sector because of the positive impacts that they may have in such areas as community cohesion, social inclusion, local pride and identity. However, events can also have negative social impacts (as set out in Chapter 14), and these can lead to both financial problems for governments and reputational problems with political implications.

11.4.3 Public sector event financing

Governments around the world are becoming commissioners of services from the private and third sectors, meaning that they increasingly commission specialist event producers to deliver their events. This is in line with the more strategic marketing orientation in local government that was identified by Pugh and Wood (2004) when they looked at local authority events. These developments form part of a changing public sector paradigm in which government is seen as enabling and facilitating, rather than directly delivering the full range of public services.

CASE STUDY 11.3

Private companies delivering public sector events

Event name: NHS Institute for Innovation and Improvement Alumni Conference
Event category: public sector event
Venue and location: Excel, London, UK
Audience: 1200 delegates
Website: http://www.worldevents.com/index.shtml

This one-day conference was held in 2006 to celebrate fifty years of management training schemes in the National Health Service, the UK's publicly funded healthcare system. It had the dual role of bringing together professionals from within the NHS and promoting the NHS to a media and stakeholder audience.

The NHS commissioned a private sector event management company – World Events – to produce and manage this event. World Events provides international events management services, producing hundreds of events each year for both private and public sector clients:

> World Events is an international event agency. Founded in 1986, the company has 130 full time staff and a further 100 trained staff who work with us on a part time basis. Offices are located in Europe, USA and Asia with a revenue in excess of €46.7m/£39.8m/$57.7m. World Events is ranked in the top ten event management agencies in Europe and has won numerous industry awards for the work it has conducted for its clients.
>
> (World Events 2011)

For this event, World Events' role included:

- event design – developing a theme
- recruiting sponsors and exhibitors to help fund the conference
- marketing the event
- bookings using a bespoke web presence and online booking system
- sourcing keynote speakers and a facilitator
- operations management
- catering.

The event format involved keynote presentations, workshop sessions, debate and discussion. There was a significant use of technology during the event and it was produced to a very high standard in terms of decor and operations management. Delegate feedback was very good, with the following data recorded by World Events:

- 75 per cent got a good impression of the future vision
- 87 per cent more likely to take part in activity post-conference
- 83 per cent would use website to remain informed
- 80 per cent found the event useful and enjoyable.

Study activity

What are the benefits to the National Health Service of commissioning a private company to produce an event like the one outlined in Case Study 11.3? Do you think the public sector has the capability to produce outstanding events?

11.5 The third sector

Between the private and public sectors, and often bridging the two in practical terms, is the third sector. Known historically as the 'charitable' or 'voluntary' sector (Shone and Parry 2010), when it comes to events management, contemporary third sector organisations often still contain a strong voluntary and/or charitable component, but they may act in entrepreneurial, businesslike ways that do not conform to older stereotypes of village fête committees and well-meaning volunteer organisations. Many third sector organisations channel public sector funding to the community level, delivering services in communities, and increasing numbers of them engage in forms of social enterprise – generating profitable business for socially sustainable ends. Such businesses have often evolved from charitable and voluntary groups that wished to avoid the constraints imposed by the regulation of charities and sought to develop a more entrepreneurial attitude to social change. The Social Enterprise Coalition, a representative body for social enterprise in the UK, states: 'Social enterprises are businesses driven by a social or environmental purpose. There are 62,000 of them in the UK, contributing over £24bn to the economy, employing approximately 800,000 people' (SEC 2011).

For example, the Play House, in Birmingham, is an educational theatre company that operates as a social enterprise. Every year, the company produces more than 1000 touring theatre events for schools and young people, and it typically involves around 25,000 people in its work. To achieve recognition as a social enterprise, it has demonstrated that more than 50 per cent of its income comes from trading, that at least 50 per cent of the company's profits are spent on socially beneficial purposes, and that, if it ceased trading, its assets would be distributed for socially and environmentally beneficial purposes. Meeting these requirements allowed the Play House to be awarded the government-sponsored 'Social Enterprise Mark', which allows potential funders and partners to have confidence in its social responsibility (Play House 2011; Social Enterprise Mark 2011).

11.6 Events in the third sector

Third sector organisations operate in the same social and economic climate as any other form of business, so it should come as no surprise that the third sector has embraced the growth in the planned events sector as vigorously as its private and public sector counterparts. Third sector organisations carry out three main roles in the event industry, as shown in Figure 11.5.

11.6.1 Venue management and ownership

Third sector organisations, such as charities, community organisations and social enterprise, can own and/or manage event venues. In the UK, local government will often retain legal

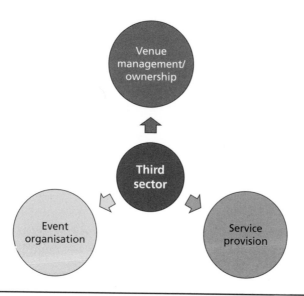

Figure 11.5 The roles of the third sector in events

Image 11.2 The Hub, Cape Town, South Africa
Source: Gallo Images / Getty Images

ownership of a range of possible event venues, but the day-to-day management of these venues will be provided by a third sector organisation. This system ensures that the venue is run in accordance with the public sector's commitment to public value, but it removes many of the costs and complications of management from the public sector.

Other third sector organisations own venues outright and use them to generate income to help them meet their social, cultural or environmental goals. An example is the Hub, in Cape Town, South Africa. This venue was set up to support local third sector groups and to encourage innovation in social enterprise. It does this by providing networking, meeting and work space for social enterprises, along with an exhibition and event space with catering facilities. The Hub makes its spaces available for private hire to generate income, and also hosts its own events on such topics as climate change, social entrepreneurship and new technologies (Hub Cape Town 2011)

11.6.2 Service provision

Third sector organisations can be involved with both indirect and direct service provision for events. Within communities, third sector groups can provide services relating to neighbourhood management, crime reduction, the maintenance of public space and youth work that help to create a stable and secure environment for events. In addition, they can provide direct services, such as catering, volunteers, and advice and consultations. In Manchester, Good Mood Food provides catering services for the local events industry, mainly for small- to medium-size business events and private functions. The firm is a social enterprise that offers training, employment and volunteer opportunities for individuals suffering from mental health problems, and it also campaigns to highlight the links between good food, health and mental well-being (Good Mood Food 2011).

11.6.3 Event organisation

Third sector organisations stage events to gain publicity for their social goals, to raise funds, and/or for training and networking purposes. The third sector is very diverse, including every-thing from international non-governmental organisations (NGOs) to small local campaign groups. Because of this diversity, third sector organisations are involved in staging a wide range of events, including:

- cultural events
- networking events
- conferences
- community festivals
- fundraising events.

The last two categories in this list are characteristic of third sector events activity. Festivals are discussed in depth in Chapter 13, but fundraising events have a specific and prominent role within the third sector, so are explored in more detail below.

11.6.4 Fundraising events

Fundraising events, of which there are many different types, are extremely common within the third sector. Getz (2007: 26) suggests a list of events which commonly fulfil a fundraising function:

- gala dinners
- concerts
- entertainment shows
- sponsored endurance events
- celebrity sports
- auctions.

Webber (2004) provides a categorisation of fundraising events which helps to explain their various objectives (see Table 11.1).

However, as Webber goes on to show, such events, in themselves, are not very efficient in terms of income generation (see Table 11.2). Instead, they should be seen as part of a more strategic approach to fundraising that includes relationship-building and increasing awareness if their potential for charitable giving is to be fully exploited.

Table 11.1 Types of fundraising events

Source: Webber 2004

Fundraising event	Objective
Donor development	To generate additional income from existing supporters
Rewarding current supporters	To maintain the enthusiasm and engagement of current supporters
New support generation	To attract new supporters
Networking	To increase networking opportunities between supporters and potential supporters
Awareness raising	To develop awareness of the cause for which funds are being raised; to maintain awareness of the cause in the minds of supporters, public and the media

Table 11.2 Productivity of different fundraising methods

Source: Webber 2004

Fundraising method	Income raised per pound spent
Legacies	43.3
Committed giving	3.7
Memberships	2.7
Local fundraising	2.3
Fundraising events	2.2
Direct marketing	2.0
Not from individuals:	
Trusts	9.9
Corporate	4.7

CASE STUDY 11.4

A fundraising event for a social enterprise

Event name: A Big Night Out with Jamie
Event category: third sector event
Venue: St Paul's Cathedral, London
Date: 11 November 2010
Audience: 250-plus
Website: http://www.fifteen.net/abignightoutwithjamie/Pages/default.aspx

The Big Night Out with Jamie is an annual fundraising event for Fifteen – a social enterprise set up by celebrity chef Jamie Oliver:

> It exists to inspire disadvantaged young people – homeless, unemployed, overcoming drug or alcohol problems – to believe that they can create for themselves great careers in the restaurant industry.
> The Fifteen restaurants serve food of the highest quality made from the best ingredients: their kitchens are where the apprentices learn their trade, and their profits help fund the programme.
>
> (Fifteen Foundation 2011)

The event was structured around a four-course meal designed by Jamie Oliver, but it also incorporated musical entertainment and a charity auction which raised £25,000. The total amount of money raised by this event was £200,000.

Reporting on the event, the Fifteen Foundation make use of testimonials from attendees to demonstrate its success:

> What an amazing venue, I never thought in my lifetime I would stand next to Nelson's tomb with a mojito in my hand. It was great to see the fantastic work done by the Fifteen Foundation. I loved the wheel of fortune game, even if Tash on our table won all the Golden Prizes and walked off with a Plasma TV and an Apple Mac! The Auction prizes were once again exciting and unique. All in all a fabulous night out. Thank you Fifteen!
>
> (Julia Newnham, British Leisure)

> You can rely on Jamie's Big Night to be great fun. The food (as you'd expect) is always delicious and the entertainment is starry. It is a fabulous way for us to thank customers while at the same time raise money for a great cause.
>
> (Tom Weldon, Penguin UK)

Study activity

Use the internet to identify a charity in which you have an interest. Put yourself in the place of an event manager seeking new business in the third sector. How would you pitch an event concept to fundraising managers in the charity you have selected? What can an event offer them that differs from other, more economically productive, forms of fundraising?

11.7 Other not-for-profit events

11.7.1 Political and state events

Political events are held by political organisations and governments. They include party conferences, protests, trade union meetings and policy launches. These vary in scale from national party conferences, to large-scale political protests (such as demonstrations against meetings of the G20), to local-level activist group meetings.

Van Wyk (2005: 468) defines a political event as:

> carefully planned, organised, managed and implemented/hosted even by political office bearers either in government, interest groups, civil society members or outsourced to event managers. Furthermore this event has a political or public nature with a political purpose or message, with the intention to reach as many people as possible by a variety of means such as hosting an event, marketing and the media, and the intention to reach a specific objective or a number of objectives.

State events are ceremonies that are held to mark occasions of national significance, such as the opening of parliament, the inauguration of a leader or the commemoration of a conflict. They possess their own intrinsic socio-cultural significance, but also have an economic impact, often attracting high numbers of tourists. Among the specific challenges posed by political and state events with very high media profiles are issues of media management, political and cultural relationships, crowd management and security.

Van Wyk (2005) illustrates the scale of such events by citing two examples of South African presidential inaugurations:

- 1999 – 55,000 attendees, including thirty heads of state from other countries and 5000 foreign dignitaries.
- 2004 – 45,000 attendees, including thirty-five heads of state from other countries.

CASE STUDY 11.5

A radical political event

Event name: Mutiny
Event type: political event
Venue: Resistance Gallery, London, UK
Audience: 200
Website: http://jointhemutiny.wordpress.com/about/

Mutiny events are radical political gatherings that take place on a bi-monthly basis at the Resistance Gallery in Bethnal Green, London. They have been developed and are produced by a non-hierarchical, loosely affiliated group of individuals and are open at the planning stage to anyone who wants to contribute or become involved in the event to join the group. The aim of the Mutiny events is to create new ways for people to engage with the political situation in the UK and worldwide by bringing together journalists, performers, academics, poets, artists and musicians in events that mix entertainment and debate with very high levels of audience participation. They are examples of a new generation of political events that have emerged across the world as young people, in particular, move away from mainstream forms of political engagement and create forms of political practice that make greater use of creativity, participation and activism in their design.

> We want to change the world. We want to see an end to the carbon economy, to the global dominance of the American military complex and sweatshops abroad and call centres in the UK. At the same time we want to spend an evening with friends, enjoying a drink and the spectacle of alternative films and documentaries, performances and poetry, comedy and art installations.
>
> (Mutiny 2011)

The content of each Mutiny event is themed by discussion on topics that have included money, love, the media, fashion and education. The format changes for each event, but will typically involve a panel discussion, individual speakers, musical performances, exhibition of art, and a great deal of audience interaction and debate. In addition, Mutiny events make use of social media, including Twitter and Facebook, to involve people who are unable to attend in person and to collect feedback throughout the night from the audience.

Using the internet, what examples of political events at the activist level can you find in your region? What can event managers learn from these events in terms of audience participation, marketing and social media? What could students of events management and professional event managers contribute to the growth and development of such events?

11.7.2 Faith events

Faith events are diverse in size and reach – from intimate meetings of a few individuals, to organised faith services and celebrations, to the largest single event in the world in terms of attendance: the Hajj in Mecca, Saudi Arabia. This annual religious pilgrimage is undertaken by approximately 3.4 million people every year (Raj *et al.* 2009).

Faith events often play a key role in the lives of individuals and families, marking significant life events such as births, deaths and weddings. Other faith events form part of the official calendar of a country or culture, reflected in public holidays such as Mexico's Feast of the Dead (Getz 2007) and Christmas. Typically, a formal faith event is followed by a more secular celebratory event, such as a wedding reception or meal. Pilgrimage is another type of faith event, where individuals follow a particular path to reach a sacred destination of importance to their faith.

In 2010, Pope Benedict XVI, the head of the Roman Catholic Church, visited the UK for the first time. His multi-event tour included Glasgow, Edinburgh, Birmingham and London. As this was an official state visit, the host country was expected to meet many of the costs of the tour, with the eventual cost to the public finances estimated at between £12 million and £20 million. There were three ticketed events, with an aggregate audience of approximately 225,000 people (*Guardian* 2010).

Industry voice

Leon Panitzke, director, Verve Communications

Verve is a full-service communications company, with a focus on PR and communications. Events management is one of the things that we're involved with, but it's something that I've personally been focused on entirely for about three years now. We have eight full-time staff, so we're quite a small, specialist agency, with a main focus on working with the public sector. We work with local councils, some government departments and National Health Service (NHS) trusts. We also have a wide pool of associates, so when we have to ramp up for bigger events, we can draw on this talent pool.

I'm a director of Verve, and have been since 2005, when the company was set up. As a director, I'm the main point of contact for our client, and it's also my job to project-manage the whole event, from start to finish. So, I'll be involved from the outset, from the original brief, through to writing the project plan and liaising with all the partners, and because we're quite heavily involved with the public sector, one of my main jobs is pulling together quite complex partnerships.

An event that we managed for the London Development Agency (LDA), which was called the 'Personal Best' recognition ceremony, was for over 1000 people at the O2. That came out of a conversation with a public sector colleague who said they were looking for some support for an event. They didn't have the budget to run an event along the same lines that they did two or three years ago, when the public finances were more generous (they'd run an event the previous year at Wembley Arena). So, we worked with the LDA to put together a programme and we introduced a jobs and skills fair to the event, which they hadn't done before. That was an idea that came out of the initial meeting. I was involved in all aspects of the event from the proposal stage, then working with twenty-eight different London boroughs. We had five months to create the event from scratch, including involving a number of celebrities and politicians. It was a really good example of partnership working really well, because having to deal with that number of different public bodies was quite problematic.

A lot of the small-scale events that we do tend to be consultation exercises: for example, we worked on something called 'A Picture of Health for South East London', which is the biggest-ever consultation exercise carried out for the NHS in London. We carried out a consultation with over a million people, which is pretty massive, but the events themselves tended to be quite small scale and deliberative, with maybe fifty to a hundred people at public events. Obviously, the job there is to make sure that everybody who *should be* consulted *has been* consulted, and that it's not just a rubber-stamping exercise, because the process has to be robust enough to stand up to a judicial review, should that ever happen. Most of the consultation events we've done are about public bodies trying to engage stakeholders and talking to residents. For example, a health body wanting to close an A and E department is always going to cause outrage, so the organisation has to prove that they've carried out a full and proper consultation exercise.

We are definitely a private sector organisation, because we are a limited company, but I would say 95 per cent of our business at the moment comes from the public sector. We will now have to look at adapting to the new financial climate, as lots of the funding that's been there in the past for public sector organisations to put on events won't be around. We are looking at different funding mechanisms and different ways of doing business. Some of my public sector clients have had meetings with me recently to ask how they can actually make money from some of the events which they used to put on for free. A lot of private sector events companies will be looking at those financial models over the coming years.

11.8 Summary

In this chapter, we have seen that the rapid recent growth of the events industry in the private sector has been matched by that in the public and third sectors. The public sector carries out a range of roles in the events industry – from regulation, taxation and oversight through to event production and marketing. Increasingly, however, the public sector seeks to commission specialist event managers and event production companies to deliver events on its behalf. Meanwhile, the third sector is growing in importance, both socially and economically, as the relationships between the state, the private sector and citizens develop in advanced economies. Organisations such as social enterprises and charities are active in the events industry, producing events and providing services for them. Other forms of not-for-profit event have their own specific characteristics and do not fit into the neat categories of private, public and third sectors. In this chapter, we have looked briefly at political, state and faith events as examples of these.

Future event managers will need to develop relationships not just with other private sector organisations but with public bodies and those in the third sector. Increasing numbers of events management students will work in these sectors after graduation. In this area, both nationally and internationally, there are complex relationships of regulation, partnership and funding that impact on successful events management. Keeping abreast of local developments and national trends will therefore be a key skill for future event managers in all kinds of organisation.

Further reading

Foster, G., Doherty, B., Mason, C., Meehan, J. and Meehan, K. (2010) *Management for Social Enterprise*, London: Sage. A very useful practical text on creating and managing social enterprises.

Raj, R. and Morpeth, D. (2007) *Religous Tourism and Pilgrimage Management*, Oxford: CABI. Covers an important area for events management in terms of visitor numbers and global reach that is currently under-researched in the events management literature.

Shone, A. and Parry, B. (2010) The Events Business: Supply and Suppliers, in *Sucessful Event Management: A Practical Handbook* (3rd edn), Hampshire: Cengage Learning. Provides a useful analysis of the different sectors involved in delivering events and the relationships between them.

Chapter 12

Corporate events

Contents

12.1 Aims

By the end of this chapter, students will be able:

- To evaluate the role of events in a corporate context.
- To recognise the importance of corporate events for brand awareness, image enhancement, staff development, motivation and profile-raising.
- To analyse a range of corporate events and their respective target markets.
- To consider the strategic business objectives and motivations of corporate events management.
- To examine the key contemporary issues faced in corporate events management.

12.2 Introduction

Corporate events are produced by or for businesses, with a primary purpose of supporting business growth. This distinguishes them from other forms of events, whose aims may be more cultural, political or sporting. Corporate events are broad, however, and can encompass many other kinds of events. Getz (2007) goes as far as to say that some events have become 'corporatised': some events are distinguished as significant corporate events by the significance and size of the corporate sponsorship, branding and hospitality on offer, such as the international circuit of Formula One motor-racing. Masterman (2004) notes that corporate hospitality, advertising and branding are prevalent at many events and, although this chapter focuses on the more orthodox business-to-business (B2B) and business-to-customer (B2C) events of the corporate events industry, it is important to recognise the corporatisation of many events as a consequence and cause of the professionalisation of the events industry and of its economic significance.

As mentioned in previous chapters, a recent business trend has been a new emphasis on experiential marketing and the 'experience economy' (Pine and Gilmore 1999), with companies seeking to influence their potential consumers though the provision of memorable and enjoyable experiences, leading to a growth in a newer form of corporate event that can often appear to be cultural or spontaneous in nature, but which actually promotes specific products and services. When, in 2009, the global advertising agency Saatchi and Saatchi recruited the singer Pink to lead a karaoke session for 13,000 people in Trafalgar Square, London, for the mobile phone network T-Mobile, the event provided material for a major advertising campaign and a viral marketing push that helped the company to promote itself as innovative, exciting and enabling (Whitehead 2009). Corporate venues such as shopping centres and megastores are also now animated through the staging of events in order to enhance the retail experience (Getz 2007). At the extreme end is the Dubai Shopping Festival, launched in 1996 to promote the economic development of the Gulf state. The six-week-long festival is focused in the second-largest shopping mall in the world, the 6.5-million-square-foot 'Mall of the Emirates', and it has become a major feature of the global corporate events calendar, attracting more than 5 million visitors in 2008 (MyDSF 2010).

The B2B sector of the corporate events industry has seen the most significant growth over the last two decades. Originating in North America's political and religious congresses in the nineteenth century, and in conventions of professional associations (Bowdin *et al.* 2011), Europe and North America witnessed the rise of planned business events, such as conferences and networking events, in the early twentieth century, but their growth has been most dramatic

Table 12.1 Factors influencing the growth of corporate events

Internal	External
Increasing corporate visibility	Globalisation of markets
Driving sales	Municipal promotional strategies
Improving staff morale	Technological advances
Broker relationships between firms	Developments in travel

since the late 1980s in the Asia–Pacific region (Weber and Ladkin 2003). This growth in the corporate events sector has been influenced by a combination of internal and external factors, as set out in Table 12.1.

Internally, large companies are increasingly placing events within the mainstream of their activities, with some employing in-house event managers and the majority outsourcing event design and production to contractors (O'Toole and Mikolaitis 2002). This mainstreaming has come about as contemporary business models have begun to emphasise the importance of relationship-building between staff and with external partners and customers as a key mechanism for improving profitability.

Externally, socio-economic pressures have also contributed to the growth of corporate events. Cities looking to maximise their income from visitors have invested heavily in conference centres and travel hubs to attract high-spending business tourists, enabling the staging of high-profile, global corporate events on a dramatic scale and introducing new competitive pressures into the market as corporations compete to produce the most high-impact events. Globalisation has also opened up new markets for companies, with those looking to achieve global competitiveness now obliged to achieve visibility on new scales. Finally, the rapid pace of growth and technological development in the travel industry has meant that it has become both more practical and increasingly cost-effective for companies to support their staff to travel and network at greater distances.

Although corporate events have been the fastest-growing sector of the events industry (O'Toole and Mikolaitis 2002), as well as the sector with the highest yields, the Exhibition for the Incentive Business Travel and Meetings' (EIBTM) *Trends and Market Report 2010* confirms that such events have been hardest hit by the economic crisis that began in 2008: 'As corporate profits have fallen in most countries over the past year, companies have reacted with an array of cost-cutting measures related to their employees' business travel and their participation in meetings and business events' (Davidson 2010). This reduced demand within the corporate events market is likely to have a number of effects, including an excess of event venues and event production resources, reducing the profitability of the corporate events sector in the short to medium term as the purchasers of these products and services benefit from oversupply. In this climate, it is vital that future event managers are able to identify and respond confidently and flexibly to changes within the corporate events sector.

Many authors use the MICE acronym (Meetings, Incentives, Conferences and Exhibitions) to describe the various aspects of the corporate events industry (e.g. Bowdin *et al.* 2011), or place corporate events within a broader framework of 'organisational events' or 'business and trade events' (e.g. Shone and Parry 2010; Getz 2005). However, the MICE categorisation, which was developed in the business tourism literature of the 1980s, needs revisiting and updating to reflect changes in the nature of the contemporary market place; and the overarching category of organisational events does not differentiate sufficiently between various organisational contexts, including party political conferences, charitable events, World Expos and business conferences. To address this issue, we have updated the MICE model below, and have provided a detailed description, with contemporary examples, for each category.

12.3 Categorisation

In order to gain a real insight into this key area of the events industry, it is necessary to analyse the specific events covered by the umbrella term 'corporate events' in more detail. These events are easily categorised as MINCE:

- Meetings and conferences
- Incentives
- Networking events
- Corporate hospitality
- Exhibitions and trade shows.

Study activity

Using the internet and trade publications, locate a recent event that relates to each of the five 'MINCE' corporate event categories. Identify the suppliers and the target market for each event. Complete Table 12.2.

Table 12.2 Categories of corporate events

Category	Event name	Suppliers/Audience
Meetings and conferences		
Incentives		
Networking events		
Corporate hospitality		
Exhibitions and trade shows		

12.3.1 Meetings and conferences

12.3.1.1 Definition

Conferences and meetings bring together groups of people with commonalities of interests in order to interchange ideas (Shone and Parry 2010). These events are characterised by their focus on business, trade or politics, so they are B2B rather than B2C.

Image 12.1 Attendees applauding at a conference
Source: Stockbyte / Getty Images

The conference and meeting market has traditionally been the most prolific sector of corporate events, with recent research by Eventia suggesting that each UK conference venue held, on average, 375 events between 2006 and 2008, generating an overall market value of £7.2 billion (Eventia 2009). This market therefore makes a significant contribution to the overall UK economy, and it is equally significant in many other countries throughout the world.

12.3.1.2 Characteristics

According to the ICCA (International Congress and Convention Association), a conference is 'a participatory meeting designed for discussion, fact-finding, problem solving and consultation, with a specific objective in mind' (ICCA 2010). Conferences vary in size, length and content, but they are typified by their focus on one particular topic, discussed during a plenary session of keynote presentations and panel discussions and often accompanied by breakout sessions and workshops. They are professionally organised and predominantly fee-charging, with a published programme of speakers and activities. Conferences are often supported by sponsors, and they can be either one-off events or held periodically.

There has been little research into what motivates audiences, or delegates, to attend conferences, because, as Getz (2007) suggests, it is widely assumed that people attend primarily to fulfil part of their business or job description. Whilst this assumption is partially correct, the major motivation for attending conferences could be divided into 'content' (the information attendees are given) and 'networking' (the information and people they meet).

Meetings are less formal gatherings but they are still an important component of the corporate events industry. They are usually held off-site, with a chairperson and a specific agenda, focused on a very specific issue. They involve attendees from various organisations, all of whom share similar business interests. Meetings tend to be smaller in scale than conferences, which gives each attendee a greater opportunity to contribute to the agenda, debate or discussion.

Study activity

For the past thirty years, the Confederation of British Industry (CBI) has hosted an annual conference that attracts hundreds of attendees, including senior government ministers, shadow ministers, global and UK business leaders and key principals from public bodies. In 2009, a particularly impressive programme included the British Prime Minister and both main opposition party leaders.

The Power-Gen Asia Annual Conference is an example of what Bauer *et al.* (2008) call a 'mega-business event'. It is run by the Penwell Corporation, a B2B media company, over three days and features twenty-five conference sessions, one hundred and twenty specialist speakers and over seven thousand delegates.

Look at the websites of both of these conferences – http://www. cbi2009conference.org.uk and http://www.powergenasia.com – and identify the reasons why delegates attend them. Write down five of the most important reasons for each conference. What lessons can you, as future event managers, learn from these successful events?

12.3.1.3 Key issues

There are four key components in the organisation of successful conferences and meetings, as outlined in Figure 12.1.

In order to deliver a successful meeting or conference, the organiser must first have a clearly defined concept and a robust programme. A conference programme includes details of the keynote speaker(s), a list of contributors with brief annotations of their subject areas, information on breakout sessions and workshops, plans for networking opportunities and full conference timings, including food and beverage breaks. The importance of getting the content of the programme right cannot be overstated – it is this content that provides one of the two key motivations for the target market to attend.

Once the programme has been established, finding a venue that suits the event becomes a priority. The importance of this aspect of corporate event planning is explored in more detail later in this chapter.

Another consideration is the target market – clearly identifying who will attend and why they should want to is pivotal to the success of any conference or meeting. As conferences are fee-generating, they are often deemed successful only in terms of their return on investment (ROI) and the income that they generate from delegate fees.

Creating and implementing an effective marketing plan is crucial to any event's success (see Chapter 7 for more information). Securing sponsorship is another vital component of conference delivery, as revenue from sponsorship often funds the event and drives budgeting (see Chapters 6 and 7).

Figure 12.1 Key components for conference and meeting events management

12.3.1.4 Trends

As Bowdin *et al.* (2011) note, technological innovation impacts on many aspects of event management. However, some recent technological developments, especially in the fields of emerging technologies, such as video presence and high-speed data networking, have had a particularly significant impact on the design, marketing and delivery of corporate events. As the use of personal technology increases, conference and meeting organisers have had to think creatively and offer something more than the traditional conference formula. The industry has therefore seen a growth in webinars, teleconferencing and videoconferencing (Davidson 2010).

In addition to the increased opportunities offered by technology, external factors, such as environmental concerns (Getz 2005), and major international incidents, such as 9/11, the SARS outbreak and various conflicts and wars, have changed how, why and under what circumstances people are prepared to travel (Allen 2008). However, ultimately the conferences and meetings industry is centred on face-to-face interaction, the sharing of ideas, and networking with like-minded individuals. Organisers therefore have to work hard to ensure that the programming of their conference or meeting offers something that cannot be captured through technology alone. The programme has to convince the target market that they have to *be* there, or else they will miss out (Haug 2010).

Another innovation which is steadily growing in popularity is 'unconferencing'. This typically still involves face-to-face meetings and dialogue between attendees. However, it differs from a traditional conference in terms of design. Wolf *et al.* (2011) have published a case study of an unconference held by a Swiss technical university – ETH Zurich. The event design included a general introduction from the university's vice-president; a structured process to ensure that each participant met at least five other participants; an 'ideas market', during which fifty ideas were proposed, examined and selected or abandoned by the entire audience; a reception and dinner that included external experts who helped to continue to shape these ideas; a panel of judges who watched the ideas being pitched; and a people's jury in which participants pitched ideas to each other.

CASE STUDY 12.1

Lift10 explores the concept of technology and connects people

Event name: Lift10
Event type: conference
Venue: Geneva International Conference Centre, Geneva, Switzerland
Date: 4–7 May 2010
Attendance: 1000 delegates
Sponsors: one global partner, ten main partners and dozens of event partners and supporters
Website: http://liftconference.com/lift10

The event started on Tuesday evening with a meeting at the organiser's offices followed by pre-conference drinks. The conference started fully the following morning, with a briefing from the founders of Lift followed by nine workshops. In the afternoon, the plenary session began with a welcome speech, followed by two plenary sessions on various topics, featuring ten speakers. These sessions comprised demos, speeches and open stages. In the evening, a partner event featured eight start-up companies presenting their new products, followed by cocktails and fondue.

A similar pattern was followed on Thursday, with the addition of prize-giving, Lift experience exposition and an invitation to a local festival during the evening.

On Friday, there were specialist workshops before a plenary session brought all the delegates back together to share their inspirational stories and wrap-up the conference. In the evening, there was a networking event at La Sip, which included complimentary drinks and DJ sets.

The principal innovation at this event was the 'Lift Experience', described by the organisers as follows:

> Think of a huge space where new media artists and interaction designers are invited to display pieces that address the conference topics in a different way. Meet other attendees and get inspired by a series of projects aiming to provoke a dialogue between people with different backgrounds and cultures from all over the world.
>
> (Lift 2011)

12.3.2 Incentives

12.3.2.1 Definition
The term 'incentives' covers a wide range of events, including trips and travel, training, away-days and team-building. The incentives branch of the events industry has long been seen as a particularly lucrative one (Bowdin *et al.* 2011), and it continues to survive despite the global economic crisis that began in 2008, reflecting the key role that events of all kinds now play in corporate activities.

12.3.2.2 Characteristics
Incentive trips are defined by Davidson (2003) as exceptional travel trips that employees receive from their employer as prizes for winning a competition related to their jobs. The purpose of such trips is to encourage staff to meet certain business objectives. However, a more comprehensive view of the sector shows that, whilst incentive trips are still the largest component of incentive travel, the sector has grown to include a wider range of activities. A more relevant term, 'incentive travel', is becoming prevalent, as it relates to incentive trips *and* to destination management and exploration and familiarisation trips – journeys arranged by external agencies in order to allow stakeholders to experience specific destinations, activities or venues.

Other incentive events are event-based activities that focus on staff development. Training events, away-days and team-building activities all have as their primary focus motivational experiences for participants in order to achieve specific organisational goals or to increase performance levels (SITE 2010). This side of the industry is growing steadily, with a proliferation of such incentives as 'It's a Knockout' days – in which co-workers form teams and complete huge inflatable obstacle courses, often in fancy dress – or 'Olympiad' days – where colleagues compete in their own mini-Olympics. More often, incentive trips that work towards building the motivation of attendees take the form of cooking days, treasure hunts and quizzes.

As the economy grows and contracts, the incentives market usually follows suit. In boom times, spending tends to increase, with trips organised to more distant and exotic locations; during recessions, cost-cutting often leads to shorter trips to cheaper destinations (Davidson 2010).

12.3.2.3 Key issues
Incentive events are widely recognised as useful management tools, as they are effective means of recognising and rewarding employees (Davidson 2003). However, offering incentive events is not the only way to reward employees: cash bonuses, promotions, gifts and profit-related pay are all frequently used by the corporate sector. Given the number of alternatives, and the high cost in financial and human resource terms that incentive events represent for organisations, the question is: why do companies continue to rely on such events? The answer lies in the reward economy and the motivational needs of potential attendees. In order for an incentive event to succeed, the venue, location and event programme must all be attractive to the potential attendees; organisers must also strive to communicate the offering effectively – building up awareness and anticipation is key (Severt and Breiter 2010).

An important consideration for organisers of incentive events is the demographic make-up of attendees. Whilst there may be some commonalities, these are not necessarily related to age, sex, education or cultural background – the only real commonality is the sharing of a job or working for the same organisation. This makes planning for an incentive event that will appeal to a target market of various demographics both complicated and delicate.

In 2010, CMM Incentives organised Vie at Home's annual incentive trip to reward the cosmetic company's top performers. Seventy consultants and managers were taken on a four-day trip to Cape Town, where they stayed in the Table Bay Hotel. Activities included: a trip in a cable-car up Table Mountain, with drinks and canapés served at the top; a Winelands Discovery Adventure; whale-watching on a sunset cocktail cruise; a gala dinner at the Cape of Good Hope Castle; and a farewell picnic at the Kirstenbosch Gardens. The event manager had three key criteria for selection of the destination: flight time, time difference and weather. But they also took into consideration the profile of the group – which was likely to be all-female and aged between twenty and sixty (Harwood 2010).

12.3.2.4 Trends
The EIBTM's *Trends and Market Report* (Davidson 2010) indicates that the economic downturn of 2009 affected incentive travel more than any other sector of the corporate events industry. It predicts that, during future periods of economic crisis, incentive groups will be smaller and incentive trips will visit less ostentatious destinations in order to reduce accusations of extravagance. Supporting this theory, *Conference and Incentive Travel* magazine reported that 'Axa Life has scaled down its incentive travel programme for the next two years in response to the fallout from the financial crisis. The insurance giant's UK division is cutting back on overseas trips, but will continue to run prize programmes and small rewards' (Henderson 2010).

12.3.3 Networking events

12.3.3.1 Description
In the past ten years, the focus of corporate events has shifted to a concentration of outcomes. Businesspeople have become more selective in the events they attend, and the motivation for attendance is no longer solely focused on the content of the event but also, and importantly, on the quality and relevance of the other attendees to the guests' corporate objectives. The importance of face-to-face meetings with colleagues, associates, consumers and/or potential clients has never been more strongly emphasised by event participants.

Many organisations see business networking as a low-cost marketing method to develop sales opportunities and contacts (Business Balls 2010). Others see it as an environment in which they can share ideas and keep abreast of industry developments, or as an essential tool in career development that provides an opportunity to forge key business relationships through personal interaction. The events industry has responded to these developments by providing event spaces that facilitate opportunities to meet and greet interested and interesting parties in a networking-enabled environment.

These networking events include small-scale lunches and dinners, drinks receptions, product launches, conventions, congresses, awards ceremonies and symposia. The main focus is on providing networking opportunities – for sponsors to meet potential new clients; for large brands to raise awareness among a particular audience; for companies to demonstrate their new products to potential purchasers; and for association members to share ideas and innovations as well as to keep abreast of industry developments.

12.3.3.2 Characteristics
Association networking events are organised by trade bodies and professional/industry associations to communicate with their members. They provide opportunities for associations to discuss key issues and to share relevant information with their respective audiences (Allen

et al. 2011). Since the late 1990s, these events have become central to the events industry, forming a key revenue stream for event professionals. They have continued to deliver throughout the financial crisis, with the EIBTM's 2010 report indicating that the association sector has been less affected by the economic climate than the rest of the corporate sector (Davidson 2010).

Association networking events include conventions, congresses, symposia, summits and awards ceremonies. The first four of these are similar in form to conferences, but are usually larger in size and are often repeated annually. They can be held on a regional scale, such as the Regional Asthma Summit, held annually in Yorkshire and Humberside, UK; a national scale, such as the French Teachers Association Congress, held in the Gambia for the first time in January 2010; or an international scale, such as the G8 and G20 summits, held in Canada in 2010, which attracted 700 official delegates as well as a large number of accompanying guests. Many people will be familiar with the format of awards ceremonies, such as the internationally renowned Oscars. A large and robust industry specialises in corporate award ceremonies; usually (though not always), these are run by or for professional and industry associations. Examples include the Professional Beauty Awards, the Chemical Industry Association Awards and the Music Industry Association Awards.

Uniquely, these association networking events often have the same audience at each event. The priority is to ensure audiences are kept abreast of developments in their professional fields and given ample time to network with colleagues and associates (Allen *et al.* 2011).

The other side of the networking events industry is typified by events run *by business for business (B2B)*. The primary goal of these events is to encourage business networking or the promotion and marketing of a specific product or brand. They tend to be less formal than other corporate events, and often concentrate on the social side of networking. Examples include intimate lunches, dinners, drinks receptions, private members' clubs events and product launches. The Supper Club, founded in 2003 by the entrepreneur Duncan Cheatle, is attended by a group of UK entrepreneurs who share knowledge, contacts, best practice and experiences. Its primary function is to encourage peer-to-peer learning, and it actively excludes any organisation that may try to use the network for self-promotion. The Supper Club offers its members structured forums, social events and subject-specific dinners. By 2010, it had already hosted 560 events and its membership had increased significantly – unsurprisingly, as its members reported an average growth in sales of 26 per cent in 2009 (Supper Club 2010).

12.3.3.3 Key issues and trends

Networking event managers have to be forward thinking, giving their participants new experiences and unique opportunities to meet colleagues and associates. The industry has recognised the need to drive networking forward as well as the reluctance of some participants to participate in traditional networking, which is often seen as a contrived and jaded concept. Successful organisers continue to devise new ways to ensure that target markets will want to attend their events and that participants will interact when they attend them. There is often a multitude of interests in one room, with guests from a variety of demographic backgrounds, though participants will usually share a common focus. This, coupled with the negative connotations of the word 'networking', has resulted in a need to try innovative ideas. For instance, the London networking events organisation Business Junction joined forces with the Circus Space to create a unique networking event in which participants enjoyed a free forty-minute juggling session followed by a networking lunch (Business Junction 2010).

In recent years, numerous organisations have emerged that utilise new technology at their networking events. One particularly popular tool is 5 Minute Networking software – an event facilitation system that fuses the concept of speed dating with the principles of business

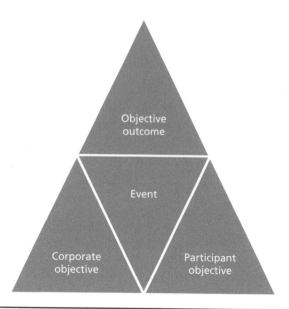

Figure 12.2 Achieving outcomes at networking events

networking. The software seating programme initiates introductions while the database keeps track of who has met whom at previous events. The process continues after the event via the software company's website (5 Minute Networking 2010).

Whilst there has been a move towards incorporating some innovation into networking events, the industry generally remains convinced that interpersonal relationships and face-to-face opportunities are still the best networking tools. This was confirmed by a survey of 600 executives conducted by Hilton Hotels, which found that face-to-face meetings are still considered more effective and productive than those utilising recent innovations in communications technology (Arvey 2009). Networking events therefore still tend to follow the formula of: a corporate objective (usually a brand, product or key issue that needs promoting or discussing); the participant's objective (to meet colleagues or associates, increase business interaction or gain awareness of new developments in their field of interest); and a networking opportunity (an event that allows all parties to interact face-to-face). These three segments can be viewed (as in Figure 12.2) as the base and centre of a pyramid, building towards the key motivation behind the event (the outcome).

Study activity

Networking events are at their most successful when people with shared interests interact with each other face-to-face. With the continued advances in technology and the internet, will this situation change? Using the internet, find one example of a networking event that does not rely on interpersonal exchanges and occurs with guests in different times/places.

12.3.4 Corporate hospitality

12.3.4.1 Definition

Corporate hospitality events have as their focus the entertainment of key clients in order to improve or cement business relationships. These events therefore involve an element of networking. However, they should not be confused with networking events – there is a clear difference between the two. A corporate hospitality event is a hosted event that forms part of another public live event; in essence, it is an event within an event. Key clients are invited, at no charge, to one event by a particular 'host' organisation. When they arrive at that event, the host organisation will have a hospitality suite for the private use of these invited guests. This suite will offer a premium view of the event itself, plus complimentary food and drinks.

12.3.4.2 Characteristics

In the past, corporate hospitality events happened mostly at sporting events, such as the Olympics, the French Open Tennis Championships and the Super Bowl. However, in recent years, there has been a move towards alternative corporate hospitality events, with an increasing number of cultural events providing opportunities to host key clients. Examples of these are boxes at large arenas to watch music concerts, premium seats at the theatre and movie premieres, tickets for opening days of flower shows, and VIP areas at festivals. Corporate hospitality events are, by their very nature, one-offs, although corporate clients may well rent the same box at a sporting ground or return to the same festival with different clients every year. They usually last one day or less, and the hosting organisation covers all costs.

A typical corporate hospitality event involves a welcome drink, premium views of the event, usually from a box, complimentary drinks throughout the event and food – sometimes a seated meal, sometimes canapés. There is often a gift for guests to take away at the end of the event.

The corporate hospitality organiser Keith Prowse has various video clips of such events on its website, http://www.keithprowse.co.uk/KP/VirtualTours.aspx.

12.3.4.3 Key issues

The corporate hospitality events industry places great importance on the guest experience. The success of a corporate hospitality event is largely dependent on the success of the hosting at the event itself, aided by a smooth invitation and acceptance process. The hosting at the event therefore has to be carefully planned and managed, with all of the guests' needs catered for by the event organiser so that the host can concentrate on cementing business relationships and potentially creating new opportunities. As Davidson (2003: n.p.) states,

> 'Relationship management' is the phrase used to describe the technique of forming close bonds with those people who are important to the competitiveness and profitability of a company . . . [C]orporate hospitality can be a highly effective method of establishing and maintaining a positive image for the company that invests in it, and ultimately improving their business performance.

The role of brand association is also important: the choice of event is informed by the impression that it will make on the host organisation's key clients. A brand such as Cartier hosts its key clients at various international polo events because it wishes to be associated with high-end experiences. (The relationship between sponsorship of events, corporate hospitality hosting and brand association is discussed in detail in Chapter 7.)

The Bureau of Investigative Journalism conducted an investigation into the effectiveness of corporate hospitality in 2010. This revealed that the UK's most senior civil servants were wined and dined by major corporations and interest groups on more than 3100 occasions over a period of three years. The accountants PricewaterhouseCoopers and KPMG were the most active hospitality providers, although Fujitsu, BT, Deloitte and arms giant BAE were significant players, too. In an article about the investigation, Curtis and Evans (2010) noted that David Hartnett – the Permanent Secretary for Tax at HM Revenues and Customs – accepted invitations to eat and drink 107 times over the three-year period: 'Hartnett sat down with representatives of the "big four" accountancy firms 27 times . . . Corporate hospitality is part of Hartnett's approach to raising tax from big firms. Rather than confronting them, he has relied on persuading them to pay their share of tax.'

HM Revenues and Customs defended Hartnett's activities by saying that he engaged with

> people from all sectors of the economy in meetings which take place inside and outside office hours. The relationships that Dave has forged have enabled HMRC to transform its relationships with business and other taxpayers. This has made a significant contribution to the increased tax yield HMRC has achieved in the period.
>
> (Curtis and Evans 2010)

12.3.4.4 Trends

The global economic crisis that began in 2008 has resulted in a move away from traditional, lavish corporate hospitality events as organisations cut their spending. Some of these changes have been relatively low key – sparkling wine has replaced champagne, and canapés have replaced dinner. Others changes have been more dramatic. There has been an increase in daytime events, and educational elements have been added to some corporate hospitality events. Such events are still seen as valid and successful marketing tools (Bell 2009), but organisations have increasingly realised that they need to be more of a justifiable business proposition in order to remain a viable option for guests.

12.3.5 Exhibitions and trade shows

12.3.5.1 Description

At the most basic level, exhibitions and trade shows involve a large number of manufacturers and retailers displaying a selection of their products to potential buyers and/or the general public. Exhibitions can therefore be for a consumer target market or for business purposes (the latter events are also known as trade shows). They take place in large, purpose-built venues – such as the ExCel Centre in London, the Vietnamese National Convention Centre or the San Diego Convention Center – are usually held on an annual basis, and often attract an international audience.

It is important to note that the typologies 'fair', 'convention' and 'exposition' are sometimes used to describe exhibitions and trade shows (see, for example, Bowdin et al. 2011 and Allen et al. 2011). Conventions tend to be organised by associations or professional bodies for their members, and the term 'exposition' (expo) tends to be applied to larger-scale exhibitions. The primary difference between a fair and an exhibition is that fairs place more emphasis on entertainment by including live demonstrations related to the industry as well as live music, celebrity guest appearances, and so on. Exhibitions, on the other hand, are likely to host accompanying conferences or seminars, which enable visitors to meet and speak to individual companies and organisations from the industry in question. This obviously increases opportunities for networking and also allows influential figures from the industry to present their latest innovations and policies on a more intimate scale than at the exhibition itself.

In recent years, there has been increasing use of the term 'confex' to describe a conference and an exhibition taking place simultaneously at the same venue, with the same overall purpose and content. These events might prioritise the conference, with a small accompanying exhibition; or they might lead with the exhibition and run a small-scale conference alongside. International Confex is a leading UK event that delivers a comprehensive showcase of UK venues and event services and promotes the best of the international events industry during an exhibition that is attended by over 1000 exhibitors. The 10,000 visitors to the exhibition are also invited to attend the accompanying conference – Confex Knowledge. This features keynote addresses from industry specialists and seminar sessions that explore key areas of industry debate, marketing and business skills (International Confex 2010).

12.3.5.2 Characteristics

The key characteristic of any exhibition or trade show is that it is a marketing or communication tool. The benefits of these events are that they allow direct customer contact, provide a platform for products and services, and create marketing opportunities by allowing the media to focus on companies or products (UFI 2011).

Exhibitions and trade shows can be divided into two categories: those that communicate primarily with a consumer target market (the general public); and those that focus on a specific business or trade. It is useful to explore these two areas separately, as the management of each kind of event requires significantly different approaches.

Consumer exhibitions and shows are open to the general public. They charge an entrance fee and are centred on such themes as cars, fashion and travel (Getz 2007). They sometimes move around the country, but, more often than not, they return to the same venue each year. Competition in this sector is fierce, and there are usually a number of exhibitions vying for the same target market.

Consumer-led exhibitions are seen as beneficial for all stakeholders as 'manufacturers test new products at shows, retailers try to sell and the consumer is searching for both ideas and entertainment' (Getz 2007: 40). An example of a large consumer exhibition is the Clothes Show Live, which takes place annually in Birmingham, UK, and regularly attracts 170,000 visitors and hundreds of exhibitors (Clothes Show Live 2010).

As Getz (2007) suggests, trade exhibitions and shows are invitation based, and are usually staged for a specific business purpose or related to an association membership. Their primary function is therefore to promote or sell a product from a particular area of business. They allow visitors to evaluate products side-by-side, keep abreast of industry developments and meet suppliers directly.

The International Consumer Electronics Show is the largest trade show in America, hosting 2500 exhibitors every year. It is not open to the general public, and visitors must work in the consumer electronics industry to attend. The event attracts 126,000 of these industry professionals annually. In addition to being invited to the exhibition, they can attend a conference that runs alongside it and enjoy numerous entertainment options, such as competitions, concerts and celebrity guests (International Consumer Electronics 2010).

A growing number of exhibitions and trade shows are now targeting a cross-sector market: these are known as hybrid shows. Their main target market may be the professionals from a specific industry, but they realise that their content will be of interest to the general public as well. In order to maximise their potential audience (and therefore their profit), they stage events that will appeal to both.

An example of a hybrid exhibition is Tattoo Jam, a three-day tattoo convention, which takes place annually at Doncaster Racecourse, UK. It features 300 working artists and traders in the Lazarus Exhibition Hall and has separate function rooms for workshops, seminars and live entertainment. Two days of the exhibition are open to the general public, while the third is reserved for registered tattooists, piercers, guests and associated traders. Tattoo Jam is run by the publishers of *Skin Deep*, *Skin Shots International* and *Tattoo Master* magazines and the organisers of another tattooing event, Tattoo Freeze. (For the organiser's perspective, see Big Tattoo Planet 2009.)

12.3.5.3 Key issues

Staging an exhibition is a very complex events management skill. A daunting array of operational planning is required when dealing with such a large-scale event. In fact, lead times, from the original concept development through to delivery of the event, can be as long as two years. The exhibition event manager can be dealing with anything from 100 to 3000 separate exhibitors as well as sponsors, caterers, venue, client, audio-visual providers and so on. The build-up and breakdown of an exhibition are particularly complex and need to be managed with tight control. At the same time, exhibition event managers need to comply with a number of regulations, laws, permits and licences, including various Health and Safety Acts (1974, 1981, 1999), Electricity at Work Act 1998, Building Standards and Regulations, Lifting Operations and Lifting Regulations and so on (see AEO, BECA and EVA 2002 for a comprehensive list).

12.3.5.4 Trends

UFI, the Global Association of the Exhibition Industry, published its fifth Barometer Survey in July 2010 (UFI 2010). This report suggested that there would be an increase in turnover during 2010, although Europe faced a longer recovery delay than the Asia–Pacific region and the Americas. The Middle East–Africa region appears to have been less severely affected by the economic downturn than the other regions, with most companies declaring a stable profit in 2010. Surveyed organisations identified the state of the national/regional economy as the most important issue facing their business in 2011.

The Asian trade fair market is experiencing significant expansion, and Vincent Gérard, UFI's managing director, commented,

> While the exhibition industry in the US and Europe struggled to find their feet in 2009, Asia posted another year of substantial growth. As China, Asia's largest trade fair market, grew by nearly 7% and the region as a whole grew by 3.8%, it is clear that in 2010 and beyond the global exhibition industry will be looking to Asia for opportunities to grow existing events as well as launch new ones.
>
> (UFI 2010)

CASE STUDY 12.2

IMEX

Event name: IMEX
Event type: exhibition
Venue: Messe Frankfurt, Germany
Date: 25–27 May 2010
Attendees: 9000 visitors, including 3800 hosted buyers and 5000 trade visitors
Sponsors: approximately one dozen partners
Website: http://www.imex-frankfurt.com

IMEX, in Frankfurt, is the essential worldwide exhibition for meetings and incentive travel. In 2010, it hosted 3500 exhibitors from 157 countries representing national and regional tourist offices, major hotel groups, airlines, destination management companies, service providers, trade associations and more. There was also a politicians' forum for twenty-eight international politicians, fourteen other forums, an education programme featuring over eighty sessions, CSR drop-in power sessions, a gala dinner and an awards ceremony.

A record number of over 3800 hosted buyers from more than sixty markets attended 2010's show, out of a visitor total of nearly 9000. Long-haul buyers made up nearly 25 per cent of the total buyers, a rise of 10 per cent compared to 2009. Eastern European buyers also rose – from 11.5 per cent to 14 per cent of the total. Just over 60 per cent of the buyers were from the traditional and established European markets.

In 2010, online individual and group appointments rose to an unprecedented 57,000 – a rise of 14 per cent on the previous year – with diary messages exchanged between buyers and exhibitors rising by 9 per cent, to just over 12,000. The mood amongst buyers and exhibitors was positive and optimistic, with many reporting increases in levels of business and appointment numbers.

Source: IMEX 2010

12.4 Key logistical issues for corporate events

12.4.1 When do corporate events take place?

Corporate events have peak and off-peak seasons. Traditionally, few corporate events took place in December, July or August, as organisations' employees were often on long Christmas or summer holidays. However, as consumption and demand have grown over the past five years, and as the recession has resulted in a drive towards businesses working harder to attract and retain clients, the peaks and troughs have flattened out, with the peak season now stretching from the very start of February right into July and commencing again in the first week of September. Figure 12.3 illustrates the changes that have occurred in the peaks and troughs of a typical event season.

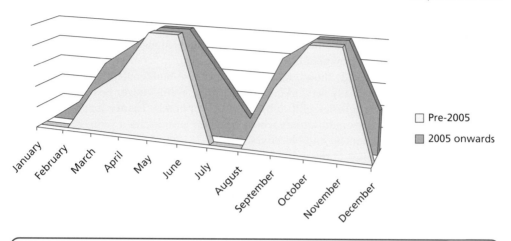

Pre-2005

2005 onwards

Figure 12.3 Peaks and troughs of an event season

The day of the week on which a corporate event takes place is a key decision for the event manager. Choosing the wrong day impacts on the number of attendees registering and severely jeopardises the success of the event. With the notable exception of corporate hospitality, corporate events with businesses as their target market (B2B) tend to take place during the working week. Mondays and Fridays are less popular, as business guests are often away from the office (on long weekends) or are unwilling to attend an event that has elements of socialising at the start and end of the week. The majority of B2B corporate events therefore take place on Tuesday, Wednesday or Thursday. These events are often run during business hours: attendees tend to view them as work, so they are usually unwilling to give up their free time to attend.

The notable exception to these unwritten rules of timings are corporate hospitality events, which take place throughout the year, on any day of the week, including weekends, and usually outside of office hours. Attendees tend to view these events as entertainment and enjoyable, so they are willing to give up their free time to attend. Events run for members of associations or for consumers are also less stringent about avoiding Mondays and Fridays and often take place over weekends – the perception being that guests are interested enough in the product or in the activities of their association that they will happily invest their spare time in attending an event.

It is essential that corporate hospitality event managers check calendars for the relevant industry. For instance, there would be little point running an event aimed at university academics in August, when they take time away from the office to write and prepare for the following year. Similarly, if possible, corporate events should not be scheduled to clash with major sporting events. Sometimes, however, this is unavoidable. One of the authors once held an event on FA Cup Final day. Three-quarters of the invited audience stated they would not attend if they could not watch the match, so screens were erected around the venue, and the entire programme was rearranged to ensure that guests could see the whole game, if they so desired.

Event managers should also keep track of national holidays. Bank holidays, school holidays, religious festivals and related holidays should all be avoided, unless the event has a specific and related theme.

The key is to choose a date that maximises the potential target market – event managers should identify the best date with the least number of obstacles for their invited guests.

12.4.2 Where do corporate events take place?

As we have seen earlier in this chapter, corporate events come in many shapes and sizes. They can be local, national or international, and whilst some of them (conferences, meetings, conventions, exhibitions and trade shows) take place in purpose-built conference and exhibition centres, many others (especially networking and incentive events) might be held in high-end restaurants, museums, art galleries, golf clubs, vineyards or hotels. There is an ever-increasing number of venue finders – organisations whose sole aim is to locate a venue that perfectly complements the event's content and objectives.

Of course, the venue must fit the general event requirements of size, capacity, location and so on (all of which are explored in detail in Chapter 4). However, beyond these logistical requirements, the corporate event manager will choose the venue on the basis of their perception of stakeholders and target market. The image that the venue projects and the message that it sends to the target market are key considerations in corporate events, where image is a large part of the whole event concept. A venue such as the Ritz Hotel in London gives an event an air of formality, wealth and top-class service with first-class food, whereas the Moulin Rouge in Paris is more risqué, with an image of informality, entertainment and fun. These images do not just reflect on the event itself, but send deeper messages about the organisers, their products and their work philosophies.

Moreover, the choice of venue often relates to the type of event that is being staged. Corporate events sometimes rotate around regions (or even countries), so the choice may be limited to a certain location. Similarly, they are often staged alongside other, more established events. For example, the number of corporate events will mushroom whenever a mega-event is in town, as skilful event managers attempt to exploit the sudden proximity of their target markets by inviting them to smaller-scale events. For instance, there is always a city- or nation-wide peak in corporate events just before, during and immediately after the FIFA World Cup or the Olympics.

For these reasons, it is unwise to stick to a standardised, inflexible checklist of venue criteria. Each venue choice is so specific to the event that a new checklist should be devised every time a venue search is launched. Choosing the correct venue is the most important decision a corporate event manager can make.

Study activity

A key client has commissioned you to produce a corporate event. The client runs a high-level accountancy firm specifically for entrepreneurs turning over at least £1 million a year. The entrepreneurs all currently run their own businesses in a diverse range of industries. The brief is given below:

- Event: evening networking drinks reception.
- Attendees: fifty of our most important customers. They are all entrepreneurs and each of their companies generates over £1 million a year. They are mostly men in their forties and fifties.
- Location: Central London.
- Date: a Tuesday, Wednesday or Thursday in May.

- Budget: £100 per head.
- Additional notes:

  ○ We would like a unique venue, preferably one that our customers will not have visited before.
  ○ As our customers are high earners, the venue should be high end and glamorous.
  ○ We will require canapés and cocktails on arrival, plus drinks throughout the evening.
  ○ There should be room for twenty-five staff members, in addition to the invited guests.
  ○ We will need to be able to make speeches.

Visit http://www.uniquevenuesoflondon.co.uk or http://www.venuefinder. com and identify the best venue for the event. In a small group, prepare a five-minute pitch for your venue proposal, clearly showing how your choice will add value to the event.

12.5 The corporate event customer

The term 'customer' can be confusing when applied to events. For corporate events, the customer can be either internal or external. Internal customers are people who work for the organisation arranging the event: for example, a meeting for a board of directors or a training day for a team from the shop floor. External customers come from outside the organisation. They are people with whom the organisation already does business, or with whom it would like to do business, or with whom it wishes to communicate in order to satisfy corporate objectives. This distinction between internal and external customers is important for the event manager, as they must identify the target market clearly in order to deliver an event successfully.

Uniquely in corporate events, the customer is not only the customer of the event (the delegate in a conference or the visitor to the trade show) but the customer of the corporation organising or hosting the event. In this sense, corporate events have a dual purpose: they must satisfy the wants, needs and demands of the *event* customer, but their primary purpose is to satisfy the wants, needs and demands of the *corporate* customer.

Corporate events allow organisations to maintain and develop business relationships, close deals and make sales, meet with competitors' clients, and work towards the overall corporate objective. Corporate event managers therefore need to develop an understanding of the customer's desires in order to ensure that the event meets their expectations and perceptions from both event *and* coroprate perspectives (see Figure 12.4).

These events therefore focus on the recruitment and retention of corporate customers. Corporate events are designed to build, increase and protect corporate loyalty. This is a driving force in corporate events, which in turn form part of a wider continuum of business communication and marketing. The need to impress, entertain and get to know customers in order to build loyalty explains why corporate events place considerable emphasis on providing networking opportunities.

Figure 12.4 Corporate event customer satisfaction model

The hosts of corporate events are responsible for ensuring that the networking is effective, but it is the event manager's responsibility to ensure that the logistical and operational aspects are right. Everything that happens at these events is a direct reflection on the host organisation. Any impressions that are made will ultimately inform the customer's business decision. Will they want to do business with an organisation that serves bad food or allows an event to run over the advertised finish time?

These impressions also relate to the corporation's brand, product or message. As Allen *et al.* (2011) suggest, events aimed at external customers measure their success through, among other things, a change in attitude or perception. This is echoed by a study conducted by Nguyen and Leblanc (2001: 227), in which the authors discovered that 'the degree of customer loyalty has a tendency to be higher when perceptions of both corporate reputation and corporate image are strongly favourable'.

Consideration should also be given to another form of corporate event customer – the sponsors who are often involved in such events. Satisfying these people, along with other external stakeholders, such as associations and media partners, can be as important as pleasing the event customers, as they often provide the revenue and/or the promotion for the event. (Sponsorship is considered in more detail in Chapter 7.)

Whilst the global economic downturn has resulted in a change in the corporate events sector – with lower budgets and less extravagance in evidence – the building of corporate loyalty through the perceptions that are created at events continues. As Kastelein (2010) reports, 'organisations continue to spend on such events to maintain healthy client/customer relationship. The desire for maintaining and strengthening customer or employee relationship is expected to drive companies to seek corporate hospitality services.' In fact, the UK corporate hospitality market is predicted to explode to £1.5 billion by 2015, partly fuelled by opportunities created by large-scale sporting events, such as the 2012 London Olympics (Kastelein 2010).

Comic-Con

Event name: Comic-Con
Event category: see Study Activity, below
Venue: San Diego Convention Centre, California, USA
Date: 22–25 July 2010
Attendees: 125,000 visitors
Sponsors: nine main sponsors, including Sony, Warner Brothers, Walt Disney, Universal Pictures and Penguin Books
Website: http://www.comic-con.org

Comic-Con takes place in a large (460,000-square-foot) exhibition hall and features 5445 exhibitors from comic-book and mainstream publishing, film studios, computer game companies and music companies. The first Comic-Con, in 1970, focused on comics and science-fiction novels and had a small, specialist audience. It is now the most visited exhibition-style event in the United States, reflecting the fact that comic-book characters have moved into the mainstream with such

Image 12.2 Comic-Con International, San Diego
Source: Sandy Huffaker / Getty Images

films as the *Batman* and *Superman* franchises and the recent *X-Men* trilogy. The event combines a major exhibition with a range of conference sessions attended by movie stars, writers, film producers and artists. In addition, there are a number of interactive sessions where attendees can collect autographs, play games involving their favourite characters, attend workshops and buy products – 1500 of which were exclusively released at Comic-Con in 2010.

The way in which Comic-Con has developed over the past forty years exemplifies two key trends that have been discussed in this chapter. First, its growth illustrates how important events have become in the corporate landscape. In marketing terms, the participation of large numbers of blue-chip media companies in what was previously a niche event demonstrates the value that they place on the event as a pipeline to new customers – for promoting their new products and increasing sales of their existing lines. There is a B2B aspect to this, too, as toy manufacturers, such as Mattel and Hasbro, increasingly exhibit at Comic-Con in a bid to persuade the media companies who are in attendance to develop films based on their toys (White 2010).

Second, the conference has developed as an experiential marketing event on a huge scale. Alongside the exhibition, the programme of associated events delivers a range of experiences for dedicated fans and a general leisure audience. Over the past few years, the fastest-growing events have been those targeted specifically at families and female attendees as the industries involved in Comic-Con have targeted new markets in what was previously a male-dominated sphere. One of the major selling-points for this event is the presence of celebrities who speak on panels, sign autographs and meet fans. In 2010, the roll-call included Scarlett Johansson, Robert Downey Jr., Daniel Craig and Angelina Jolie.

Study activity

Explore the Comic-Con 2010 website at: http://www.comic-con.org/cci/.

1 List the main features of the event. How would you categorise it: as a conference, an exhibition or a confex? Is it primarily B2C or B2B?
2 What features of the event make use of experiential marketing techniques? How important are these to the success of Comic-Con?
3 Is the Comic-Con model suitable for all corporate events? What can corporate event managers learn from the growth and success of Comic-Con?

12.6 Corporate event evaluation

As with all event typologies, evaluating the success of a corporate event is essential. Without measures in place that reveal the return on investment (ROI) and the satisfaction levels of internal and external stakeholders (often known as return on objectives (ROO)), the value of the event will remain undetermined and no lessons can be learned or advantages exploited.

Event evaluation for corporate events takes two forms. First, the 'hard' factors should be assessed. This mainly involves looking at the budget and final costings to decide if the event has been a financial success. However, the second form of evaluation is perhaps more important for a corporate event. This involves evaluating the 'soft' factors, such as enhancing loyalty among customers, aligning individual goals with corporate goals, and strengthening relationships (Hall 2009).

Corporate event evaluation typically begins with some form of financial modelling to ensure the 'hard' factors are assessed effectively, while a survey or questionnaire might be handed out for completion by delegates either at the event or immediately after it. Thereafter, focus groups might be held to evaluate success; reports might be carried out that can quantify increased business as a direct result of the event; 'wash-up' meetings with key stakeholders, such as sponsors, might be held; and in-depth monitoring of the level of PR or marketing for a set time after the event might be employed.

Some, or all, of these methods are used to create a final report that reflects the success (or failure) of the entire event in terms of how well it met the client's objectives and investment goals, and its legacy.

Industry voice

Donna Galbraith, head of events, Caspian Publishing

My role as head of a department specialising in corporate events offers a broad variety of tasks and responsibilities, but there are still days that follow a particular pattern. For example, many of our awards ceremonies and conferences are annual events, so they can feel as if they follow a set cycle. However, our events still challenge me every year. There can be a speaker with excessive expenses that you have to deal with, a hundred extra vegetarians who turn up unexpectedly to an event, and tight security requirements for a member of the royal family or a government minister. Something can always happen that takes you by surprise and you have to think on your feet. The main speaker can pull out an hour before, or the event overruns and you need to move the coffee break to a different room to speed things up. It sounds simple, but it can be difficult to break the news to several sponsors who have their stands in the *other* coffee area!

Over the past eight years, the team at our company has run events for diverse clients, which include corporate giants such as Lloyds, HSBC and KPMG, membership bodies, such as the CBI (Confederation of British Industry) and the Chemical Industries Association, as well as many events that celebrate the diversity of women in business. I have worked with entrepreneur and diversity specialist Pinky Lilani OBE since 2004. Running the Asian Women of

Achievement Awards with her has proved one of my greatest privileges, and one of my greatest challenges! It is currently one of our largest events and guests come from all sorts of organisations.

My average day has changed over the past eight years, since I began as an events assistant. I think it's very important that anyone who starts out in events is prepared to do a lot of administration, experience some frustrations and embark on a journey, gaining more experience as they progress. It can take time to get to where you want to be, and it isn't as glamorous as it often appears, either! For example, at awards, you usually have only about ten minutes to get dressed up to meet guests. Despite the drawbacks, my job is still incredibly exciting and I have met people and seen places that I don't think I could have done in another job.

There are seven of us and I run the team. I am lucky to work with a great group. As the event director, I deal with team management matters which include holiday requests, career development and workloads. Every Monday, we start with a team meeting, so everyone can say what they are doing. This is very helpful for me in order to facilitate the distribution of work. The meeting also includes a catch-up with our marketing department. We liaise with them – looking at copy for emails and working out from our data who the mailings should go out to. On top of this, I am also responsible for liaising with senior managers within the company; together, we decide on the events team strategy for each year and we work together to deliver outcomes that affect the entire business. My department is one of the biggest revenue earners in the company – as such, management and the board consider it a priority and I am required to report to them on a weekly basis.

As well as managing the team and liaising with management, I am responsible for the overall delivery of the fifty-plus events we run every year. I need to negotiate with all our suppliers to get the best deals and draw up and maintain all the budgets (each event has its own one). On a daily basis, I'll be required to give final approval of marketing and PR strategies, select suppliers, agree finance decisions and keep a close eye on the client and sponsor relationships.

I am the main contact for our key sponsors and clients. I'll probably have at least one weekly conference call a day with one of our events' headline sponsors or with a client. Increasingly, I view myself as a relationship manager; once the sponsors come on board, we look after them and we work with them to help them to achieve their objectives. Occasionally, we might not be able to deliver their requests and I have to manage that reality, which isn't always easy.

There are often many stakeholders involved in a single event. These can range from event partners who might receive a cut of the profits in exchange for marketing to their contacts, providing speakers for the event, etc. to headline sponsors, category sponsors (with awards) and associate sponsors, as well as the many people involved internally with the event at my company. There are many people to please. For example, when putting a room plan together for a dinner of 400 guests, everybody needs a good view of the stage. All of their logos need to feature strongly on the backdrop. There is a lot to think about and it can feel like a juggling act.

It is a great feeling, though, when you know the event has gone well. You've pulled it off and the clients are happy, too. However, it's my experience that the event manager can usually be their own biggest critic. The day after an event usually involves me being at my desk early, coordinating with the PR team to maximise press and debriefing with all the stake-holders and my team. As an event manager, you are always striving to improve your events – next time can always be bigger and better!

12.7 Summary

This chapter has provided an overview of a diverse and dynamic sector of the events industry. It has focused on a broad sweep of corporate events, and the significance of technological and business developments for the sector have been noted. Corporate event managers face challenging times in the short to medium term as the world economy recovers from the financial crisis of 2008 and the recessions that have followed in Western countries, but with the largest growth area for corporate events being Asia, it is likely that opportunities will continue to present themselves for entrepreneurial event managers and organisations to grow their businesses in an extremely competitive market. Events have become central to the way that many companies do business in the twenty-first century and this, along with innovations in emerging technologies, means that successful event managers need to keep pace with a vibrant and globalised industry.

Further reading

Bowdin, G., Allen, J., O'Toole, W., Harris, R. and McDonnell, I. (2011) *Events Management* (3rd edn), Oxford: Butterworth-Heinemann. This textbook does not cover the particular intricacies of corporate events but it does include a brief discussion of them in Chapter 1.

Davidson, R. (2008) What Does Generation Y Want from Conferences and Incentive Programmes? Accessed at: http://www.fcb.fi/UserFiles/fcb/File/pdf/R_Davidson/RD_What% 20Does%20Generation%20Y%20want%20from%20Conferences%20and%20Incentive %20Programmes.pdf. An investigation into the way in which conferences and incentive programmes can be designed in such a way that they appeal to members of the Y Generation – the youngest and fastest-growing consumers of conference and incentive events. The article examines these customers' particular motivations and needs.

Getz, D. (2007) *Event Studies*, Oxford: Butterworth-Heinemann. This text includes a rather complex dissection of the industry, but it is useful for the paragraph on various aspects of the exhibition industry and for its discussion on World Fairs in Chapter 2.

Chapter 13

Cultural events and festivals

Contents

13.1 Aims

By the end of this chapter, students will be able:

- To define the different categories of cultural events and festivals.
- To explore key management issues for these types of events.
- To analyse the challenges involved in marketing cultural events and festivals.
- To discuss the ways in which cultural events and festivals can contribute to cultural and social change.

13.2 Introduction

Cultural events and festivals are major sectors of the events industry and are key drivers of the tourism and service economies in all the major developed economies and in most countries around the world. Cultural events are hugely diverse in nature, from a Coldplay tour to the Cannes Film Festival and celebrations of identity and nationality. The calendar of festivals within just one country will inevitably be crowded with religious, seasonal and community festival events.

This chapter provides an overview of the cultural events and festivals sector. The aim is to introduce the reader to the variety of different events and festivals in this category and to draw their attention to some key management processes involved in producing this diverse group of special events.

13.3 Cultural events

The word 'culture' is notoriously difficult to define (Ali Knight and Robinson 2004). Some authors place cultural events under the more general category of 'special events' (Raj *et al.* 2008), whilst others include a separate category of 'cultural events' in their typologies of events, but separate these artistic events from other kinds of cultural expression, such as festivals of identity and community (Bowdin *et al.* 2006; Getz 2005). Sonder (2004) unites many of the kinds of events described in this chapter through the concept of 'entertainment', but elsewhere this term has been seen as separate, almost by definition, from the arts (Hughes 2006) which make up so much of our cultural practices. The term 'cultural events' takes a more holistic view of human activity and those events which emphasise the cultural, as opposed to other, aspects of our lives.

Any definition of cultural events needs to differentiate these events from others that are more easily defined as business events, sports events or mega-events, for example, whilst also remaining sufficiently open to cover the broad range of events that take place within the big tent of 'culture'. To resolve this, we can introduce two definitions of cultural events. The first, conceptual definition allows us to incorporate a diversity of events within the framework of cultural events, whilst the second provides a stable base from which to move forward and discuss the management issues associated with staging these events.

13.3.1 Conceptual definition

Cultural events are associated with expressions of 'culture', but what does this term mean, if anything? The cultural economist Arvo Klamer (2002: 1) describes the diversities of culture and their significance:

> It may be a bridge, a piece of wood. Or a temple, a windmill, a painting, a piece of furniture, a mask, jewel, bead. It may even be a language, a ritual, or a practice. Whatever it is, it differs from other goods because people may consider it a symbol of something – a nation, a community, a tradition, a religion, a cultural episode.

To discuss the management of cultural events, it is necessary to elaborate on this list of cultural forms to produce one that resembles cultural forms as we experience them in the events market place; but even then the list is remarkably diverse. Within it, there are events in which culture is understood anthropologically – in Raymond Williams' (2010) terminology, as 'a way of life' – as well as events that are better understood as expressions of an aesthetic culture (see Table 13.1).

Terry Eagleton (2000:1) sounds a note of caution here:

> It is hard to resist the conclusion that the word 'culture' is both too broad and too narrow to be greatly useful. Its anthropological meaning covers everything from hairstyles and drinking habits to how to address your husband's second cousin, while the aesthetic sense of the word includes Igor Stravinsky but not science fiction.

Whilst this overview of the diversity of culture as a concept gives us a framework for identifying cultural events, if we are to move on to a consideration of their management, there is a need for a more 'greatly useful' definition that event managers can operationalise.

Table 13.1 Categorising cultural events

Anthropological		Aesthetic	
Type	Example	Type	Example
National cultural	St Patrick's Day in New York	Arts	Wagner Festival in Bayreuth
Religious	Divali in Bradford	Music	Bonnaroo Festival in Tennessee
Ethnicity	Mela in Oslo	Heritage	Festival of the Olive in New South Wales
Sexuality	Manchester LGBT Festival		
Community	Notting Hill Carnival in London		

13.3.2 Operational definition

Getz (2007: 31) defines cultural celebrations as 'solemn or joyous events that have cultural meaning', but this anthropological definition does not capture the aesthetic components of culture, packaged together by many authors as 'merely' entertainment events. In response to this, and taking on board the conceptual framework of culture set out above, we can devise a more open definition of cultural events as those that either present a particular expression of culture or aim to represent the cultural expressions of specific groups.

13.4 Festivals

Festivals are extremely common forms of cultural practice and, although many have long histories, the majority have been founded much more recently (Getz 2005). The International Festivals and Events Association estimates that there are over 4.5 million recurring festivals worldwide each year (IFEA 2009: 1)

Festivals are both a particular kind of cultural event, each with its own history and tradition, and a specific celebratory form, with structural elements that can be used within a range of cultural traditions. Sonder (2004: 18) groups together parades, fairs and festivals as 'particular types of themed events that may simultaneously contain historical, cultural, ceremonial, religious, patriotic and social themes'.

The term 'festival' is used by event organisers to describe a broad range of event forms – from short celebrations of a particular place or culture to events that extend over weeks and can involve vast numbers of venues and performers.

> Each summer people visit Edinburgh from every corner of the globe and enjoy three exhilarating weeks of the very best in international opera, music, drama and dance. Come with us on a journey of discovery in 2010 and celebrate the colour, the passion and the drama of the Edinburgh International Festival.
>
> (Edinburgh International Festival 2010)

> For the whole weekend commencing Saturday 4 September 2010 the town of Faversham will be home to the annual Faversham International Hop Festival. A traditional, fun festival set in the picturesque medieval town's square and surrounding streets, celebrating the olden days of hop picking in Kent. With music to suit eclectic tastes, children's entertainers, professional street theatre, stilt walkers, Morris dancing, craft fare, and ceilidh, it's a weekend for family and friends to enjoy!
>
> (Faversham Hop Festival 2010)

Bowdin et al. (2006) use South East Arts' categorisation to divide arts festivals into seven distincitve types:

1 High-profile celebrations of the arts.
2 Festivals that celebrate a particular location.
3 Art-form festivals.
4 Celebration of work by a community of interest.
5 Calendar.
6 Amateur arts festivals.
7 Commercial music festivals.

Cultural events and festivals

We can add to this list by reference to the conceptual framework for cultural events, above, to produce a more comprehensive list of festivals generally:

8 Celebrations of the expressions of specific cultural groups.

Getz (2007: 31) offers a simple, clear definition of festivals as 'themed, public celebrations', which he concedes does not 'do justice to the richness and diversity of meanings' attached to this kind of event. This difficulty stems from the historical and fundamental role that festivals have played in human culture – as celebratory, commemorative or ritualistic events. Perhaps the first festival took place in 534 BC in Greece in honour of the God Dionysus, and there are records of festivals playing important social and cultural roles from the twelfth century to the present day in Europe (Quinn 2005). Some writers even place the 'carnival-esque' experience of festivals at the heart of an understanding of how society manages itself and is governed. For theorists such as Bakhtin (1984), festivals offer a short period of time when we can rebel against, challenge and reimagine society, before we are obliged to return to an altered, but mainly pre-served, social reality.

Because festivals and society are so intertwined, it can be very difficult to isolate the elements that define 'a festival', so it is perhaps useful to consider a loose arrangement of elements that combine to produce a festival event:

● themed content
● the presence of multiple individual events
● possibilities for participation
● extension in time and space
● celebratory or commemorative functions.

Each of these elements creates a set of management challenges that will be present to a greater or lesser degree in every festival.

CASE STUDY 13.1

New Orleans Mardi Gras

Location: New Orleans, USA
Event type: festival
Attendees: 1,500,000

From the beginning of the twentieth century until the present day, New Orleans in Louisiana in the south of the United States has been known as a cultural and leisure destination, with a reputation built on cultural events (especially music), festivities and culinary specialities. A river city, New Orleans has hosted cotton, petroleum and shipbuilding industries. In recent years, and in similar fashion to many industrial cities in the developed world, its economy has been restructured as manufacturing and production jobs have moved to lower-wage economies. In this period, the city has turned increasingly towards the service sector, within which it specialises in tourism and cultural production. The most famous of the city's many cultural events is the Mardi Gras.

This festival originated in France. It was brought to America in the 1700s and has been held in New Orleans every year since the 1800s on the day before Ash Wednesday in the Catholic calendar. On Mardi Gras, almost the entire city shuts down, with businesses closing and a public holiday for residents. Roads throughout the central area of the city are closed and become parade routes, decked out in purple, green and gold. These are the 'official colours' of the festival and stand for justice, faith and power. Over the whole Mardi Gras period, the city hosts hundreds of individual cultural events.

The festival today

In 2010, around 1.5 million people came to New Orleans during Mardi Gras. The festival brings approximately $322 million into the local economy, yet the

**Image 13.1
Parade float at
Mardi Gras**
Source: Cheryl Gerber /
Getty Images

city government does not fund or actively support it, other than by providing permits and licences for the parades and associated events.

The festival is arranged by the coordinated actions of non-profit organisations known as 'krewes', which work together to choose the themes of parades, outfits and schedules. Krewes take their names from ancient mythology or the areas of the city where they are based. More than fifty of these krewes currently organise Mardi Gras.

As well as being a major tourist and cultural event, the festival performs a commemorative and celebratory role for the communities of the city. As the imported tradition of Mardi Gras developed in the city, a parallel set of events began to emerge, with the excluded black communities of New Orleans forming into krewes and reclaiming areas of the city against the local history of racism and slavery. As American society has become more integrated, these parades of 'Mardi Gras Indians' have been integrated into the wider festival. They are no longer seen as dangerous and exotic, but as part of the core event itself.

Challenges

As the Mardi Gras celebrations have grown in the city, annual visitor numbers have risen year on year. This creates problems of congestion and overcrowding, and difficulties for the local tourism industry in meeting this highly seasonal demand for accommodation, transport and hospitality.

Mardi Gras is now a global media product, with live television broadcasts by *Entertainment Tonight*, MTV and the Playboy Channel within the US every year, and reports on a worldwide scale by global media networks. This prominence has also attracted big-name brands to the event, with parade floats and events carrying sponsorship from the likes of Bacardi rum, Southern Comfort, Coors beer, Kool cigarettes and others. This has led to concerns that local people are being increasingly excluded from this global media event in the interests of high-spending tourists and sponsors.

There are also social problems associated with this increased profile. The festival increasingly attracts large groups of students on 'Spring Break' and parties of other visitors intent on drinking and partying. These attendees rarely participate in the parades and indeed show little interest in any of the cultural traditions of the event. Mardi Gras evolved as a religious and then a community festival, but it is now in danger of gaining a reputation for antisocial behaviour.

In the wake of Hurricane Katrina and the devastation of much of the city, Mardi Gras has the potential to unite the city and bring in much-needed investment, but it faces significant challenges if it is to maintain the support of local people as well as corporate sponsors.

Sources: Fox-Gotham 2002, 2005; Mardi Gras New Orleans 2010

What role does Mardi Gras play in the life of New Orleans? Do other festivals play similar roles in other cities?

In the following sections, we shall describe specific cultural event and festival forms in detail and then analyse the particular management functions that are associated with them.

13.5 Types of cultural events and festivals

13.5.1 Music events and festivals

Music events are by far the largest element of the whole events sector. In the United Kingdom, 60 million visits are made to music concerts each year, generating around £1.9 billion (Mintel 2008). They vary greatly in form and style, from individual performances in bars and community centres to multi-day touring music festivals. However, they can be categorised into four main types: the first two view music events from the perspective of the artist, whilst the second two take an organisational perspective.

13.5.1.1 Music concerts
Music concerts are one-off music events that attract an audience because of the presence of an individual performer or a small number of performers appearing together.

13.5.1.2 Music tours
Tours involve repeated performances by an individual performer or group of performers, moving between different venues. Touring occurs at three different scales: regional, national and international. Regional touring is usually carried out by artists with low national profiles, or artists working within very localised musical scenes. National tours take place when an artist's profile has developed to a level where they are gaining national media exposure. International touring is usually commercially viable only for the most successful artists.

13.5.1.3 Music programmes
Performance venues seek to design programmes (see the section on programming, below) that will attract event attendees to a venue throughout the year. These programmes can involve a succession of events featuring individual artists, or longer-term residencies where one artist or group of artists become a regular feature of a particular venue.

13.5.1.4 Music festivals
Music festivals are a growing phenomenon, with the British market for this categorisation alone including over 600 annual events. The outdoor rock and pop music festival market in Britain has seen an increase of 71 per cent since 2003 (Anderton 2008). Although other music genres also make use of the festival form (e.g. the annual Prague Spring Festival of classical music and JazzFest in Berlin), the rock and pop festival market is the most dynamic and attracts the largest

audiences. These large events draw on a recent countercultural tradition in popular music and offer a packaged, multi-day experience that promises not only a procession of high-profile and credible musical entertainment but camping on site and a recreation of the glory days of the Woodstock era. One of the aspects of event design that separates festivals from other music events is the provision of non-music attractions, such as catering, accommodation, secondary events and retailing, all of which must be present in order to generate an 'authentic' festival experience (Bowen and Daniels 2005).

This phenomenon is not limited to Europe. As the events market matures in other regions, a similar growth in the outdoor festival market is occurring. In Taiwan, the Spring Scream Festival has grown from hosting twelve bands in 1994, when it began, to hosting 200 bands across nine stages over a four-day event that attracted 300,000 attendees in 2008, grossing £86 million in revenue (Wang and Weng 2008).

13.5.2 Film events and festivals

Film events come in a number of forms, including screenings in cinemas or less unorthodox settings, promotional events, and festivals. Screenings follow a very standardised format that offers little scope for customisation by event managers, and promotional events can be best understood from a marketing perspective. This section will therefore concentrate on film festivals and the niche market for specialist screenings.

Film festivals can be analysed in two ways: the promotional services that they provide to the film industry; and the networking and development opportunities they provide to film professionals.

Film festivals vary enormously in size – from the Cannes Festival in France, with 350,000 attendees and an economic impact of $97 million (Grunwell and Ha 2008), to the Sundance Independent Film Festival in the US, with around 50,000 annual visitors, to small local and regional events.

Cannes is the world's most important film festival. It was launched in 1946 and takes place every year in the south of France. As well as bestowing a prestigious set of awards upon films entered in its competition, it generates promotional opportunities for films through screening opportunities and media exposure. In 2009, the festival's budget was £23 million, of which around half comes from the French state, with the rest being contributions from the film industry. In total, 299 feature films were shown at Cannes in 2009, along with 47 short films. These films were seen by 350,000 attendees, of whom 24,827 were accredited as professionals from the film sector. Reporting from Cannes were 3469 accredited journalists.

At the opposite end of the scale from the grandeur of Cannes are the 'Secret Cinema' events that have been running in London since 2008. Originally conceived by independent short-film

Table 13.2 Elements of a film festival

Promotional services	Development opportunities
Film screenings	Technical exhibits
Marketing support	Networking events
Awards	Educational activities

Image 13.2 Bollywood actress Aishwarya Rai on the red carpet at the 64th International Cannes Film Festival
Source: AFP / Getty Images

producers Future Shorts, the events take place monthly and are announced just two days, or sometimes only a few hours, beforehand to members of an internet mailing list. Attendees have only vague ideas of the choice of film before it starts, passed on through instructions to act or dress in a particular way as a member of the audience. The Secret Cinema events specialise in showing independent, arthouse and little-known films to a self-selecting audience of film fans who expect an immersive experience that uses elements of event design to enhance the film experience through themed venues and supplementary performances. A recent review in *Empire* magazine gives an evocative description of the atmosphere at a screening of Wim Wenders' 1987 film, *Wings of Desire*:

> Inside, past the couple kissing at the bottom of the stalled escalator, the specially-designed posters . . . and the buzzing TVs was a rather cavernous upstairs, all black walls, decaying furniture and a pleasantly melancholy band playing at a cafe bit in the corner. A couple of small rooms were decorated like a child's room, and a small library (again, that should've helped me twig, but no) before we headed into the auditorium itself – where we were greeted by a circus. The Circus Alekan, in fact, which finally did give it away: it's going to be *Wings of Desire*!
>
> The floor of the theatre was set up with a mini sawdust ring, a juggler, a trapeze artist, ringmaster, knife-thrower and victim target. After a quick circus performance, a musical interlude, short film *Splitting the Atom* and a bit more trapezery, the Wim Wenders film finally got underway. The reaction when the title card came up was interesting: hardly

anyone left immediately, although about six people in my line of vision left during the running time, which is probably a good result for an arthouse film being shown to a general audience.

(O'Hara 2010)

These unorthodox events have proven so successful at generating a marketing buzz and media interest that they are now produced 'in partnership' with Microsoft, which uses them to promote its web technologies and smartphone software applications – an example of a synergetic partnership between a cultural and a business organisation, with both gaining from the relationship.

13.5.3 Community festivals and events

A community-themed festival or event is a 'public themed celebration which can act as a catalyst for demonstrating community values and culture' (Jepson *et al.* 2008: 2). A community represented through this process could be distinguished by its:

- nationality
- ethnicity
- sexuality
- interest
- place.

Festivals play an important role in helping to create and support community identities through celebration, preservation and renewal of the cultural identities and practices of a group of people. Huang *et al.* (2010: 254) define community-based festivals (CBF) more specifically as 'essentially small scale, bottom up, and run by one or more volunteers for the benefit of the locality. They take place in rural or semi-rural areas with the primary goal of providing cultural and entertainment benefits for locals and visitors.'

Although the majority of CBFs certainly are low-profile, small-scale events, many festivals and cultural events that have developed within specific communities now attract large audiences and have national and sometimes even international profiles. In some cases, transnational communities (Aksoy and Robins 2004) formed through diasporas and other migrations have generated international networks of cultural events and festivals, such as the annual Chinese New Year celebrations, held in China Towns in most of the world's major cities, or the festivals that are connected through the European Mela Network. The Mela was 'a festival tradition serving to celebrate ethnic community and folk cultures and identities in India, but increasingly becoming a showcase for global and hybridised cultural forms related to Indianness' (Carnegie and Smith 2006: 256).

CASE STUDY 13.2

Manchester's LGBT Festival

Location: Manchester, UK
Event type: community festival
Attendees: 42,000

Manchester Pride is an example of a festival associated with a community of sexuality. Hughes (2006) writes that this is just one example of a huge range of 'Gay Pride' events, including marches, festivals and parades. Interpride, the international organisation for lesbian, gay, bisexual and transgender (LGBT) festival events, has 143 member organisations in 20 global regions (Interpride 2010).

Manchester's LGBT Festival was founded in the 1990s during a period when a gay community was developing in a regenerating area centred on Canal Street, formerly an industrial part of the city. The festival celebrates and gives voice to the gay community of Manchester, and performs a charitable function by raising money for LGBT groups and AIDS prevention and awareness campaigns.

In 2009, the festival attracted 42,000 visitors to a four-day programme of events centred on the August Bank Holiday. The most recent figures indicate that the festival contributes in excess of £17 million per year to the local economy. The festival parade, which moves throughout the city, attracted upwards of 250,000 people. The entire programme included:

- the main festival parade
- street markets
- music events
- a funfair
- sports events
- lectures and discussion events.

Since 2003, a charitable organisation called Manchester Pride has been organising the festival. Its mission statement describes the work it does:

> Manchester Pride is an annual festival by and for lesbian, gay, bisexual and transgender people, working towards the involvement of different sectors of the community, and raising funds for LGBT and HIV organisations. Manchester Pride provides opportunities for empowerment, participation, representation, access, and celebration, encouraging pride, respect and partnership working.
>
> (Manchester Pride 2010)

13.5.4 Arts events and festivals

Arts events and festivals can focus on the performing arts, the visual arts, sonic art, or a combination of all three. They are the most common type of festival event (Allen *et al.* 2008)

The performing arts include, but are not limited to, dance, theatre and opera (Kotler and Scheff 1997). Often magical entertainment, circus arts and comedy are included within this framework, sharing common elements of performance, venue type and consumer. Performing arts events can take place on a one-off basis, as tours, as serial events or in festival format.

Arts events that are in the fields of visual and sonic arts can include short-term exhibitions of art and opening events (Getz 2005), as well as festivals. Longer-term exhibitions of artworks are covered by the substantial literature in the field of museum and gallery management. Axelsen and Arcodia (2005) suggest that these short-term cultural events are little understood within the events management literature, despite their prominence within the visual arts field, with gallery managers increasingly using them to attract visitors and promote sales of specific artists and works. They suggest that these events are worthy of further exploration within the field of events management for three main reasons:

- They offer another perspective on events management as a subject and as a set of management techniques that can be incorporated into the development of subject knowledge and good practice in the industry.
- The art market is becoming less producer-led and more consumer-led, in common with the wider cultural industries, so understanding the art event consumer helps art event managers to meet the needs of the art market.
- Boundaries between high and low art have become blurred and there is a growing market of event consumers for art forms that have traditionally been seen as elitist, such as the visual arts.

An example of this kind of short-term event is Soundwalk – an annual one-day event that brings together international sound artists in Long Beach, California. The 2009 Soundwalk involved fifty artists from around the world, who collaborated to create a set of temporary sound art installations: 'The evening operates under the concept of a one-night multi-sensory experience as conveyed through sound art that is situated in various indoor and outdoor spaces throughout the East Village Arts District in Downtown Long Beach' (Soundwalk 2010). The Soundwalk events showcase the work of an emerging group of sound artists and introduce members of the public to a new artistic practice:

> This year, FLOOD [the event organisers] will be exploring 'connectivity' by expanding both geographically and conceptually. The activation of 1st Street as a 'sound corridor' will connect the Arts District with Pine Avenue, thus offering both participants and attendees interesting new contexts in which to exhibit and to experience art set forth in sound.
>
> It has been FLOOD's aim to raise awareness as well as engender an appreciation for alternative artistic practices by exposing audiences, along with the larger community, to aesthetic sensibilities and innovative approaches that exist outside those of the contemporary mainstream.
>
> (Soundwalk 2010)

Serial events are unique to the performing arts. They involve repeated performances of the same event over an extended period and, in the case of contemporary mega-musicals, often simultaneously in several venues in different countries. The musical *Mamma Mia* has been seen by over 40 million people worldwide, grossing an estimated $2 billion at the box office in more than twenty countries. This is the serial reproduction of one 155-minute performance.

In many instances, a variety of art forms are programmed together in 'combined arts festivals' (CAFs) (Finkel 2006). The majority of these festivals are produced outside of the commercial sector and are often produced and/or promoted by local authorities. Finkel profiles the Lichfield Festival, which has been running for twenty-five years in a small town near Birmingham, UK. It currently runs for ten days across fifteen venues. A total of 61 events made up the programme for the 2003 festival, of which 27 (44 per cent) were music and 13 (21 per cent) were film. There were also seven drama and five visual arts events.

Finkel suggests that there is increasing local and regional competition between CAFs in the UK, as local authorities come to see them as key tools for enhancing destination image and boosting tourism.

13.5.5 Literary events and festivals

Literary events and festivals are a growing sector of the cultural events industry. They vary in size and scope, but include:

- commercial book launches
- book clubs and reading groups
- talks and readings given by authors
- literary festivals.

Commercial launch events are organised by book publishers and generally take place in book shops for a small audience or at trade fairs (see Fenich 2005). The largest trade fair, in Frankfurt, attracted 299,000 visitors in 2009 (Buchmesse 2010).

Book clubs and reading groups are small, locally organised events that are usually informal in nature. However, Burwell (2007) notes that their increasing popularity, especially in the women's' market, has led to them being targeted by publishing companies as an effective mechanism for generating word-of-mouth publicity for books. They have also become a feature of mass media and celebrity culture, with celebrity endorsements allied to publishers' more traditional marketing efforts. The most successful of these has been Oprah Winfrey's Book Club, with *Time* magazine reporting:

> It's the greatest force in publishing today, with the power to raise authors from the dead (Leo Tolstoy) or crucify them on the national stage (James Frey). The all-powerful Oprah's Book Club is not so much a club as a ruthlessly influential marketing vehicle, with the power to fundamentally alter best-seller lists, Amazon rankings and royalty payments. Sure, the 'club' has 2 million 'members' and a web site that provides a space for users to share thoughts on featured titles, read excerpts and get advice like, 'How to Read a Hard Book'. But in the 12 years Oprah's Book Club has existed, its significance has been – from the perspective of authors and editors, at least – not its sense of community, but its influence on sales, which has been known to increase a print run fivefold.
>
> (Pickert 2008)

Despite the commercial success of endorsed reading groups such as Oprah's, at the level of the individual event these book clubs are locally organised and, whilst they may make use of centrally (often publisher-) produced reading notes and supplementary material, they tend to involve no more than a dozen people at any one time. Literary festivals, by contrast, can attract thousands of times more visitors and are being developed in a number of countries, capitalising on the maturation of the festival market. These festivals combine authors' talks, catering, accommodation, retail and secondary events within the traditional festival spatial and temporal arrangements of a bounded site over multiple days.

The Hay Festival of Literature and the Arts is a charitable organisation that has promoted the Hay-on-Wye literary festival since 1988. Beginning as a small event that aimed to build on the tradition of bookselling in a small town in Wales, by 2010 it had set itself the target of attracting 100,000 people to a festival that Bill Clinton described as 'Woodstock for the mind' (BBC 2009). In that year, speakers included Pervez Musharraf, the former President of Pakistan, whilst previous headliners have included Archbishop Desmond Tutu and Paul McCartney, demonstrating that the original aims of promoting the book trade have widened to include a range of intellectual activities. The Hay Festival has also recently expanded internationally, to include parallel events in:

- Segovia, Spain
- Alhambra, Spain
- Cartagena, Colombia
- the Maldives
- Zacatecas, Mexico
- Nairobi, Kenya
- Beirut, Lebanon.

The festival in Kenya shows how literary festivals, as one kind of cultural event, can be developed to address broader social issues as well as being successful commercial events in their own right:

> Storymoja Hay Festival Nairobi is a three-day celebration that will provide opportunities for the meeting of minds and sharing of ideas between storytellers and the public. The Festival will act as a platform for readers, writers, listeners and thinkers and provide exposure to some of the world's leading names in literature as well as some up-and-coming authors. It will also provide space for the culmination of the active participation 'Kenya Get Reading Campaign' workshops for students, which Storymoja have cultivated alongside universities and schools over the last two years.
>
> Storymoja Hay Festival Nairobi offers an opportunity to bring much-needed focus on the importance of literacy in improving people's day-to-day lives, helping improve social cohesion and informed decision-making in an atmosphere of relaxed enjoyment.
>
> (Storymoja Hay Festival Nairobi 2009)

Study activity

Visit the website for the Storymoja Hay Festival in Nairobi: http://www.hayfestival.com/storymoja/index.aspx?skinid=10. Explore the programme for the event and answer the following questions:

- What are the various elements of the festival?
- How international is the festival?

- What are the aims of the festival?
- Who sponsored the event? Why do you think they wanted to be associated with it?

13.6 Programming cultural events and festivals

Although the idea of programming is used across the events industry, the term is used in a specific way for cultural events and festivals. In this instance, it describes the process of choosing and presenting a set of events that are joined together by venue, content or organisation. It is a central concept for understanding the management of cultural event organisations and cultural event venues, such as theatres and concert halls (Cuadrado-Garcia and Perez-Cabenero 2005). Programming in this manner should be distinguished from the concept of developing a programme for an event, which involves assembling the elements of event design for a single event within a theme (e.g. Getz 2005; Sonder 2004; Allen *et al.* 2008).

Castaner and Campos (2002) identify the factors involved in the programming decision-making process that event managers go through when designing a programme of cultural events. These can be divided into environmental and cultural factors that impact upon an organiser's ability to develop innovative programmes within a specified form.

13.6.1 Environmental factors

These can be divided into macro-, meso- and micro-level influences on the cultural organisation. Macro factors come from the external environment, such as changes in legislation, changes in society and the influence of other organisations. Micro factors are internal to the organisation and include its strengths and weaknesses, its level of available resources, and human resource issues. Meso factors refer to those influences that span the internal and external operating environments, such as relationships with particular funding bodies and sponsors, and organisations working in partnership.

These environmental factors, taken together, form the practical horizons of what a cultural organisation will be able to programme within a venue or a festival.

13.6.2 Cultural factors

In order to understand the programming process fully, it is necessary to examine cultural factors, too. These factors are both internal and external to an organisation and relate to the cultural orientations of the audience and to the orientations of the cultural programmers themselves. The influence of inherently conservative audiences or programmers will produce 'safe' programmes that avoid risk in order to consolidate existing audiences. Meanwhile, audiences and programmers who are enthusiastic about cultural innovation will exert pressure that produces more innovative, creative programming, even though this carries the risk of alienating the existing audience.

Successful programming works through a creative tension between conservative and innovative approaches to programming decision-making, within a set of environmental constraints that are specific to every cultural organisation.

Allen *et al.*'s (2008: 454) discussion of the factors influencing the development of a programme for a *single* event shows that the process of event design and the development of

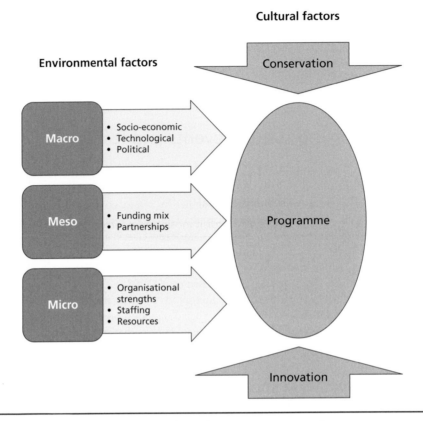

Figure 13.1 Determinants of cultural event programming

multiple-event programmes operate under a similar set of constraints. The authors explain that the programme for a single event depends on:

- the expectations of the audience
- the constraints of the venue and the infrastructure
- the culture of the client and the main sponsors
- the availability of elements of the staging and their relationship to each other
- the logistics
- the creative intent of the event team.

Cultural programmes can be expressed according to four main stylistic conventions, as shown in Table 13.3.

Assassi (2005) carried out a study of French theatres to determine the characteristics of performing arts programming decision-making and discovered four elements of this process, as shown in Figure 13.2.

The *reactive component* of programming relates to the box-office potential of a cultural event, expressed either as an attendance figure or as an income stream. The *relational component* is a measure of how far the programme is designed as a response to feedback from and interaction with cultural consumers. The *proactive component* describes how the programming

Table 13.3 Programming styles

Programming style	Example
Thematic	A concert season programmed in partnership with a scientific organisation, themed on the relationship between music and science
Temporal	A programme of outdoor theatre events during the summer in the grounds of a country estate
Disciplinary	A visual arts festival
Audience constituency	A festival of Kurdish music and poetry

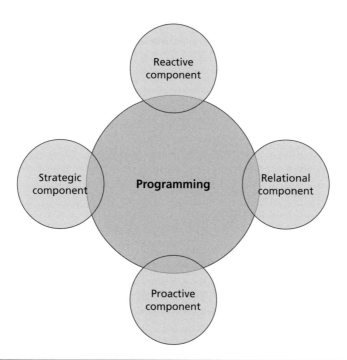

Figure 13.2 Components of programming
Source: Adapted from Assassi 2005

decisions reflect the cultural objectives of the organisation. Finally, the *strategic component* refers to how far the programming decisions meet the broad strategic aims of the organisation.

According to this model, successful programming will be a mix of all four of these elements, with the split between the requirements of reactive and non-reactive elements determined by the financial situation and profit-driven motivation of the organisation involved.

- Use the three models set out in this section to analyse the programming of a major national cultural venue or festival in your country.
- How useful do you find each model in understanding the programming decisions of the organisation?
- What information do you need to help you to carry out this analysis?
- What recommendations can you make for developing the programming strategy of your chosen organisation?

13.7 Marketing cultural events and festivals

Consumers are presented with an ever-increasing volume of marketing messages for cultural activities, due to the growth of the 'cultural industries' and the extension of the market place into their leisure time (Hesmondhalgh 2007). Cultural organisations are competing for consumers' attention, not only against other cultural organisations but with other 'agents of leisure', such as cinemas, leisure centres, digital broadcasters and shopping malls. In order to gain a competitive advantage, they now make use of sophisticated marketing techniques. This has been a relatively recent development, with the controversies over the commercialisation and commodification of culture now playing a less prominent role in cultural management discourse than when such concepts as 'arts marketing' first appeared in the 1980s. In 1986, in a rhetorical style that mirrored concerns about the pernicious role of money in the arts field, Hans Haacke wrote:

> Trained by prestigious business schools, they are convinced that art can and should be sold like the production and marketing of other goods. They make no apologies and have few romantic hang-ups.
>
> It is expected that the lack of delusions and aspirations among new arts administrators will have a notable impact on the state of the industry. Being trained primarily as technocrats, they are less likely to have an emotional attachment to the peculiar nature of the product they are promoting. And this attitude, in turn, will have an effect on the type of products they are promoting. And this attitude, in turn, will have an effect on the type of products we will soon begin to see.
>
> (Haacke, cited in Chong 2002: 2)

Twenty-five years later, Haacke's predictions have failed to materialise, and the field of cultural events is more diverse and widespread than ever. New technologies, innovative funding regimes and the growth of cultural sponsorship have all helped to support a global cultural sector that is recognised by most developed nations as fundamental to their economic success and cultural identity. This diverse group of cultural producers within the 'cultural industries' (Hesmondhalgh 2007) make use of the full repertoire of marketing strategies and techniques that were explored in Chapter 7. However, when considering cultural events specifically, we can make use of two models that help event managers to develop both their marketing strategies and the cultural form in which they are working. These models are the concept of the 'cultural consumer' and the group of social marketing techniques known as 'audience development'.

13.7.1 The cultural consumer

Kolb (2005) sets out four core challenges facing cultural organisations in the competition for consumers:

1 Cultural marketers can no longer assume that they know what the consumer wants from the cultural experience.
2 Consumers living in a multi-media, cross-cultural environment will want more combinations of art forms and new delivery methods.
3 Cultural marketers must target packaged events to specific market segments.
4 These packaged events must provide multiple benefits to meet consumer needs, whilst fitting within consumers' time and budget constraints.

Bearing in mind these constraints, Kolb goes on to suggest that, when faced with this level of uncertainty within an organisation and the cross-cultural, multi-media competencies and expectations of cultural event attendees, there is a need for a specific cultural segmentation model for cultural consumers. This is in line with Getz's (2005) recommendation to use product-related variables when segmenting the market for an event. This model of the 'cultural consumer' can be used by cultural event managers to attract specific groups of attendees through the design and marketing processes. It first classifies the consumer in terms of their engagement with the cultural form or event (see Figure 13.3).

This model shows cultural consumers segmented into five groups, each of which is represented to a different degree for different cultural forms within a total population of cultural consumers. *Petty producers* have developed such a strong level of engagement with the culture that they have started to create it at an amateur level. They are looking for cultural experiences that allow them to participate in production or that offer opportunities for their advancement or development within their preferred cultural field.

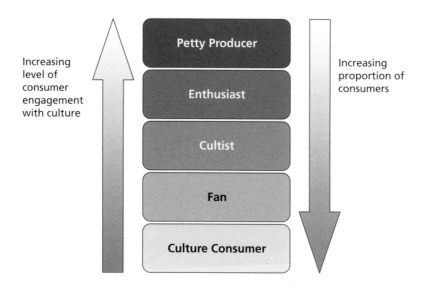

Figure 13.3 Cultural consumers
Source: Adapted from Kolb 2005

Those within the *enthusiast* segment of the cultural consumer market place have an excellent knowledge of the cultural form that goes beyond mere attachment to a particular individual, group or venue. They are very knowledgeable about their chosen field and it is a significant element in their social and friendship networks. This group of event consumers will be attracted to cultural events and festivals that are innovative and have a clear relationship to the traditions associated with their cultural form.

Cultists are a heavily specialised segment of this market who have developed attachments to specific events, stars or groups. They are characterised by the lengths they will go to in order to indulge their interests, both financially and temporally. They will seek out events that are

Table 13.4 Cultural consumer model applied to theatre events

Type of consumer	Example consumption activity	Value to the organisation
Petty producer	Begins to write and get involved in amateur theatre. Prepared to spend for 'important/exclusive' events.	Can generate new cultural workers and products. Audience for specific high-value events.
Enthusiast	Studies a course in theatre history. Prepared to travel widely and invest in their interest.	Part of valuable networks that can be accessed for marketing purposes. Potentially a large attendee group, but often dispersed. Market for high-value events.
Cultist	Attends all events featuring a specific film star.	A reliable audience with patterns of repeat attendance. Likely to consume cult-related products, such as exclusive events and signings, and to purchase related merchandise. Part of valuable networks of cultists.
Fan	Excited by music, theatre and productions starring certain TV or film personalities.	A large audience group that can be targeted using specific events or programming.
Cultural consumer	Will attend the theatre as part of an evening out or in response to a marketing campaign that emphasises entertainment, price and/or convenience.	This is the mass audience for all culture. Theatres will need to attract these people to develop sustainable audiences to support wider programming aims and ensure financial survival.

related to their particular interests and those that give them opportunities to meet like-minded consumers.

A *fan* is similar to a cultist, but will devote less time and money to pursuing their interest. This allows fans to have multiple allegiances and to be more open to developing new cultural interests. They are attracted by the familiarity of the form or content of the event, or the connection between the event and another which they have attended in the past.

The majority of the population – the mass audience for cultural events and festivals – can be classified as *cultural consumers*. They do not have specialist cultural event interests, but consume culture as part of day-to-day life. For these consumers, factors such as convenience and cost are key elements in their decision-making processes, as are the effects of reference groups.

Kolb's model is important for understanding the marketing of cultural events and festivals as it shows how different kinds of cultural consumers have specific, event-related expectations and desires, which will influence their value to a cultural organisation in terms of income or programming choices. However, cultural organisations seek to develop both the cultural forms in which they work and the audiences for their work. This idea of 'audience development' is fundamental to understanding the relationship between the marketing goals of a cultural event and its broader cultural mission.

Study activity

As the marketing manager of a contemporary pop music venue in a large city, how would you go about attracting the various segments of the cultural market place – as defined in Kolb's model – for your events?
  Use the following questions as a guide:

- Which segment(s) would you focus on and why?
- How would you effectively market your event to your chosen segment(s)?
- How would your chosen segment(s) influence the event design process?

13.7.2 Audience development

Audience development is an umbrella term for techniques and approaches that are designed to increase audiences for cultural events. While these have much in common with general marketing approaches, cultural organisations employ them in the hope of achieving broader goals. (In this sense, they are a form of social marketing.) These goals include cultural, financial and social objectives, and the innovative aspect of audience development is combining these within the field of cultural management, as is shown in Figure 13.4.

These objectives relate to the internal and external relationships of a cultural organisation. Some of these relationships are grounded in the mission of the cultural organisation, such as a commitment to develop a particular cultural form, whilst others focus on external factors, such as the requirements of funding bodies or a relationship with the local community.

Audience development aims to break down barriers to access and deliver new audiences for cultural events by changing perceptions and behaviours of potential and existing event attendees. These changes will then lead to attendees

Cultural events and festivals

- attending an unfamiliar cultural form
- attending more frequently
- attending new venues
- transforming from lapsed into regular attendees
- forming closer bonds with a cultural organisation
- becoming donors of time or money
- increasing level of interaction within their social groups and the wider community.

Within cultural event and festival organisations, audience development is a cross-functional activity that requires the participation of the whole organisation. Successful audience development requires that cultural producers, marketers, educational professionals and strategists work

Figure 13.4 Audience development goals

Table 13.5 Audience development relationships and activities

Organisational goal	Relationship to organisation	Outcomes
Cultural	Internal	Enhancing understanding of a cultural form
		Building support for cultural innovation
	External	Developing dialogue with an audience
Financial	Internal	Increasing revenue
		Developing loyalty
	External	Meeting criteria of funding bodies
Social	Internal	Providing an educational experience
	External	Addressing issues of social exclusion
		Providing therapeutic benefits

together to align the activities of an event organisation with audience development plans. Kawashima (2006), having conducted a review of audience development practices in the cultural sector, shows the multiple benefits of pursuing such strategies:

- providing financial security
- increasing opportunities for cultural production and participation
- promoting individual development and fulfilment for audiences
- promoting social cohesion.

All of these outcomes are dependent on increasing *participation* in cultural events. McCarthy and Jinnet (2001), in a study of arts organisations in the United States, found three ways in which participation can be increased:

- *Diversifying participation* involves attracting event attendees who would not normally attend a cultural event. Such people will need to be convinced of the benefits of attending, so this form of developing participation is the most time and resource intensive.
- *Broadening participation* involves attracting more people to an event, from a pool of likely cultural event attendees. To broaden participation successfully, it is important to broaden the scope of your marketing activities to provide information about your programmes and events to those who are already interested in your type of cultural event but who have not previously attended. Marketing messages that emphasise price and convenience are also be appropriate for this strategy.
- *Deepening participation* involves strengthening the engagement of your existing audience. This can be accomplished through educational and special event programming, encouraging your existing audience to invest more in the organisation and to become increasingly loyal towards it.

Organising a variety of audience development techniques within these categories gives a useful overview of the diversity of audience development practices within the cultural sector (see Table 13.6).

Table 13.6 Audience development techniques

Participation strategy	Benefits to the organisation	Example techniques
Diversifying	Attracting new event attendees Developing new sources of revenue Generating support for cultural innovation	Producing new cultural forms: for example, staging performances of new musical forms or programming a season of films targeted at specific potential attendees Changing the environment, mood and/or tone of a venue or event Developing new customer service strategies

Participation strategy	Benefits to the organisation	Example techniques
		Programming events that cross over cultural forms
Broadening	Increasing audience size	Marketing development:
	Developing sustainable revenue streams	Pricing structure and incentives
		Communications
	Consolidating support for cultural innovation	Collaborative events with other providers
Deepening	Increasing audience loyalty	Event interpretation: for example, pre- and post-event talks, access to rehearsals and/or venue tours
	Increasing audience spending	
	Extending support for cultural innovation	Educational activity: for example, workshops, summer schools and/or master classes
		Increasing opportunities for feedback from and dialogue with event attendees

---

CASE STUDY 13.3

Battersea Arts Centre

Location: London, UK
Venue type: arts venue
Attendees: various

The Battersea Arts Centre (BAC) has developed an exemplary approach to audience development work. The centre aims to develop participation in each of the three principal ways through an integrated audience development strategy called the 'Ladder of Development'.

The BAC has occupied the former town hall in Battersea, South London, on a succession of ad hoc leases since 1982, but it has now been granted a 125-year lease in recognition of both the role it plays in developing new theatrical work for the British and European theatre circuit and its significance in the local community. Fully 95 per cent of the work performed at the BAC has been developed in the building, and several of its shows have gone on to national and even international success, such as *Jerry Springer: The Opera*.

The Ladder of Development is an example of an audience development strategy that aims to include the local community, develop new audiences and support cultural innovation. It does this by providing space for the creation of new works and allowing audiences to experience this work as it is being developed. New theatre productions are performed from their 'scratch' versions right through to finished plays. The BAC contains a number of spaces, including a café/bar area and black-box-style performance areas, each of which is suited to a different level of audience participation.

At the beginning of a production's life, scratch performances and readings can take place informally, for instance in a cabaret style in the café area, with very high levels of audience feedback and participation. At such performances, audience members are frequently free to choose what they pay, meaning that the BAC has a steady stream of interactive, accessible events running in the building. As a production develops, it usually moves to a succession of other performance spaces in the building, where it is viewed by invited audiences of critics and members of the public before a full press night is held. As a performance moves up this Ladder of Development, the production team receives support from the BAC's in-house team of experienced producers and advisers, who help the event to reach its full potential. Eventually, the production will leave the BAC to tour or take up residence elsewhere.

This approach to development means that the BAC has the opportunity to develop new audiences for its events by supporting cultural innovation. It does this through an audience development strategy that aims to diversify, broaden and deepen participation through the production of multiple, parallel events and the creation of a range of opportunities for audience engagement.

Figure 13.5 The BAC's Ladder of Development

Study activity

Visit the Battersea Arts Centre's website: http://www.bac.org.uk. Analyse its current programme of events using the Ladder of Development model and answer the following questions:

● How many events are taking place this month?
● Which rung of the 'ladder' does each event currently occupy?
● How could you, as a potential event attendee, participate in these events?

13.8 The public role of cultural events and festivals

Cultural events and festivals are increasingly forming part of public sector strategy (Bowdin *et al.* 2010), usually linked to economic development through increased tourism, secondary spending or business development. Recently, they have also been promoted as vehicles for developing social capital and/or community cohesion through ideals of participation and the representation of excluded groups in the public sphere.

Hall and Rusher (2004) set out five perspectives from which the intersection of public policy and events can be studied:

● The political nature of the event policy-making process.
● Public participation in the event planning and policy process.
● The sources of power in event policy-making.
● The exercise of choice by public officials in complex policy environments.
● Perceptions as to the effectiveness of event policies.

Quinn (2005: 927) notes that there has been a 'reconceptualisation of the festival as a useful strategy for the contemporary city to adopt in the attempt to reposition and differentiate itself in an increasingly competitive world'. This new world for cities has been developed through new approaches to urban management that emphasise competitiveness and integration, structural changes in economic production that have seen Western cities deindustrialise and develop their service sectors, and the use of cultural industries to restructure wealth and job creation. All of this has taken place in a globalising system that has produced urban areas of incredible cultural diversity.

For example, the city of Manchester has seven designated 'pillar' events that together form a key part of the city's economic, tourism and community development strategies:

● Enchanted Evenings – combined arts festival
● Starbucks Manchester Jazz Festival
● D.Percussion – a music festival
● Manchester Pride
● Manchester Literature Festival
● Villa Espana Manchester Food and Drink Festival
● Manchester 'Smile' Comedy Festival.

These events contribute at least £49 million to the city's economy through direct and indirect event expenditure by 505,000 attendees (Jura Consultants 2006).

The European Festival Association (EFA 2010) states that festivals:

- Inspire citizens through the arts, challenge and offer them occasions to broaden their horizons.
- Help deconstruct stereotypes.
- Promote a creative society that sustains and develops quality of life, social well-being and equal opportunities for all.
- Boost geographic, social and generational solidarity by bringing people together through inventive and participatory initiatives.

However, one should not view these positive economic and social effects as inevitable. Hosting cultural events and festivals can have both positive and negative impacts, so the event manager must work hard to maximise the former while minimising the latter. Moscardo (2008) provides a useful summary of the range of negative and positive impacts that event hosting can have on a location (see Table 13.7).

Table 13.7 Summary of event and festival impacts
Source: Moscardo 2008

Category	Positive	Negative
Economic	Direct income Multiplier effect Employment	Loss-making events Increased prices for locals Opportunity costs
Tourism	Enhanced destination image Extension of tourism season	Risk of reputation damage
Physical	New facilities and infrastructure Regeneration of rundown areas	Environmental damage Overcrowding Congestion
Socio-cultural	Social opportunities for locals Improved social networks	Commodification of culture Antisocial behaviour Dissatisfaction with event image
Psychological	Enhanced sense of community Excitement Pride	Conflict
Regional community development	Enhanced skills for volunteers and participants Support for other regional products and services	Conflict with other regional activities

In Serbia, the EXIT Music Festival was held for the first time in 2000. This event demonstrates how the political and social potential of cultural festivals and events can be realised in a way that moves beyond the prevailing instrumental analyses of cultural events and festivals in the literature.

CASE STUDY 13.4

EXIT

Location: Novi Sad, Serbia
Event type: music festival
Attendees: 50,000

The first EXIT Festival was held in the summer of 2000 and was conceived as a protest against the Milosevic regime in Serbia, which was seen as illegitimate and repressive by many of the country's citizens. The tag-line of this first event was 'Exit from ten years of madness' – in reference to the government – and it was held to coincide with the presidential elections as a way of mobilising young people to become more involved in politics.

> After 10 years of darkness, people who are not old enough to remember the good old days decided, since they couldn't move out of the country of darkness, to give themselves, their friends and their city some sort of happening to revive the cultural scene of Novi Sad . . . Free concerts, performances, parties, stands and film projections were frequented by the youth . . . from Novi Sad, but also many visitors came from the region, other cities and other countries. 34 large concerts were held that featured the biggest local bands, 12 theatrical performances, more than 120 films were shown (some were premiered in Novi Sad), 20 stands, 40 huge parties, 11 performances.
>
> (EXIT 2010)

After the overthrow of Milosevic, the festival moved into the mainstream, and it has been funded and supported by a range of public bodies that see it as a key means of establishing national identity in the wake of two decades of conflict and of presenting a fresh destination image to the international tourism industry.

The festival today

The festival is held in the former fortress of Petrovardin, a military fortification built in the seventeenth century and of immense cultural and symbolic significance as a relic of the former power of the region in European affairs.

EXIT is now the largest music festival in South-East Europe: in 2009 more than 50,000 people attended on each day of the four-day event. It takes place across twenty stages and features hundreds of music performers. The festival has mainly promoted electronic music and it is particularly renowned for techno, but over the past three years it has widened its appeal to include rock and pop acts.

As well as being a major event in the European festival circuit, comparable to Glastonbury in England and the Love Parade in Berlin, EXIT promotes peace, democracy, multiculturalism and human rights. This is a key element in the identity of the festival as a commercial brand and as an expression of contemporary Serbian culture and identity. The majority of attendees come from neighbouring former Yugoslavian states, and recent research has shown that most of them believe that EXIT has made a significant contribution to improving Serbia's image in the rest of the world.

Sources: Lukic-Krstanovic 2008; Zakic *et al.* 2009; EXIT 2010

Study activity

In what ways does the EXIT Festival contribute to the development of local and national identities?

Industry voice

Steph Walker, general manager, Christchurch Arts Festival, New Zealand

The Christchurch Arts Festival has been running since 1995 in the largest city in the South Island of New Zealand. It is governed by a charitable trust, but is also one of four major events in the Christchurch City Council's events strategy, which means we work very closely with the council. (Interestingly enough, we are only part of their events strategy, and have nothing to do with any council arts staff.) The council is also our biggest funder. The festival is multi-disciplinary, meaning we showcase the best music, theatre, dance, visual arts and ideas from New Zealand and the world.

Usually, the festival runs in the centre of the city, with a busy programme over seventeen straight days, but in light of the earthquakes that happened in 2010 and 2011, we completely recontextualised the event. First, none of our original venues were left standing and the central city was closed to the public. People were staying more in the suburbs where they live, so we opted to take the shows out around the city to meet them. Second, we changed the format of the festival so that it would run over eight consecutive weekends. There hasn't been much cultural activity in the city, so we wanted to ensure our audiences weren't too overwhelmed! Third, we sought sponsorship to make ticket prices cheaper. We knew that our audiences could not currently afford to go to many shows, especially those who were hit hard by the earthquakes. Finally, we revisited the programme. We wanted the festival to be heart-warming and fun, so we edited out any shows that had darker themes or simply weren't appropriate any more. What we have ended up with is a new way of running an arts festival in New Zealand, and we are tremendously excited about this. I always think that an arts festival should mirror the situation of the city it resides in, and this is a great example of that.

My daily routine varies greatly – some days I might be at planning meetings for sites and buildings we are using, others I might be drafting contracts for artists and sponsors, or developing the strategies around anything from marketing to volunteers. I spend a lot of my time ensuring I know what everyone on my team of ten is up to, and developing and maintaining relationships with our key stakeholders. These start with our board, funders, sponsors and festival friends and move on to suppliers, staff, volunteers and artists. I work closely with the director of the festival on the programme, and then with all the other staff members to make sure the logistics of the festival run smoothly. At a certain point in the festival planning you have the programme locked down and sent to the printers. That is when everything you have been planning suddenly starts to look like becoming reality. It is incredibly exciting when you know you have a great festival on your hands!

The main challenge of an arts festival – or other cultural event – is that you often rely on the programme to attract audiences. If you don't get the programme right, then you certainly see a drop in attendance. The box-office risk is also a big worry in that respect. It takes a lot of audience development to gain an audience that will go to whatever you programme in the festival, and when your festival is every two years, as ours is, you have to find ways of constantly keeping it in people's minds. We're trying to use online tools as a way of doing this – things like Facebook, Twitter and regular e-mail newsletters. Many festivals go down to a skeleton staff between festivals, so sometimes this side of festival management gets forgotten.

Once you get closer to the actual festival, the marketing plan is very important. Many festivals will pick 'hero shows' which form the backbone of their marketing, and then do some generic marketing of the festival alongside this. We chose not to highlight particular shows for the 2011 festival, and instead pushed the festival as a whole. However, we used advertising and promotions with print, radio and online media to push shows to different audiences. The great thing about the Christchurch Arts Festival is the wide variety of shows we have, and we want to attract just as wide a variety of audiences to the shows, too.

13.9 Summary

This chapter has set out a framework within which one can identify a set of events and festivals that can be grouped together as 'cultural'. Bringing these events together is a response to the way in which the huge diversity of human cultural expressions has imploded under the pressures of globalisation and marketisation to form the 'cultural industries' from which so many of our leisure and social experiences are drawn. Concepts such as the 'cultural consumer', 'audience development' and 'programming' unify the cultural events sector and help event managers to transfer knowledge between different events and festivals to produce successful events in an increasingly crowded cultural market place.

Further reading

Kolb, B. (2005) *Marketing for Cultural Organisations* (2nd edn), London: Thompson. A very useful, practical book that covers marketing from planning to evaluation, with a specific focus on the cultural sector.

Picard, D. and Robinson, M. (2007) *Festivals, Tourism and Social Change*, Clevedon: Channel View Publications. Contains a range of case studies showing the social and cultural impacts of cultural events and festivals.

Chapter 14

Event impacts, sustainability and legacy

14.1 Aims

By the end of this chapter, students will be able:

- To evaluate the role of a range of impact measurements in evaluating events.
- To evaluate the positive and negative impacts of a range of events.
- To analyse and design sustainable events.
- To explain the concept of event legacy.
- To discuss the role of events in the new economics.

14.2 Introduction

This chapter will provide an overview of a range of perspectives on the impacts of events. Different kinds of impacts will be explored, using examples, and the varied ways of measuring these impacts will be discussed. The issue of event legacies will be introduced, along with a scale of event impacts, showing the important long-term and wide-ranging effects that are the hallmarks of a legacy scheme.

It is through the measurement of event impacts, across a range of domains, that we can evaluate the sustainability of an event and begin to understand the place of green events within the event industry. Event sustainability is the measure of the contribution made by event impacts to positive change in external fields, including the environment, social justice and economic justice.

14.3 Event impacts

Event impacts can be split into three categories, as shown in Figure 14.1.

Personal impacts are covered in more detail in Chapter 3. Suffice to say here that they can include:

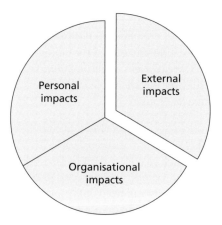

Figure 14.1 Event impacts

- Positive experiences, expressed as:

  ○ perceptions that the event met or exceeded expectations
  ○ satisfaction, happiness
  ○ attitude change (towards the events, sponsors, causes, or events in general)
  ○ fundamental personal change in terms of lifestyle, personality or values.

- Negative experiences, expressed as:

  ○ perceptions of poor value-for-money
  ○ no intent to repeat event experience
  ○ lack of satisfaction
  ○ failure to meet expectations (Getz 2007).

Organisational impacts can include:

- Financial impacts – revenue generation, profit- and loss-making activity.
- Human resource impacts – recruitment and retention, motivation of staff, training oppor-
  tunities.
- Impacts on organisational capacity – growth, skills development, client acquisition.
- Marketing impacts – profile-raising, word-of-mouth, media attention.

In this chapter, the focus will be on the *external impacts* of events and on the interactions between the events industry, the economy, the environment, society and culture.

14.3.1 Economic impacts of events

Economic impact assessments have been used to justify government support for events and in making decisions about investing in the events industry, including the construction of conference and exhibition venues as well as their supporting infrastructure, such as roads and hotels. For example, the Walter E. Washington Convention Center cost $800 million to build, funded by a bond issue backed by the District of Columbia. The district government justified this significant public sector investment by pointing to the positive impact that the construction of the venue would have on the local and regional economies, and the ongoing economic benefits that the venue would generate once it had been built. It has been estimated that the convention centre has generated 17,000 jobs and annually adds $1.4 billion to the economies of Washington and the District of Columbia (Morgan and Condliffe 2006; DC Convention 2007).

Morgan and Condliffe (2006) set out the three steps necessary to develop a methodology for assessing the economic impacts of an event:

1 Define the geographical area under study – this could be the town, city, district, region or country where an event takes place.
2 Identify the industries from which to collect data to assess direct impacts. For example, for investments in infrastructure and venues, you will need to collect construction industry data, while assessment of tourism impacts will need data from the leisure and hospitality sectors.
3 Collect data on or estimate the direct impacts of the event on the industrial sectors that have been identified.

Within this third point, a range of different approaches can be used to measure economic impact. It is important to be able to distinguish between the economic activity within an area independent of the presence of an event and when that area is influenced by an event. For this reason, it is always important to have baseline data of economic activity so that changes can be measured. Three of the most frequently used methods of calculating economic impacts are explained below.

14.3.1.1 Multiplier effects

Multiplier calculations are the most frequently used method for evaluating the economic impacts of events. Multipliers capture the direct and indirect spending associated with events by calculating the money spent by attendees on attending the event itself *and* the extra spending in the economy that is facilitated by this initial injection. The extent to which the initial attendee spend generates additional spending is known as the multiplier effect. As Carlsen (2004: 247) explains, 'The size of the multiplier effects will be determined by the extent to which the economy can retain the additional event-related expenditure in the local economy.' This relates to the concept of 'leakage' – the movement of event-related expenditure outside the geographical area within which impacts are being assessed. For example, a percentage of the revenue generated by a touring performance by the Rolling Stones at the O2 Arena in London will flow out of the event hosting area and return to the Netherlands, where the band members are registered for tax purposes. This is a leakage of money from the event area to another area, so it cannot be included in the local economic impact of an event and must be subtracted from a multiplier calculation.

A model setting out the various aspects of a multiplier calculation is given in Figure 14.2. By calculating the spending under each of the three categories in this figure, the total spending generated by an event can be calculated. This can then be used to produce a figure that demonstrates the impact of event spending on the local economy.

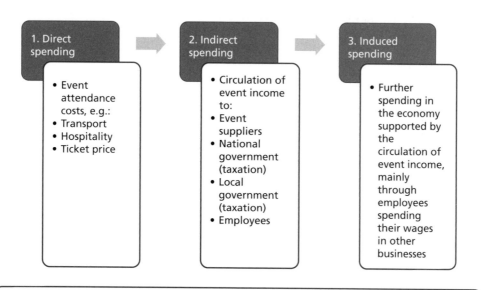

Figure 14.2 Aspects of multiplier calculations

There are two ways of calculating a multiplier:

Direct spending + Indirect spending / Direct spending = Multiplier

or

Direct spending + Indirect spending + Induced spending / Direct spending = Multiplier

The more commonly used first type does not include induced spending as this is usually difficult to estimate.

Dwyer *et al.* (2000) used a multiplier to predict the economic impact of the Gay and Lesbian Mardi Gras in New South Wales, Australia, based on the impacts of previous events in the region. The multiplier of 1.2 was applied to show that for every dollar spent on the event, an additional 20 cents was generated in the economy. This allowed the authors to show that the event, which generated $33.96 million of direct spending, contributed a total of $40.75 million to the regional economy.

Tribe (2005) shows the direct relationship between a multiplier value and leakage in the economic impacts of an event (Table 14.1).

14.3.1.2 Input–output analysis

Input–output modelling has a 'before and after' perspective on the economic impacts of events. The economic data used to carry out this form of analysis come from national-level statistical data that describe the economic relationships between various industrial sectors and regions. In the United Kingdom, these data are collected by the Office for National Statistics and are organised according to Standard Industrial Classification (SIC) codes, which categorise every business by industrial sector. The data show the contribution made by each industrial sector to the economy and give multiplier values that demonstrate how much an extra investment in any particular sector will contribute to the broader economy. By calculating the amount of income generated for each industrial sector by an event (for example, attendee spending on transport or hospitality), it is then possible to apply the multipliers given in the input–output table for that sector to calculate the value added to the economy by the event.

Table 14.1 The multiplier–leakage relationship
Source: Adapted from Tribe 2005: 271

Value of multiplier	Leakages from the local economy	Impact of expenditure on the local economy
High	Low	High
Low	High	Low

CASE STUDY 14.1

The economic impact of the Kaustinen Folk Music Festival

Location: Kaustinen, Keski-Pohjanmaa, Finland
Event type: cultural event
Attendees: 100,000
Website: http://www.kaustinen.net/english

The Kaustinen Folk Music Festival was founded in 1968 and has taken place every year since then in Kaustinen, a small municipality in Finland with a population of 4308. Each July, the town plays host to more than 100,000 visitors for nine days. The programme is diverse, featuring more than 3000 solo artists, bands and dance troupes from the folk music field, as well as Finnish pop stars and 'world music' artists. The festival has grown from an initial regional audience of around 18,000 to become a cultural tourist destination with a specialist global audience.

Tohmo (2005) set out to measure the economic impact of this festival, using an input–output methodology. The research team designed and administered a survey of event attendees, measuring demographic information, length of stay and expenditure on a range of goods and services. They found that the average attendee spend was €133, with the largest categories being hotels and restaurants (35 per cent) and tickets for events (27 per cent).

Using input–output data for the festival's region provided by the Finnish government – including the multiplier data for each industrial sector – the researchers related attendee spending in each category of their survey to its eventual contribution to the regional economy. For example, spending of €474,726 in hotels and restaurants in the region was calculated as generating a total of €612,871 in the regional economy. This was arrived at by calculating the multiplier effects associated with every aspect of the hotel and restaurant sector's interaction with other industrial sectors, including, for example, suppliers, the inputs of the education system to their staff's skills, public administration, clothing manufacture and construction. The aggregate multiplier effect for all of these interactions was calculated as 1.2910. The calculation using this input–output data was as follows:

> Total attendee spend in each industrial category × Aggregate multiplier effect from each category = Total impact of spending in hotels and restaurants: €474,726 × 1.2910 = €612,871

When this formula had been followed for each category of spending identified in the researchers' survey, it was calculated that the festival brought an additional €1.35 million of spending into the regional economy, and that this generated direct and indirect economic impacts of €1.67 million.

14.3.1.3 Cost–benefit analysis

This method of analysis places values on the costs associated with staging an event and the benefits that it generates. These two values are then compared and the event is deemed viable if the benefits outweigh the costs. This is a very simple method of calculating the economic impacts of an event and is often used as a starting point for economic analysis in the planning stages. It can, however, be used in a more sophisticated way by including the tangible and intangible aspects of event costs and benefits. Carlsen (2004) provides a description of the tangible and intangible elements of a cost–benefit calculation, as outlined in Tables 14.2 and 14.3.

The advantage of this method of analysis is that it allows for the incorporation of what economists call 'externalities'. These are aspects of the event that cannot be accounted for in direct economic terms; they appear in Carlsen's framework as the intangible costs and benefits. Traditionally, investment decisions have been made on the basis of return on investment (ROI) models which make calculations such as those given above. However, contemporary events management takes into account these externalities in the production of sustainable events. The next two sections look at two categories of externality in event planning: environmental impacts and socio-cultural impacts.

Table 14.2 Tangible costs and benefits of events
Source: Carlsen 2004: 253

Tangible costs	Tangible benefits
Capital and construction costs	New facilities and venues
Wages and other employment costs	Employment for event employees
Additional essential services cost (e.g. police, sanitation, road maintenance)	Increased tourism expenditure before, during and after the event
Long-term event facilities maintenance	Positive media coverage and images

Table 14.3 Intangible costs and benefits of events
Source: Carlsen 2004: 253

Intangible costs	Intangible benefits
Crowding and inconvenience	Enhanced community pride
Noise and visual pollution	Cultural renewal
Personal crime and property damage	Increased interest and investment in host destination
Resident exodus and tourist avoidance of event area	Enhanced commercial and residential property values

14.3.2 Environmental impacts of events

The environment, in its natural or physical aspects, is a core part of the event product. The staging of an event in a particular country, region or locality implies a set of relationships to the environment which are reciprocal in nature. The climate, landscape and setting of an event venue impact on the attractiveness and success of that event and are, in turn, acted on by the presence of the event.

In order to carry out an evaluation of the environmental impacts of an event, it is necessary to collect data in the following categories:

- Baseline environmental data for the location of the event, before the event takes place.
- The primary impacts of the event on the environment, such as the construction of facilities and infrastructure, waste management and the carbon footprint of the event itself.
- The secondary impacts of the event, such as congestion and pollution caused by travel to and from the venue and the use of accommodation by attendees.

No event will ever have zero environmental impacts, so it is incumbent upon event managers to develop management strategies that maximise positive impacts and minimise negative ones. Positive impacts can include the construction of zero-carbon facilities and the contribution that events can make to the physical improvement of town and cities. Negative environmental impacts associated with events include resource consumption, noise, and the carbon footprint of the event itself and the travel associated with it.

David (2009) shows the energy consumption associated with the attendance of one consumer at an event, depending on their mode of travel (Table 14.4). For self-propelled travel, the energy needs are met through the consumption of foodstuffs, but for automated transport the energy comes from burning carbon in fuel.

Getz (2007: 315) suggests a number of techniques that can be used to minimise the negative impacts of events:

- *Impacts of event travel* – Support mass-transit travel solutions, concentrate multiple events in one location, stress small-scale events.
- *Investment in event infrastructure and venues* – Avoid sensitive areas, impose design standards, implement sustainable development practices.
- *Event activities* – Require green event practices, clean up after events, and educate visitors.

Table 14.4 Transport energy intensity
Source: David 2009

Means of transport	Energy consumption per passenger kilometre (KJ)
Aircraft	6000
Train	2100
Coach	2100
Car with 1–4 passengers	1900–7800
Cyclist	120
Pedestrian	250

CASE STUDY 14.2

Managing environmental impacts at the Bonnaroo Festival

Location: Tennessee, USA
Event type: music festival
Attendees: 70,000-plus

Bonnaroo is one of the largest music festivals in the US, taking place over four days each year in Manchester, rural Tennessee, sixty miles outside Nashville, and regularly attracting more than 70,000 attendees. This event has attracted significant attention for its green policies, becoming one of only two US winners of the Greener Festival Award in 2008 and 2009, and marketing itself with messages of environmental responsibility and sustainability. The event is also highly regarded within the American music industry, described by *Rolling Stone* magazine as 'The American music festival to end all festivals' (cited in Arik and Penn 2005: 5).

> Bonnaroo is committed to investing the extensive time and resources necessary to be a leader in creating a sustainable festival. From our inception, the festival has strived to make the most sustainable choices while maintaining the ultimate experience for the fan, setting the standard in sustainability and greening practices for North American festivals.
>
> The Bonnaroo Music and Arts Festival is committed to partnering with the fans, other festivals, musicians, and artists to effect change. To take our sustainability practices to the next level, the festival is a proponent of behavior changes, long-term investments, and the ripple effect of education.
>
> Bonnaroo's overarching sustainability principle is: local is sustainable. We will use this principle to guide our decisions for 2009 and beyond.
>
> (Bonnaroo Music and Arts Festival 2009)

The main focus of sustainability efforts at Bonnaroo is on influencing the behaviour of event attendees. Kennell and Sitz (2010) investigated these efforts through micro-ethnographic research during the 2009 festival, when it was headlined by the Beastie Boys, Bruce Springsteen and Snoop Dogg.

One of the researchers gained access to all areas of the festival by interning for the Planet Roo eco-village coordinator. The researcher's job involved aiding the coordinator in all operational aspects of the eco village, including vendor management for environmental organisations, stage production and artist transportation. The researcher also worked alongside a group of volunteers who concentrated on environmental initiatives and the promotion of these among event attendees. This privileged access allowed for detailed observation of the event

Image 14.1 Aerial view of the Bonnaroo Festival
Source: Douglas Mason / Getty Images

managers' efforts to minimise negative environmental impacts and the behaviour of attendees.

The festival's environmental principles are translated into practice in three key ways:

- educational activities for volunteers and festival-goers
- dedicated 'green' spaces
- embedding environmental concerns into the core values of the event.

Bonnaroo specifies education, outreach and activism as its primary greening policies; and, in an effort to maintain and improve its dedication to sustainability, it seeks to educate all parties involved in the festival. This begins with providing all Bonnaroo staff and volunteers with a 'greening handbook', distributed via email, which includes a list of festival purchasing policies and greening tips. Through this, it is hoped that Bonnaroo workers will 'make the most sustainable choices from their travel to the festival, to what they purchase while in Manchester, to how they treat the actual site'. The organisers also increase the educational aspect of the festival by: including the Bonnaroo environmental mission statement in all agreements and contracts with vendors partners and sponsors; partnering with the Carbon Shredders organisation to encourage festival-goers to pledge to reduce their carbon footprint by 10 per cent within the year; increasing sustainability signage throughout the festival grounds with the goal of educating attendees about the resources they are consuming (for example, signs about water conservation at each watering station); improving compost collection by increasing the number of manned recycling stations; and engaging a large number of volunteers to educate attendees' on the proper disposal of rubbish.

Planet Roo is placed centrally within the festival grounds and acts as a promotional hub to educate attendees on both the festival's own greening programme and broader environmental and social issues. Various organisations have booths within Planet Roo to inform festival patrons about their issue of choice, while the village also acts as the home to 'ambassadors'. The organisations, ambassadors and festival itself host panel discussions, how-to sessions and documentaries in order to encourage interest and participation in environmental activities and education.

Discussions with managers revealed that they approach greening promotion subtly – through volunteer activism and attempts to influence behaviour – because they want Bonnaroo to continue to be a sustainable event, but they do not want that to become its sole purpose or focus.

Study activity

Based on your knowledge of large events like Bonnaroo, how effective do you think the organisers' efforts will be in reducing the environmental impacts of the event? What other measures could they implement to reduce the negative impacts of Bonnaroo on the local environment?

14.3.3 Social impacts of events

There has been a relatively small amount of research into the social impacts of events, when compared with the wealth of studies on economic and environmental impacts. However, all events, not just cultural events, take place in social and cultural contexts that differ from event to event and location to location. Understanding the social implications of producing an event in a particular location is key to managing its impacts. Measurements of social impacts are usually constructed from resident perceptions of those impacts, rather than through an objective measure, due to the complexity of measuring subjective factors. This complexity makes it difficult for event managers to develop an objective social impact assessment methodology, but rather suggests that a conceptual approach is needed which identifies broad areas of impacts. Through genuine engagement with a host community, event managers might then identify particular areas of tension or positive impacts and concentrate their resources on those factors.

Whilst most measurements of social impacts on a community assess the negative implications of hosting an event, Shone and Parry (2010) point out that events also serve an important positive function in contemporary Western society. The increasing demands of work, the isolating impacts of modern media and the changing of traditional family structures have all contributed to a reduction in opportunities for social interaction. Events at the community level, and those which involve communities in their planning and execution, can therefore fulfil important human needs for association and friendship.

Small (2007) conceptualises the social impacts of an event as shown in Figure 14.3.

- *Inconvenience* – This relates to the impact of hosting an event on the day-to-day lives of a community. It includes such factors as reduced parking availability, traffic congestion, increased queuing time in local shops, and extra noise and litter.
- *Community identity and cohesion* – This element is the extent to which an event increases feelings of togetherness and identity within a community. Events which are based on authentically local cultural practices, for example, will often increase residents' feelings of identity and cohesion.

Figure 14.3 Small's social impact model
Source: Small 2007

- *Personal frustration* – This is the extent to which individual members of a community feel personally impacted by an event. Residents affected in this way feel that they are less important than event attendees during the event period and may therefore be resentful towards the event itself.
- *Entertainment and socialisation opportunities* – This identifies the extra opportunities for entertainment and social interaction that are available to residents due to the presence of an event. These opportunities can come from attending the event itself or from secondary effects in the community, such as increased numbers of tourists.
- *Community growth and development* – This element summarises the opportunities for skills development and other improving activities that become available to a community through hosting an event. This impact can be achieved through community involvement in the planning stages of an event as well as through participating in event-related activities, such as volunteering.
- *Behavioural consequences* – These are the new behaviours that can be introduced into a community through hosting an event. They can include increases in crime and vandalism, for example.

CASE STUDY 14.3

The social impacts of club culture: Ayia Napa

Location: Ayia Napa, Cyprus
Venue type: multiple nightclubs playing electronic dance music

Ayia Napa is a small town in the south-east of the Mediterranean island of Cyprus. Although the resort has been developing since the partition of the island in 1974, it has seen its most significant developments since 1995, when a British promoter began staging dance music events in the town. From the turn of the millennium, the resort became synonymous with a previously underground form of dance music culture called UK Garage, and this small town of less than 3000 residents started to play host to half a million annual visitors, mostly drawn by the music events taking place in its twenty nightclubs.

The development of this music-event-focused tourism has had a number of social impacts on the town. In 2001, a BBC reporter investigated local residents' perceptions of this new event tourism in the resort:

> Father Panayodis Papagheorghiou is one of a growing number of residents who believe the resort developed too fast. 'It was a sleeping, fishing village and the people were very innocent in many ways, they were very removed from the rest of the world. They had a very relaxed life, they worked in the fields, they came home, they went to church, they lived a very peaceful life,' he said. 'Society changed quickly and things happened, and most of the

Image 14.2 Tourists gather in the main square in Ayia Napa at night
Source: AFP / Getty Images

people have moved out of the town to the outskirts and they built new homes. They only come in to work, or to go to church. So, in that sense, the society has also been broken up.'

Andreas Chrisaphines is one of the growing number of hoteliers who fear that the resort has become a victim of its own success. He said: 'The last few years, it has been spoiled by the youngsters who come making a lot of noise, made the families really run away from the place. Measures should be taken to stop this clubbing. The police should be strict with them as well and I think the government should take all the measures necessary to avoid clubbing in this area.'

(Morgan 2001)

Saveriades (2007) conducted a series of seven focus groups with Ayia Napa residents to investigate their perceptions of the social impacts of the increase in tourism. Although residents emphasised the economic benefits of the changes that have taken place in Ayia Napa, they were generally pessimistic about the social impacts of this new form of tourism. They saw negative social impacts caused by imported social concepts such as materialism, sexual permissiveness expressed in modes of dress and promiscuity, and the abuse of recreational drugs and alcohol.

These social and moral importations were seen as affecting the life of the community in two ways: first, by affecting the day-to-day quality of life of residents and, second, by influencing Cypriots (especially the younger generation) to adopt the behaviours and attitudes of pleasure-seeking event tourists.

Study activity

Using Small's social impact model, analyse the information in the Case Study 14.3. How can you categorise the negative social impacts according to Small's model and how could you develop strategies to achieve more positive outcomes?

14.4 Measuring impacts and evaluating events

To understand the impacts of an event fully, it is necessary to carry out an evaluation. This is a process of checking performance against a set of predefined criteria. It is the method by which you measure the success of an event and is the first stage of the planning process for the next event. Getz (2005: 377) sets out seven practical reasons for investing management time and resources in the process of evaluation. It enables the event manager to:

- identify and solve problems
- find ways to improve management
- determine the worth of the event or its programmes
- measure success or failure
- identify and measure impacts
- satisfy sponsors and other stakeholders
- gain acceptance, credibility and support.

Evaluation should be an ongoing process that is built into the management of an event, and it should draw on a number of quantitative and qualitative sources of data. Some areas of evaluation require both kinds of data in order to arrive at a holistic understanding of a particular set of impacts.

We can see from Table 14.5 that evaluation requires the synthesis of information from three perspectives, and it is only by combining these three perspectives that a systematic evaluation can be conducted (see Figure 14.4).

Table 14.6 categorises sets of data into each of these three perspectives and suggests methodologies for collecting this information.

Table 14.5 Evaluation data sources
Source: Adapted from Shone and Parry 2010: 246

Quantitative data	Qualitative data
Attendee statistics, including market segmentation data	Attendee perceptions
Sales figures	Interviews with attendees and staff
Financial reports and accounts	Management notes and commentary
Economic impact analysis	Social impact analysis
Environmental impact analysis	Environmental impact analysis
Social impact analysis	

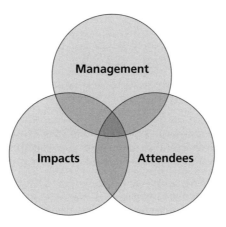

Figure 14.4 Perspectives in event evaluation

Table 14.6 Evaluation data sets

Evaluation perspective	Data sets	Suitable methodologies
Management	Financial information	Audit of financial records and accounts
	Attendee statistics, including market segmentation data	Analysis of booking data Attendee survey

Evaluation perspective	Data sets	Suitable methodologies
	Management notes and commentary	Analysis of meeting records and staff communications
		Interviews with management staff
	Staff perceptions of the event	Interviews with staff
		Staff surveys
Attendees	Attendee perceptions of the event	Interviews
		Surveys
		Analysis of social media related to the event
Impacts	Economic impacts	Quantitative economic impact analysis
	Environmental impacts	Quantitative and qualitative environmental impact analysis
	Social impacts	Quantitative and qualitative social impact analysis

14.5 Event sustainability

Event managers have ethical and, increasingly, legal responsibilities to produce events that are 'socially, culturally and environmentally responsible' (Getz 2005: 123). They also have responsibilities to their colleagues and stakeholders that relate to the health of their own organisation. Getz (2005: 123) goes on to state, 'Sustainable events are those which maximize benefits in each of these categories while minimizing negative impacts; sustainable events are those which can endure indefinitely without consuming or spoiling the resources upon which they depend, including the vital resource base of community goodwill and support.'

The most widely quoted definition of 'sustainability' was set out by the United Nations World Commission on Environment and Development after the Rio Earth Summit in 1992: 'Sustainable development is development that meets the needs of the present without compromising the ability of future generations to meet their own needs' (UNCED 1992: 1.1). This overarching definition is now applied to many aspects of human activity, including business, urban planning, policy development and, increasingly, events management. In recent years, growing acceptance of the probability of catastrophic climate change, as well as research into the social and cultural aspects of event impacts, has forced the events industry to reflect on its sustainability as a whole as well as the sustainability of individual events and event organisations. This reflection has prompted the development of new industry standards and awards, as well as the growth of a new kind of 'green event'.

Since 1992, the media, governments, interest groups and citizens have increasingly focused on issues of sustainability, and in particular on those issues associated with the environment and climate change. In these cases, most attention has been paid to the issue of resource use, especially the depletion of natural resources and the use of fossil fuels in transport and industry. To achieve the targets set by the Intergovernmental Panel on Climate Change, we need to reduce our global carbon emissions by 85 per cent by 2050, compared to 1990 levels. However, between 1990 and 2009, global carbon emissions actually *rose* by 40 per cent (Jackson 2009). This pessimistic outlook for the global climate places a moral obligation on all citizens to act in a sustainable way, in order to allow future generations to live their lives in similarly favourable conditions to our own.

However, event managers work in resource-intensive economies, which place significant demands on them in terms of profitability and growth. Devoting resources to pursue what are sometimes seen as abstract moral objectives can generate difficulties in this regard, especially in a competitive operating environment. Nevertheless, there is certainly a growing sector of green events – defined by Laing and Frost (2010: 262) as an event that 'has a sustainability policy or incorporates sustainable practices into its management and operations' – with the events industry becoming more sustainable in response to external pressure from government and broader society.

Although there is no international consensus on the relative national contributions to sustainable development and climate change reduction that should be made by each country, most governments have national policies on sustainable development. These policies relate to areas of government activity that directly impact on events management, such as transport policy, infrastructure development, energy and taxation. For instance, following the Stern Review of Climate Change Economics for the UK Treasury in 2006, the UK government passed a Climate Change Act that requires all businesses to report on their carbon emissions and sets new targets for businesses and local authorities in respect of their waste management (DECC 2008).

In addition to governments, two other external forces are driving the events industry towards greater sustainability: sponsors and consumers. Companies with a commitment to sustainability will seek to sponsor events that support this commitment and help them to broadcast it to a wider audience. The growth of corporate social responsibility (CSR) within corporations, and pressure from lobby groups, has meant that many large organisations now see sustainability as a core part of their brand and insist that this is reflected in the events they sponsor. Changing consumer preferences also have a direct impact on event management, with potential customers refusing to attend some events because of a perceived lack of sustainability.

CASE STUDY 14.4

The BS8901 standard for event sustainability

BS standards are British industrial standards that provide a guarantee to a consumer or service user that a product meets an agreed national benchmark for quality in its field. BS8901 was launched in 2007 as the standard for sustainable events. The standard is not for the event itself but for the management system through which it is produced. The aim of the standard is to provide a benchmarking process against which sustainable events management practices can be managed, giving the assurance that an event produced by a company that has been awarded BS8901 will have been produced to the highest standards of sustainability. The standard does not refer to any objective measures of sustainability, such as acceptable levels of carbon intensity for event processes or minimum standards for social impact assessment, but instead seeks to ensure rigour in sustainability planning and 'continuous improvements' in sustainable outcomes from these plans.

The awarding body, BSi Management Systems, identifies three 'tiers' of the events industry to which the standard can be applied: Tier 1 are event owners; Tier 2 are event managers; and Tier 3 are event suppliers. BSi claims that the standard can be applied equally to 'all types of events, from the local craft show to the London 2012 Olympics' (BSi 2009: 1), and, indeed the London Organising Committee of the Olympic Games has stated that it aims to be compliant with BS8901 and expects its suppliers to do the same.

BSi identifies three phases of sustainable events management:

- Phase 1 – Planning. The first phase is about planning the event and requires an organisation to define its policy and commitment to sustainable development. It requires you to identify key stakeholders, the sustainability issues and set key performance indicators for improved event sustainability.
- Phase 2 – Implementation. Phase 2 requires you to define responsibilities, ensure staff are sufficiently well trained and competent and provide sufficient resources to implement and operate your events management system. It also requires you to manage your supply chain.
- Phase 3. The final phase is about monitoring, measuring and evaluating the event in relation to the management system and the objectives set, and then taking action to continually improve event performance.

To gain BS8901 certification, an event organisation must be independently audited to ensure that its processes meet the standards set out in the detailed technical specification for the standard and, following a successful audit, the organisation can claim that it is BS8901 compliant and is entitled to use this on its marketing material.

Study activity

Look at the Earls Court and Olympia Venues organisation's sustainability web page: http://www.eco.co.uk/p/bs-8901/35. EC&O claims that it has received bookings on the basis of the sustainability credentials that it has gained after being awarded BS8901. As an event manager, what incentives would you have to book EC&O venues for your events? Could you justify paying a premium rate to do so?

14.6 Event legacies

The concept of 'legacy' refers to those impacts of an event that continue to be felt long after the event has concluded. Elsewhere, these impacts are referred to as 'long-term effects' (e.g. Bowdin *et al.* 2006). Typically, these are measured over years or even decades. When planning for very large and mega-events, the potential legacy benefits are often used to convince licensing authorities and investors to commit to the event. Gold and Gold (2009) note that in Olympic circles 'legacy' has acquired almost magical status in its ability to convince and persuade. Indeed, the majority of the supposed benefits of staging a mega-event tend to be expressed in terms of legacy. In 2007, the Olympic President Jacques Rogge said: 'Legacy is our *raison d'être*. It ensures that the Olympic Games are more than metres and medals . . . Values, partnership and legacy are all required to turn the Olympic Games into an enduring celebration of the human spirit. Once an Olympic City, always an Olympic City. Wherever the Games have appeared, cities are changed forever' (quoted in Gold and Gold 2009: 16).

It is tempting to view legacy in purely positive terms, but, of course, the impacts of any event can be positive or negative. Preuss (2007) sets out a series of positive and negative, tangible and intangible legacy effects associated with staging an event (see Table 14.7).

14.7 Events and the new economics

Following the economic crisis of 2008 and the global recession that followed, there has been an upsurge of interest in both new economic models and new ways of doing business, which will have a significant impact on the events industry in the future. The largest and fastest-

Table 14.7 Legacy impacts
Source: Preuss 2007

Legacy impact	Tangible	Intangible
Positive	New infrastructure	Destination image/reputation
	Urban realm improvements	Renewal in community spirit
	Increased tourism	Increased regional cooperation
	Urban regeneration	Formation of popular memories
	Additional employment	Educational opportunities
	Inward investment and company relocation	Production of new ideas and cultural forms
Negative	Debts from construction	Opportunity costs
	Debts from delivery	Socially unjust displacements
	Redundant infrastructure	Unjust distribution or resources
	Increases in property costs	

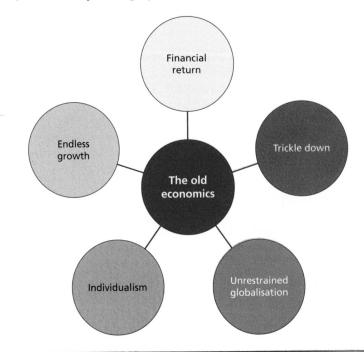

Figure 14.5 The old economics
Source: Adapted from Harvey 2007

growing sector of the industry has been the corporate sector (O'Toole and Mikolaitis 2002), but this has been hit hard by a global decline in business spending (EIBTM 2010). A period of economic restructuring in the advanced economies is now taking place, and the events industry of the future may play a different role in the public, private and third sectors from the one it does now.

The old economics is a way of thinking about the structure of society and economies from the start of the last major period of crisis and restructuring in the mid-1970s to the economic crisis of 2008. In this model, unrestrained globalisation and the individual pursuit of private profitability were seen as the preconditions for a period of endless economic growth. The measure of the success of this system was taken to be financial return, and a succession of policy-makers in American and Western European governments believed that the benefits of this growth would trickle down to the less advantaged members of society, creating a situation where everyone benefited from the financial success of a few. In 2008, as a credit crunch and a banking crisis began to escalate, it became clear that this model was no longer functioning. The global connectedness of finance and the concentration on profitability above all other considerations had produced an economic system in which everyone was vulnerable to the poor judgement and mistakes of a few. During the subsequent period of public spending cuts, private sector job losses and economic contraction, increased attention has been paid to new ways of thinking about our economic system.

Under the old economics, events management was studied as a subject area that had its roots in profit-making service industries, especially tourism, and events management education was based on models from business education. Often, policy-makers would look to event strategies and venue construction as forms of economic development to replace declining industries. The

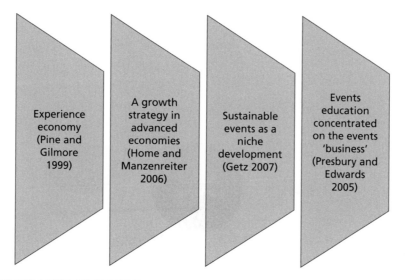

Figure 14.6 Events in the old economics

growth in the events sector was viewed as a consequence of the move towards the 'experience economy', in which commerce and consumption are based on participation in experiences rather than on traditional relationships of production and distribution. Until very recently, discussions of sustainability have been on the margins of event management – treated as an area of potential specialisation – in a way that has mirrored the role of sustainability within the wider economy.

The new economics (Boyle and Simms 2009) consists of a range of innovative methods for growing economies and implies a new set of relationships between the public and private sectors. Under the new economics, financial institutions and economic policy serve broader goals of increasing human welfare within limits that are ecological and social in nature. This model recognises that the old economics did not pay sufficient attention to its environmental and social impacts and seeks to address this through a concentration on localities, as opposed to global growth. It also appeals to the human capacity for cooperation, rather than individualism.

The new economics forces us to consider the future of the events industry in terms of impacts and sustainability in a much more profound way than has been the case up to now. The logic of the experience economy is now being extended beyond the business world, with some authors talking about the 'festivalisation' of everything, or the 'experience society' (Carmago 2007). In this way of thinking, events have a much greater role to play in the public and third sectors as well as the private sector. They provide the means to achieve a diverse range of social outcomes, including community cohesion, educational development, support for families and regional development. In this paradigm, sustainability has to be mainstreamed into organisations and event programmes, becoming a core element of business rather than something that can be incorporated on a piecemeal basis or merely as an attempt to gain market share with eco-conscious consumers.

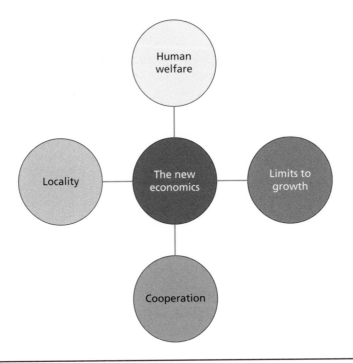

Figure 14.7 The new economics

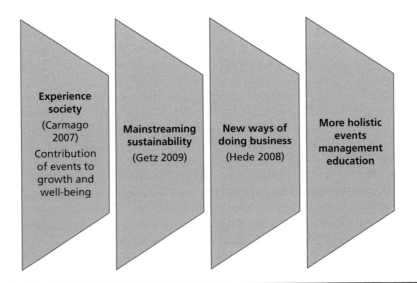

Figure 14.8 Events in the new economics

Choose a type of event (e.g. mega-event, community festival or sports event). Make the case for hosting the event in your region, first within the framework of the old economics and then within the framework of the new economics. Which of these frameworks would be more successful, and why, when presenting your proposal to:

- Local residents?
- Potential sponsors?
- Local politicians?

The new economics suggests that a more holistic approach to the study of events management is needed – one that places events within their social, economic and cultural contexts. It will also require event managers of the future to develop new skills and become aware of new business practices, two of which are outlined below.

14.7.1 Social return on investment (SROI) models

SROI is a modelling technique that accounts for broader aspects of the value created by investment than those produced by standard accounting models (Boyle and Simms 2009). It shares much with 'triple bottom line' (TBL) and 'social accounting' methods in that it considers the social and cultural impacts of spending, and it is increasingly being promoted within the fields of social enterprise and public policy.

SROI is based on principles that emphasise the specificity of the local socio-economic context of investment, and it is concerned with measuring the sustainable creation of social value. It can measure the value of the social impacts created by an event and provides a monetised indictor of this value:

SROI = value of event impacts / value of event spending

The value of the impacts is calculated by focusing on four areas (adapted from Rotheroe and Richards 2007: 34):

1 *Stakeholder engagement* – Event stakeholder objectives are identified and made central to the process.
2 *Materiality* – Focusing the analysis of impacts on those areas determined as important to the event stakeholders, who will be both within and outside an event management organisation: for example, local residents and sponsors.
3 *Impact map* – Using a cause-and-effect chain from inputs through to outputs, outcomes and impacts. Develops a pathway to understand how the event causes changes in its external environment.
4 *Appreciation of deadweight* – Calculating the proportion of outcomes that would have occurred regardless of the presence of the event.

This approach to placing a financial value on event impacts has much in common with TBL accountancy practices. It places ecological and social impacts alongside financial information to report on event performance in three categories, rather than the traditionally dominant 'bottom line' of profit and loss. Hede (2008) discusses the TBL model as reflecting the three interests of event stakeholders:

- economic interests
- social interests
- environmental interests.

Hede identifies two overarching groups of event stakeholders whose interests should be taken into account in this reckoning of event impacts (see Table 14.8).

14.7.2 Social enterprise

Social enterprises are businesses that exist to fulfil a social or environmental purpose. They generate profits, but invest those profits back into the business or into the communities in which they are based. In the UK alone, there are more than 62,000 social enterprises, employing around 800,000 people and generating more than £24 billion for the economy (Social Enterprise Coalition 2010). Social enterprises are alternative forms of business to conventional profit-making organisations, but more entrepreneurial and less bureaucratic than registered charities. This new form of organisation is a fast-growing sector, offering opportunities to develop new businesses within the new economics model. As the events industry restructures to meet the needs of the post-financial crisis economy, social enterprise will become a more common model for events businesses to adopt. An example of an events social enterprise is the Conference Consortium, established in 2005 by a group of third sector organisations, government agencies and trade unions to stage conferences, exhibitions and seminars relating to issues of drug and alcohol use and harm prevention (Conference Consortium 2010).

Table 14.8 Event stakeholders
Source: Hede 2008

Individual level	Organisational level
Residents	Community groups
Shareholders	Government
Tourists and attendees	Sponsors
Volunteers	Media
Event employees	Business

Industry voice

Chris Dixon, arts development officer, Ashford Borough Council, UK

My role is to provide leadership and encouragement as well as enabling resources to nurture arts development and cultural events throughout the borough. This includes strategically positioning the arts and culture in Ashford so that cultural activity and organisations can support and achieve a variety of improvements in local life. My role also includes direct delivery of specific projects and events to continue growing a creative buzz.

When I came into post, Ashford was highlighted as an area of weakness in Kent (and the region) for culture. Therefore, my day-to-day focus for initiating and delivering a project is not so much wrapped up in the quality end product (as a commercial enterprise would be), but ensuring that the project is successful in being a driver for prosperity and social cohesion, stimulating inward investment, supporting job creation and improving student retention – to name but a few of the impacts that cultural events in the borough are planned to have.

Balanced with these goals and ambitions is the ever-growing concern of the impacts of the global economic crisis on our current financial climate and widespread cuts in public spending. However, it could be argued that a recent key achievement – over the past year or so – has been the council's ability to continue to safeguard and extend our local events programme as well as continue to support many arts organisations that deliver on the council's current priorities. We have also continued to secure significant funding in this time of austerity to begin providing the necessary infrastructure (buildings and platforms) to support future cultural events for the town.

I'm currently in the middle of delivering a new major event where we have secured £55,000 of external funding to promote a series of arts and performances under the banner of 'Revealing Ashford'. This project came about as I saw an opportunity to develop the council's relationship with key arts stakeholders, to encourage partners to work together in collaboration and work as a collective towards Ashford being seen from the outside as an influential, connected, cultural and confident destination. Many of the events will purposely coincide with key milestone achievements for the Ashford arts scene.

Revealing Ashford has kick-started the process of artists and event organisers responding to a wide brief that supports and strengthens Ashford's geographical and cultural position in artistically interesting and experimental ways. The programme includes an international collective of dancers from Paris, Brussels, Lille and London travelling to Ashford to create and perform new work over a weekend, reinforcing and promoting Ashford's unique and direct transport routes. Residents and businesses are busy creating and hosting displays of trees and the woodland to highlight the rural identity and green infrastructure the borough has to offer. An internationally renowned orchestra is working with local schools and composers to perform a world premiere piece of work to celebrate the first arts season in a new venue that is being developed. And young people are engaging with a contemporary art gallery that has recently opened in the town to create and present their own films using the latest technology. All of this serves to uncover (or reveal) Ashford's new cultural spaces, connectivity and creative ideas. This upsurge in cultural events will help to rebrand the town in the eyes of visitors, residents and investors.

The biggest challenge so far in this new venture has been trying to bring the wide variety of delivery partners 'around the table' to work together, to collaborate on research, share intelligence and capture data, to improve a historically dormant audience.

At this stage, I'm still unsure whether Revealing Ashford will achieve all these things or provide a lasting legacy for the arts in the borough: for example, furthering Ashford's brand of 'Best Placed in Britain . . . for the Arts'. However, I am confident that we have taken significant steps in raising our game in the arts world, making culture a valued and recognised part of everyday life, and maximising the impacts that supporting cultural events can have on a town.

14.8 Summary

In this chapter, a range of perspectives on the impacts of events has been covered. First, three different techniques for calculating economic impacts were explained. Second, the environmental impacts of events were explored. Finally, the social impacts of events were identified. In each of these sections, a case study was included to help readers see how these concepts can be applied in practice, while study activities gave readers the opportunity to develop their own expertise in these areas. The sections on sustainability and legacy put these individual impacts into a broader context.

The events industry, like all other industrial sectors, will have to change and adapt as the consequences of the economic crisis play out over the next ten years. The last section of this chapter dealt with some of the new economic ideas that are currently influencing business and government policy, and offered two examples of the new business practices that are emerging in the present period. It is clear that the event managers of the future will have to possess skills in impact assessment and will need to be able to apply these in an environment of increasing ecological and social change.

Further reading

Boyle, D. and Simms, A. (2009) *The New Economics: A Bigger Picture*, London: Earthscan. Begins by setting out the conditions leading up to the economic crisis of 2008 and goes on to sketch out the principles of the new economics in a practical, clear way.

Picard, D. and Robinson, M. (2007) *Festivals, Tourism and Social Change*, Clevedon: Channel View Publications. Contains a range of case studies showing the social and cultural impacts of cultural events and festivals.

Raj, R. and Musgrave, J. (eds) (2009) *Event Management and Sustainability*, Oxford: CABI. An edited collection that covers a range of social, economic and environmental aspects of event sustainability.

Chapter 15

Events and the media

Contents

15.1 Aims

By the end of this chapter, students will be able:

- To define event media.
- To understand the role of the media in modern events.
- To identify what is required to manage media coverage of events.
- To predict the challenges inherent in modern coverage of events.

15.2 Introduction

This chapter focuses on media coverage as a mediated reality between those directly involved in an event and its wider stakeholders. Media coverage has been responsible for revitalising certain events and even re-engineering how events are organised and delivered. Media coverage not only increases sponsorship exposure among a much wider audience but significantly shapes international perceptions of events, resulting in important new challenges to their planning, management, delivery and legacies. In some cases, media coverage can overshadow the main event objectives, and even 'hijack' the impact of their planned outcomes. However, many of the challenges that event planners face in obtaining media coverage, whatever the size of the event, can be overcome, and an attempt to understand how the media operates might well contribute to a more successful event.

Event managers face an increasingly challenging media environment, irrespective of geographical location, and they cannot ignore the importance of being effective managers of the media. The increased fragmentation of the media in general means that there are many more points of contact for event planners to consider. They must also come to terms with the new social media platforms, such as Facebook, Twitter and YouTube, which present fresh opportunities and challenges. They must bear in mind that the media have the potential to make or break an event, so they should understand how to make best use of this influence, while at the same time ensuring that it is not allowed to destroy the reputation of an event. The media, while very powerful and hungry for stories, works in a particular way, so an understanding of its rituals and procedures should lead to a much stronger mutual working relationship. It is therefore vital to understand all aspects of the media, its key players and the roles they occupy. The event team should make informing the media an important part of its overall tasks, in an attempt to maintain interest in the run-up to an event and during its staging. There should also be a plan to deal with any stories that might damage the reputation and standing of the event, with crisis management built into the overall event planning process.

15.3 What is the media?

The media can be defined as any communication medium that is designed and managed by an owner with the aim of informing or entertaining an audience (Katz 2007). Also referred to as the mass media, it is a form of communication that operates on a large scale, reaching and involving most people in society. Originally, the written word was the most effective way of communicating with an audience, but then this was superseded by the arrival of radio and television. Distinctions were then made between print and electronic media. However, given the introduction of web-based technology, a newspaper can now be in print format and/or in an

> ### Table 15.1 Components of the media
> Source: Adapted from Katz 2007

Print media	Electronic media	Social media
Newspapers	Television	Facebook/LinkedIn
Magazines	Radio	Twitter
Outdoor billboards	Internet	Blogs
Direct mail	Podcasts	

electronic version on a website (Katz 2007). Such is the rise of the web as a means of obtaining news that many newspapers in the United States are now facing closure as their sales plummet.

There is much discussion about what the media is, and the elements shown in Table 15.1 (adapted from Katz 2007) are somewhat different from those itemised by McQuail (2002), who suggests that the media consists of newspapers, magazines, film, radio, television and recorded music. To this, we must add social media, such as Facebook and Twitter, which offer opportunities to events managers to pass information on to their stakeholders, as will be discussed in more detail later in this chapter.

Newspapers and TV stations, in particular, are investing heavily in their websites, which require a constant supply of stories and regular updating. For many people, the media fills a large part of their social and leisure time, so the stories and images it relays can be highly influential. It is the role of the media to convey information and entertainment to a variety of audiences, ranging from individuals to companies and other organisations (Katz 2007). While the media is not always seen as a positive force in advanced societies, and it is often considered to be too powerful, it cannot be ignored. It communicates with millions of people (Williams 2003), and it has the potential to change their attitudes towards specific events. It is worth considering the various components of the media in order to establish which represents the best choice when looking to communicate with an event audience.

15.3.1 Television

Television is possibly the most powerful of all media, given the size of the audience it can reach. Some television stations are owned by the state, and as a general rule they do not attract advertising revenue, whereas others are owned by private companies and usually generate income from advertising and sponsorship. The majority of these stations are viewed predominantly in their countries of origin, so they usually target the domestic market, although some programmes can be viewed in more than one country. Satellite television companies are generally multi-country and may specialise in specific areas, such as music and sports. Event managers can send information to television news programmes or specialist programmes in order to publicise their events. In some cases, they might secure a television interview, although this is advisable only if they are competent and feel confident that they will be able to hold their own with the interviewer (Baines *et al.* 2005).

It is perhaps harder to gain publicity on television than in any other media, but that should not put off the ambitious event manager, as the sheer size of the audience means that the event may well receive a significant and instant boost if it is covered on TV.

15.3.2 Radio

The number of radio stations has grown significantly over the past twenty years, primarily through the proliferation of new private stations. Most countries also have national radio stations that are usually aimed at specific target markets. A private commercial station usually looks for news items to fit into its hourly bulletins, with local stations concentrating on local events. Event managers should look to establish links with their local stations because they offer a targeted audience and can deliver instant news. The latter can be especially useful if attendees need to be given last-minute information, for instance about traffic delays or congestion near the event.

15.3.3 Newspapers

There are significant differences in the availability of national and local newspapers, depending on the country. For instance, in the USA, there are many regional newspapers; whereas in the UK, national tabloids enjoy much wider circulations than local newspapers. All newspapers attempt to inform and entertain their readers through print and photographs. While they generate some revenue through direct sales, their main income comes from advertising, so they cannot afford to offend the companies and organisations that buy advertising space.

15.3.4 Magazines

It is important to recognise the two broad categories of magazine: consumer magazines, aimed predominantly at individuals; and trade magazines, which are read mainly by people who work in a particular business area. Event managers tend to make use of both categories to promote their events: for instance, details of a music festival might appear in both the *NME* and in trade magazines aimed at the catering industry. All magazines produce reader data and media packs to encourage companies to buy advertising space, and these are useful for the event manager to check whether the attendee profile of their event matches that of the magazine reader.

15.3.5 Social networking sites

Social networking sites – such as Facebook, LinkedIn and Twitter – offer new ways of communicating with stakeholder groups. These sites bring together like-minded people and allow them to maintain dialogue with family, friends or business associates. Companies are increasingly using these sites to build contact lists of people who are interested in particular events or products. According to the website Football Marketing, as many as 14 million fans have visited Manchester United's Facebook site, with around 200,000 of them posting regularly (Football Marketing 2011). Glastonbury Festival also has around 160,000 members on its official Facebook page.

15.4 The role of the media in events management

When considering the media and events management, we must first look at the media's impact on society as a whole. A news story has the potential to reach millions of people within a very short period of time. Such is the power of the media that political groups are increasingly using it to inform the public of their activities. In terms of events management, the media plays a significant role in informing stakeholder groups about the importance of events, while at the same time making some events the focus of their stories. The 2010 Commonwealth Games in Delhi were dominated by media stories of poor facilities and problems with stadium management, even though, in reality, this was a relatively successful event in a developing country.

It might be argued that event managers are in competition with each other in pursuit of media coverage to increase interest in, or encourage people to attend, their events. The fact is that the events industry needs the media to help make events more prominent and increase awareness levels. With heightened awareness, there is a greater chance of enhanced ticket sales. Given the increase in satellite communication, the media is able to transfer information about events instantly all around the world to media partners in other countries. Bowdin *et al.* (2010) even suggest that some events may be created for media consumption, and that a TV audience may dwarf the number of attendees. They then suggest that 'integration of the event with the media provides greater exposure to the event' (Bowdin *et al.* 2010: 638), which means that if the event organisers treat the media as potential partners, the latter will be more likely to support the event. The goal of developing relationships with the media is therefore to generate publicity, which Kitchen (1997: 7) states is 'information from an outside source used by the news media based on its news value or information perceived by the media as relevant to its audiences'. Should the media endorse information in this way, that improves the event's relationship with its target audience. Even murderous regimes have understood the importance of utilising the power of the media: for instance, in 1978, the Argentinian military dictatorship hired a leading US public relations agency to improve its public image in the run-up to the FIFA World Cup.

15.4.1 Media events

A media event is either planned specifically to appeal to the media or simply receives extensive coverage because various media outlets feel it will be of interest to their audiences. While it is difficult to manufacture a media event, recognising when this happens is critical and might even form part of an overall plan for dealing with the media. These events are usually significant, sometimes on a global scale. They have been called 'a unique media genre that results when television's visual and narrative power taps into public fascination with a story that transcends daily experience' (Rivenburgh 2002: 32). People feel compelled to watch such an event, and in many cases a broadcaster and its audience will adjust their schedules in order to cover and see it. One example is when a national sports team progresses into the final of a major tournament. Even though the rights to broadcast the match might be owned by one key media supplier, others will still cover the story in depth.

15.4.2 Media rights

Media companies often pay a high premium to secure the rights for a particular event. The value of these broadcasting agreements is based on the amount of interest that such events generate among a television audience (which, for many major events, is likely to be a global audience). In the case of a major music festival, the media company that pays for exclusive broadcasting coverage will also invest heavily in promoting its involvement in the event and producing additional programmes. For instance, it might make a programme about setting up the event or one that shows its history. This programme might then hold a competition in which audience members can win tickets for the event or meet performers.

When a media company pays for exclusivity, it is important that the event manager does not breach the conditions of their agreement and allow rival broadcasters too much access. So, for instance, they should be careful not to leak stories to rival media groups or even answer every question that they receive about the event.

In order to improve the ratings for its main coverage of an event, a television company might include features in its main news programming. This reflects the importance of the event to the broadcasting organisation, rather than its importance to a wider audience, but it can serve to increase the event's popularity.

Study activity

For the following day-long events, suggest news stories that you think will be covered by the media. You should focus on participants, sponsors, attendees and spectators, and should suggest which media outlets might be interested in the stories.

1 A local music festival, with fifty acts, whose aim is to promote multiculturalism in the community.
2 An international trade fair for food and drink companies, with at least forty countries represented.
3 A five-kilometre fun run in fancy dress to raise money for disadvantaged children.

15.5 The media and links to stakeholders

Table 15.2 identifies stakeholder groups that are important to event managers. Each of these stakeholders can influence the outcome of an event, so the event manager must communicate with all of them. As it is difficult and resource intensive for the event manager to contact such a wide range of stakeholders individually, they can provide information to the media in the hope that this will then be shared with the wider stakeholder group. While the media is listed as just one of a number of stakeholder groups in the table, it is a crucial resource for event managers as it can be used to influence all of the other groups.

Event organisers have access to a range of communication tools with which they can reach the most important stakeholder groups. It may well be impossible to communicate directly with all of the stakeholder groups listed in Table 15.2, perhaps due to budget or time constraints, so it is essential to prioritise them on the basis of their importance to the event. For large groups (such as attendees), media with a broad reach (such as television and newspapers) may be most effective, and these media might also get a message to other stakeholder groups. However, the event manager needs to ensure that they always communicate with particular stakeholder groups in the most appropriate way, which means tailoring messages to specific audiences. For instance, it is probably best to contact government departments personally – through letters and face-to-face meetings. Many media organisations – especially local radio stations and newspapers – are increasingly reliant on receiving news rather than using their own journalists to find it, so they are more likely to reproduce press releases.

Table 15.2 Stakeholder groups and communication tools

Stakeholder groups	Communication tools
Attendees at the event (past, present or future)	Television
	Radio
Event suppliers/agents	Newspapers
Community (location of event)	Magazines
Media	Specialist publications
Financial community/investors	Website
Sponsors	Social media (Facebook, Twitter, etc.)
National/local government	Personal letters
Employees/volunteers	Meetings
Potential employees/volunteers	Newsletter
Opinion leaders or formers	Direct mail

Study activity

What are the key messages that an event organiser should be trying to get across to their stakeholders?

CASE STUDY 15.1

Working effectively with the media: lessons from the Millennium Dome

Location: London, UK
Event type: cultural event
Attendees: 8 million

In order to celebrate the Millennium in 2000, the British government commissioned the building of a landmark project in a run-down, former dockland area of Greenwich, London. The Dome, as it became known, housed a number of sponsored exhibitions that celebrated scientific and cultural achievement. It was relatively popular with visitors, attracting around 8 million over the course of the year, most of whom were highly satisfied with their visit, according to surveys (Paraskevas 2000). However, the total number of visitors was well below the project's very ambitious target, and the media repeatedly criticised the whole event, labelling it a failure and a waste of money. This antipathy seems rather strange, given the large number of visitors and their general satisfaction. So, is it possible that the event organisers upset the media in some way and that this was the catalyst for the year-long negative coverage?

The organisers certainly did not underestimate the importance of the media, and they tried to do everything in their power to accommodate and curry favour with key players. For instance, many newspaper editors and their families were invited to the lavish and exclusive opening-night ceremony on 31 December 1999. The organisers knew that they had to impress these important media figures if they were to generate positive coverage, so they made sure that the editors were among the first groups to travel on the newly completed underground line. This would take them directly to the Dome, and the idea was that the editors would see the new building in all its splendour as they emerged from the station after a short, fifteen-minute journey from Central London. Unfortunately, though, the train was delayed, and many distinguished guests – including the editors – had to wait in increasingly exasperated queues for over an hour. This incident severely damaged the reputation of the Dome's managers, and the newspaper editors were in no mood to forgive what they viewed as an embarrassing disaster.

Nevertheless, after the Dome closed at the end of 2000, the events industry came to its rescue. A decade after it had first opened, the Anschutz Entertainment Group (AEG), a US company, had turned it into one of the most successful multi-purpose event arenas in the world. With a capacity of 20,000, it now regularly hosts high-profile music events, NBA basketball games and other major events, and it is a venue for the 2012 London Olympics. AEG also took over management of the Thames Riverboat Service, which transports visitors from Central London directly to the venue.

A building that was once derided now receives almost universally positive publicity, and AEG enjoys excellent relationships with the local, national and international media.

15.5.1 Working with journalists

Many event managers do not have experience of working closely with journalists. However, along with many other people, they may have preconceived ideas of what journalists are like. Many commentators talk of a new breed of journalist who could not be more different from the traditional reporter who was forever in pursuit of a lead, knocking on doors and interviewing members of the public. These new journalists spend most of their time at their desks, trawling the internet to find the latest information that they need for their stories. This phenomenon presents new opportunities for any event organiser who is willing to provide the media with consistently good copy. Given the value of achieving widespread media coverage for events, the event manager should do everything in their power to make the journalist's job as easy as possible by supplying them with high-quality material. Once the journalist starts to trust a particular source of information, they are likely to keep coming back for more stories.

Newspapers are now being produced both online and in print, which has created even more demand for stories. Events are perfectly equipped to meet this demand, and frequently provide great news stories that are usually well received by the journalists' audiences. Developing effective long-term relationships with the media should therefore be the goal of every event manager.

15.5.2 Working with the media at an event

Given the importance of the media to the event organisers, it is vital to ensure that their needs are catered for at events. It is vital to designate specific media areas where the reporters can produce the material that is needed for their particular medium. This usually entails setting up a press room with refreshments and perhaps even administrative support – all of which should make it easier for the journalists to write their (hopefully favourable) copy. Elsewhere, the media should be provided with photo opportunities and press passes that enable them to move around the venue with ease.

15.6 Media management

Getz and Fairley (2004) considered the management of media at four different sporting events in Australia. Their paper contained interesting observations about the means employed by event organisers to develop their relationships with the media, and these can serve as guidelines for other event managers:

1 Employ a media relations officer to feed stories to the media and create media interest.
2 Advertise in local magazines or newspapers, and especially in special interest magazines, to promote the event.
3 Develop an event website to provide information to the media and other stakeholders.
4 Host media-familiarising tours of the event.
5 Organise media events to involve the media more closely with the event.
6 Monitor all media coverage, possibly through an agency.
7 Keep sponsors informed of media coverage.
8 Employ a professional camera operator to capture images.
9 Create video 'postcards' and stories to send to the media.
10 Employ a photographer to develop digital images to send to the media.
11 Develop long-term media relationships.

This is a crucial checklist for event managers and highlights areas where new skills or additional resources might be required. It is important to recruit the right people for these tasks, as dealing with the media demands considerable experience and understanding of how the system works. Employing a media relations officer will probably represent a new cost for the event, but hiring such a specialist – someone who is comfortable dealing with the media and knows how to create stories – should show a return on the investment.

How would you suggest an event manager might maximise coverage of their event in the media?

15.6.1 Creating news stories

It is important to understand the relationship between the media and advertisers when submitting information to the former. Advertising revenue usually represents the largest income stream for a media organisation, especially a small-scale one, so placing an advert for an event in the local paper will not only provide information for the target audience but help to build up a close, mutually beneficial relationship with the newspaper itself. Some publications also feature 'advertorials' – combined adverts and news stories. These can be a useful way of increasing the column inches devoted to an event. After all, the newspaper's editor might decide that an event is worth only four lines and no photo on an inside page, rather than the front-page splash that the event organiser had expected. Nevertheless, an experienced media relations officer should understand that any amount of coverage is valuable.

There will be several opportunities to work closely with the media during larger events, including tours to the venue to give journalists more insight into the event. The media also now make extensive use of websites to gather information, so setting one up should be a priority for any event manager. Obviously, the website should be carefully managed to ensure that it releases only the appropriate information to the media and other stakeholders.

The event organiser must collect and monitor data about all the media coverage that has been generated, either by members of the media themselves or through press releases. While this research can be carried out by the event team itself, it might be better managed by a specialist agency that has the resources to monitor global media coverage as well as local stories. It is also important for sponsors to be kept informed of any coverage that they have received, as sponsorship deals can sometimes be improved on the basis of early positive coverage.

It bears reiterating that event organisers should try to help the media as much as possible. For instance, an event is much more likely to receive a favourable write-up if the journalist is sent a pin-sharp digital image rather than a poor-quality photo (Getz and Fairley 2004). Video 'postcards' and stories are also useful tools for publicising an event. Some event managers might think that the media should incur the costs of producing such material, as they will be using it to fill their pages or their news bulletins. However, the initial outlay will be recouped many times over if the material forms the basis of a five-minute segment on a local news programme or a half-page feature in a newspaper. The event manager should strive to produce media kits and press packs that give more information than a simple press release, and they should present it in a format that the media can use immediately (Shone and Parry 2010).

15.6.2 Media and sponsorship

As we saw in Chapter 7, sponsorship is an important element in events management. While media organisations sometimes sponsor events and promote their links to them, they are not always willing to promote other event sponsors in their coverage. They will usually mention a title sponsor – if the event officially carries the name of that sponsor – but at other times they will instruct their camera operators to avoid showing a sponsor's name, particularly during

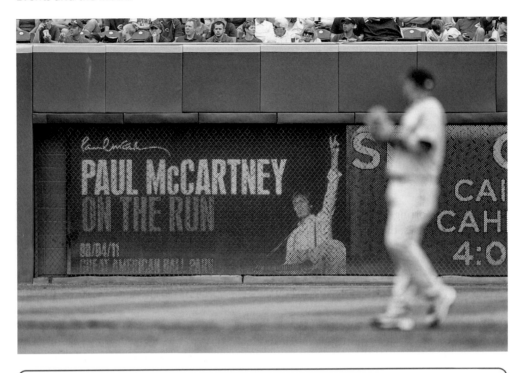

Image 15.1 Paul McCartney advertisement at a baseball game
Source: Joe Robbins / Getty Images

interviews that take place with sponsors' names and logos in the background. Consequently, many sponsors' logos are only partially shown or are out of focus during TV coverage of events.

Why do the broadcasters go to such lengths to keep the sponsors' names out of shot? The answer is simply that they are trying to protect their own advertisers (if they are a commercial station) or are trying to prevent sponsors from gaining free air time and name awareness (if they are state owned). Nevertheless, sponsors will pay heavily for events that receive wide media coverage, as these give them golden opportunities to expose their names to a large audience.

There is clearly a link between the media and sponsorship, and the event manager must be aware of its importance. Their aim should be to gain widespread media coverage for their event and then to use that coverage to leverage better sponsorship deals. Having secured these deals, they should work with the sponsors to devise a plan for maximum media presence during the event. Of course, television coverage of an event like a music festival might also generate more interest in the event itself and encourage viewers to attend the following year.

15.6.3 Media and logistics

One important consideration for an event manager is the area that is assigned to the media, because, as Bowdin *et al.* (2010) suggest, their presence might well be disruptive. This is particularly true when the arena has limited space, as is the case at many sporting events. How much space will be needed for technical support staff, and where will they stay if they need to be present at the event for more than one day? At mega-events, such as the Olympics, as many as 8000 journalists might cover an event with only 2000 participants (Horne 2007). Specialist press areas are created for many major events. In the case of major sporting events, such as the FIFA World Cup Final, journalists tend to occupy areas that are converted back to seating areas for spectators once the main event has concluded.

CASE STUDY 15.2

NBA and European football television contracts

Many sporting events receive significant income through the sale of media rights. In most cases, the largest figure comes from television rights. Clearly, many events make for excellent television programmes that generate high viewing figures, so media companies are now prepared to pay much more than the event organisers could possibly generate in ticket sales. Such is the value of these media deals that the broadcasters wield significant influence over the event organisers and even dictate when some events take place. For instance, Monday night football games – which are now so common in television schedules around the world – were initiated by media companies looking to fill a previously little-watched slot. Many events are now timed to suit the largest global TV audiences, rather than the live attendees or even the local TV audience. This has certainly had an impact: several studies have shown that attendance at the event itself usually falls when a game is shown live on television (Borland and MacDonald 2003; Forrest et al. 2006; Buraimo et al. 2010).

The figures in Table 15.3 show that the television rights for the NBA were around $500,000 a year in 1980, but this has now risen to just under $1 billion per year. This deal allows media companies to televise all of the games, and to show live action on internet channels or through mobile technology. It is around 20 per cent higher than the previous deal and four times higher than the deal struck in 2001.

In 2008, the new TV deal for the English Premier Football League began. It was worth £1.7 billion over three years, covered 138 live matches, and was granted to Sky and Setanta, although the latter went bankrupt not long after the deal had been signed. While this deal is the highest for any football league in the world, it is still dwarfed by those negotiated by American sports.

Like the NBA, the Premier League negotiates deals on behalf of all the clubs in the league. However, Spanish football clubs negotiate their own deals. This means that the two biggest clubs – Real Madrid and Barcelona – account for 43 per cent of all football TV revenue in Spain, with the remaining 57 per cent split between the other sixteen clubs in the top division.

Perhaps the key question, given the annual increase in payments for media rights, is just how high media companies might be prepared to go to secure exclusive rights to these major sporting events in the future. The fact that the media are now prepared to pay such huge amounts suggests that rights used to

Table 15.3 NBA cable television contracts
Source: Inside Hoops 2011

Year	Broadcaster(s)	Value of contract
1979–80 to 1981–82	USA	$1.5 million/3 years
1982–83 to 1983–84	USA/ESPN	$11 million/2 years
1984–85 to 1985–86	TBS	$20 million/2 years
1986–87 to 1987–88	TBS	$25 million/2 years
1988–89 to 1989–90	TBS/TNT	$50 million/2 years
1990–91 to 1993–94	TNT	$275 million/4 years
1994–95 to 1997–98	TNT/TBS	$397 million/4 years
1998–99 to 2001–02	TNT/TBS	$840 million/4 years
2002–03 to 2007–08	TNT	$2.2 billion/6 years
2008–09 to 2015–16	ABC/ESPN/TNT	$7.4 billion/8 years

be sold far too cheaply, to the benefit of the media companies and the detriment of the clubs, so the price might well continue to rise. On the other hand, if TV deals have now peaked and start to decline, this will obviously have a significant impact on sporting events organisers, who have perhaps become too reliant on the media to finance their events. Certainly, organisers should not underestimate the importance of negotiating media deals and should have a clear idea of the value of their product to the media.

Study activity

What do you think are the key developments in events media coverage over the past twenty years?

15.7 The impact of media coverage on events

Media coverage – be it positive or negative – invariably has some impact on an event. Getz *et al.* (2007) found that many festival organisers in Australia and Sweden believed that the media had more impact than any other group of stakeholders. They also learned that the local media in Sweden was the most effective means of changing people's perception of a music festival (from negative to positive). The importance of generating goodwill for an event through the media is also a priority when local government has pledged its financial support to an event and needs positive feedback from the local community. In this case, communication with the community is almost entirely facilitated through media coverage.

15.7.1 Valuing media coverage

Carlsen *et al.* (2001) highlight frequent criticism of the Australian government by rival political parties and the media, who often claim that events have lost money and have had negative rather than positive impacts. By contrast, positive media coverage can certainly contribute to the success of an event, and there are a number of ways of evaluating this. Such evaluation will help the event planner to understand the impact of media coverage and will provide data that can then be used for setting objectives in future event plans.

Perhaps the most commonly held view is that any story about an event in the media is free publicity and therefore promotes the event (Dwyer *et al.* 2001). The simplest way to evaluate this impact is to time the length of the report (if it is broadcast media) or to calculate the number of column inches (if the story appears in print). However, this technique has its critics, and it is certainly the crudest way of evaluating impact.

Cutlip and Center suggest that the first stage in assessing impact should be to compare the number of messages sent to the media with how many of those messages subsequently appear in print or on TV (Broom 2008). The next stage uses generall viewing or readership figures to calculate how many people were likely to have seen the messages. Finally, further, more targeted research is undertaken to ascertain how the messages influenced people's attitudes to the event.

McNamara (2005) suggests that various forms of research – surveys, interviews and focus groups – should be carried out before, during and after an event to assess its impact. However, perhaps the most frequently used method for evaluating coverage in the media is advertising equivalency (see Chapter 7 for details of this technique). This is of limited use, though, because it does not take into account the quality of the coverage and the extent to which it reaches the event's target group and stakeholders. Coverage in a specialist publication about music festivals with a readership of only 20,000 might impact on many more potential attendees than an article in a regional newspaper with a readership of 100,000. Here, it is vital to understand who the key event stakeholders are and how they might best be reached through the media.

Brassington and Pettitt (2003) suggest that media coverage should be monitored for its 'tone'. While this is a subjective way of measuring coverage, the main emphasis is on trying to gauge whether the coverage is 'favourable' and/or 'prominent'. The most effective means of testing the impact of this type of coverage is to undertake attitude research before and after an event to monitor any changes in attitude. A clear example of attitude measurement was the IPSOS survey (IPSOS 2010), which showed that Londoners' attitudes to hosting the 2012 Olympic Games had changed: by July 2010, 73 per cent were in favour, compared with 69 per cent four years earlier.

15.7.2 Working with the events media

Anyone writing press or media releases must remember that the media are only interested in news stories: that is, any story that editors or producers believe will be of interest to their audiences. This can be frustrating for event managers. Their primary goal might be to inform potential attendees of the start date for a festival, but the media might only be interested in a quirky detail relating to a group of volunteers or the venue. While this generates some publicity for the event, it does not contain the main message that the organisers wish to get across. It is also important to understand that there is never enough space to cover every aspect of every story, and the media are usually inundated with stories that they generate themselves or have been given via press releases.

Media coverage is very competitive, and a newspaper might not publish an article on an event if its leading competitor has already broken the story. The quality of information sent to the media may also result in a story not being published or broadcast. Unfortunately, many press releases are simply not newsworthy as they tend to read more like adverts for the event. If we consider trying to generate coverage for a music festival, then the story might not necessarily be the festival itself, but the fact that one of the groups consists of a group of high-profile actors. The story of the festival should flow naturally from this story, but the main emphasis will remain on the group. The fact that you have reduced the event's carbon footprint might not be considered newsworthy by a major newspaper, but a specialist publication might find it fascinating. The event manager must therefore understand the priorities and interests of various media in order to increase the chances of the story being covered amd reaching the target audience.

15.7.3 How to write a news or press release

A news release is sent to TV and radio stations, while press releases provide information for newspapers and magazines. It is very important to follow certain principles when sending information to the media. The event manager should research all of the specialist publications that are likely to feature events, and should consider their exact requirements and the main points of contact.

The event team should be familiar with how a newsroom operates. A local radio station that broadcasts a news bulletin every hour usually employs only a handful of staff, so they are highly unlikely to answer phones minutes before the bulletin goes out on air. The newsroom is a busy, hectic place as deadlines approach, and, as ever, event managers should do everything in their power to make the journalists' lives easier. They should not pressurise editors to cover their stories, because in the media – in contrast to other business sectors – persistence usually does not pay off and it can create the wrong impression. If the editorial team do not think a story should be covered, then that is the end of the road for that story – at least until the next opportunity to publicise it arises.

If an event manager manages to secure coverage on radio or television, obviously they should make every effort to comply with the broadcaster's wishes. For instance, if a radio statio wants to conduct an interview on its breakfast show and asks the event manager to be at the studio by 6 a.m., it would be unwise for the event manager to ask if this could be changed to 8 a.m. Attempting to dictate the schedule to a programme editor in this way will often result in the item being dropped altogether, meaning that the event manager loses precious free publicity as well as the opportunity to communicate information to key stakeholders.

Holden and Wilde (2007) devised a template that is generally suitable for press and news releases (but always make sure that you follow publications' and broadcasters' individual guidelines for press releases, if they have them):

TODAY'S DATE
This allows the department receiving the press/news release to assess its newsworthiness. Never send out a release that was dated some time ago.

FOR IMMEDIATE RELEASE

It goes without saying that you have sent this at the right time for it to be used. If the story is not ready to be released, do not send it.

HEADING OR HEADLINE

Your target publications will probably be better at writing headlines than you are, so anything you write here is likely to be changed, but it is still worth putting down something. Practise writing headlines of fewer than ten words, and *always* include the most important and interesting points.

FIRST PARAGRAPH

Remember that the rest of the press release might not be used (or even read), so it is important that the main facts of the story are included in the first paragraph. It might read like a summary of the rest of the press release.

You should include the 5Ws: who, what, why, when and where:

- Who is the story about? (In this case the event, the team and/or the participants.)
- What are you going to do?
- Why are you going to do this?
- When will it happen? (It is important to provide dates and times.)
- Where will this event take place? (If the release is about an event that has already taken place, make this clear.)

SUBSEQUENT PARAGRAPHS

These expand on the basic information given in the first paragraph. However, try to limit the whole text to about one side of A4. If the publication/broadcaster needs more information, the editorial team will contact you. Remember that good communication is possible in very few words.

INCLUDE QUOTATIONS

Try to include a quotation in the release. This could come from a participant at the event or from a member of the management team, but you should always ensure that the journalists who receive the press release are in no doubt about who is being quoted.

'ENDS'

Centre this word at the end of the press release so that the journalist can see where it finishes.

NOTES FOR EDITORS

Here you can include some additional background information for the editor. You might re-emphasise the name of the event or its website address at this point.

CONTACT DETAILS

Make sure that the journalists can get hold of you easily if they need to follow up the story. Ensure that your phone is always switched on: if an editor needs to check something and is unable to get hold of you, the chances are that they will drop the story. Include details of your website and politely suggest that the editor can find additional information there.

PHOTOGRAPHS

Digital cameras have made it much easier for everyone to produce professional-looking photographs. It is often worth including a photograph, but only if it is appropriate for your press release. Check with each publication which format they prefer. A recurring criticism is that photographs do not have sufficiently high resolution for print purposes. Remember that if the story is interesting, the publication might well send its own photographer to get a picture.

15.7.4 Avoiding problems with press and news releases

Compiling and sending out a press/news release is time consuming, so it is important to get it right. The following points should help the event manager to avoid some common mistakes when producing and distributing their releases.

15.7.4.1 An advert disguised as a release

It is natural for an event manager to want to advertise their event in the media, especially if they believe they can do so for a fraction of the cost of buying conventional advertising space. Consequently, the news release is often seen as a way of gaining maximum publicity for very little outlay. However, editorial staff will immediately throw such obviously self-serving releases straight in the bin. The key to a successful release is to create a story that will be of interest to the publication's target audience while still containing a clear link to and information about the event itself.

15.7.4.2 Poorly constructed media releases

Event managers sometimes send out releases that contain mistakes, miss the publication's or broadcaster's deadline, or lack key information. Journalists are busy people, and they always have alternative stories to cover, so they will not accept such sloppiness. Again, the release will go straight in the bin.

15.7.4.3 Contact details are missing or incorrrect

Plenty of work usually goes into producing press and news releases, so it would be a terrible shame if all your effort succeeded in arousing the interest of an editorial team, only for them to be unable to get hold of you to follow up the story. Journalists work to tight deadlines, so if they cannot contact you easily and quickly, they will move on to something else.

15.7.4.4 The story has been used elsewhere

In an attempt to gain maximum coverage, it is standard practice to send the release to as many media contacts as possible. However, it is important to remember that some major publications will not cover a story that has already featured in the pages of a rival.

15.7.5 Holding a press conference

A press conference enables the event planner to assemble important members of the press, television and newspapers and facilitates a two-way flow of information. Imagine all of the most important media people in one place, all fighting to ask the key question before relaying the answer back to their readers, listeners or viewers. They will generate interest in the event

Image 15.2 Billabong sponsorship of surfing at a press conference
Source: ASP / Getty Images

and awareness levels will rise dramatically. It is a straightforward process and merely requires a venue that can comfortably accommodate all of the invited journalists, with a stage area for the event representatives.

However, you should not understimate the amount of time that will need to be devoted to organising such an event, nor the skills and time required to answer all of the journalists' questions at the conference itself. Also remember such conferences are not cheap for the media companies that agree to attend – they will have to dispatch camera crews, technicians and recording equipment, as well as their reporters – so it is vital not to waste their time with a poor presentation. If the ultimate goal is to persuade the general public that you are staging an important and professionally run event, then the first people you have to convince are the reporters. So you should only ever arrange a press conference when you have something important to say – something that cannot be communicated in a press release.

You must also be realistic and objective about the importance of your event before arranging a press conference. They are usually worthwhile only for big, significant events. The media are likely to attend only if they believe they are going to come away with a major news story that will be of interest to their readers and viewers – so holding a press conference simply to announce the dates of an annual festival, for instance, will generally be a waste of time.

In some cases, such as when an event has received negative publicity, the event team might be desperate to call a press conference to give their side of the story. But you should always remember that you can never force the media to attend, so the story you have to tell must be of interest to them, too.

15.8 Crisis management for event managers

Crisis management (CM) planning begins with identifying crises – or 'known knowns' (Regester 2008; Horne 2007) – that might impact on an event. The next stage is to prepare a response, which will enable the event team to be ready for action should the worst happen. Crises will obviously be of interest to the media, and to other stakeholders, so the CM plan must contain key media outlets' contact details and draft press releases that, with some modifications, could be used immediately. These crisis communication plans will enable the event manager to 'deal with the media in a demanding situation' (Jefkins 1994: 52) and will hopefully prevent that 'demanding situation' from becoming a major controversy. If there is crowd disorder at a music festival, the event organisers should immediately inform the media that procedures are in place to deal with the situation and avoid injury to attendees. Of course, crowd disorder at a major festival is a great news story for the media, so they will not ignore it, but they cannot be allowed to think that it has occurred because of the organisers' negligence, as that could have disastrous consequences for the event owners. Feeding key information to the media might kill off the story before it has a chance to develop, and it also allows the event organisers to communicate with a wider audience to show that their event is professionally managed.

Regester (2008) suggests that an event organiser who reacts positively and decisively to a crisis situation might even be viewed in a more positive light once it is over. The message is quite simple for all event managers: make yourself accessible to the media and put your side of the story, as this will reduce the risk of journalists going to other sources for their information.

Study activity

There are crowd problems at the entrance to your event and ten people have been injured and taken to hospital. Thankfully, they are not seriously injured, but the press have picked up on the story and they are trying to blame your organisation for the incident. Some journalists are suggesting that you could have done more to prevent the overcrowding and a rumour is circulating that excessive drinking might have exacerbated the problem. The reputation of your event is clearly at stake, and you need to show that you are a responsible event organiser.

Produce a 100-word report in the form of a press release to show that you took all possible steps to prevent the overcrowding and address all of the accusations that are being made against you.

Case Study 15.3 illustrates the problems encountered by the media in state-controlled countries like China, and how the Western media attempt to expose government interference in events. In the case study, while the Chinese government appears to be hiding any problems from the press, the Western press are doing everything in their power to highlight any weaknesses. The lessons for event managers are that they must be aware of political intervention and indeed must be conscious of the need of governments that host mega-events, like the Olympic Games, to run them successfully. There is usually some indication of potential issues prior to an event taking place, so event organisers should monitor press coverage carefully and identify any areas that might become problematic later.

CASE STUDY 15.3

The media representation of Beijing 2008 Olympic volunteers

Location: Beijing, China
Event type: mega-event
Attendees: 7,000,000

Many events now rely heavily on the goodwill of volunteers to provide professional assistance and reduce their overall operating costs. Among other reasons, people volunteer simply to be part of a memorable event, to have a chance of getting close to their heroes, to meet and develop friendships with other volunteers, and to gain work experience that might enhance their chances of gaining full-time employment in the future.

Wilson (2000) defines volunteering as any activity in which time is given freely to benefit another person, group or organisation, whereas Stebbins (1996) classifies it as a leisure pursuit. The cost savings to an event organiser can be considerable: as many as 70,000 largely unpaid volunteers assisted at the 2008 Beijing Olympics.

Analysis of the media representation of volunteers at the Beijing Olympics in 2008 identified two main themes. The first was that the volunteers were mainly Chinese, altruistic and friendly, having overcome intense competition in order to participate in the event. By contrast, the second theme, mainly originating in foreign online reports, suggested that these volunteers were ineffective in their roles because they lacked essential skills and instead functioned covertly as tools of the Chinese state to promote fakery. For instance, some stories suggested that they were used as seat-fillers to make events look more successful and also acted as plain-clothes security personnel. Other reports stated that they were mistreated by the organisers and consequently did not enjoy the volunteering experience.

The foreign press also criticised the number of volunteers, their lack of training and their poor language skills. By contrast, many articles in the Chinese press emphasised that the volunteers were making huge sacrifices, but ultimately increasing their chances of future employment. It was apparent that the foreign media tended to report the negative aspects of the volunteers, while the Chinese press countered this with praise for the hard work that they were doing on behalf of the nation.

This case study shows that the international media were suspicious of China's attempts to conceal any weaknesses in its delivery of the Games, so they accused the government of using excessive numbers of volunteers to ensure that the event ran smoothly. The implication was that these volunteers were not treated as well as those at Western events, and that many of them were unhappy with their volunteer experience.

Source: Bladen 2010

Industry voice

Ryan Oliver, support manager, Bozboz

I work in a full-service digital agency based in Brighton. We specialise in websites specific to the music industry and have undertaken online marketing campaigns for record labels, festivals, musicians and event venues. This involves making sure that event information and related marketing materials are disseminated effectively across a wide range of websites and social media platforms.

One of Bozboz's organisational strengths is that we are full service. This means that we are able to offer personal attention to all areas of a project in-house, rather than outsourcing certain elements according to our own particular specialisms. This enables us to have a joined-up approach and facilitates great communication at every stage, from the initial brief to post-launch marketing campaigns and beyond.

I have an incredibly varied role, with no two work days the same. However, I generally spend the first portion of my day responding to any late night and early morning e-mails that have come in. Many days will see me meeting with clients to discuss new projects and ongoing strategies, looking at developing trends within search marketing and social media, and making recommendations to our clients and my colleagues about the best way that these might be implemented within our ongoing projects.

E-marketing and social media offer huge advantages over traditional marketing mediums. You can get a lot more feedback on the success of your communications from an e-marketing campaign than by paper advertising. This is achieved by examining factors such as click-through rates, bounce rates and analytical data. These statistics can be used to tailor future communications and greatly enhance their effectiveness, as campaigns progress by looking at what has worked well (and what hasn't) and troubleshooting according to these parameters.

Social media is a fantastic promotional tool for the events industry, as it enables both direct and real-time communication with your target market and your existing customers. It is possible to field questions and comments about an event through sites such as Facebook and Twitter as they come in. It also enables organisers to humanise the brand on a level that can be very difficult to achieve through more traditional marketing.

Recently, we were tasked with overseeing a social media strategy for the We, The People Festival, which took place on 4–5 June in Bristol Harbour, featuring artists including the Streets, Chase & Status, Example, Doom and many more. In a twelve-week period, we grew the festival's Facebook group to nearly 5000 'likes' and interacted directly with the fan base live from the event. This direct, grass-roots approach enabled questions about the festival to be answered quickly and allowed the fan base to feel a greater level of affinity with the festival and the artists than would otherwise have been possible. In turn, this generated more sales for the event and deepened the loyalty of existing customers.

Event managers who make use of social media need to be prepared to enter a role where they don't necessarily leave their job at the door as they leave the office. Often, the peak time for interaction will be outside of 'normal' working hours. If you are overseeing a social media campaign, you are essentially acting as the mouthpiece of the organisation. Find a voice that is structured towards your demographic, while being natural, friendly and approachable.

15.9 Summary

The events industry is coming to terms with the importance of the media and the need to develop very strong relationships with media companies, but there is still a long way to go. The media thrive on the news stories that events present to them, which they need to keep their audiences entertained. Event managers and the media are entering a new area where greater emphasis is being placed on developing mutually beneficial relationships. The fragmentation of the media and the introduction of new media, such as Facebook and Twitter, also mean that the event manager has to work hard to understand the changing needs of the media, and to develop new skills for working with the media.

New television deals for leading sporting events are driving these events forward, and they now provide the largest revenue streams for many individual sports clubs. The case studies in this chapter have shown how the media have been largely successful in developing top-quality events by providing income for those events in return for media coverage. Obviously, event managers need to keep abreast of current deals, and they should keep a careful eye on how they develop in the future.

The media's role is changing at a rapid rate, so event managers must be prepared to devote time, energy and money to developing their relationships with the press and broadcasters. They must have a good understanding of how publicity is generated, and must be able to calculate the value of the extra awareness that this creates. Finally, they should develop an appreciation of how media organisations work, which will enable them to send out the most appropriate information at the right time.

Further reading

Getz, D., Andersson, T. and Larson, M. (2007) Festival Stakeholder Roles: Concepts and Case Studies, *Events Management*, 10: 103–122. This article considers the role of stakeholders at festivals. It is one of the leading papers in this research area.

Horne, J. (2007) The Four 'Knowns' of Sports Mega-Events, *Leisure Studies*, 26 (1): 81–96. This article looks at the under-researched area of crisis management and discusses the key factors that might threaten a major sporting event.

References

1 Introduction to events management

BBC (2005) Diana's Funeral Watched by Millions [online]. Available at: http://news.bbc.co.uk/onthisday/hi/dates/stories/september/6/newsid_2502000/2502307.stm. Accessed 29 June 2011.

Bladen, C. and McKechnie, A. (n.d.) Professionalization and the Events Industry, Unpublished paper.

Bowdin, G., Allen, J., O'Toole, W., Harris, R. and McDonnell, I. (2011) *Events Management* (4th edn), London: Elsevier.

Britain for Events Report (2010) [online]. Available at: http://www.britainforevents.co.uk. Accessed 29 June 2011.

China People's Daily (2008) China to Revive Traditional Festivals to Boost Traditional Culture [online]. Available at: http://english.peopledaily.com.cn/200506/25/eng20050625_192259.html. Accessed 29 July 2011.

CTHRC (2011) Emerit Professional Certification [online]. Available at: http://cthrc.ca/en/programs_services/skills_training_upgrading_and_certification/emerit. Accessed 29 July 2011.

Dragon Boat Net (2011) The Paddlers Site [online]. Available at: http://dragonboatnet.com/. Accessed 29 June 2011.

EMBOK (2011) Introduction [online]. Available at: http://www.embok.org. Accessed 29 June 2011.

Getz, D. (2005) *Event Management and Event Tourism*, New York: Cognizant Communications.

Getz, D. (2007) *Event Studies*, Oxford: Butterworth-Heinemann.

Getz, D. (2008). Event Tourism: Definition, Evolution, and Research, *Tourism Management*, 29 (3): 403–428.

Goldblatt, J. (2008) *Special Events: The Roots and Wings of Celebration*, Chichester: John Wiley and Sons.

Goldblatt, J. (2010) *Special Events: A New Generation and the Next Frontier*, Chichester: John Wiley and Sons.

Greenwood, E. (1957) Attributes of a Profession, *Social Work*, 2 (3): 45–55.

Hoyle, E. and John, P. (1995) *Professional Knowledge and Professional Practice*, London: Cassell.

Ibrahim, Y. M. (1997) Day after Diana's Funeral, Britain Continues to Grieve [online]. Available at: http://partners.nytimes.com/library/world/diana/090897diana-dayafter.html. Accessed 29 June 2011.

IFEA (2009) The Power of Celebration [online]. Available at: http://www.ifea.com/joomla1_5/

index.php?option=com_content&view=article&id=180&Itemid=306. Accessed 10 May 2009.

Maslow, A. H. (1943) A Theory of Human Motivation, *Psychological Review*, 50 (4): 370–396. Available at: http://psychclassics.yorku.ca/Maslow/motivation.htm. Accessed 29 June 2011.

Millerson, G. (1964a) Dilemma of Professionalism, *New Society*, 4 June.

Millerson, G. (1964b) *The Qualifying Associations*, London: Routledge and Kegan Paul.

Trollope, A. (ed.) (1859) *The Bertrams*, Gloucester: Michell Sutton.

Wilensky, H. (1964) The Professionalization of Everyone?, *American Journal of Sociology*, 69: 142–146.

Woods, J. (2009) Speakers' Corner for the 21st Century [online]. Available at: http://www.telegraph.co.uk/culture/art/5949162/Speakers-Corner-for-the-21st-century.html. Accessed 29 June 2011.

2 Managing event projects

Bowdin, G., Allen, J., O'Toole, W., Harris, R. and McDonnell, I. (2011) *Events Management* (4th edn), Oxford: Butterworth-Heinemann.

Doran, G. T. (1981) There's a SMART Way to Write Management Goals and Objectives, *Management Review*, November: 35–36.

Dulewicz, V. and Higgs, M. (2005) Assessing Leadership Styles and Organisational Context, *Journal of Managerial Psychology*, 20 (1): 105–123.

Frame, J. D. (1995) *Managing Projects in Organizations* (2nd edn), San Francisco: Jossey-Bass.

Goldblatt, J. (2005) *Special Events: Event Leadership for a New World* (4th edn), Chichester: John Wiley and Sons.

Kolltveit, B. J., Karlsen, J. T. and Gronhaug, K. (2007) Perspectives on Project Management, *International Journal of Project Management*, 25: 3–9.

LaBrosse, M. (2007) The Evolution of Project Management, *Employment Relations Today*, Spring: 97–104.

Lewin, K., Lippitt, R. and White, R. K. (1939) Patterns of Aggressive Behavior in Experimentally Created Social climates, *Journal of Social Psychology*, 10: 271–301.

Maylor, H. (2010) *Project Management* (4th edn), Harlow: Pearson.

Nicholl, K. (2010) Glastonbury Loses Battle of Portaloo: 2012 Festival off because Olympics Needs All the Police and Portable Toilets, *Daily Mail*, 16 October [online]. Available at: http://www.dailymail.co.uk/news/article-1321160/Glastonbury-2012-cancelled-London-Olympics-need-police-Portaloos.html. Accessed 12 November 2010.

Pinto, J. K. (2010) *Project Management*, New Jersey: Pearson.

Project Management Certification Website [online]. Available at: http://www.pmcertification.net/. Accessed 25 September 2011.

Schwalbe, K. (2009) *An Introduction to Project Management* (2nd edn), Boston: Cengage.

Shone, A. and Parry, B. (2010) *Successful Event Management* (3rd edn), Hampshire: Cengage Learning.

Silvers, J. R. (2007) *Risk Management for Meetings and Events*, London: Elsevier.

Turner, J. R. (1999) *The Handbook of Project-based Management* (2nd edn), Berkshire: McGraw-Hill.

Turner, R. T., Muller, R. and Dulewicz, V. (2009) Comparing the Leadership Styles of Functional and Project Managers, *International Journal of Managing Projects in Business*, 2 (2): 198–216.

Wysocki, R. K. (2007) *Effective Project Management* (4th edn), Indianapolis: Wiley.

3 Event design and production

Published sources and presentations

Berridge, G. (2006) *Event Design for Experience*, Oxford: Butterworth Heinemann.

Bowdin, G., Allen, J., O'Toole, W., Harris, R., and McDonnell, I. (2006) *Events Management* (2nd edn), Oxford: Butterworth Heinemann.

Brown, S. and James, J. (2004) Event Design and Management: A Ritual Sacrifice?, in Ian Yeoman *et al.* (eds) *Festival and Events Management*, Oxford: Butterworth-Heinemann.

Burr A. (2006) The 'Freedom of the Slaves to Walk the Streets': Celebration, Spontaneity and Revelry versus Logistics at the Notting Hill Carnival, in David Picard and Mike Robinson (eds) *Festivals, Tourism and Social Change: Remaking Worlds*, Clevedon: Channel View.

Clawson, M. (1963) *Land and Water for Recreation: Opportunities, Problems and Policies*, Chicago: Rand McNally.

De Bono, E. (1967) *New Think: The Use of Lateral Thinking*, London: Avon Books.

De Bono, E. (1976) *Teaching Thinking*, London: Penguin.

De Bono, E. (2006) *Lateral Thinking: The Power of Provocation*, Clive: De Bono Thinking Systems.

Getz, D. (2007) *Events Studies*, Oxford: Butterworth-Heinemann.

GLA (2004) *Notting Hill Carnival: A Strategic Review*, London: GLA.

Goldblatt, J. (2005) *Special Events: Event Leadership for a New World* (4th edn), Chichester: John Wiley and Sons.

Goldblatt, J. (2010) *Special Events: A New Generation and the Next Frontier*, Chichester: John Wiley and Sons.

Jensen, R. (1999) *The Dream Society: How the Coming Shift from Information to Imagination Will Transform Your Business*, New York: McGraw-Hill.

Maclachlan, D. L. C. (1989) *Philosophy of Perception*, Englewood Cliffs: Prentice-Hall.

Malouf, L. (1999) *Behind the Scenes at Special Events: Flowers, Props and Design*, New York: Wiley.

Monroe, J. C. (2005) *Art of the Event: Complete Guide to Designing and Decorating Special Events*, New York: Wiley.

Pavlov, I. P. (1927) *Conditioned Reflexes: An Investigation of the Physiological Activity of the Cerebral Cortex*, translated and edited by G. V. Anrep, London: Oxford University Press.

Pine, B. J. and Gilmore, J. H . (1999) *The Experience Economy*, Cambridge, MA: Harvard Business Review.

RHS (2009) Press release, 27 November.

RHS (2010) Press release, 14 May.

Schön, D. (1987) Educating the Reflective Practitioner, presentation to a meeting of the American Educational Research Association, Washington, DC.

Shone, A. and Parry, B. (2010) *Successful Event Management* (3rd edn), Hampshire: Cengage Learning.

Skinner, B. F. (1957) *Verbal Learning*, New York: Appleton-Century-Crofts.

Skinner, B. F. (1974) *About Behaviorism*, New York: Knopf.

Watt, D. C. (1998) *Event Management in Leisure and Tourism*, Harlow: Longman.

Zeithaml, V., Bitner, M. and Gremler, D. (2006) *Services Marketing*, Berkshire: McGraw-Hill.

Websites

http://press.rhs.org.uk/RHS/files/26/26a4dc16-6ac9-4bb1-8295-ed34f78eb57e.pdf.
http://www.bbc.co.uk.
http://www.dailymail.co.uk.
http://www.embok.org.
http://www.juliasilvers.com.
Richardson, T. (2010) Chelsea Flower Show 2010: Field of Dreams, *Daily Telegraph* [online].
    Available at: http://www.telegraph.co.uk/gardening/chelseaflowershow/7763358/Chelsea-
    Flower-Show-2010-Fields-of-dreams.html. Accessed 7 November 2011.

4 Event operations

Abbott, J. L. and Abbott, S. M. (2000) The Importance of Proper Crowd Management and
    Crowd Control in the Special Events Industry, in J. Allen, R. Harris, L. K. Jago and A. J.
    Veal (eds) *Events beyond 2000: Setting the Agenda, Proceedings of the Conference on
    Evaluation, Research and Education, Sydney, July 2000*, Sydney: Australian Centre for
    Event Management, University of Technology.
Abbott, J. L. and Geddie, M. W. (2001) Event and Venue Management: Minimizing Liability
    through Effective Crowd Management Techniques, in *Event Management*, 6: 259–270.
Actionsustainability (2011) BS8901: Make Your Event Sustainable [online]. Available at: http://
    www.actionsustainability.com/news/198/BS-8901-Make-your-event-sustainable. Accessed
    24 February 2011.
Allen, J., O'Toole, W., Harris, R. and McDonnell, I. (2010) *Festival and Special Event
    Management* (5th edn), Queensland: John Wiley and Sons Australia.
BBC (2010) Stampede at German Love Parade Festival Kills 19 [online]. Available at: http://
    www.bbc.co.uk/news/world-europe-10751899. Accessed 30 December 2010
Berlonghi, A. (1995) Understanding and Planning for Different Spectator Crowds, *Safety
    Science*, 18: 239–247.
Bowdin, G., Allen, J., O'Toole, W., Harris, R. and McDonnell, I. (2010) *Events Management*
    (3rd edn), Oxford: Butterworth-Heinemann.
BSI (2010) The BS8901 Standard [online]. Available at: http://www.bsigroup.co.uk/en/
    Assessment-and-Certification-services/Management-systems/Standards-and-Schemes/BS-
    8901. Accessed 16 December 2010.
Cherubini, S., Iasevoli, G. and Lauretta, G. (2007) Events Ticketing Management: The Case
    of the Olympic Winter Games Torino 2006 and the FIFA World Cup Germany 2006,
    presentation at Marketing, Trends in Europe Conference, Paris, 26–27 January.
Corbin Ball Associates (2011) QR Codes for Meetings [online]. Available at: http://www.
    corbinball.com/articles_technology/index.cfm?fuseaction=cor_av&artID=6491. Accessed
    19 May 2011.
EventScotland (2006) *Events Management: A Practical Guide*, Edinburgh: EventScotland.
Francisco, L. (2008) Always Prepare for the Worst, *Event Magazine*, January.
Francisco, L. and Quainton, D. (2008) Second Lapland-Style Attraction Closes as Alton Towers
    Offers Free Alternative, *Event Magazine*, December [online]. Available at: http://www.
    eventmagazine.co.uk/news/867875/Second-Lapland-style-attraction-closes-Alton-Towers-
    offers-free-alternative. Accessed 17 May 2011.
Fruin, J. (1984) Crowd Dynamics and Auditorium Management, *Auditorium News* [online].
    Available at: http://www.crowdmodelling.com/Fruin2.html. Accessed 4 November 2011.

Fruin, J. (2002) The Causes and Preventions of Crowd Disasters [online]. Available at: http://www.crowdsafe.com/FruinCauses.pdf. Accessed 24 February 2011.

Getz, D. (2007) *Event Studies*, Oxford: Butterworth-Heinemann.

Goldblatt, J. (2008) *Special Events: The Roots and Wings of Celebration*, Chichester: John Wiley and Sons.

Health and Safety Executive (HSE) (1999) *The Event Safety Guide*, Norwich: HSE Books.

Health and Safety Executive (HSE) (2000) *Managing Crowds Safely*, Norwich: HSE Books.

Jenner, T. (2010) Whose Queue is it Anyway: A Study of Responsibilities for Post-event Queuing, *Journal of Crowd Safety and Security Management*, 2 (1): 15–23.

Matthews, D. (2008) *Special Event Production: The Process*, Oxford: Butterworth-Heinemann.

New York Times (2003) Woman Killed at Festival [online]. Available at: http://www.nytimes.com/2003/09/01/us/woman-killed-at-festival.html?ref=burningmanfestival. Accessed 9 June 2011.

Oakes, S. and North, A. C. (2008) Using Music to Influence Cognitive and Affective Responses in Queues of Low and High Crowd Density, *Journal of Marketing Management*, 24 (5–6): 589–602.

Quainton, D. (2010) ISO to Create Global Event Standard, *Event Magazine*, January [online]. Available at: http://www.eventmagazine.co.uk/news/975911/ISO-create-global-event-sustainability-standard. Accessed 28 December 2010.

Tum, J., Norton, P. and Wright, J. N. (2006) *Management of Event Operations*, Oxford: Butterworth-Heinemann

Shelby, B., Vaske, J. J. and Heberlien, T. A. (1989) Comparative Analysis of Crowding in Multiple Locations: Results from Fifteen Years of Research, *Leisure Science*, 11: 269–291.

Shone, A. and Parry, B. (2010) *Successful Event Management* (3rd edn), Hampshire: Cengage Learning.

Silvers, J. (2004) *Professional Event Coordination*, New Jersey: John Wiley and Sons.

5 Managing the event human resource

Berridge, G. (2007) *Event Design for Experience*, Oxford: Butterworth-Heinemann.

Bitner, M. J. (1993) Managing the Evidence of Service, in E. E. Scheuing and W. F. Christopher (eds) *The Service Quality Handbook*, New York: Amacom.

Bladen, C. (2009) *Towards an Olympic Volunteering Legacy: Proceedings of the 2008 People, Place, Enterprise: The Olympic Legacy Conference*, London: University of Greenwich.

Booms, B. and Bitner, J. (1981) Marketing Strategies and Organizational Structures for Service Firms, in J. Donnelly and W. George (eds) *Marketing of Services*, Chicago: American Marketing Association.

Bowdin, G., Allen, J., O'Toole, W., Harris, R. and McDonnell, I. (2010) *Events Management* (3rd edn), Oxford: Butterworth-Heinemann.

Boxall, P. and Purcell, J. (2008) *Strategy and Human Resource Management*, Basingstoke and New York: Palgrave Macmillan.

Brown, S. and James, J. (2004) Event Design and Management: A Ritual Sacrifice?, in Ian Yeoman *et al.* (eds) *Festival and Events Management*, Oxford: Butterworth-Heinemann.

Coyne, B. and Coyne, E. (2001) Getting, Keeping and Caring for Unpaid Volunteers for Professional Golf Tournament Events, *Human Resource Development International*, 4 (2): 199–216.

Cuskelly, G., Hoye, R. and Auld, C. (2006) *Working with Volunteers in Sport: Theory and Practice*, London: Routledge.

Elstad, B. (2003) Continuance Commitment and Reasons to Quit: A Study of Volunteers at a Jazz Festival, *Event Management*, 8 (2): 99–108.

Festinger, L. (1957) *A Theory of Cognitive Dissonance*, Stanford: Stanford University Press.

Flashman, R. and Quick, S. (1985) Altruism is Not Dead: A Specific Analysis of Volunteer Motivation, in L. Moore (ed.) *Motivating Volunteers*, Vancouver: Vancouver Volunteer Centre.

Getz, D. (2007) *Events Studies*, Oxford: Butterworth-Heinemann.

Goldblatt, J. (2010) *Special Events*, Chichester: John Wiley and Sons.

Gorge Group (1994) Getting Results in Network Organisations, presentation at the ASTD annual conference, Anaheim.

Hackman, J. R. and Oldham, G. R. (1976) Motivation through Design of Work, *Organizational Behaviour and Human Performance*, 16: 250–279.

Kolb, D. A. (1984) *Experiential Learning Experience as a Source of Learning and Development*, New Jersey: Prentice-Hall.

Maslow, A. H. (1943) A Theory of Human Motivation, *Psychological Review*, 50 (4): 370–396.

McCurley, S. and Lynch, R. (1998) *Essential Volunteer Management* (2nd edn), London: Directory of Social Change.

Pfeffer, J. (1998) *The Human Equation*, Boston: Harvard Business School Press.

Pilbeam, S. and Corbridge, M. (2006) *People Resourcing: HRM in Practice*, New Jersey: Financial Times/Prentice-Hall.

Schein, E. (2010) *Organizational Culture and Leadership*, San Francisco: Wiley.

Shone, A. and Parry, B. (2010) *Successful Event Management* (3rd edn), Hampshire: Cengage Learning.

Stebbins, R. A. (1996) Volunteering: A Serious Leisure Perspective, *Non-Profit and Voluntary Sector Quarterly*, 25 (2): 211–224.

Toffler, A. (1990) *Powershift: Knowledge, Wealth, and Power at the Edge of the 21st Century*, New York: Bantam Books.

Torrington, D., Hall, L. and Taylor, S. (2009) *Human Resource Management* (7th edn), London: Pearson Education.

Tyson, S. and York, A. (2000) *Essentials of HRM* (4th edn), Oxford: Butterworth-Heinemann.

Van der Wagen, L. (2007) *Human Resource Management for Events: Managing the Event Workforce*, Oxford: Elsevier.

Walton, J. (1999) *Strategic Human Resource Development*, Harlow: Pearson Education.

6 Event finance

Masterman, G. (2009) Financial Planning and Control, in *Strategic Sport Event Management*, London: Butterworth-Heinemann.

Owen, G. (1994) *Accounting for Hospitality, Tourism and Leisure*, London: Pitman Publishing.

Phoenix, F. and Wilson, R. (2009) Managing Events, in K. Bill (ed.) *Sport Management*, Exeter: Learning Matters.

Running Sports (2007) Managing Events: What Do I Need to Know about Organising an Event? [online]. Available at: http://www.runningsports.org/club_support/all_resources/quick_guides/managing_events.htm. Accessed 7 November 2011.

Watt, D. C. (1998) Funding, in *Event Management in Leisure and Tourism*, Harlow: Longman.

Wilson, R. (2011) *Managing Sport Finance*, Abingdon: Routledge.

Wilson, R. and Joyce, J. (2008) *Finance for Sport and Leisure Managers: An Introduction*, Abingdon: Routledge.

7 Event marketing

Allen, J., O'Toole, W., Harris, R. and McDonnell, I. (2011) *Festival and Special Events Management*, New Jersey: Wiley.

BDS (2010) Sponsorship [online]. Available at: http://www.sponsorship.co.uk/in_sponsorship/in_sponsorship.htm. Accessed 31 October 2011.

Blythe, J. (2009) *Principles and Practice of Marketing*, Hampshire: Cengage Learning.

Booms, B. and Bitner, J. (1981) Marketing Strategies and Organizational Structures for Service Firms, in J. Donnelly and W. George (eds) *Marketing of Services*, Chicago: American Marketing Association.

Bowdin, G., Allen, J., O'Toole, W., Harris, R. and McDonnell, I. (2011) *Events Management* (4th edn), Oxford: Butterworth-Heinemann.

Burton, M. (2011) Mike Burton Events Management Company [online]. Available at: http://www.mikeburton.com. Accessed 14 June 2011.

Chaffey, D., Ellis-Chadwick, F., Johnston, K. and Mayer, R. (2006) *Internet Marketing: Strategy, Implementation and Practice*, London: Prentice-Hall.

De Pelsmacker, P., Geuens, M. and Van den Burgh, J. (2010) *Marketing Communications: A European perspective*, London: Prentice-Hall.

Fink, J. S., Trail, G. T. and Anderson D. E. (2002) Environmental Factors Associated with Spectator Attendance and Sport Consumption Behaviour: Gender and Team Differences, *Sport Marketing Quarterly*, 11: 8–19.

Goldblatt, J. (2011) *Special Events: A New Generation and the Next Frontier*, New Jersey: Wiley.

Holden, P. R. (2008) *Virtually Free Marketing*, London: A & C Black.

Holden, P. R and Wilde, N. P. (2007) *Marketing and PR*, London: A & C Black.

Hoyle, L. H. (2002) *Event Marketing: How to Successfully Promote Events, Festivals, Conventions and Expositions*, New York: Wiley.

Kahle, L. R., Kambara, K. M. and Rose, G. M. (1996) A Functional Model of Fan Attendance Motivations for College Football, *Sport Marketing Quarterly*, 5 (4): 51–60.

Kim, N. and Chalip, L. (2004) Why Travel to the FIFA World Cup? Effects of Motives, Background, Interest and Constraints, *Tourism Management*, 25: 695–707.

Lagae, W. (2005) *Sports Sponsorship and Marketing Communications: A European Perspective*, London: Prentice-Hall.

Lovelock, C. and Gummerson, E. (2004) Whither Services Marketing? In Search of a New Paradigm and Fresh Perspectives, *Journal of Service Research*, 7 (1): 20–41.

McDonald, M. and Wilson, H. (2011) *Marketing Plans: How to Prepare Them, How to Use Them* (7th edn), London: Wiley.

Melnick, M. J. (1993) Searching for Sociability in the Stands: A Theory of Sports Spectating, *Journal of Sport Management*, 7, 1: 44–60.

Mintel (2006) *Sponsorship*, London: Mintel International Group Limited.

Mintel (2009) *Sports Sponsorship*, London: Mintel International Group Limited.

Nicholson, R. E. and Pearce, D. G. (2001) Why Do People Attend Events: A Comparative Analysis of Visitor Motivations at Four South Island Events, *Journal of Travel Research*, 39: 449–460.

O'Neill, M., Getz, D. and Carlsen, J. (1999) Evaluation of Service Quality at Events: The 1998 Coca-Cola Masters Surfing Event at Margaret River, Western Australia, *Managing Service Quality*, 9 (3): 156–165.

Rines, S. (2002) Guinness Rugby World Cup Sponsorship: A Global Platform for Meeting Business Objectives, *International Journal of Sports Marketing and Sponsorship*, 4: 449–465.

Skinner, B. E. and Rukavina, V. (2003) *Event Sponsorship*, New York: Wiley.

Sneath, J. Z., Zachary Finney, R. and Close, A. G. (2005) An IMC Approach to Event Marketing: The Effects of Sponsorship and Experience on Customer Attitudes, *Journal of Advertising Research*, December: 373–381

Solomon, J, (2002) *An Insider's Guide to Managing Sporting Events*, Champaign: Human Kinetics.

Stotlar, D. (2005) *Developing Successful Sports Marketing Plans*, Morgantown: Fitness Information Technology.

Topping, A., Collinson, P. and Walsh, F. (2011) Olympics: Man Gets £11,000 of Tickets after Bidding for £36,000', *Guardian* [online]. Available at: http://www.guardian.co.uk/sport/2011/jun/01/olympics-man-wins-tickets-bidding. Accessed 29 August 2011.

Wakefield, K. L. (2007) *Team Sports Marketing*, Oxford: Butterworth-Heinemann.

8 Event health, safety and risk management

Published and general online sources

Abbott, J. L. and Abbott, S. M. (2000) The Importance of Proper Crowd Management and Crowd Control in the Special Events Industry, in J. Allen, R. Harris, L. K. Jago and A. J. Veal (eds) *Events beyond 2000: Setting the Agenda, Proceedings of the Conference on Evaluation, Research and Education, Sydney, July 2000*, Sydney: Australian Centre for Event Management, University of Technology.

Abbott, J. L. and Geddie, M. W. (2001) Event and Venue Management: Minimizing Liability through Effective Crowd Management Techniques, *Event Management*, 6: 259–270.

AEO, BECA and EVA (2002) *The Guide to Managing Health and Safety at Exhibitions and Events: 'The Red Book'* (2nd edn), Berkhamstead: AEO, BECA and EVA.

AEO, AEV and ESSA (2010) *E-Guide 2010* [online]. Available at: http://www.aeo.org.uk/files/eguide_2011_version1.pdf. Accessed 4 November 2011.

Al-Bab.com (2011) The Hajj Pilgrimage to Mecca [online]. Available at: http://www.al-bab.com/arab/background/hajj.htm. Accessed 9 June 2011.

Allen, J., O'Toole, W., Harris, R. and McDonnell, I. (2008) *Festival and Special Event Management* (4th edn), Queensland: John Wiley and Sons.

BBC (2001) Hajj Perils, Ancient and Modern [online]. Available at: http://news.bbc.co.uk/1/hi/world/middle_east/1203697.stm. Accessed 9 June 2011.

BBC (2008) Scores Die in India Temple Crush [online]. Available at: http://news.bbc.co.uk/1/hi/world/south_asia/7643373.stm. Accessed 9 June 2011.

Big Lunch, The (2011) About the Big Lunch [online]. Available at: http://www.thebiglunch.com. Accessed 9 June 2011.

Bowdin, G., Allen, J., O'Toole, W., Harris, R. and McDonnell, I. (2010) *Events Management* (3rd edn), Oxford: Butterworth-Heinemann.

Challis, B. (2009) After the Great White Tragedy: Where Now with the Crowd Safety Legislation?, *Music Law Updates*, December [online]. Available at: http://www.musiclawupdates.com/articles/ARTICLE%2009GreatWhite.htm. Accessed 9 June 2011.

Cornish, S. C. (2010) An Examination of the Crowd Management of Traditional Events: Prospects for the 21st Century, *Journal of Crowd Safely and Security Management*, 2 (1): 6–14.

Crowd Dynamics (2011) Website [online]. Available at: http://www.crowddynamics.com. Accessed 14 February 2011.

References

Glastonbury Festivals (2002) *The Report of the Licensing Working Group* [online]. Available at: http://www.glastonburyfestivals.co.uk/_assets/pdf/educational-resources/3TheReview.pdf. Accessed 9 June 2011.

Glastonbury Festivals (2011) *Crowd Control* [online]. Available at: http://www.glastonbury festivals.co.uk/_assets/pdf/educational-resources/10CrowdControl.pdf. Accessed 9 June 2011.

Hartley, H. (2002) A Party on the River: The 1989 *Marchioness* Disaster: Regulation of Safety on the River Thames and the 'Political Economy' of Risk, *World Leisure Journal*, 44 (4): 30–43.

Health and Safety at Work Act (1974). Available at: http://www.legislation.gov.uk/ukpga/1974/37/contents. Accessed 9 June 2011.

Health and Safety Executive (HSE) (1999) *The Event Safety Guide*, Norwich: HSE.

Health and Safety Executive (HSE) (2000) *Managing Crowds Safely: A Guide for Organisers at Events and Venues*, Norwich: HSE.

Health and Safety Executive (HSE) (2002) *COSHH: A Brief Guide to the Regulations*, Norwich: HSE.

Health and Safety Executive (HSE) (2003) *Health and Safety Regulations: A Short Guide*, Norwich: HSE.

Health and Safety Executive (HSE) (2009) *Working with Substances Hazardous to Health: What You Need to Know about COSHH*, Norwich: HSE.

Health and Safety Executive (HSE) (2010) Example Risk Assessment for a Village Hall [online]. Available at: http://www.hse.gov.uk/risk/casestudies/villagehall.htm. Accessed 12 February 2010.

Health and Safety Executive (HSE) (2011) *Five Steps to Risk Assessment*, Norwich: HSE.

Hede, A. (2007) Managing Special Events in the New Era of the Triple Bottom Line, *Event Management*, 11: 13–22.

Lenton, S., Boys, A. and Nothcross, K. (1997) Raves, Drugs and Experience: Drug Use by a Sample of People who Attend Raves in Western Australia, *Addiction*, 92 (10): 1327–1337.

Maritime and Coastguard Agency (2005) *Formal Safety Assessment & Research Projects of Domestic Passenger Vessel Standards*, London: HMSO.

NFPA (2011) Nightclubs/Assembly Occupancies [online]. Available at: http://www.nfpa.org/itemDetail.asp?categoryID=633&itemID=21073&cookie%5Ftest=1. Accessed 9 June 2011.

Robideaux, C. (2009) Wrongful Death Suit Settled Involving Wal-Mart 'Black Friday' Stampede [online]. Available at: http://www.youtube.com/watch?v=Wsa4BYcwII0. Accessed 9 June 2011.

Shone, A. and Parry, B. (2010) *Successful Event management* (3rd edn), Hampshire: Cengage Learning.

Silvers, J. (2004) *Professional Event Coordination*, New Jersey: John Wiley and Sons.

Slapper, G. (2007) Corporate Manslaughter Law is a Vast Improvement, *The Times* [online]. Available at: http://business.timesonline.co.uk/tol/business/law/article2097907.ece. Accessed 28 December 2010.

Sky News (2010) Cambodia: 456 Dead in Festival Stampede [online]. Available at: http://news.sky.com/skynews/Home/World-News/Cambodia-Stampede-Kills-378-People-In-Phnom-Penh-During-Water-Festival-Say-Officials/Article/201011415822127?lid=NewsYourWay_ARTICLE_15822127_Cambodia_Stampede_Kills_378_People_In_Phnom_Penh_During_Water_Festival_Say_Officials. Accessed 9 June 2011.

Tarlow, P. E. (2002) *Event Risk Management and Safety*, Chichester: John Wiley and Sons.

Tum, J., Norton, P. and Wright, J. N. (2006) *Management of Event Operations*, Oxford: Butterworth-Heinemann.

Upton, M. (2008) *Safe Event Management*, paper presented at Theatre Managers Association Conference, 10 June. Available at: http://www.crowdmodelling.com/2008_upton.pdf. Accessed 4 November 2011.

USA Today (2008) RI Club Fire Released from Prison [online]. Available at: http://www.usatoday.com/news/nation/2008-03-19-4281531984_x.htm. Accessed 9 June 2011.

YouTube sources

Deputy Collector Revokes Permission Granted for Chakraview Music Festival in Agonda. Available at: http://www.youtube.com/watch?v=Yevh3NNYnmI. Accessed 9 June 2011.

German Love Parade Raw Video Footage from Associated Press. Available at: http://www.youtube.com/watch?v=4WnV74PW4bo&feature=related (images and comments may be disturbing). Accessed 9 June 2011.

German Love Parade Stampede Kills 18. Available at: http://www.youtube.com/watch?v=YwxBRrY8Vco. Accessed 9 June 2011.

Sky Sports News: Hillsborough Disaster 20th Anniversary. Available at: http://www.youtube.com/watch?v=pPAD1Q2jzVI. Accessed 9 June 2011.

Stampede Kills 378 during Cambodian Festival. Available at: http://www.youtube.com/watch?v=3_VqI2TY-H0. Accessed 9 June 2011.

The Big Lunch 2011. Available at: http://www.youtube.com/watch?v=jG6KorBRRkc. Accessed 9 June 2011.

Wal-Mart Stampede Death Lawsuit. Available at: http://www.youtube.com/watch?v=Wsa4BYcwlI0. Accessed 9 June 2011.

9 Sporting events

Published sources and presentations

Agrawal, J. and Kamakura, W. A. (1995) The Economic Worth of Celebrity Endorsers: An Event Study Analysis, *Journal of Marketing*, 59: 56–62.

Amato, C. H., Okelshen-Peters, C. L. and Shao, A. T. (2005) An Exploratory Investigation into NASCAR Fan Culture, *Sport Marketing Quarterly*, 142: 71–83.

Ambrose, P. J. (2004) Drug Use in Sports: A Veritable Arena for Pharmacists, *Journal of the American Pharmacists Association*, 44 (4): 501–516.

Andersson, T. (2001) Swedish Football Hooliganism 1900–1939, *Soccer and Society*, 2 (1): 1–18.

Arnett, D. B. and Laverie, D. A. (2000) Fan Characteristics and Sporting Event Attendance Examining Variance in Attendance, *International Journal of Sports Marketing and Sponsorship*, 23: 219–238.

Barget, E. and Gouguet, J.-J. (2007) The Total Economic Value of Sporting Events: Theory and Practice, *Journal of Sports Economics*, 8 (2): 165–182.

Beckett, A. H. and Cowan, D. A. (1979) Misuse of Drugs in Sport, *British Journal of Sports Medicine*, 12: 185–194.

Branscombe, N. R. and Wann, D. L. (1991) The Positive Social and Self-Concept Consequences of Sports Team Identification, *Journal of Sport and Social Issues*, 152: 115–127.

Bush, V. D., Bush, A. J., Clark, P. and Bush, R. P. (2005) Girl Power and Word-of-Mouth Behaviour in the Flourishing Sports Market, *Journal of Consumer Marketing*, 22 (5): 257–264.

References

Cousens, L., Babiak, K. and Slack, T. (2001) Adopting a Relationship Marketing Paradigm: The Case of the National Basketball Association, *International Journal of Sports Marketing and Sponsorship*, 2: 331–355.

Crawford, M., Donnelly, J., Gordon, J., MacCallum, R., MacDonald, I., McNeil, M., Mulhearn, N., Tilston, S. and West, G. (2001) An Analysis of Consultations with the Crowd Doctors at Glasgow Celtic Football Club, Season 1999–2000, *British Journal of Sports Medicine*, 35: 245–250.

Crespo, A. H., Garcia de los Salmones, M. M., Agudi San Emeterio, A. and del Bosque, R. (2003) Analisís de los Factores de la Calidad Percibida en los Espectaculos Deportivos Aplicación al Fútbol Professional, paper presented at the Congreso Mundial de Gestión Económica del Deporte, Barcelona, 14–15 May.

Dickie, J. F. (1995) Major Crowd Catastrophes, *Safety Science*, 18: 309–320.

Duke, V. and Crolley, L. (1994) *Argy-Bargy at the Match: Football Spectator Behaviour in Argentina*, European Studies Research Unit Working Paper, University of Salford.

Duke, V. and Crolley, L. (2001) Fútbol, Politicians and the People: Populism and Politics in Argentina, *International Journal of the History of Sport*, 18 (3): 93–116.

Emery, P. R. (2002) Bidding to Host a Major Sports Event: The Local Organising Committee Perspective, *International Journal of Public Sector Management*, 15 (4): 316–355.

Giulianotti, R. (2002) Supporters, Followers, Fans and Flaneurs: A Taxonomy of Spectator Identities in Football, *Journal of Sport and Social Issues*, 261: 25–46.

Hamilton, G. (2004) Watch Boca Juniors Play River Plate in Buenos Aires, *Observer*, 4 April.

Hightower, R., Brady, M. K. and Baker, T. L. (2002) Investigating the Role of the Physical Environment in Hedonic Service Consumption: An Exploratory Study of Sporting Events, *Journal of Business Research*, 55: 697–707.

Humphreys, B. R. and Ruseski, J. E. (2008) Estimates of the Size of the Sports Industry in the United States, paper presented to the International Association of Sports Economists, Gijon, Spain, 8–11 August.

Hunt, K.A., Bristol, T. and Bashaw, R. E. (1999) A Conceptual Approach to Classifying Sports Fans, *Journal of Services Marketing*, 136: 439–452.

Jowdy, E. and McDonald, M. A. (2003) Relationship Marketing and International Fan Festivals, *International Journal of Sports Marketing and Sponsorship*, 4: 295–312.

King, A. (1997) The Lads' Masculinity and the New Consumption of Football, *Sociology*, 31 (2): 329–346.

Lowry, T. (2004) The Prince of NASCAR, *Business Week*, 3871: 90.

Malcolm, D. (2002) Football Business and Football Communities in the Twenty-first Century, *Soccer and Society*, 13: 102–113.

Masterman, G. (2009) *Strategic Sports Management* (Olympic edn), Oxford: Butterworth-Heinemann.

Pennington-Gray, L. and Holdnak, A. (2002) Out of the Stands and into the Community: Using Sports Events to Promote a Destination, *Events Management*, 7: 177–186.

Preuss, H. (2005) The Economic Impact of Visitors at Major Multi-sport Events, *European Sport Management Quarterly*, 5 (3): 281–301.

Preuss, H. and Solberg, H. A. (2006) Attracting Major Sporting Events: The Role of Local Residents, *European Sport Management Quarterly*, 6 (4): 391–411.

Redhead, S. (1997) *Post-Fandom and the Millennial Blues: The Transformation of Soccer Culture*, London: Routledge.

Sandvoss, C. (2003) *A Game of Two Halves: Football, Television and Globalization*, London and New York: Routledge.

Small, K. (2007) Social Dimensions of Community Festivals: An Application of Factor Analysis in the Development of the Social Impact Perception (SIP) Scale, *Event Management*, 11: 45–55.

Spencer, N. E. (2004) Sister Act VI: Venus and Serena Williams at Indian Wells: 'Sincere Fictions' and White Racism, *Journal of Sport and Social Issues*, 28 (2): 115–135.

Stewart, B. Smith, A. C. T. and Nicholson, M. (2003) Sport Consumer Typologies: A Critical Review, *Sport Marketing Quarterly*, 12: 206–216.

Sutton, W. A., McDonald, M. A. and Milne, G. R. (1997) Creating and Fostering Fan Identification in Professional Sports, *Sport Marketing Quarterly*, 61: 15–22.

Tanaka, T. (2004) The Positioning and Practices of the 'Feminized Fan' in Japanese Soccer Culture through the Experience of the FIFA World Cup Korea/Japan 2002, *Inter-Asia Cultural Studies*, 51: 52–62.

Tapp, A. and Clowes, J. (2002) From 'Carefree Casuals' to 'Professional Supporter', *European Journal of Marketing*, 3611 (12): 1248–1269.

Tomlinson, M., Buttle, F. and Moores, B. (1995) The Fan as Customer: Customer Services in Sports Marketing, *Journal of Hospitality and Leisure Marketing*, 3 (1): 19–36.

Wakefield, K. L. and Sloan, H. J. (1995) The Effects of Team Loyalty and Selected Stadium Factors on Spectator Attendance, *Journal of Sport Management*, 9 (2): 153–172.

Westerbeek, H. M., Turner, P. and Ingerson, L. (2002) Key Success Factors in Bidding for Hallmark Sporting Events, *International Marketing Review*, 19 (3): 303–322.

Wilde, N, (2009) Interview with Orlando Salvestrini, President of Marketing, Boca Juniors, *International Journal of Sports Marketing and Sponsorship*, 10 (3): 2–5.

Wong, L. L. and Trumper, R. (2002) Global Celebrity Athletes and Nationalism: Fútbol, Hockey and the Representation of Nations, *Journal of Sport and Social Issues*, 26 (2): 188–194.

Websites

Charlton Athletic Community Trust: www.cact.org.uk.

FA: www.thefa.com/TheFA/England2018.

FIFA: www.fifa.com/mm/51/53/98/safetyregulations.

Guardian: www.guardian.co.uk/football/2010/dec/02/mike-lee-qatar-world-cup-bid.

Managing sporting events: www.helpforclubs.org.uk.

New York Yankees: www.newyork-yankees.mlb.com.

Olympic Games: www.olympic.org.

Phoenix Suns: www.nba.com/suns.

Sheffield Hallam FC: www.theoldestfootballgroundintheworld.com/history.

Sport Business magazine: www.sportbusiness.com.

10 Mega-events

Andranovich, G., Burbank, M. and Heying, C. (2001) Olympic Cities: Lessons Learned from Mega-event Politics, *Urban Affairs*, 23 (2): 113–131.

Atkinson, G., Mourato, S., Symanski, S. and Ozdemiroglu, E. (2008) Are We Willing to Pay Enough to Back the Bid? Valuing the Intangible Impacts of London's Bid to Host the 2012 Summer Olympic Games, *Urban Studies*, 45 (2): 419–444.

Baim, D. (2009) Olympic-driven Urban Development, in G. Poynter and I. MacRury (eds) *Olympic Cities: 2012 and the Remaking of London*, Farnham: Ashgate.

References

Balibrea, M. P. (2001) Urbanism, Culture and the Post-industrial City: Challenging the 'Barcelona Model', *Journal of Spanish Cultural Studies* 2 (2): 187–210.

Bianchini, F. (1993) *Cultural Policy and Urban Regeneration: The Western European Experience*, Manchester: Manchester University Press.

Bladen, C. (2009) Towards an Olympic Volunteering Legacy, in J. Kennell, E. Booth and C. Bladen (eds) *The Olympic Legacy: People, Place Enterprise: Proceedings of the First Annual Conference on Olympic Legacy, 8 and 9 May 2008*, Greenwich: Greenwich University Press.

Boykoff, J. (2011) Anti Olympics, *New Left Review*, 67: 41–59.

Boyle, P. and Haggerty, K. (2009) Spectacular Security: Mega-events and the Security Complex, *International Political Sociology*, 3 (3): 257–274.

Brunet, F. (2009) The Economy of the Barcelona Olympic Games, in G. Poynter and I. MacRury (eds) *Olympic Cities: 2012 and the Remaking of London*, Farnham: Ashgate.

Carlsen, J. and Taylor, A. (2003) Mega-events and Urban Renewal: The Case of the Manchester 2002 Commonwealth Games, *Event Management*, 8 (1): 15–22.

Diamond, J. and Liddle, J. (2005) *Management of Regeneration*, Abingdon: Routledge.

Evans, G. (2005) Measure for Measure: Evaluating the Evidence of Culture's Contribution to Regeneration, *Urban Studies*, 42 (5/6): 959–983.

FIFA (2002) 41,100 Hours of 2002 FIFA World Cup TV Coverage in 213 Countries [online]. Available at: http://www.fifa.com/newscentre/news/newsid=84258.html. Accessed 26 October 2011.

FIFA (2007) No.1 Sports Event, press release [online]. Available at: http://www.fifa.com/mm/document/fifafacts/ffprojects/ip-401_06e_tv_2658.pdf. Accessed 4 October 2011.

Garcia, B. (2004) Urban Regeneration, Arts Programming and Major Events: Glasgow 1990, Sydney 2000 and Barcelona 2004, *International Journal of Cultural Policy*, 10 (1): 103–118.

Garcia, B. and Miah, A. (2004) Non-accredited Media, the Olympic Games, the Media and the Host City: The British Academy 2004 Project, *Culture @ The Olympics*, 6: 1–7.

Getz, D. (2007) *Event Studies*, Oxford: Butterworth-Heinemann.

Girginov, V. and Parry, J. (2005) *The Olympic Games Explained*, Abingdon: Routledge.

Giulianotti, R. and Klauser, F. (2009) Security Governance and Sport Mega-events: Toward an Interdisciplinary Research Agenda, *Journal of Sport and Social Issues*, 34 (1): 1–13.

Guala, C. (2009) To Bid or not to Bid: Public Opinion before and after the Games: The Case of the Turin 2006 Winter Olympic Games, in J. Kennell, E. Booth and C. Bladen (eds) *The Olympic Legacy: People, Place Enterprise: Proceedings of the First Annual Conference on Olympic Legacy, 8 and 9 May 2008*, Greenwich: Greenwich University Press.

Hill Dickinson LLP (2008) Official Partners [online]. Available at: http://www.08business connect.com/detail/Hill_Dickinson_LLP/45/80.aspx. Accessed 16 January 2010.

Horne, J. and Manzenreiter, W. (2006) An Introduction to the Sociology of Sports Mega-events, *Sociological Review*, 54 (2): 1–24.

Istanbul 2010 (2011) Benefits for Istanbul [online]. Available at: http://www.en.istanbul2010. org/AVRUPAKULTURBASKENTI/istanbulakatkilari/index.htm. Accessed 28 April 2011.

Jonas, A. and Ward, K. (2002) A World of Regionalisms? Towards a US–UK Urban and Regional Policy Framework Comparison, *Journal of Urban Affairs*, 24 (4): 377–401.

Kennell, J. and Macleod, N. (2009) A Grey Literature Review of the Cultural Olympiad, *Cultural Trends*, 18 (1): 83–88.

Lee, C., Song, H. and Mjelde, J. (2008) The Forecasting of International Expo Tourism Using Quantitative and Qualitative Techniques, *Tourism Management*, 29: 1084–1098.

Lee, C. and Taylor, T. (2005) Critical Reflections on the Economic Impact Assessment of a Mega-event: The Case of the 2002 FIFA World Cup, *Tourism Management*, 26: 595–603.

Liverpool08 (2008) Commercial Support [online]. Available at: http://www.liverpool08.com/commercial/. Accessed 16 January 2010.

Liverpool08 (2009) *Liverpool08 European Capital of Culture: The Impacts of a Year Like No Other*, Liverpool: Liverpool08.

McGuigan, J. (1996) *Culture and the Public Sphere*, Abingdon: Routledge.

Morgan, K. (2002) The New Regeneration Narrative: Local Development in the Multi-level Polity, *Local Economy*, 17 (3): 191–199.

Persson, C. (2002) The Olympic Games Site Decision, *Tourism Management*, 23: 27–36.

PODIUM (2009) About Us [online]. Available at: http://www.podium.ac.uk/about-us. Accessed 16 January 2010.

Preuss, H. (2005) The Economic Impact of Visitors at Major Multi-sport Events, *European Sport Management Quarterly*, 5 (3): 281–301.

Roberts, K. (2004) *The Leisure Industry*, London: Palgrave.

Roberts, P. (2000) The Evolution, Definition and Purpose of Urban Regeneration, in P. Roberts and H. Sykes, *Urban Regeneration*, London: Sage.

Roche, M. (2000) *Mega-events and Modernity: Olympics and Expos in the Growth of Global Culture*, Abingdon: Routledge.

Shulenkorf, N. (2005) *Oktoberfest Munchen: The World's Largest Public Event*, Nordestet: Grin Verlag.

Smith, A. (2007) Large-scale Events and Sustainable Urban Regeneration: Key Principles for Host Cities, *Journal of Urban Regeneration and Renewal*, 1 (2): 1–13.

Smith, A. and Fox, T. (2007) From Event-led to Event-themed Regeneration: The 2002 Commonwealth Games Legacy Programme, *Urban Studies*, 45 (5): 1125–1143.

Tarlow, P. (2002) *Event Risk Management and Safety*, New York: John Wiley and Sons.

Theodoraki, E. (2007) *Olympic Event Organisation*, Oxford: Butterworth-Heinemann.

Vickery, J. (2007) *The Emergence of Culture-led Regeneration: A Policy Concept and its Discontents*, Centre for Cultural Policy Studies Research Paper No. 9, University of Warwick.

Weed, M. (2008) *Olympic Tourism*, Oxford: Butterworth-Heinemann.

11 Events in the public and third sectors

Allen, J., O'Toole, W., Harris, R. and McDonnell, I. (2008) *Festival and Special Event Management* (4th edn), Oxford: John Wiley and Sons.

Bærenholdt, J. and Haldrup, M. (2006) Mobile Networks and Placemaking in Cultural Tourism: Staging Viking Ships and Rock Music in Roskilde, *European Journal of Urban and Regional Studies*, 13 (3): 209–224.

Barker, M., Page, S.-J. and Meyer, D. (2001) Evaluating the Impacts of the 2000 America's Cup on Auckland, New Zealand, *Event Management*, 7: 79–92.

Bridgestone Arena (2011) Home Page [online]. Available at: http://www.bridgestonearena.com/. Accessed 18 February 2011.

British Visits and Events Partnership (BVEP) (2010) *Britain for Events*, London: BVEP.

Carson, L. (2001) Innovative Consultation Processes and the Changing Role of Activism, *Third Sector Review*, 7 (1): 7–22.

City of Toronto (2011) *Community Consultation Meetings Notice, March 2011*, Toronto: City of Toronto.

Create London (2010) *Create09 Festival Report*, London, Create London.

Event Scotland (2009) *Scotland: The Perfect Stage*, Edinburgh: Event Scotland.

References

FEI (2011) *Birmingham City Council Events Strategy 2008–2012* [online]. Available at: http://www.feiuk.com/Case_Study_02.asp. Accessed 17 January 2011.

Fifteen Foundation (2011) A Big Night out with Jamie [online]. Available at: http://www.fifteen.net/abignightoutwithjamie/Pages/default.aspx. Accessed 18 February 2011.

Getz, D. (2005) *Event Management and Event Tourism*, New York: Cognizant Communication.

Getz, D. (2007) *Event Studies: Theory, Research and Policy for Planned Events*, Oxford: Butterworth-Heinemann.

Good Mood Food (2011) Good Mood Food [online]. Available at: http://www.goodmoodfood.org/. Accessed 18 February 2011.

Guardian (2010) Pope's Visit: An Interactive Guide [online]. Available at: http://www.guardian.co.uk/world/interactive/2010/aug/25/popes-visit-interactive-guide-uk. Accessed 18 February 2011.

Hiller, H. (2000) Mega-events, Urban Boosterism and Growth Strategies: An Analysis of the Objectives and Legitimations of the Cape Town 2004 Olympic Bid, *European Journal of Urban and Regional Studies*, 24 (2): 439–458.

Hjalager, A.-M. (2009) Cultural Tourism Innovation Systems, *Scandanavian Journal of Hospitality and Tourism*, 9 (2–3): 266–287.

Hub Cape Town (2011) The Events [online]. Available at: http://capetown.the-hub.net/public/events.html. Accessed 18 February 2011.

Jago, L., Chalip, L., Brown, G., Mules, T. and Ali, S. (2003) Building Events into Destination Branding: Insights from Experts, *Event Management*, 8: 3–14.

Jefferson Centre (2002) *Citizens Jury: Global Climate Change*, St Paul: Jefferson Centre.

Maenning, W. and du Plessis, S. (2009) Sport Stadia, Sporting Events and Urban Development: International Experience and the Ambitions of Durban, *Urban Forum*, 20 (1): 61–76.

Mutiny (2011) Join the Mutiny [online]. Available at: http://jointhemutiny.wordpress.com. Accessed 18 February 2011.

Nashville Predators (2011) Bridgestone Arena [online]. Available at: http://www.nashvillecorporatepartnerships.com/bridgestone_arena/bridgestone_arena.html. Accessed 18 February 2011.

Play House, The (2011) About Us [online]. Available at: http://theplayhouse.org.uk/about/. Acecssed 17 February 2011.

Pugh, C. and Wood, E. (2004) The Strategic Use of Events within Local Government: A Study of London Borough Councils, *Event Management*, 9: 61–71.

Quinn, B. (2003) Symbols, Practices and Myth-making: Cultural Perspectives on the Wexford Festival Opera, *Tourism Geographies*, 5 (3): 329–349.

Raj, R., Walters, P. and Rashid, T. (2009) *Events Management: An Integrated and Practical Approach*, London: Sage.

Roskilde Festival (2011) Frontpage [online]. Available at: http://www.roskilde-festival.dk/uk/. Accessed 18 February 2011.

SEC (2011) About Social Enterprise [online]. Available at: http://www.socialenterprise.org.uk/pages/about-social-enterprise.html. Accessed 17 February 2011.

Shone, A. and Parry, B. (2010) *Successful Event Management* (3rd edn), Hampshire: Cengage Learning.

Social Enterprise Mark (2011) The Play House [online]. Availble at: http://www.socialenterprisemark.org.uk/profile/theplayhouse. Accessed 17 February 2011.

Sport England (2011) England Athletics: Responding to Your Views [online]. Available at: http://www.englandathletics.org/page.asp?section=1287andsectionTitle=Consultation. Accessed 22 June 2011.

Stokes, R. (2007) Realtionships and Networks for Shaping Events Tourism: An Australian Study, *Event* Management, 10: 145–158.

Stokes, R. and Jago, L. (2007) Australia's Public Sector Environment for Shaping Event Tourism Strategy, *International Journal of Event Management Research*, 3 (1): 42–53.

UNESCO (2011) The World Water Day is Discussed in a Hearing in Brazil [online]. Available at: http://www.unesco.org/new/en/brasilia/about-this-office/single-view/news/the_world_water_day_is_discussed_in_public_hearing_in_brazil/. Accessed 22 June 2011.

Van Wyk, J. (2005) Managing Political Events, in D. Tassiopolous (ed.) *Event Management: A Professional and Developmental Approach*, Lansdowne: Juta

Webber, D. (2004) Understanding Charity Fundraising Events, *International Journal of Nonprofit and Voluntary Sector Marketing*, 9 (2): 123–124.

Wood, E. (2009) An Impact Evaluation Framework: Local Government Community Festivals, *Event Management*, 12: 171–185.

World Events (2011) Our Company [online]. Available at: http://www.worldevents.com/ourcompany/. Accessed 18 February 2011.

12 Corporate events

5 Minute Networking (2010) Taking the Work out of Networking [online]. Available at: http://www.5minutenetworking.com. Accessed 4 October 2011.

AEO, BECA and EVA (2002) *Guide to Managing Health and Safety at Exhibitions and Events*, London: AEO, BECA, EVA.

Allen, J. (2008) *Event Planning: The Ultimate Guide to Successful Meetings, Corporate Events, Fund-raising Galas, Conferences, Conventions, Incentives and Other Special Events*, Sydney: John Wiley and Sons.

Allen, J., O'Toole, W., Harris, R. and McDonnell, I. (2011) *Festivals and Special Events Management* (5th edn), Milton, Queensland: John Wiley and Sons.

Arvey, R. D. (2009) Why Face to Face Business Meetings Matter: The Hilton Family Group [online]. Available at: http://www.iacconline.org/content/files/WhyFace-to-FaceBusiness MeetingsMatter.pdf. Accessed 4 November 2011.

Bauer, T., Law, R., Tse, T. and Weber, A. (2008) Motivation and Satisfaction of Mega-business Event Attendees: The Case of ITU Telecom World 2006 in Hong Kong, *International Journal of Contemporary Hospitality Management*, 20 (2): 228–234.

Bell, L. (2009) Corporates Question Value of Hospitality in Economic Climate [online]. Available at: http://www.citmagazine.com/news/rss/902048/Corporates-question-value-hospitality-economic-climate/. Accessed 4 October 2011.

Big Tattoo Planet (2009) Tattoo Jam 2009 [online]. Available at: http://www.bigtattooplanet.com/features/convention/tattoo-jam-2009. Accessed 6 October 2011.

Bowdin, G., Allen, J., O'Toole, W., Harris, R. and McDonnell, I. (2011) *Events Management* (4th edn), Oxford: Butterworth-Heinemann.

Business Balls (2010) Home Page [online]. Available at: http://www.businessballs.com/business-networking.htm. Accessed 3 August 2010.

Business Junction (2010) Home Page [online]. Available at: http://www.businessjuntion.co.uk. Accessed 9 August 2010.

Clothes Show Live (2010) Event Info [online]. Available at: http://www.clothesshowlive.com/event-info. Accessed 10 August 2010.

Curtis, P. and Evans, R. (2010) Tax Boss Most Wined and Dined Mandarin', *Guardian* 17 June [online]. Available at: http://www.guardian.co.uk/business/2010/jun/17/hmrc-head-tax-corporate-entertainment. Accessed 5 August 2010.

References

Davidson, R. (2003) *Business Travel: Conferences, Incentive Travel, Exhibitions, Corporate Hospitality and Corporate Travel*, Harlow: Pearson.

Davidson, R. (2010) *Trends and Market Report* [online]. Available at: http://www.eibtm.com/page.cfm/T=m/Action=Press/PressID=5. Accessed 5 August 2010.

Eventia (2009) *The UK Market Trends Survey*, n.p: Eventia.

Getz, D. (2005) *Event Management and Event Tourism*, New York: Cognizant.

Getz, D (2007) *Event Studies*, Oxford: Butterworth-Heinemann.

Hall, A. (2009) ROI: Measured, Guaranteed, *Corporate Meetings and Incentives*, September: 19.

Harwood, S. (2010) Vie at Home's Cape Town Incentive [online]. Available at: http://www.citmagazine.com/news/1009048/Vie-Homes-Cape-Town-incentive/. Accessed 31 July 2010.

Haug, L. (2010) Lift Lab [online]. Available at: http://liftlab.com/. Accessed 28 July 2010.

Henderson, N. (2010) Axa Life Cuts back Incentive Travel Programme [online]. Available at: http://www.citmagazine.com/news/search/965058/Axa-Life-cuts-back-incentive-travel-programme/. Accessed 31 July 2010.

ICCA (2010) Events and Education [online]. Available at: http://www.iccaworld.com/evps/. Accessed 4 October 2011.

IMEX (2010) Press Releases [online]. Available at: http://www.imex-frankfurt.com/press.php?action=showstory&newsid=230. Accessed 7 August 2010.

International Confex (2010) Home [online] Available at: http://www.international-confex.com. Accessed 10 August 2010.

International Consumer Electronics (2010) Home [online]. Available at: http://www.cesweb.org. Accessed 7 August 2010.

Kastelein, R. (2010) UK Corporate Hospitality Market to Explode to £1.5 Billion by 2015 [online]. Available at http://www.euticketnews.com/20100708845/uk-corporate-hospitality-market-to-explode-to-p15-billion-by-2015.html. Accessed 5 August 2010.

Lift (2011) Lift10 [online]. Available at: http://liftconference.com/lift10. Accessed 4 October 2011.

Masterman, G. (2004) A Strategic Approach for the Use of Sponsorship in the Events Industry: In Search of a Return on Investment, in I. Yeoman, M. Robertson, J. Ali-Knight, S. Drummond and U. McMahon-Beattie (eds) *Festival and Events Management: An International Arts and Culture Perspective*, Oxford: Butterworth-Heinemann.

MBD (2009) UK Corporate Hospitality Market Report [online]. Available at: http://www.mbdltd.co.uk/UK-Market-Research-Reports/Corporate-Hospitality.htm. Accessed 4 October 2011.

MyDSF (2010) Dubai Festival City [online]. Available at: http://mydsf.ae. Accessed 5 August 2010.

Nguyen, N. and Leblanc, G. (2001) Corporate Image and Corporate Reputation in Customers' Retention Decisions in Services, *Journal of Retailing and Consumer Services*, 8 (4): 227–236.

O'Toole, W. and Mikolaitis, P. (2002) *Corporate Event Project Management*, New York: John Wiley and Sons.

Pine, B. J. and Gilmore, J. H. (1999) *The Experience Economy*, Cambridge, MA: Harvard Business Review.

Severt, K and Breiter, D. (2010) The Anatomy of an Incentive Travel Program, Research Funded by the Incentive Research Foundation [online]. Available at: http://www.incentivemotivate.com. Accessed 28 July 2010.

Shone, A. and Parry, B. (2010) Successful Event Eanagement (3rd edn), Hampshire: Cengage Learning.

SITE (2010) Home [online]. Available at: http://www.siteglobal.com. Accessed 28 July 2010.

Supper Club (2010) The Story [online]. Available at: http://www.supper-club.net/thestory. Accessed 10 August 2010.

UFI (2010) The Global Exhibition Barometer [online]. Available at: http://www.ufi.org/Public/Search.aspx?Clef_SITESMAPS=584&SEARCH=Global+barometer. Accessed 4 August 2010.

UFI (2011) UFI Mission & Figures [online]. Available at: http://www.ufi.org/Public/Default.aspx?Clef_SITESMAPS=69. Accessed 13 May 2011.

Weber, K. and Ladkin, A. (2003) The Convention Industry in Australia and the United Kingdom: Key Issues and Competitive Forces, *Journal of Travel Research*, 42: 125–132.

White, M. (2010) Comic-Con's Grown up Nerds Give Mattel, Hasbro New Toy Pitches [online]. Available at: http://www.bloomberg.com/news/2010-07-22/comic-con-s-grown-up-nerds-give-mattel-hasbro-new-way-to-pitch-girls-toys.html. Accessed 22 July 2010.

Whitehead, J. (2009) Pink and 13,000 Volunteers Converge on Trafalgar Square for T-mobile Ad [online]. Available at: http://www.brandrepublic.com/news/902483/Pink-1300-vounteers-converge-Trafalgar-Square-T-Mobile-ad/. Accessed 10 August 2010.

Wolf, P., Hansmann, R. and Troxler, P. (2011) Unconferencing as Method to Initiate Organizational Change: A Case Study on Reducing CO2 Emissions of a University, *Journal of Organisational Change Management*, 24 (1): 112–142.

13 Cultural events and festivals

Aksoy, A. and Robins, K. (2004) Parting from Phantoms: What is at Issue in the Development of Transnational Television from Turkey, in J. Friedman and S. Randeria (eds) *Worlds on the Move: Globalisation, Migration and Cultural Security*, London: I. B. Tauris.

Ali-Knight, J. and Robertson, M. (2004) Introduction to Arts, Culture and Leisure, in I. Yeoman, M. Robertson, J. Ali-Knight, S. Drummond and U. McMahon-Beattie (eds) *Festival and Events Management: An International Arts and Culture Perspective*, Oxford: Butterworth-Heinemann.

Allen, J., O'Toole, W., Harris, R. and McDonnell, I. (2008) *Festival and Special Event Management* (4th edn), Queensland: John Wiley and Sons.

Anderton, C. (2008) Commercialising the Carnivalesque: The 'V' Festival and Image Risk Management, *Event Management*, 12: 39–51.

Arts Council England (2004) *Festivals and the Creative Region*, London: ACE.

Assassi, I. (2005) The Influence of Theaters' Programming Strategy on Their Relations with Artistic Production Companies: An Analysis Based on the French Experience, paper presented at the 8th International Conference on Arts and Cultural Management, 3–6 July, Montreal, Canada.

Axelsen, M. and Arcodia, C. (2005) Conceptualising Art Exhibitions as Special Events, *Journal of Convention and Event Tourism*, 6 (3): 63–80.

Bakhtin, M. (1984) *Rabelais and his World*, Indianapolis: Indiana University Press.

BBC (2009) Woodstock for the Mind is Belfast Bound [online]. Available at: http://news.bbc.co.uk/1/hi/northern_ireland/8003768.stm. Accessed 26 October 2011.

Bowdin, G., Allen, J., O'Toole, W., Harris, R. and McDonnell, I. (2006) *Events Management* (2nd edn), Oxford: Butterworth-Heinemann.

Bowdin, G., Allen, J., O'Toole, W., Harris, R. and McDonnell, I. (2010) *Events Management* (3rd edn), Oxford: Butterworth-Heinemann.

Bowen, H. and Daniels, M. J. (2005) Does the Music Matter? Motivations for Attending a Music Festival, *Event Management*, 9 (3): 155–164.

References

Buchmesse (2010) Frankfurter Buchmesse 2010 [online]. Available at: http://www.buchmesse. de/. Accessed 9 May 2010.

Burwell, C. (2007) Reading *Lolita* in Times of War: Women's Book Clubs and the Politics of Reception, *Intercultural Education*, 18 (4): 281–296.

Carnegie, E. and Smith, M. (2006) Mobility, Diaspora and the Hybridization of Festivity, in D. Pickard and M. Robinson (eds) *Festivals, Tourism and Social Change*, Clevedon: Channel View Publications.

Castaner, X. and Campos, L. (2002) The Determinants of Artistic Innovation: Bringing in the Role of Organisations, *Journal of Cultural Economics*, 26: 29–52.

Chong, D. (2002) *Arts Management*, Abingdon: Routledge.

Cuadrado-Garcia, M. and Perez-Cabenero, C. (2005) The Process of Programming in the Performing Arts: An Empirical Research in Spain, paper presented at the 8th International Conference on Arts and Cultural Management, 3–6 July, Montreal, Canada.

Eagleton, T. (2000) *The Idea of Culture*, Oxford: Blackwell.

Edinburgh International Festival (2010) Home Page [online]. Available at: http://www.eif.co. uk/. Accessed 9 May 2010.

EFA (2010) Home Page [online]. Available at: http://www.open-the-door.eu/. Accessed 10 May 2009.

EXIT (2010) Exit Festival [online].Available at: http://eng.exitfest.org/. Accessed 9 May 2010.

Faversham Hop Festival (2010) Home Page [online]. Available at: http://www2.swale.gov.uk/ hopfestival/. Accessed 9 May 2010.

Fenich, G. (2005) *Meetings, Expositions, Events and Conventions: An Introduction to the Industry*, New Jersey: Pearson Prentice-Hall.

Finkel, R. (2006) Tensions between Ambition and Reality in UK Combined Arts Festival Programming: Case Study of the Lichfield Festival, *International Journal of Event Management Research*, 2 (1): 25–36.

Fox-Gotham, K. (2002) Marketing Mardi Gras: Comodification, Spectacle and the Political Economy of Tourism in New Orleans, *Urban Studies*, 39 (10): 1735–1756.

Fox-Gotham, K. (2005) Tourism from above and below: Globalisation, Localisation and New Orleans's Mardi Gras, in *International Journal of Urban and Regional Research*, 29 (2): 309–326.

Getz, D. (2005) *Event Management and Event Tourism*, New York: Cognizant Communication.

Getz, D. (2007) *Events Studies*, Oxford: Butterworth-Heinemann.

Grunwell, S. and Ha, I. (2008) Film Festivals: An Empirical Study of Factors for Success, *Event Management*, 11: 201–210.

Hall, C. M. and Rusher, K. (2004) Politics, Public Policy and the Destination, in I. Yeoman, M. Robertson, J. Ali-Knight, S. Drummond and U. McMahon-Beattie (eds) *Festival and Events Management: An International Arts and Culture Perspective*, Oxford: Butterworth-Heinemann.

Hesmondhalgh, D. (2007) *The Cultural Industries* (2nd edn), London: Sage.

Huang, J., Li, M. and Cai, L. (2010) A Model of Community-based Festival Image, *International Journal of Hospitality Management*, 29 (2): 254–260.

Hughes, H. L. (2006) Gay and Lesbian Festivals: Tourism in the Change from Politics to Party, in D. Pickard and M. Robinson (eds) *Festivals, Tourism and Social Change*, Clevedon: Channel View Publications.

IFEA (2009) The Power of Celebration [online]. Available at: http://www.ifea.com/joomla1_5/ index.php?option=com_contentandview=articleandid=180andItemid=306. Accessed 10 May 2009.

Interpride (2010) Current Members [online]. Available at: http://www.interpride.org/interpride-members. Accessed 9 May 2010.

Jepson, A., Wiltshier, P. and Clarke, A. (2008) Community Festivals: Involvement and Inclusion, paper presented at the CHME International Research Conference, Strathclyde Business School, University of Strathclyde, 14–16 May, Glasgow.

Jura Consultants (2006) *Economic Impact Assessment: The Pillar Events*, Edinburgh: Jura Consultants.

Kawashima, N. (2006) Audience Development and Social Inclusion in Britain, *International Journal of Cultural Policy*, 12 (1): 55–72.

Klamer, A. (2002) On the Economics of Arts and Culture [online]. Available at: http://www.klmar.nl/art.htm. Accessed 26 July 2005.

Kolb, B. (2005) *Marketing for Cultural Organisations* (2nd edn), London: Thompson.

Kotler, P. and Scheff, J. (1997) *Standing Room Only: Strategies for Marketing the Performing Arts*, Oxford: Blackwell.

Lukic-Krstanovic, M. (2008) The Festival Order: Music Stages of Power and Pleasure, *Issues in Ethnology and Anthropology*, 3 (3): 129–143.

McCarthy, K. and Jinnet, K. (2001) *A New Framework for Building Participation in the Arts*, New York: RAND.

Manchester Pride (2010) Who Are We [online]. Available at: http://www.manchesterpride.com/aboutus/whoarewe. Accessed 19 May 2010.

Mardi Gras New Orleans (2010) Mardi Gras New Orleans [online]. Available at: http://www.mardigrasneworleans.com/. Accessed 9 May 2010.

Mintel (2008) *Music Concert Events and Festivals*, London: Mintel Group.

Moscardo, G. (2008) Analysing the Role of Festivals and Events in Regional Development, *Event Management*, 11: 23–32.

O'Hara, H. (2010) Secret Cinema, the Experience [online]. Available at: http://www.empireonline.com/empireblogs/empire-states/post/p783. Accessed 18 May 2010.

Pickard, D. and Robinson, M. (eds) (2006) *Festivals, Tourism and Social Change*, Clevedon: Channel View Publications.

Pickert, K. (2008) Oprah's Book Club [online]. Available at: http://www.time.com/time/arts/article/0,8599,1844724,00.html. Accessed 19 May 2010.

Quinn, B. (2005) Arts Festivals and the City, *Urban Studies*, 42 (5/6): 927–943.

Raj, R., Walters, P. and Rashid, T. (2008) *Events Management: An Integrated and Practical Approach*, London: Sage.

Sonder, M. (2004) *Event Entertainment and Production*, Hoboken: John Wiley and Sons.

Soundwalk (2010) Home Page [online]. Available at: http://www.soundwalk.com/. Accessed 9 May 2010.

Storymoja Hay Festival Nairobi (2009) Home [online]. Available at: http://www.hayfestival.com/storymoja/index.aspx?skinid=10. Accessed 18 May 2010.

Wang, Y. C. and Weng, A. (2008) Indies Music, Festivities and 'Spring Scream': A Taiwanese Case of Cultural Tourism, *Proceedings of the 19th Annual Conference of Chinese Management Educators*, Toronto, 24–26 July: 455–463.

Williams, M. and Bowdin, G. (2007) Festival Evaluation: An Exploration of Seven UK Arts Festivals, in *Managing Leisure*, 12 (2): 187–203.

Williams, R. (2010) *Keywords: A Vocabulary of Culture and Society*, London: Fontana Press.

Yeoman, I., Robertson, M., Ali-Knight, J., Drummond, S. and McMahon-Beattie, U. (eds) (2004) *Festival and Events Management: An International Arts and Culture Perspective*, Oxford: Butterworth-Heinemann.

Zakic, L., Ivkov-Dzigurski, A. and Curcic, N. (2009) Interaction of Foreign Visitors of the

EXIT Music Festival with Domestic Visitors and Local Population, *Geographica Pannonica*, 13 (3): 97–104.

14 Event impacts, sustainability and legacy

Allen, J., O'Toole, W., Harris, R. and McDonnell, I. (2008) *Festival and Special Event Management*, Milton: Wiley.

Arik, M. and Penn, D. (2005) *Economic Impact of Bonnaroo Music Festival on Coffee County: Report Prepared for Axis Ventures*, Knoxville: Axis Ventures.

Morgan, T. (2001) Cypriot's Club Culture Fear [online]. Available at: http://news.bbc.co.uk/1/hi/world/europe/1417977.stm. Accessed 19 September 2010.

Bonnaroo Music and Arts Festival (2009) Home Page [online]. Available at: http://www.bonnaroo.com/. Accessed 12 May 2009.

Bowdin, G., Allen, J., O'Toole, W., Harris, R. and McDonnell, I. (2006) *Events Mangement* (2nd edn), Oxford: Butteworth-Heinemann.

Boyle, D. and Simms, A. (2009) *The New Economics: A Bigger Picture*, London: Earthscan.

Brundtland Commission (1987) Report of the World Commission on Environment and Development: Our Common Future [online]. Available at: http://www.un-documents.net/wced-ocf.htm. Accessed 20 October 2010.

BSi (2009) *Make Your Event Sustainable*, London: BSi.

Carlsen, J. (2004) The Economics and Evaluation of Festivals and Events, in I. Yeoman, M. Robertson, J. Ali-Knight, S. Dummond and U. McMahon-Beattie (eds) *Festival and Events Management: An International Arts and Culture Perspective*, Oxford: Butterworth-Heinemann.

Carmago, P. (2007) Using Tourist Resources as Tools for Teaching and Creating Awareness of Heritage in a Local Community, in G. Richards (ed.) *Cultural Tourism: Global and Local Perspectives*, New York: Howarth Press.

Conference Consortium (2010) About Consortium [online]. Available at: http://www.conferenceconsortium.org/about-consortium.html. Accessed 10 October 2010.

David, L. (2009) Environmental Impacts of Events, in R. Raj and J. Musgrave (eds) *Event Management and Sustainability*, Oxford: CABI.

DC Convention (2007) Washington Convention Centre Authority Concludes Bond Sale: Press Release [online]. Available at: http://www.dcconvention.com/PressRoom/PressReleases/PressReleasePages.aspx?id=93&year=2007. Accessed 20 October 2010.

Department for Energy and Climate Change (DECC) (2008) Climate Change Act 2008 [online]. Available at: http://www.legislation.gov.uk/ukpga/2008/27/contents. Accessed 1 November 2010.

Derrett, R. (2003) Making Sense of How Festivals Demonstrate a Community's Sense of Place, *Event Management*, 8: 49–58.

Dwyer, L., Mellor, R., Mistilis, N. and Mules, T. (2000) Forecasting the Economic Impacts of Events and Conventions, *Event Management*, 6: 191–204.

EIBTM (2010) Trends and Market Report [online]. Available at: http://www.eibtm.com/page.cfm/T=m/Action=Press/PressID=5. Accessed 5 August 2010.

Getz, D. (2005) *Event Management and Event Tourism*, New York: Cognizant Communication.

Getz, D. (2007) *Event Studies*, Oxford: Butterworth-Heinemann.

Getz, D. (2009) Policy for Sustainable and Responsible Festivals and Events: Institutionalisation of a New Paradigm, *Journal of Policy Research in Toursm, Leisure and Events*, 1 (1): 61–78.

Getz, D. and Andersson, T. (2008) Sustainable Festivals: On Becoming an Institution, *Event Management*, 12: 1–17.

Gold, J. and Gold, M. (2009) Riding the Mexican Wave: Deciphering the Meaning of Olympic Legacy, in J. Kennell, E. Booth and C. Bladen (eds) *People, Place, Enterprise: Proceedings of the First Annual Conference on Olympic Legacy*, London: GUP.

Harvey, D. (2007) *A Brief History of Neoliberalism*, Oxford: Oxford University Press.

Hede, A.-M. (2008) Managing Special Events in the New Era of the Triple Bottom Line, *Event Management*, 11: 13–22.

Horne, J. and Mazenreiter, W. (2006) An Introduction to the Sociology of Sports Mega-events, *Sociological Review*, 54 (2): 1–24.

Jackson, T. (2009) *Prosperity without Growth: Economics for a Finite Planet*, London: Earthscan.

Kennell, J. and Sitz, R. (2010) Greening Bonnaroo: Exploring the Rhetoric and Reality of a Sustainable Festival through Micro-ethnographic Methods, paper presented at the Global Events Congress IV, Leeds, 14–16 July.

Laing, J. and Frost, W. (2010) How Green Was My Festival: Exploring Challenges and Opportunities Associated with Staging Green Events, *International Journal of Hospitality Management*, 29: 261–267.

Morgan, A. and Condliffe, S. (2006) Measuring the Economic Impacts of Convention Centre and Event Tourism: A Discussion of the Key Issues, *Journal of Convention and Event Tourism*, 8 (4): 81–100.

Morgan, T. (2001) Cypriots' Club Culture Fear [online]. Available from: http://news.bbc.co.uk/1/hi/world/europe/1417977.stm. Accessed 19 September 2010.

O'Toole, W. and Mikolaitis, P. (2002) *Corporate Event Project Management*, New York: John Wiley and Sons.

Pine, B. J. and Gilmore, J. H. (1999) *The Experience Economy*, Cambridge, MA: Harvard Business Review.

Presbury, R. and Edwards, D. (2005) Incorporating Sustainability in Meetings and Event Management Education, *International Journal of Event Management Research*, 1 (1): 30–45.

Preuss, H. (2007) The Conceptualisation and Measurement of Mega Sport Event Legacies, *Journal of Sport and Tourism*, 12 (3–4): 207–227.

Raj, R., Walters, P. and Rashid, T. (2009) *Events Management: An Integrated and Practical Approach*, London: Sage.

Rotheroe, N. and Richards, A. (2007) Social Return on Investment and Social Enterprise: Transparent Accountability for Sustainable Development, *Social Enterprise Journal*, 3 (1): 31–48.

Saveriades, A. (2007) A Sociometric Examination of Perceptions of the Impact of Contemporary Tourism on Society in the Tourist Resort of 'Ayia Napa', Cyprus: A Qualitative Approach, *Society and Leisure – Montreal*, 30 (1): 177–195.

Shone, A. and Parry, B. (2010) *Successful Event Management: A Practical Handbook* (3rd edn), Andover: Cengage.

Small, K. (2007) Social Dimensions of Community Festivals: An Application of Factor Analysis in the Development of the Social Impact Perception (SIP) Scale, *Event Mangement*, 11: 45–55.

Social Enterprise Coalition (2010) About Social Enterprise [online]. Available at: http://www.socialenterprise.org.uk/pages/about-social-enterprise.html. Accessed 9 November 2010.

Tohmo, T. (2005) Economic Impacts of Cultural Events on Local Economies: An Input–Output Analysis of the Kaustinen Folk Music Festival, *Tourism Economics*, 11 (3): 431–451.

Tribe, J. (2005) *The Economics of Recreation, Leisure and Tourism* (3rd edn), Oxford: Butterworth-Heinemann.

United Nations Commission on Environment and Development (UNCED) (1992) Our Common Future [online]. Available at: http://www.un-documents.net/ocf-02.htm. Accessed 01 November 2010.

15 Events and the media

Baines, P., Egan, J. and Jefkins, F. (2005) *Public Relations: Contemporary Issues and Techniques*, Oxford: Elsevier.

Bladen, C. R. (2010) Media Representation of Volunteers at the Beijing Olympics, *Sport in Society*, 13 (5): 784–796.

Borland, J. and MacDonald, R. (2003) Demand for Sport, *Oxford Review of Economic Policy*, 19 (4): 478–502.

Bowdin, G., Allen, J., O'Toole, W., Harris, R. and McDonnell, I. (2010) *Events Management* (3rd edn), Oxford: Butterworth-Heinemann.

Brassington, F. and Pettitt, S. (2003) *Principles of Marketing*, New Jersey: Prentice-Hall.

Buraimo, B., Paramio, J. L. and Campos, C. (2010) The Impact of Televised Football on Stadium Attendances in English and Spanish League Football, *Soccer and Society*, 11 (4): 461–474.

Carlsen, J., Getz, D. and Soutar, G. (2001) Event Evaluation Research, *Events Management*, 6: 247–257.

Chalip, L., Green, B. and Hill, B. (2003) Effects of Sport Event Media on Destination Image and Intention to Visit, *Journal of Sport Management*, 17: 214–234.

Broom, G. M. (2008) *Cutlip and Center's Effective Public Relations* (10th edn), London: Prentice-Hall.

Deloitte and Touche (2008) Football Money League Report [online]. Available at: http://www.deloitte.com/view/en_GB/uk/industries/sportsbusinessgroup/b54ae8e99defd110 VgnVCM100000ba42f00aRCRD.htm. Accessed 4 November 2011.

Dwyer, L., Mellor, R., Mistilis, N. and Mules, T. (2001) A Framework for Assessing 'Tangible' and 'Intangible' Impacts of Events and Conventions, *Events Management*, 6, 175–189.

Football Marketing (2011) Home Page [online]. Available at: http://www.football-marketing. com. Accessed 2 June 2011.

Forrest, D., Simmons, R. and Buraimo, B. (2006) Broadcaster and Audience Demand for Premier League Football, in C. Jeanrenaud and S. Késenne (eds) *The Economics of Sport and Media*, Gloucester: Edward Elgar.

Getz, D., Andersson, T. and Larson, M. (2007) Festival Stakeholder Roles: Concepts and Case Studies, *Events Management*, 10: 103–122.

Getz, D. and Fairley, S. (2004) Media Management at Sport Events for Destination Promotion: Case Studies and Concepts, *Events Management*, 8: 127–139.

Holden, P. and Wilde, N. (2007) *Marketing and PR*, London: A&C Black.

Horne, J. (2007) The Four 'Knowns' of Sports Mega-Events, *Leisure Studies*, 26 (1): 81–96.

Inside Hoops (2011) NBA TV Contracts [online]. Available at: http://www.insidehoops.com/ nba-tv-contracts.shtml. Accessed 31 October 2011.

IPSOS (2010) Survey [online]. Available at: http://www.ipsos-mori.com/Assets/Docs/Polls/ olympics-2012-survey-for-bbc-london-july-2010-topline.pdf. Accessed 1 June 2011.

Jefkins, F. (1994) *Public Relations*, London: McDonald and Evans.

Kitchen, P. J. (1997) Integrated Marketing Communications in US Advertising Agencies: An Exploratory Study, *Journal of Advertising Research*, September–October: 7–16.

Katz, H. (2007) *The Media Handbook*, New Jersey LEA.

McNamara, J. (2005) *Public Relations Handbook*, Australia: Archipelago Press.

McQuail, D. (2002) *McQuail's Mass Communication Theory*, London: Sage.

Paraskevas, A. (2000) Dream on but Realise the Basics: Insights from Visitor Satisfaction, the Case of the Millenium Dome, paper presented at the 1st International Conference on Tourism, Recreation and Leisure, Athens, Greece, 24–26 August.

Regester, M. (2008) *Risk Issues and Crisis Management in Public Relations*, London: Kogan Page.

Rivenburgh, N. (2002) The Olympic Games: Twenty-first Century Challenges as a Global Media Event, *Sport in Society*, 5 (3): 32–50.

Shone, A. and Parry, B. (2010) *Successful Event Management: A Practical Handbook* (3rd edn), Andover: Cengage.

Stebbins, R. A. (1996) Volunteering: A Serious Leisure Perspective, *Non-Profit and Voluntary Sector Quarterly*, 25 (2): 211–224.

Williams, K. (2003) *Understanding Media Theory*, London: Arnold Publications.

Wilson, J. (2000) Volunteering, *Annual Review of Sociology*, 26: 215–240.

Index

Figures, Plates and Tables are in **bold**